Praise for *Trail of Feathers*

"All the pieces of a brilliant true-crime story are here: an exotic location, mysterious circumstances, and a complex, endearing victim."
—*Chicago Tribune*

"[Rivard] writes with clarity and sensitivity. He imbues common stories with an engaging universality, and he brings often unfathomable issues of international relations and cultures in conflict to the human level."
—*St. Louis-Post Dispatch*

"[G]rimly compelling.... Read it and never again will you go into the wild unprepared." —*Newark Star-Ledger*

"Robert Rivard has written a book about many things—murder, justice, friendship, journalism, international relations—but *Trail of Feathers* is most eloquently the story of Philip True, a reporter who wandered with an open heart into a closed and unknowable world. It's a clear-headed, riveting book that deserves comparison with Jon Krakauer's *Into the Wild*, another unforgettable portrait of a tragic pilgrim."
—STEPHEN HARRIGAN, author of *The Gates of the Alamo*

"Justice in Mexico is elusive. Mr. Rivard chased it for years, and his tangled encounters with Mexican courts, lawyers, and two presidents provide some of the book's most fascinating pages ... the twists and turns of the legal process eventually become as intriguing as True's hike across the mountains. What seems an open-and-shut case becomes anything but.... Mr. Rivard, in his self-effacing way, emerges as a quietly heroic figure in this story. In military fashion, he simply refused to leave a man in the field. 'True's last trek might have been a personal quest, but for journalists, he died as a reporter because he was a reporter,' he writes. 'That meant something.'"
—WILLIAM GRIMES, *New York Times*

"Rivard tells this murky story exceedingly well." —*The Boston Globe*

"A bold and heartbreaking book. . . . The book is many things at once: A wildlife adventure story and true-crime tale; an account of True's own off-beat life (aspects of which he had never shared even with his wife); Rivard's personal quest to find True and then to avenge his murder; and an analysis of how politics and the U.S. and Mexican governments both helped and hindered the investigation of the first modern-day homicide of a foreign correspondent on Mexican soil. . . . The details are heartbreaking not only because of True's tragic end but also because of Rivard's personal connection to his former reporter. . . . [E]nthralling." —LISE OLSEN, *The Houston Chronicle*

"Robert Rivard's *Trail of Feathers* is a powerful, important story, filled with intrigue, insights, fascinating characters, and high drama. It's a potent, revealing non-fiction book that reads like a novel. This is a haunting, riveting work as timely as tomorrow's headlines." —DAN RATHER

"Philip True was the epitome of a reporter's reporter, at least as described in this moving account of his murder in a remote corner of western Mexico. . . . Rivard thoroughly fleshes out True . . . and such characters as the sullen Huichols accused of the murder, the delusional crusader defending them, and Mexican president Vicente Fox. . . . Rivard's engaging, compassionate . . . story goes beyond the tragedy of True's death to include the vast, beautiful and troubling world of Mexico itself, 'where people are preyed on by the very forces that exist to protect them.'" —*Publishers Weekly*

"[An] extraordinarily gripping, rare insider's account of the whole affair. . . . Rivard brings an unexpected literary flourish to his telling, exploring with great compassion the deeper sources of True's life and journalism, alongside a revealing, memoiristic reflection on his own life and career, including some searing mea culpas, that give the book a powerful emotional resonance. . . . *Trail of Feathers* emerges as an exemplary work of literary journalism, unique in its balance of hard-edged reporting and ambitious reaches into the profound implications of the Philip True saga."

—John Phillip Santos, *The San Antonio Express-News*

"After an American journalist is murdered in a remote area of Mexico, his editor pursues the truth—and the killers—with astonishing fidelity and tenacity.... At times the narrative feels like a Latin-American *Bleak House*, where truth and justice seem incidental ..."

—*Kirkus Reviews*

"*Trail of Feathers* is tremendous for the way it digs into enormous issues of history, poverty, and bilateral misperceptions. Moreover, when it comes to editorial perseverance, Rivard is the gold standard.... Long after True's case faded from the news, Rivard remained relentless. The case consumed his life when he could have dismissed the whole thing as further proof of Mexican corruption and inscrutability. It's enough to make reporters wonder whether their own editors, in these days of ceaseless budget cuts, could equal Rivard's effort in pursuing justice for True and his widow.... In the meantime, *Trail of Feathers* stands as testimony that despite all that has changed in Mexico, it remains a country where justice isn't given, it must be taken." —*Columbia Journalism Review*

"Aptly labeled a 'true crime/memoir,' it's not just one story of crime and punishment, but also an exploration of deeply hidden personal secrets, bonds between men, the nature of contemporary journalism, cultural differences, the nature of justice and, ultimately, what one editor believed he owed a friend and reporter.... Rivard ... imbues common stories of human frailty and triumph with an engaging universality, and he brings often unfathomable issues of international relations and cultures in conflict to the human level. More important, he has submitted a far more intimate true-crime book than the market has seen in many years.... *Trail of Feathers* deftly explores the effects of a single choice as they ripple outward. Philip True's ill-fated journey set in motion several other journeys, some of which have not yet ended. That might be an uncomfortable conclusion for mass-market true-crime fans, but it's real. It's true." —*Denver Post*

"[Rivard's] writing is . . . crisp and fresh . . . emerging with luminous salience is this: More fierce even than True's murder was the determination of his family and colleagues. They would not permit Mexican authorities to make a murder akin to an insignificant feather, easily blown away by the winds of indifference."

—DANIEL DYER, *Cleveland Plain Dealer*

"This is the powerful, riveting true story of a reporter's slaying in Mexico and his editor's search for justice. . . . Suspenseful, atmospheric, and deeply moving, *Trail of Feathers* is more than a mere true crime tale. It is an indictment of justice south of the border and one man's determination to find true justice for a former colleague."

—*Tucson Citizen*

"Rivard's book *Trail of Feathers: Searching for Philip True* is part tribute to True, but a warts-and-all tribute. It also is part autobiography, but a warts-and-all autobiography. On both counts, it is an unusual and superb book. Rarely are authors so candid about dead colleagues and about themselves. . . . Each story is told sensitively. Rivard manages to write page after page without sounding an insincere note. *Trail of Feathers* is a triumph, managing to uplift even as it chronicles degradation. . ." —STEVE WEINBERG, *The Oregonian*

TRAIL OF FEATHERS

ROBERT RIVARD

PublicAffairs *New York*

TRAIL OF FEATHERS

Searching for Philip True

A REPORTER'S MURDER IN MEXICO
AND HIS EDITOR'S SEARCH FOR JUSTICE

First published in hardcover in 2005 in the United States by PublicAffairs™, a member of the Perseus Books Group.
Published in paperback in 2006 by PublicAffairs™.

Book design and composition by Mark McGarry, Texas Type & Book Works
Set in Fairfield

Library of Congress Cataloging-in-Publication Data
Rivard, Robert, 1952–
Trail of feathers : searching for Philip True / by Robert Rivard.
p. cm.
"A reporter's murder in Mexico and his editor's search for justice."
Includes bibliographical references.
HC: ISBN-13 978-1-58648-222-0; ISBN-10 1-58648-222-X
1. True, Philip, d. 1998—Death and burial. 2. Murder victims—Mexico. 3. Foreign correspondents—Crimes against—Mexico—Case studies. 4. Murder—Mexico—Sierra Madre Occidental—Case studies. 5. Murder—Investigation—Mexico—Case studies.
6. Huichol Indians. I. Title.
HV6535.M42S54 2005
364.152'3'09723—dc22   2005045822

PBK: ISBN-13 978-1-58648-455-2; ISBN-10 1-58648-455-9

10 9 8 7 6 5 4 3 2 1

To Monika,
faithful companion on life's journey, and to Nick and Alex,
as they embark on their own.

Contents

Author's Note

On the morning of November 27, 1998, Philip True, the Mexico City correspondent for the *San Antonio Express-News*, walked out his front door to a waiting taxi summoned from the corner *sitio*. Martha, his Mexican-born wife, was four months pregnant with their first child and not yet showing. She stood by and watched as her husband and the driver wrestled True's heavy backpack into the car's small trunk for the ride to the airport and his flight to Guadalajara.

It was the Friday after Thanksgiving Day. The American holiday is not celebrated in Mexico, but True had scrounged through Mexico City's open-air markets, tracking down everything he needed to prepare an elaborate farewell feast of roast goose with all the trimmings. Before every great trip, Philip always told Martha, a great meal.

At 50, True had a rugged, weathered face but was boyishly lean and fit, an outdoors devotee bound for a long awaited ten-day trek into the remote canyon country of western Mexico. True's outing would be both wilderness quest and journalistic exploration of the reclusive Huichol (wee-chole) Indians, whose small villages and outlying ranches were spread along the deep folds of the Sierra Madre Occidental.

True gave his wife one last kiss and climbed into the taxi. "If I'm not back in ten days, come looking for me," he said, then waved good-bye through the open window as the taxi disappeared from view up the steep, winding street.

No one who knew True ever saw him alive again.

True was my reporter. I was his editor. We were not close friends, but we had much in common: difficult home lives we fled as teenagers, years of blue-collar work as directionless young men, and a backdoor entrée into newspaper reporting that gave each of us a new start in life. The many intersections of our two lives began long before we met.

We came from distant corners of the United States, yet somehow made our way to the same small daily newspaper in the same small city on the Texas–Mexico border. More than a decade separated our arrival in Brownsville. But it was there, where the muddy waters of the Rio Grande flow downstream and empty into the Gulf of Mexico, that each of us began to pursue a reporter's life working south of the border. Our paths crossed for the first time in San Antonio in 1992; soon afterward, True and I found ourselves working together at the same South Texas newspaper. My own rise from reporter to senior editor positioned me to send True to live and work south of the border, just as I had once lived and worked south of the border. Years later, fate led me south once more, this time not on assignment, but in search of my lost reporter.

Philip True was a journalist with working-class roots and no known family other than Martha; he had little to say about his own past life. He was openly skeptical of anyone in power, in government, and even at his own newspaper. He wrote with great craft and empathy about the poor and the powerless. It was his keen appreciation for the redeeming qualities of people living on the margins that made his best stories so memorable.

Only after his disappearance did I learn that True was a devoted walker, in the wilderness definition of the word. He savored every opportunity to leave behind his everyday existence to venture into the unknown, sometimes with a friend or girlfriend but usually alone. Retracing his life much later, I figured that True had spent an entire year sleeping outdoors on treks, camping and cycling trips, and hitchhiking adventures. He never stopped.

"Walking in the wilderness," True told his Mexico City therapist, Sara Delano Rojas, in one particularly revealing remark, "helps me put back together the pieces of my broken soul."

News of True's long-planned trek caught me by surprise when I learned he was missing. I had covered civil wars and repression in Central America in the 1980s, so his disappearance was deeply unsettling news. I knew what could befall a reporter traveling alone in the lawless backcountry. I wondered why True had set out without a companion.

As Martha and the newspaper launched a search, I realized I could not stay in San Antonio while others went into the mountains. So I went looking for True, fearing the worst, hoping for the best. Only one thing was certain: we were going to find him, no matter what.

Days after his reported disappearance, our small search party came upon True's remains in a hidden grave, deep in the Chapalagana canyon, which translates from the Huichol language to Canyon of the Twisted Serpent. He had been murdered, the first accredited U.S. journalist to suffer such a fate in Mexico in modern times.

Many of Mexico's ancient peoples such as the Olmecs and the Aztecs have disappeared, declined, or assimilated. Others, such as the Maya and the Zapotecs, have somehow survived while suffering the theft of ancestral lands, the indifference of a distant central government, and the twin burdens of poverty and prejudice. In a country with hundreds of identifiable indigenous groups that are mere remnants of once thriving societies, the Huichols remain Mexico's most isolated and preserved native people.

There are fewer than 20,000 Huichols, scattered in small settlements throughout the Sierra Madre, but they remain fiercely faithful to their history and traditions. They speak their own language, are known for their traditional dress and folk art, and live a simple if impoverished agrarian life. The Huichols worship gods found in nature, and their shamans, or priests, are the keepers of an ancient oral history, recounted and passed down from one generation to the next in long singsong chants.

The Huichols will walk hundreds of miles and back to find and gather peyote, a button-shaped cactus that induces hallucinations when ingested, for use in their sacred rituals. Huichol shamans, chanting ancient creation myths, gaze through this hallucinatory window into space and time, where the past and the future are both at hand. They commune with ancestors and even experience the mystical transformation of man into beast, unleashed to roam the sierra on all fours.

Following True's footsteps through the Huichol Sierra was its own strange, sometimes dreamlike odyssey. After hiking into one of the Sierra Madre's most forbidding gorges, we descended into an even deeper labyrinth, the Mexican judicial system. Our search for a missing reporter became a search for missing justice in a country where the rule of law is as fleeting and elusive as the passing spirit of a man-deer in the canyon country.

The gruesome killing of a reporter metamorphosed into a larger drama, steeped in the unresolved historical grievances that simmer in the hearts of many Mexicans. Few Americans know that the United States seized nearly half of Mexico's territory in 1848, an act regarded by many historians on both sides of the border as a blatant "Manifest Destiny" land grab. American textbooks largely ignore such history, but every Mexican student studies this defining historical episode, one that was followed by two more cross-border military incursions in the twentieth century. Cross the border to the south, even now, and you do not need peyote to sense the memories of defeat and resentment hovering in every room like ghosts. Such feelings lay beneath the surface in the True case, like shifting sands, always undermining forward movement.

Trail of Feathers took shape slowly as I lost faith in Mexico's justice system. One year, two years, five years slipped by after True's murder, the case languishing in Mexican courts while his killers went free. We met with presidents, ambassadors, governors, judges, lawyers, and investigators, all actors in the drama. All vowed justice but none could deliver. Many believed True was a victim of his own bad decisions, when in fact he was murdered in cold blood. This book began as my own final argument in the court of public opinion.

Along this path, I found the story of True's "other life," before he became a newspaper reporter at the relatively advanced age of 41. It was a story that editors had gleaned only in its vaguest outlines while he was alive. True kept that story at the bottom of his backpack, hidden from view. Finding it became the key to giving deeper meaning to his life and death.

I came to know True far better in death than in life, just as I came to know and admire Martha as a widow far better than I knew her as True's wife. In telling her husband's story, I had to choose between the truth and airbrushing his disturbing family life and years as an unfulfilled young man. I also had to share enough of my own unhappy upbringing to help readers understand the deep psychological attachment I felt to True as we pursued his killers. Digging up the past can be hurtful, but such revelations illuminate what otherwise would remain in the dark, unfathomed and beyond grasp.

The Philip True I came to know was a self-reliant, somewhat fatalistic sojourner and at times a risk taker who gave too little thought to the potential consequences of his actions, driven to know what lay over the horizon. True was no fool, but he remained an idealist into middle age, a man who regarded every stranger as a friend. As a journalist, True was a sensitive, caring witness in a part of the world where justice and hope are as scarce as water in the desert. It is a cruel irony that such a good friend of Mexico and its people died in pursuit of a story he was willing to walk through a wilderness to find and bring home.

True went in search of a threatened people and culture. What he found differed from his own idealized vision of indigenous life. Some of True's decisions on the trail, as well as his killers' motive, remain the subject of speculation. I draw my own conclusions, but I am not an objective observer. I was True's editor, his advocate in Mexico's courts, and an ally of his widow, Martha.

Trail of Feathers is a story about a quest. True's descent into the Chapalagana was the last solo trek in a lifelong journey to leave behind his past, a final walk before embracing his future as a father and husband, as a man who would no longer walk alone. Some will conclude that True's hubris led him forward on his fatal peregrination, a trespasser on closed, communal lands where distrust of strangers is born from centuries of resisting outside forces. Perhaps so, but True had visited the Huichols more than once. He believed he was welcome.

There is far more to it, something deeper than anything found at the bottom of a dark canyon. Powerful life forces breed independent spirits like True and cause them to venture forth into the unknown. Until the very end, he went searching for something he never quite found in civilization. By journey's end, we learn from reading his journal, True realized what he sought was no longer to be found on the trail but was waiting for him back home: a loving wife carrying his baby, a family he could finally call his own. By then it was too late.

Part 1

True's Route through the Chapalagana

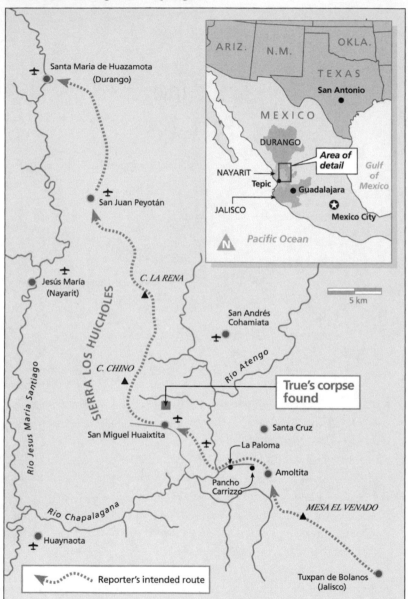

1

Agent True

As anthropologists began comparing notes on the world's few remaining primitive cultures, they discovered something unexpected. From the most isolated tribal society in Africa to the most distant islands in the Pacific, people shared essentially the same definition of what is news. They shared the same kind of gossip. They even looked for the same qualities in the messengers they picked to gather and deliver their news. They wanted people who could run swiftly over the next hill, accurately gather information, and engagingly retell it.

—Bill Kovach and Tom Rosenstiel, *The Elements of Journalism*

MEXICO CITY, MARCH 1998

Philip True had spent a lifetime preparing for this journey. Now he sat at his keyboard, writing in the early morning light and imagining the perfect trek. He would go alone, a reporter in search of a story, a walker in search of a solitary backcountry experience.

Before taking his first step into the wilderness, however, he had to sell this ambitious undertaking to editors in San Antonio—not an easy task. The story that True had in mind wasn't exactly news or even a typical feature story related to some current event. True was asking his editors to underwrite a personal quest.

After living and working for three years in Mexico City as the correspondent for the *San Antonio Express-News,* True believed he had come across the ultimate reporting foray, a solo exploration of one of the hemisphere's last surviving native cultures. The Huichols were an ancient people who had dwelled in isolation for a long time, some say for more than a thousand years. True, however, was in a hurry. In a matter of months, the rainy season would render the backcountry impassable. If he didn't go now, he'd have to wait until winter.

As True polished his story proposal, he omitted any mention of his imagined hike through the wilds. He focused instead on his planned encounter with the reclusive Huichols. To reach their remote villages, he would have to walk the footpaths that course through swallowing canyons, over soaring mesas chiseled by wind and the eons, and up and down the steep slopes of the Sierra Madre. The Huichol world is caught in another time, largely devoid of roads, electricity, running water, and telephones. Often the only sounds are the sounds of nature.

I have come across what I think would make a good story; if not for the news side, certainly for one of the Sunday sections.

The Huichol Indians live in Mexico's last true wilderness, the Sierra Madre Occidental of northern Jalisco, Nayarit and Durango. It is John Huston country: a 100-mile wide swath of big-boned mountains and rolling mesas cut by vertical river canyons.

In an area of tens of thousands of square miles, there are only a handful of dirt roads. To get anywhere, you most often have to walk or ride horses.

The good stories, True believed, were always found "out there" somewhere, in places that required perseverance to reach. Stories about man versus nature, man versus man: peasants caught in the global economy, drought gripping helpless farmers, the poor sold short by politicians, a ragtag army of Mayans taking up arms against the Mexican government in Chiapas.

True liked to work far from the press pack. He rebelled when given conventional story assignments, especially ones that required a coat and tie or attendance at a press conference with self-important government officials playing to the cameras amid the jangle of cell phones.

True the reporter, like True the backpacker, was a solo artist. He worked better alone. Even *Express-News* photographers, who admired his ground-level view of Mexico, his Spanish fluency, and his disciplined work ethic, found True difficult to work with at times. It wasn't that he didn't appreciate the importance of visual journalism; True himself was an amateur photographer. No, True simply plunged ahead single-mindedly, not taking into account the photographer's need to work at a more measured pace, to put subjects at ease, to work in just the right light.

Most of his workdays in Mexico City began with a call to his editor in the San Antonio newsroom, checking in, talking news developments and story ideas, assessing the competition, and trolling for the latest gossip. Despite that lifeline, True faltered when it came to navigating the newsroom where he had never physically worked. As a bureau reporter, he knew few of his newsroom colleagues. Playing politics, lobbying senior editors—these were skills that eluded him.

On one visit to headquarters, True showed up in worn jeans and leather huaraches on his bare feet, hardly the uniform of a professional journalist visiting the home office for his annual review. Until he was instructed otherwise, True made little effort to drop by the offices of top editors while on home leave. He took it personally when editors resisted his story ideas, as if they were slighting his good work or questioning the judgment of their correspondent on the ground.

What he lacked in political skills, however, True made up with a passion for chasing after good stories, no matter how hard the pursuit. His distrust of people in power and his working-class roots made True an especially sensitive reporter in a time and place when many in the media world came from more privileged circumstances than the people they covered.

The Huichols have evolved a cultural expression at least as colorful as the Chiapan Maya. Their white cotton suits are extensively embroidered in red, blue and yellow; they wear beaded necklaces and wristbands; their shamans don hats decked with mirrors, eagle and parrot feathers. Peyote is an integral part of their worship of nativist gods. Their life has been studied by anthropologists for decades.

Unlike the highland Maya, the Huichols have retained a certain joy in their life. A day near a Huichol community is marked by the nearly constant sound of children laughing and playing. This kind of joy gives them a certain integrity in their being that allows them to welcome in strangers, something the Maya are usually loath to do.

Few reporters would have conceived a similar story pitch. True, however, had been an outdoorsman since his teenage years in Southern California, and he prided himself on his fitness and adventurous spirit.

"He never knew a fat day in his life," said Joe Vasquez, True's best friend at San Fernando High School outside Los Angeles. The two cruising buddies and gymnastic team members learned early on to watch each other's backs in a school ruled by feuding white, black, and brown gangs.

True had taken many memorable trips over the years, some alone, some with Vasquez or Peter Harris, his off-campus roommate at the University of California–Irvine, some with girlfriends. Several times he had met trouble along the way: thieves on Alaska's Chilkoot trail, a pack of threatening drunks on a Nova Scotia peninsula, maniac truckers in Mexico. But when it came time to plan his next wilderness excursion, True seemed oblivious to the possibility of new dangers.

Pitching his journey into Huichol lands, True painted an irresistible landscape of a forgotten civilization preserved like an ancient insect in amber. All but invisible to the outside world, the Huichols lived in a forgotten place, a largely blank space on the map, yet endangered on all sides by encroaching modernity. In that seductive landscape, True did not see himself as a stranger or a trespasser. He didn't see himself as part of the story. He was just a good reporter serving as a bridge between his readers and a lost world.

The Huichol lifestyle has been affected by contacts with Mexican mestizo culture, but remains remarkably intact. Outside a handful of small towns, wheels do not exist. A small hand grinder for corn-meal is the usual concession to modernity (although a battery-driven boom box is occasionally seen). Distant communications are still conducted with a column of smoke.

That lifestyle now stands on the cusp of dramatic change. This month, the Mexican government strung electric lines to the town of Tuxpan de Bolanos. After a series of confrontations between Huichols and mestizo Mexicans living on disputed communal lands last year, other resources (and the government agents that accompany them) are now making their way into the back country. There is a building boom in the 300-person community.

A look at Huichol country as it confronts this influx of modernity would be a fascinating, wonderfully visual piece. The countryside, the people and their ceremonies are breathtaking and accessible. The Huichols are at once adaptive and open to change, while representing one of Mexico's vanishing indigenous cultures.

True described a world unknown to his editors or readers. He seemed gripped by the possibility of walking out of the late twentieth-century commotion of Mexico City and, all alone, entering a place lost in time.

The proposed trek combined two of the three great passions in his life: testing himself in the wilderness and unearthing great newspaper stories. Martha (pronounced Már-ta, in the Spanish style) was Philip's other great passion. She slept peacefully in the bedroom next to Philip's home office as he put the finishing touches on his story proposal.

Sometimes at work in his Mexico City home, True paused to savor this place and point in his life. Less than a decade earlier, he had been driving an aging red van and hanging wallpaper in Long Island, chasing clients for cash advances. He had lived with a cast of ever changing roommates in shared apartments, taking up with some new girlfriend even as he skirted the unpleasant aftermath of a breakup with another.

Now, at age 50, after almost ten years in the newspaper business, True was greeting each new day alongside a smart, beautiful woman who had been his wife for six years. He was the Mexico City correspondent for an ambitious regional newspaper, a daily read from San Antonio, "the Alamo City," all the way south to the border, serving one of the greatest concentrations of Mexican Americans in the United States. People there cared about his stories.

Philip and Martha, along with his cranky parrot, Fidel, lived in a small, comfortable home in one of Mexico City's most desirable neighborhoods, the rent and most of their other living expenses paid by the newspaper. Fewer than twenty-five other U.S. newspaper journalists enjoyed the same lifestyle. Fortune came late in life for True, but when it did come, it was sweet and it was satisfying.

At the same time, the jumping off place for Huichol country, the 16th century mining town of Bolanos, is of interest in its own right. Colonial ruins line the town's cobbled streets. The place was nearly abandoned between 1940 and 1970, when the price of silver brought several mines back into production.

Its mayor is the rarest of things: a decent PRI politician. He has a hat full of ambitious schemes to try to bring further prosperity to Tuxpan de Bolanos and the Huichol country, few of which will probably fly in this era of reduced developmental resources from Mexico City. He also eats peyote buttons, of which he had three on a shelf behind his desk when I spoke with him.

There is a beautiful story within all of this. Interested?

True carefully reviewed his work and then hit the send button. It was time to brew an espresso, wake up Martha, who headed a non-profit environmental agency in Mexico City, and then head out for a seven-mile jog and a new day.

*

Fred Bonavita, the tall, white-whiskered editor who oversaw the *Express-News* bureaus in Washington, Texas, and Mexico, opened the waiting e-mail from the correspondent he affectionately called "Agent True." Bonavita had listened to True rehearse his pitch over the telephone; now he read the e-mail. It would fall to Bonavita to persuade senior editors to let True make the trip.

John MacCormack bestowed the nickname on True. MacCormack was the newsroom's most respected reporter and something of a legend around the state for turning up leads that broke open the long dormant investigation into the murder of atheist Madeline Murray O'Hare. MacCormack also served as Bonavita's unofficial deputy, and in that role fielded his own fair share of morning calls from the Mexico City correspondent. The nickname captured True's streak of independence and his knack for being in the right place at the right time.

Bonavita and True were ten years apart in age, but they enjoyed a kind of father–son relationship, the wiser, more experienced and grounded Bonavita guiding the more emotional, sometimes hotheaded True. The two men developed a close relationship, each at the distant end of a telephone line. Bonavita, a former reporter and now a few years from retirement, was held in high regard by his troops in the field. He exerted a calming influence on far-flung reporters working alone, and he knew how to polish a story without imposing his own voice.

Reserved and circumspect, Bonavita sidestepped open conflicts with higher-ranking editors. He never raised his familiar, scratchy voice in story meetings when he didn't get his way, and he didn't use the office e-mail system to vent. He tended to express disagreement or doubts subtly by breaking off eye contact or clearing his throat. Bonavita had learned a trick or two from the Texas politicians he spent years covering as a statehouse reporter. He knew when to push and when to yield. As much as Bonavita liked True, he saw no advantage in butting heads if there was no chance of prevailing.

Agent True's latest story proposal was a long shot. You don't give reporters weeks off to go backpacking and camping by themselves in the wilderness. What happens if real news breaks out? As editors up the line read the memo and asked questions, they slowly learned what True had left out of his pitch—he would make his journey on foot, surviving on whatever he could carry on his back through the harsh, inaccessible terrain. There were no roads or telephones and no way for editors to track him.

The whole thing was unconventional, more of a travelogue suited for *National Geographic* magazine than a newspaper story. The *Express-News* wanted its reporter to stay focused on Mexico's opening economy and the coming end of autocratic one-party rule. His proposal seemed disconnected from the biggest stories of the day in his region: Mexico's slow march toward democracy, free trade, drug trafficking, and the standoff between the government and Zapatista guerrillas in Chiapas.

The idea was met with indifference when Bonavita shared it with senior editors, among them Carolina Garcia, the recently hired managing editor who supervised the newsroom's day-to-day coverage. Garcia was poised, articulate, and well tailored, and her distinctive silvery white hair made her easy to spot in the cavernous newsroom. She had returned to her native Texas after nearly two decades in Milwaukee, and her management style at times was more formal and demanding than some at the paper were used to. "She didn't share the same interest in Mexico as other editors and didn't seem to play stories about Mexico on page one," said Bonavita.

True, naturally distrustful of management, did not like authority figures, and he did not like the new managing editor and what he saw as a corresponding decline in front-page play of Mexico and border stories. The clique of bilingual reporters in the San Antonio newsroom—many of them experienced border reporters, others with prior work experience in Mexico and Central America—shared his view.

Life looks different from the bureaus and the reporting ranks than it does from the page one meeting, when editors weigh competing stories and agendas every day. In Garcia's defense, Mexico simply wasn't generating the kind of headlines it did when the guerrilla uprising first

broke out four years earlier or when the free trade agreement was negotiated and signed in the early 1990s. Reporters and photographers
didn't care about meetings; they chased good stories and competed for
page one.

I was finishing my first year as editor after moving up from managing editor, so if attention to Mexico and the border declined, I would
have to share the blame. Frankly, I didn't see it, at least not in any systematic way. My own newspaper career had been defined in large part
by my years as a reporter working on the border, in Mexico, and in
Central America during the violent 1980s. I never thought we lost
interest in the region or the story. In any event, no one ever brought
True's proposal to my attention. It languished in the *Express-News*
computer system, one more story pitch stacked electronically in the
story queues. Bonavita advised Agent True to move on.

But his man in Mexico City had no intention of moving on or of
accepting what he interpreted as diminishing interest in his work at
headquarters. As the rainy season ended in late November, True sat
down at his computer and launched a blunt, challenging e-mail to the
managing editor and several others.

He cited a recent story in the *American Journalism Review,* published by the University of Maryland's journalism school, that singled
out True's Mexico coverage as equal to that of any of the major
national newspapers.

> The documentation is accumulating—from readers, critics and
> newspaper analysts—that, as compared not to the Texas competi-
> tion, but to the New York Times and the Los Angeles Times, the
> San Antonio Express-News' Mexico coverage, "more consistently
> reports with depth, insight and continuity as opposed to headline
> news full of sensationalism." I read that as superior coverage.

> Given the praise, not to mention the awards received by the
> Mexican bureau... over the past two years, I would imagine that
> we would want to lead with strength, and prominently feature our
> Mexican coverage in the paper. There is reason. Mexico is the

United States' second largest trading partner; billions of dollars of trade pass through San Antonio annually bound for or coming in from Mexico, and many important San Antonio business people are looking for ways to cash in on that; our city is 60% Hispanic. . . San Antonio's historic ties to events in Mexico are long and intimate.

But over the past six months it seems that the paper's Mexico news hole is closer to page nineteen than page one; thoughtful and provocative project ideas go without response; Sunday stories now appear in Sunday Insight rather than the A section, because little interest is evidenced in *longer* pieces, etc.

What is wrong with this picture?

I will be in San Antonio on home visit early in the week of Christmas (Dec. 21–25). I would like to meet with as many of you as possible to see if we can answer that question. Thanks.

After learning from Bonavita that he had failed to persuade the editors to approve his trek through Huichol territory, True quietly decided to put in for vacation time and make the trip anyway. He would share his plans with only a few key newsroom allies and colleagues in Mexico City and be back by mid-December, in plenty of time to keep his appointment in San Antonio later in the month.

The memo and its challenging tone, like True's earlier story proposal, never reached my desk. It drew an immediate rebuke from Garcia to Bonavita. The managing editor did not like a bureau reporter she had met only once challenging her news judgment. Worse, he had done so in a widely distributed memo sent to enough subordinates to ensure its quick passage into the newsroom gossip network.

True, the former labor organizer, wasn't finished. He worked the phones in search of allies. He telephoned Dane Schiller, the newspaper's border correspondent in Laredo, to recruit him to his planned Christmas week showdown with senior editors. True argued that strength in numbers would force the bosses to give ground.

Schiller, a former naval intelligence hand, was more measured. He agreed with True's assessment that Mexico had fallen off the front page, but he had promising contacts at the *Dallas Morning News* he could pursue if he grew as unhappy with his editors as True was. He advised True to cancel his planned march on Mahogany Row (as the rank and file described the well-appointed offices occupied by senior editors), who were unlikely to yield under pressure.

Bonavita knew of his reporter's planned visit home, and he intended to do all he could to prevent Agent True from provoking senior editors. True was scheduled to receive his annual performance review and salary increase on the same visit. Bonavita set out to defuse the potential problem in his written evaluation, dated December 14, 1998, which awaited Garcia's review and signature. The evaluation praised True's work over the preceding year, without assigning blame for the tensions resulting from the e-mail exchanges between True and the front office. In regard to True's initiative, Bonavita wrote, "He frequently recommends stories that might be overlooked or underplayed by the home office, although he can become quite upset when these touts don't always bear fruit."

Under "human relations/attitude": "Philip's attitude in dealing with the home office in recent weeks has suffered from a combination of things: his impatience and a slow response from San Antonio to his requests for things that earlier were done almost automatically. While Philip is entitled to complain about the former, he needs to do it through channels. Going over a person's head to the next highest editor or executive is counterproductive. Scattergun memos achieve little other than causing more problems. Philip needs a better grip on his patience."

Bonavita didn't mention any editors by name or title, and at the same time, he deftly avoided language that suggested True was the problem. His criticism of True's intemperate e-mails was mild. Bonavita, in so many words, implicitly framed True's behavior as the inevitable result of senior editors not paying attention to his work.

Bonavita concluded, "With better cooperation from the home office to keep the bureau running smoothly and with new dedication to keeping his relations with San Antonio in better shape, Philip will approach the millennium in outstanding form."

It was a piece of skilled office diplomacy. He suggested a 6 percent salary increase, double the prevailing cost-of-living increase given to most reporters that year, an unmistakable show of support.

2
Caminando/Getting Ready

All the monuments in Mexico are to violent deaths . . . Perhaps it is the atmosphere of violence—perhaps only the altitude, seven thousand odd feet—but after a few days not many people can escape the depression of Mexico City.

—Graham Greene, *The Lawless Roads*

MEXICO CITY, NOVEMBER 1998

Striding toward the setting sun in the west, True made his way along the pedestrian path paralleling the broad, busy Paseo de la Reforma. A noisy mob of automobiles crowded the capital's great historic avenue. True moved along, double-time, through the screech of tires and the blare of horns along the cinder walkway on the edge of Chapultepec Park.

Mexico City's great cultural and historical attractions beckoned all around: the National Museum of Anthropology, the Modern Art Museum, and the Rufino Tamayo Museum. Chapultepec Castle stood sentinel high on a hill where, legend goes, six boy soldiers, their ammunition exhausted as U.S. troops encircled the military school, wrapped themselves in Mexican flags and leaped to their deaths rather than surrender to the Yankee invaders in 1847.

Reforma, modeled after Europe's grandest monumental avenues, was no longer the elegant, restrained boulevard originally envisioned by its early-nineteenth-century creator and another of Mexico's foreign usurpers, Emperor Maximilian of Hapsburg. Traffic surged, slowed, and surged again in an endless, ear-splitting cycle, the futility punctuated by the occasional comic sound of a car horn tooting "La Cucaracha" or a few bars of a Mexican bullfight song. Each morning and again in the evening, Reforma was like a writhing serpent, not quite able to swallow its struggling prey of moving, mechanized humanity.

For the stalled, pent-up drivers, there were familiar diversions. Fire-eaters, dark-skinned men with bloodshot eyes, stood in midstreet. Before a captive audience, they put a match to kerosenesoaked torches and then slowly swallowed. Tourists often recoiled with horror on first witnessing the street spectacle, while locals tended to look on with indifference or amusement. The fire-eaters pleaded for spare pesos in the seconds before the light tuned green, then awaited with resignation the next wave of commuting voyeurs.

Peasant women wrapped in colorful handwoven fabrics hawked lurid afternoon tabloids and sheets of lottery tickets, their mournful faces reflecting the scarcity of takers. Young Indian children, barefoot and unwashed, scurried between lanes to peddle penny packets of chicle (chewing gum). Older boys ignored the gestures of indignant drivers and smeared windshields with greasy rags, offering to go away for spare change.

Gleaming Mercedes-Benzes and the latest SUVs idled alongside vintage Volkswagen Beetles still manufactured in Mexico and smoking old Chevrolets and Fords, unregistered relics from north of the border brought home by returning migrants. The rich and the working poor alike sparred, bumper to bumper, in a morning and evening macho Mexico City ritual set amid the capital's great, green park.

Drivers maneuvered desperately. A sudden lane change or the gain of a single car length represented victory in these petty skirmishes, finished off with hostile eye contact between victor and vanquished.

Otherwise civilized men in tailored suits and expensive sedans careened through traffic like punch-drunk boxers in the ring. As signal lights changed from red to green, vehicles surged forward like thoroughbreds breaking from the gate in a race. Cars tore by True as if their occupants were fleeing the capital, escaping an earthquake or some other natural disaster. They were only going home.

Amid the urban cacophony, True marched along the path with the discipline of a soldier. He held a stout wooden walking stick in his right hand. A red backpack rose above his head like a totem. Stiff walking shorts and heavy hiking books over thick, turned-down socks completed his outdoor ensemble.

The thin, acrid air of Mexico City, elevation 7,564 feet, could reduce visiting joggers to tears and fits of coughing. Breezes die in the winter months, trapping the hazy air in a thermal inversion that envelopes the great Valle de Mexico, a slowly sinking dry lake bed burdened with 18 million people, a figure demographers admit is only an educated guess.

True walked with the steady, practiced pace of an experienced hiker. Daily jogs for three years in one of the hemisphere's highest and most polluted cities acclimated him to the altitude and often poisonous atmosphere. Each November day, as afternoon gave way to evening, True turned away from his reporting work, changed into outdoor gear, and hoisted his backpack laden with rocks to approximate a sixty-pound trail load. His planned departure day, the morning after Thanksgiving, loomed in the weeks ahead. Every day of training counted.

Drivers busy with their own battles must have caught a glimpse of True and wondered, "¿Quién es, y a donde va?" Who is that, and where is he going?

Mexico City's traffic could have lurched to a stop, but True would not have noticed. He was in another world, visualizing his wilderness odyssey, the very walk of his life, one greater than the sum of a lifetime of camping and hiking experiences. Bigger than Big Bend, bigger than the Chilkoot trail, bigger than Arcadia National Park in Maine,

bigger than Joshua Tree National Park, bigger even than the summer
he rode his bicycle solo from coast to coast, then south through Mexico. Well, maybe not bigger than the bike ride, his first foray into
Mexico, but more adventurous and this time on foot.

True's imagined journey would be one hundred miles of solitude:
ten miles a day for ten days through the plunging canyons and
windswept mesas of western Mexico, the Sierra Madre Occidental,
the setting for so many Wild West adventures, in print and on the big
screen. His intended route traversed much of Huichol territory. If
many claimed to have visited Huichol territory, no Mexican, and certainly no reporter, had walked its length solo.

One book on his shelf, *The Man Who Walked Through Time: The
Story of the First Trip Afoot Through the Grand Canyon,* by hiking guru
Collin Fletcher, was an inspiration.

True was going where no other reporter had gone. That was the
part his editors didn't get. No one else had this story. It wasn't just a
camping trip on company time.

There was one other important consideration weighing on True as
he mopped the sweat from his brow with the red bandana tied around
his neck, something else his editors did not know: Martha was pregnant. The couple had been hoping Martha would conceive, but the
news still came as a pleasant surprise.

Philip and Martha had flown from Mexico City to Brownsville and
on to New York earlier in the fall so he could introduce her to Long
Island friends and show her the Big Apple before they headed north
to visit Montreal and Quebec. Morning sickness hit along the way.
Philip and Martha used two different home pregnancy kits to confirm
the good news.

They spent one night in Southington, Connecticut, with Jim Wieloch and his new wife, Sonia Cantú Wieloch, the older sister of
Juanita Serrano, Martha's best friend since they were teenagers in
Matamoros. Over dinner, True pulled out a map and casually mentioned his plans for the solo trek into Huichol territory.

"You don't mean you're going by yourself, do you?" Sonia asked him. "If you do, you're crazy. Martha is pregnant, and that's a dangerous place."

True just smiled. He had made many such journeys, and he had always relied on his wits to avert real trouble when serious confrontations loomed. "That's exactly what I'm going to do," True said. "I want to learn more about the Huichols and, anyway, I've been there before."

"Man, you better take a *pistola*," Sonia said.

Philip and Martha also paid a visit to Bob Horchler and his wife, Julie McDonald, in the town of Baldwin on Long Island's South Shore. True and Horchler had played in the same volleyball league in the late 1980s, and Horchler remembers watching with admiration as True matter-of-factly announced he was giving up blue-collar work to become a journalist.

"Not many people just announce they are going to change their life and then do it," Horchler said.

A year later, True was a regular contributor to *La Tribuna*, Long Island's weekly Spanish-language newspaper serving the area's growing migrant and refugee community.

"He showed me the area he was going to hike in. It wasn't a very good map. I remember how horrified I was, even though he said he had made previous trips there," Horchler said. "Phil turned to me and said, 'Bob, these people would kill you just as soon as look at you.' The comment shocked me. It was as if he knew the people there really were not friendly."

Horchler's wife was left with the same impression. "He told us about another trip he had been on where he was hassled and it just seemed dangerous to us, and Bob asked him if he should be going on such a trip now with Martha pregnant," McDonald said. "I think he felt it was going to be his last trip and he was going to do it, a last fling before settling down."

Before they left, Philip and Martha gave their hosts a gift of Mexican folk art, a clay Day of the Dead statue.

*

Back home from their travels, time was running out for True if he was really going. Martha, at age 39, was nervous about her pregnancy and had scheduled further tests at the very time her husband would be absent. She was less than thrilled about her husband's planned absence. When he returned in ten days, Philip promised Martha, he would settle down and stay close, help her get ready for the baby. He would be there for her. But first, one last solo trek.

"I was going in for an amniocentesis, and I naturally wanted him there, but he told me not to worry," Martha said. "He wouldn't be there for the test, but he would be there when the results came back. I didn't try to stop him."

Pausing, she added, "I knew there was no stopping him."

Martha resigned herself to the inevitability of this final adventure. A grateful True sensed he better go quickly and get home on time. He scheduled vacation time for the first two weeks of December as his training peaked.

As he moved along Avenida Reforma, True tried to work through his frustration with the editors in San Antonio. When he came back, True told friends in the Mexico City press corps, his hard-won story and photographs would settle the issue in his favor. Editors would forget their previous objections, publish his work, and credit him for the vacation time. That would only underscore his argument that editors needed to follow the instincts of their man on the ground in Mexico.

His promise to Martha to settle down with her and *el bebe* had been made somewhat reluctantly, True admitted to fellow correspondents who gathered for the ritual *cantina* each Friday afternoon at the Bar Nuevo Leon. He knew he was at his best—and happiest—traveling the far-flung corners of this amazing, beautiful, miserable country as a journalist. As a father, he'd have to find his stories closer to home.

As he neared the end of an exhausting, three-hour, ten-mile training walk, True turned off Reforma onto Paseo de Las Palmas, and then into his *colonia*, his neighborhood, Las Lomas de Barrilaco. He walked down Monte Ararat, named after the resting place of Noah's ark, and finally on to Sierra Amatepec. He passed the big ravine, the

Barranca Tecamachalco, where he had gathered the rocks to weight his backpack.

Las Lomas de Chapultepec is one of the capital's most desirable districts, home to many of the city's most prosperous families. Las Lomas—that's all you have to say. The broad, tree-lined avenues are home to period mansions, some barely visible behind high, guarded walls often topped with shards of broken glass to deter nimble intruders. Private security guards patrol perimeters and heavy metal gates stand in the way of would-be thieves and kidnappers, whose crime sprees had reached epidemic proportions in recent years while the government and police seemed to look on helplessly. Mexico City is a city of great wealth, grinding poverty, and corrupt authority. Those who can afford it take the necessary precautions.

Yet trouble seems a world away in Las Lomas. Shaded islands divide traffic and provide vendors with room to display cut flowers. Leafy side streets host less ostentatious homes, cloaked in blooming bougainvillea, trumpet vine, and jacaranda trees.

Las Lomas sits high above the dense smog and rampant street crime of the old central city and the surrounding barrios that sprawl endlessly into the distance, often beyond view in the sulfur and ozone-laced air. Neighbors tend to be courteous but guarded. The house next door? One might never gain more than a passing glimpse afforded by the opening of a remotely controlled gate. At day's end, rich Mexicans retreat behind high walls. Home is *la casa*, where the outside world and all its intrusions are tightly locked out. Discretion is a way of life. Outside, an informal network of drivers and bodyguards, gardeners and servants keep watch. Any disturbance in the routine is quickly spotted, considered, and, if necessary, acted on.

The drivers at the taxi stand around the corner from True's home easily recalled the gringo reporter. Of late, he had come marching by each evening, head bent low, long arms swinging, hiking boots clomping loudly on the sidewalk, the big red backpack making him appear seven feet tall. *Chisme.* Gossip. There are few secrets in the *colonia*. Why was True marching through the streets each evening dressed like

an Alpine mountaineer? Was he *loco*? Maybe. True, *dios mío*, was getting ready for a journey to the Huichol sierra, a place few Mexicans
had ever ventured or would care to venture, for that matter.

Foreigners in the *colonia* are a familiar sight. Many diplomats,
international businessmen, and journalists choose to live in Las
Lomas, where they are safe and secure, the steep rents paid by the
home office or their sponsoring organizations.

For all its history, culture, and celebrated public life, Mexico City
is one of the world's most dangerous metropolises for foreigners and
even street-smart natives. There are more organized kidnappings here
than in any other capital. Even hailing a taxi on a busy street can be
hazardous to your health, with some drivers working with gangs to
hijack unsuspecting passengers.

Victims are robbed, often raped if they are female and beaten if
they are male, murdered if they resist. Stunned passengers are forced
at gunpoint to withdraw cash from one ATM machine after another
until their bank and credit cards are spent. Victims can turn afterward
to the local police, but good luck. Chances are local police are
involved or paid off.

Another Texas journalist, Jan Reid, a writer for *Texas Monthly* magazine, recounted his near-death experience as a victim in a book aptly
titled *The Bullet Meant for Me*. Reid tried to fight back against armed
robbers in cahoots with his taxi driver. Even today, the lanky onetime
athlete with a penchant for boxing limps along with the aid of a cane,
a revolver slug still lodged in his spine.

As True neared home on his evening hike, he slowly regained an
awareness of his surroundings, leaving behind for one more day the
long, coursing canyons and narrow footpaths of the sierra. He was following the advice offered in a particularly dog-eared book on his shelf,
The Complete Walker, the best-selling trekker's bible written by Colin
Fletcher in 1968 and still in print for new generations of true believers
to discover. "Make every effort to carry the pack as often as you can in
the week or two before you head for the wilderness, if only to prepare
your hips for the unaccustomed task. Details of distance and speed

are your affair, but . . . increase the dose until at the end you're pushing sweaty hard . . . The less conscious you are, the freer, that's all."

Thanksgiving Day, November 1998.

True had his rituals. One of them was the feast that always
marked the advent of a big trip. Martha had long ceased to be amazed
by her husband's attention to detail or his tenacity in orchestrating a
memorable pretrip meal. A great journey, True believed, was preceded
by a great repast. Even in Mexico City, True was determined to celebrate Thanksgiving Day in American style, with all the trimmings. He
finally had someone to share such holidays, and both he and Martha
talked about the coming baby, still in the womb but already part of
the family. "Might as well eat well now; this is going to be the last
good meal I eat before I leave," he told Martha.

Their cozy Chapultepec home was one of the smallest on the
block, fronted by a nondescript outer wall and guarded by an ancient,
drooping cypress tree. Inside the home was warm and inviting; works
by some of Mexico's best folk artists graced the walls and shelves,
lending color and a sense of the fantastic to their surroundings.

When Philip and Martha stayed home or when friends joined
them for the evening, True commandeered the kitchen, relishing the
opportunity to demonstrate his culinary prowess. His *ceviche* was legendary among friends, more so, recalled Kim Garcia, a former roommate and fellow reporter in Brownsville, because he refused to part
with his recipe. "Philip was a good cook, but he would not give anyone the recipe," Garcia said. "I'd have to stand over his shoulder and
wring the recipe out of him, standing and watching him cook, with his
parrot on his shoulder pecking me if I got too close."

To celebrate his pending trek to Huichol territory and to mark
Thanksgiving Day, True searched Mexico City's markets for a goose,
not a common commodity, along with everything else he needed to
prepare a gourmet meal for his wife.

"He finally found a goose downtown at the Mercado San Juan, so we had goose and stuffing," Martha said. "I was watching him prepare the meal, complaining that the room smelled and that the stuffing was going to taste bad because it had oysters and plums and apricots. I was sure it was going to turn out terrible, but he kept telling me, 'Just wait, you'll see,' and he was right. We had sweet potatoes with maple and orange syrup. All the recipes were from *The Joy of Cooking*. Everything was actually very good, and I've been making it on Thanksgiving ever since."

It was Thursday, November 26. True was set to leave the next morning. But something other than his pending departure made it a special day. Thanksgiving 1991 marked the start of Philip and Martha's courtship. Theirs was a relationship that almost never happened.

True had left his adopted home in Long Island and arrived in Brownsville toward the end of 1989, having won a job at the small *Brownsville Herald* on the strength of a telephone interview with the daily's retired editor, Lavis Laney.

Brownsville is where the Lone Star State meets Mexico, a land divided only by U.S. and Mexican flags and the narrow Rio Grande. For True, who had passed through Brownsville on previous forays into Mexico and Central America, the border city was an ideal learning ground as he embarked on a new career as a newspaper man.

True had the gift of gab. Laney knew after a half hour on the telephone with him that she had found herself a natural-born reporter. He'd also be a handful. He was older than most rookies at age 41, but he was smart, bilingual, and brimming with energy and potential, eager for a challenge. Laney needed exactly that—an enterprising, Spanish-speaking reporter to cover Matamoros, the larger, poorer sister city across the river the Mexicans called the Rio Bravo. Matamoros might be a stone's throw away, but it was a different world, home to feuding drug cartels, a corrupt police force and local government, and an overcrowded prison run by the inmates.

Sure, the bars and shops and restaurants within walking distance from the bridge enjoyed a lively tourist trade, and the more adventurous gringos found their way to Boystown, the controlled *zona de toler-*

ancia (red-light district) on the city's southern outskirts. But politics, violence, and the huge gap between rich and poor were the real beat for any reporter assigned to the other side.

True jumped at the chance, despite the low hourly pay. He sold off the tools of his wallpaper trade, loaded up his van, and left Long Island for good. True had completed his transformation: the paper-hanger was now a newspaper reporter.

"When he first came he was terribly disorganized, and he talked all the time, procrastinating, always talking, having trouble working with other people," Laney said. "I remember dreading working with him on Saturdays because he was so slow helping me get the stories done."

True's habit of challenging authority didn't stop on the beat; he often brought it back into the newsroom. Rebecca Thatcher, a younger but more experienced reporter, had met True a few years earlier when he passed through on his way back to Long Island from Central America. She remembers his battles with the *Herald* city editor. Another reporter there, Kimberly Garcia, recounted one exchange she overheard.

"Philip would start debating every little change in his copy or his assignments, how he was going to spend his workday, and in that little newsroom, everyone heard everything," she said. "One time he actually asked the city editor, 'Who made you the king of writing?' I had to pull him aside and tell him that's not how you get ahead in journalism, that you have to respect the hierarchy and the editing process."

Laney said matters came to a head a few months into True's first year there. "I finally had to sit him down and tell him he had to stop talking and start working. I said it in much stronger language than that. He looked amazed, almost stunned, like no woman had ever addressed him in that voice. But he sat down and got the work done, and it seems after that he turned a corner. There is no doubt he was a very gifted writer. He always went the extra mile."

About one year after his arrival, True set out to report a story on family planning in Matamoros, a taboo topic among many in Mexico, where machismo often dictates that men, not women, control the family planning decisions. Birth control was not discussed openly, even in the 1990s, and many men resented the suggestion they use condoms or allow their wives to take birth control pills. The Catholic Church also discouraged poorly educated women, in particular, from learning about birth control options, especially abortion.

"I was working as the director of a nonprofit family planning center, and he came looking for some help with his story," Martha said. "It was probably love at first sight for him, but not for me. He called me two days later and asked me to coffee. I said no. I had a boyfriend, a very conventional boyfriend from Matamoros, a surgeon who was very involved with everyday society in Matamoros."

Philip was persistent, Martha recalled, periodically finding reasons to visit the clinic to "follow up," long after his story was published. "He kept coming around afterwards," Martha said, although a year would go by before she finally agreed to date him.

Martha learned in their periodic chats at the clinic that True was in a relationship with a Colombian woman named Clara who lived on Long Island and had recently visited True in Brownsville. Clara, a single mother, had two small children and, unknown to Martha, True had considered asking her to move down to Texas.

Martha said Philip's tenacity in pursuing her coincided with her own growing conviction that there was more to life than marriage to a hometown doctor, a commitment that would inevitably lead to having babies and giving up her career as a social worker.

"We always said Martha was very *culta*, very smart, very educated, and very independent for a woman who grew up in Mexico," said Juanita, who first befriended Martha when the two attended a Christian summer camp as young teens. "She wasn't the kind to just go along and marry someone from the right Matamoros family and stay home and make lots of babies. She had a college degree of her own and she wanted to control her own future. A lot of us with more traditional lives lived through Martha."

For their first big date, on June 13, 1991, Philip picked up Martha in his battered van and took her to dinner at Los Portales, a laid-back Matamoros landmark featuring alfresco dining amid the aroma of sizzling beef skirts, sweet onions, and sharp chili peppers. Los Portales caters to traditional Mexican families, as well as border residents comfortable with traveling a few miles inland from the river; it is somewhat removed from the venues that cater to English-only tourists. It was the kind of intimate setting where True, the gringo gone native, could show off his Spanish.

It was also Martha's thirty-second birthday. "From the night of that dinner at Los Portales we started to get serious about each other, but he still had this girlfriend in New York, and I told him I wasn't going to see him anymore until he broke up with her."

Martha knew she was gambling, but Philip would have to make up his mind. Clara had visited again recently, and had been a big hit with Philip's friends, teaching them to dance the *cumbia* at a party. Martha had no interest in developing a new relationship with a man less than fully committed.

"So he went back to Long Island to see Clara and decide if he was going to go with the Mexicana or *la guera*," Martha joked, using border slang to describe a blond woman. "That was the impression I had, not that he knew all along he was going to break up with her, more that he was going to go see her again and decide once he got up there how he really felt. He came back and said to me, 'I've ended that relationship. Now we can start our relationship here.'"

That was Thanksgiving Day 1991.

After they finished their anniversary Thanksgiving Day feast, Philip and Martha spent their last night together on Sierra Amatepec. True carefully repacked his bulging backpack, a chore he practiced beforehand to make sure he could carry enough gear and provisions to see him through ten days. He also packed two books. One was the *The Right Stuff*, Tom Wolfe's inside look at the original astronauts and their passion for living life "on the edge of the envelope," in the atmosphere and on the ground. The other volume was *In Cold Blood*, by Truman Capote.

In the weeks before his departure, Martha had asked Philip more than once for a copy of his map and itinerary. She grew irritated as the days slipped by and he continued to ignore her request. That Friday morning, Martha insisted one final time that Philip hand over his itinerary. True gave her a photocopy of a topography map showing a vast, empty region extending hundreds of miles northwest of Guadalajara into three different Mexican mountain states. Here and there small villages, some with saint's names and others with Indian names, dotted the map. Settlements on True's intended route were circled in pen. The undulating lines of the top map described a rugged, testing terrain.

After flying to Guadalajara, True intended to catch a bus north to Tlaltenango, a mestizo town of several thousand inhabitants to the north. After one night there, he would catch the second-class bus to Tuxpan de Bolanos, his gateway to the Huichol sierra and the place he described in his story proposal as a village with an honest mayor and newly installed electricity.

Martha and Philip had visited Tuxpan de Bolanos before and had been allowed to witness a sacred peyote ceremony. On another occasion, Philip returned and participated in such a ceremony, although he never wrote about his peyote-eating experience. In the course of his visits, Philip had befriended a local Huichol leader named Jesús Gonzalez. He intended to stop for a visit and present him with a gift of feathers gathered from Fidel, his molting parrot. The Huichols greatly value such feathers as representations of the animals connecting them to their spirit world.

The oldest colonial structures in Tuxpan de Bolanos were built after Spanish soldiers and missionaries arrived. The uninvited newcomers didn't find much success farther west into the Sierra Madre. The rugged terrain was one reason. The tenacity of the Huichols was another. More than any other of Mexico's many indigenous groups, the Huichols resisted total conversion to Catholicism. To this day, most traditional Huichols continue to honor their animistic gods. Their own spirituality proved to be more enduring than the grip of *conquistadores* and the Franciscan friars who accompanied them.

After one night in Tuxpan de Bolanos, a town of five hundred people, mostly Huichols, True would reach his trailhead and cross a seven-thousand-foot ridge and then pick up the path leading down into the settlement of Mesa el Venado, or Plateau of the Deer, one of many small and isolated settlements that are home to a handful of Huichol families unaccustomed to foreign visitors or even the arrival of outsiders. By then True would be beyond the reach of modern communications and heading into the heart of the Huichol sierra. If he stayed on course, trekking 10 miles a day over the increasingly rugged peaks and plunging canyons, he would need three to four days, until December 3, to reach Amoltita, another small settlement that showed up as a mere speck on True's topographical maps.

Two days and nights on the trail also would place him in San Sebastián Teponahuaxtlán, the *comunidad indigena*, or native community, that included 900 square miles of thinly-populated territory. Villages like Amoltita looked to San Sebastián as the local seat of Huichol governance, even as they also were part of a larger "municipio," or county, a geographic demarcation imposed by the Spanish *conquistadores*. The difference in the two often overlapping, poorly demarcated entities is a confusing one for outsiders seeking to establish the chain of Huichol authority. Simply put, the Huichols live under both indigenous and central government authority and law.

The remote and distant nature of life in the Huichol sierra defined how locals viewed seldom-seen outsiders. While the central village anchoring a county or indigenous community might count a few hundred to several hundred inhabitants, most Huichol families and clans were scattered through the surrounding sierra and lived an even more isolated existence. San Sebastián, for example, has a total population of 6,577 Huichols, perhaps 500 of them in the main village and the rest scattered through rugged country that totals 2,400 square kilometers or 935 square miles.

What mattered is that True also would be beyond the reach of Huichol authorities he knew in Tuxpan de Bolanos and now would be trekking through lands overseen by Huichols in San Sebastián, where he would not stop, intending only to pass through.

After Amoltita, True would descend into the Chapalagana canyon, a twisting, narrow slash in the earth extending 150 miles west. The Chapalagana River in some places was wide and deep, while in other places it was not much more than a creek, marked by the occasional deep pool, with steep canyon walls obscuring its visibility. Once True completed his descent and ascent of the great canyon, he would reach San Miguel Huaixtita, where he promised to contact Martha via a radiotelephone available there.

From his approximate halfway point, the distance between villages would lengthen but the terrain would level. True intended to hike all the way to Santa María Ocotlán, but if he fell behind schedule, he would stop earlier at San Juan Peyotán. At any point from San Miguel on, he would be within a day's walk of a village radiotelephone. At any time he could by prior arrangement summon a bush pilot based in Tepic, the capital city of Nayarit state, which runs along the Pacific Ocean.

Jesús "Chuy" López, a bush pilot who regularly flew people and supplies in and out of Huichol territory, landing at one of the small dirt landing strips built by the government, had agreed to collect True when he was ready. From there True would hop a commercial flight back to Mexico City. True was carrying more than $400 in cash, in part to buy fresh provisions on the trail, if he encountered any, and to pay the pilot for his ride back to civilization. If everything went according to plan, True would emerge from the sierra no later than December 8 or 9.

With map in hand, Martha followed Philip outside to his waiting taxi. He loaded his backpack into the small trunk of the cab, spent a few minutes sharing an emotional farewell, and then climbed into the car. "If I'm not back in ten days, come looking for me," he told his wife.

Then he was on his way.

3

A Keepsake and Family Secrets

Those who go out weeping, bearing the seed for sowing, shall come
home with shouts of joy, carrying their sheaves.

—Psalm 126:6

LONG ISLAND, NEW YORK, JANUARY 1977

Philip True left his father's funeral with a keepsake in his pocket and
a secret in his heart, one more to add to the others he kept closely
guarded.

Theodore Leonard True was only sixty-one when he died of hard-
ening of the arteries in January 1977, but nearly two decades had
passed since he and his estranged son, now twenty-nine, had lived
under the same roof in the Southern California town of San Fernando.

Bronwen Heuer, True's live-in girlfriend since they first met at the
University of California–Irvine in 1972, was waiting at the train station to welcome him home. True, who graduated ahead of Heuer in
1970, worked as a house painter while she completed her degree.
They moved east to Long Island in 1974, vaguely in search of new

opportunities, leaving behind the West Coast and the turbulent decade of the 1960s.

Heuer had driven to the local train depot at Huntington Station to await True on a stormy winter night. Area roads were slick with ice, but True seemed relieved to be back. Even long-distance telephone calls from his mother, Christeen, or his younger sister, Bonnie, which occurred only once or twice a year, were a source of obvious but unspoken anxiety for her boyfriend. Going home had been even more painful.

On the drive home, the usually talkative, good-humored True was quiet on the subject of his deceased father, the memorial service, and his contacts with family. He shifted attention to his girlfriend's driving, second-guessing her as she negotiated the falling sleet and slick roadways.

Once inside their apartment, however, True reached into his bag and withdrew an antique pocket watch, the silver casing worn with age and ornately inscribed with the initials *PB*. Philip had inherited the timepiece from his father, he told Heuer, as he carefully opened the back casing and revealed a German inscription written in Gothic letters. The engraving, dated September 14, 1885, indicated that the timepiece was a gift from Maria Hochstrasser to Paul Bleibtreu. The last line of the engraving read, "Psalm 126," the Old Testament verse bidding travelers safe passage to Zion—Jerusalem.

Philip True, it turned out, was really Philip Bleibtreu, the descendant of German immigrants. The Bleibtreus, like so many others in the immigrant rush of the late nineteenth and early twentieth centuries, had Americanized their name. Bleibtreu in German means "stay true" or "stay faithful." The shortened surname, True, was easier to spell and pronounce yet preserved the essence of the family name. More importantly, future generations of American-born Trues would blend in and thus escape the animosity directed against German-Americans during the two world wars.

True was usually reticent about his family's troubled history, but that night he opened up a bit. Perhaps it was the emotion of the moment—the trip home, the loss of his father. Despite his dismissive comments about family values and traditions, Heuer knew True cared deep down. After all, though money was scarce, True had traveled across the country in the middle of winter after receiving word of his father's death.

True's sister, Bonnie, on the other hand, never really left home. Married twice, she remained geographically close to their mother, who later moved in with Bonnie and stayed until her death in early 1998.

The True family history, in Bonnie's telling, begins soon after her paternal grandfather, Samuel Paul Bleibtreu, arrived in Southern California early in the twentieth century, leaving his young wife behind in her native West Virginia while he established a homestead and found work. Samuel was born June 12, 1885, in Tower Hill, Illinois, the eldest of two sons of Georg and Lyanna Finmann Bleibtreu, who had left the family seat in Duisburg, a bustling Rhine River port city, to seek their fortune in the New World in the early 1880s. Shortly after Samuel's birth, his parents must have accepted the pocket watch from a godmother as a baby gift to the young boy, the inscription using his middle name, Paul, a common nineteenth-century tradition associated with baptism.

Georg and a younger brother who had arrived earlier in America were ordained ministers who led congregations in various Midwestern states. Family photographs from the era suggest prosperity. The well-dressed Bleibtreus posed in nineteenth-century studios for formal portraits amid leather-bound books, imported carpets, and other such symbols. Georg sports a silver pocket watch as little Samuel grasps his hand, perhaps the same watch handed down through the generations.

Soon after arriving in the small town of San Fernando, Samuel fathered a child out of wedlock. The mistress, learning that Samuel was married and that his wife had arrived in town just as their out-of-wedlock baby was born, abandoned the newborn child on the Bleibtreus' doorstep. It was an inauspicious welcome for Lucinda "Lulu" Minear, fresh from West Virginia. Samuel and Lulu took in the baby, born June 16, 1916, and named him Theodore Leonard True. They were registered as his adoptive parents on the birth certificate. The couple's one attempt at having a child of their own produced the still-born Samuel Jr. three years later.

It was an open family secret, said Bonnie, that "Dad was a bastard." No one seemingly tried to conceal that wounding truth from Theodore as he grew up. Later, as young children, Bonnie and Philip were taken on several occasions by their father to meet his birth mother, who showed her abandoned son and his children real affection. They were never told her full name.

Samuel had established a thirteen-acre chicken and vegetable farm in the rural community of Pacoima, in the San Fernando Valley. Samuel and Lulu's farm expanded until there were a thousand egg-laying chickens housed in row after row of wooden coops, along with several acres of vegetable gardens and fruit orchards tended by Chinese immigrants. Everything was for sale at the Bleibtreus' roadside stand.

Theodore grew up working on the chicken farm and, just before turning twenty, married Christeen Mitchell, the daughter of Lulu's sister (née Minear). In effect, it was a union of first cousins, one that had all the markings of a marriage arranged by the two families. Or if Theodore and Christeen were really attracted to each other, no one on either side of the family intervened to stop the cousins from becoming husband and wife. Christeen was a fifteen-year-old eighth grade dropout and the youngest of eight siblings. She traveled cross-country by train from West Virginia to San Fernando, and the newly-weds took possession of a small cottage that was built next to the family home.

"My mom said she and my dad weren't actual cousins, technically, since my dad was a bastard child and not Lulu's real son," Bonnie said. "But my mom did tell Phil and I that she was nothing but a West Virginia hillbilly."

Despite Christeen's lowly self-image, the Minear name is a distinguished one, dating back to men who served in Washington's army during the Revolutionary War and then helped settle the area that eventually became the state of West Virginia. Like the Bleibtreus turned Trues, the Minears came over as German immigrants. The two families seemed to experience declining prospects with each generation.

Neither Philip nor Bonnie, who were estranged from each other, eulogized their father at the memorial service. What could they say before the gathering of strangers? Theodore's second wife, Ruth, controlled all aspects of the memorial service, although she and Theodore had been divorced for years and he had died alone in his one-bedroom apartment in San Fernando. Christeen, who had divorced Theodore almost twenty years earlier, did not attend. There was no minister on hand to preside.

"I was surprised how many people showed up; it was packed," Bonnie said. "My dad was a weird guy, but I guess a lot of people had no idea who he really was, and they only knew him as the nice, quiet guy who owned True's gas station there in Pacoima. If only they knew."

The same evening he unveiled the pocket watch, Philip divulged to Heuer an even more surprising discovery he and Bonnie made while searching for their deceased father's will. Theodore, perhaps atoning for his failure as a father, had assured his children over the years they would be the sole beneficiaries of a generous life insurance policy. Both son and daughter believed the love he failed to deliver in life would be made up in death with a little cold cash.

After the service, Philip, Bonnie, and her first husband, Tom Erwin, poked around Theodore's bedroom, trying to locate the policy. Their search took them into the recesses of his closet, where the siblings found a boxed collection of pornographic photographs depicting Theodore in various sexual acts with different men.

"We were shocked at first, kind of laughing in a startled, nervous way, but it was obvious these photographs were carefully preserved, his pride and joy, so we talked about it and thought it would be a good idea to bury them with him," Bonnie recalled. "My stepmother just about dropped dead when she saw what we had found. She insisted on burning them, even though she was divorced from him. She didn't want anyone to know the truth, she said, because Theodore was a real likeable person and that's the way it ought to stay.

"It turns out she had a new will too," Bonnie added, "and Phil and I only ended up getting twelve hundred bucks each, the same amount of money his two stepchildren got. Ruth got all the rest. We never found out how much, never even got to see the actual will."

A discovery of such graphic, closeted images must have disturbed True, already unsettled by sexual tensions that for years had poisoned individual family relationships. Always the stoic about his own feelings, he mentioned the incident only matter-of-factly to Heuer and never spoke about it again. "I got the feeling he didn't want to go there," she said. Like others in Philip's life, Heuer had learned not to press.

"It was just kind of understood with Phil that he wasn't close to his family, that heavy things had happened to him," said Harris, True's college roommate. "He didn't care to talk about that part of his life. It was tough for him to make an emotional connection. He was afraid of getting singed."

True, in fact, never told Heuer, Harris, or any of his other friends the even darker secret his mother had divulged to him when he had turned eighteen in 1966. Philip's father, Christeen told him, had been banished from the family house some six years earlier after she had come home and found Bonnie, nine years old at the time, naked in her parents' bed, masturbating her father. True was eleven years old at the time of the marriage breakup, but this was the first time anyone had explained his father's abrupt departure from the household.

"Both of us as young kids saw my father beat my mother plenty of times, slap her around, that kind of thing, and he was always hollering at her and telling her she was no damn good," Bonnie recalled years later. "Then one day our dad was gone and Philip didn't know why. No one told him anything."

For all those years, only mother and daughter knew the truth. Bonnie, always the obedient child, followed Christeen's whispered instructions, "Don't tell your brother," just as she had obeyed her father when he whispered, "Don't tell your mother or brother."

Christeen's revelation came as Philip became a legal adult and about the time he decided to move out and escape his mother and the disruptive succession of husbands and boyfriends who followed in his father's footsteps. For Philip, the truth was too little, too late. He left a confused, angry young man, unable to sort out or share his feelings with family or friends.

Years later, in their last visit together at their mother's funeral in January 1998, Philip told Bonnie that as a young boy and for years afterward he had mistakenly blamed his mother's flagrant promiscuity for his father's departure. That's why, Philip had thought as a young boy, his father had abandoned him without a word of comfort. Some of his anger, Philip also admitted, had been wrongly placed on his sister. Still yearning for a father in his life, Philip apologized to Bonnie, the real victim.

Theodore began abusing Bonnie in 1957, when she was seven years old. He shrewdly picked his opportunities, waiting until they were alone in the house and then coaxing his daughter into masturbating him over the kitchen sink while he talked softly to her about their "special secret."

By the time she was nine, Bonnie now realizes, her father had grown bolder and more reckless in satisfying his deviant sexual desires. Only her mother's early return from grocery shopping that day saved Bonnie from the escalating molestation.

The family breakup, True later told his high school buddy Joe Vasquez, forced him to grow up too fast and robbed him of his adolescence. The young teenager often found himself cast in the role of the man of the house.

Christeen often remarked in front of the children how much she hated her ex-husband, adding that Philip was just like him in many ways. Later she explained her divorce to Bonnie by saying, "If your father could do such terrible things to you, he could do them to Philip too." She had a way of talking about her children that inflicted pain

on the one who happened to be listening. The remark made Bonnie
think that her mother cared more about Philip than her. She, after all,
had been the real incest victim.

Philip grew up resenting the stifling relationship he had with his
mother. She was abnormally protective of her son, unable to give him
the space he needed as a teenage boy, yet she saw no problem in making him a proxy for her banished husband when it served her purposes.

In the mid-1980s, True told Annette Fuentes (who became his girlfriend after he broke up with Heuer) that his mother regularly
molested him as a young boy. She fondled her son's genitals while
making him suck her breasts, memories he blocked out for many
years and remembered only after entering therapy in his late thirties.
By then True had lost serious relationships with four women. All had
loved True, but each found his unresolved past an impossible hurdle
to a sustained, monogamous relationship. Each girlfriend urged True
to undergo therapy. Finally he took their advice.

Sara Delano Rojas, a therapist in Mexico City who worked with
Philip and Martha years later, speculated that Philip's mother had
known her husband was molesting Bonnie long before catching him
in the act in 1960, but allowed it to go on for some time because it
freed her from her husband's sexual oppression. "A mother who fails
to protect her own daughter or abuses her own son violates the most
basic relationship we know, that of mother and child," Rojas said.

In Philip's last letter to Bonnie, he shared his feelings about the
abuse and its toll on the family:

> We are both children of chaos. Both of our parents abused us
> mentally, physically and sexually. That has had consequences for
> you and me. A point I would make is that counseling (with the
> right person, of course) helps you understand all of that, both
> from the perspective of the victim (you and me) as well as those
> who practice the abuse. . . Counseling does not make you hate
> anybody; instead it helps you understand the world better, so you

can like yourself and others around you more. It also gives you power, because you know more about things.

True advised his sister to enter therapy as a way of dealing with her own troubled past and closing the distance between them. "Both of our parents did terrible things. They weren't necessarily bad people, because they were shaped by people and forces that went to work on them," True wrote. "They were never fortunate enough, as I have been, to find the self-understanding that helps them get beyond those shaping forces."

When he wrote this letter, True was forty-nine, happily married, and working as the Mexico City bureau chief of the *San Antonio Express-News*. But he was almost forty before he faced his past as he now urged Bonnie to do.

Bonnie, like so many other incest victims, kept finding herself in situations that brought back her own troubled past. "I knew he was my dad and I knew he would never do anything to hurt me," she said, recalling her betrayed innocence as a child. "My stepson, by the way, did far worse to his own little girls. He's serving a prison sentence for what he did. His girls didn't say nothing, either, until he was gone and they knew they were safe. That's just the way kids are when something bad like this happens."

The True children watched the landscape change as neighbors sold off small working farms to real estate developers, and families by the thousands eager for the new suburban lifestyle flocked to the valley. Sprouting subdivisions slowly encircled Samuel's ramshackle farm.

Lulu died in 1955, leaving little lasting impression on her young grandchildren. After her death, an aging Samuel agreed to sell several acres to homebuilders, who demolished one of the three ranch houses. Christeen and the teenagers moved into the two-bedroom house and Samuel settled into the smaller cottage. The orchards went next, then the gardens, and finally the last of the chickens as, piece by piece, the original Bleibtreu farm was sold and surrounded by look-alike homes.

Philip and Bonnie played with friends around the construction sites, building and caving in tunnels, making friends with Mexican laborers, and, after the workers left for the day, climbing over the wood-frame skeletons as if they were monkey bars on a playground.

Samuel died on Christmas Eve 1959, unaware of the disturbing events next door that would come to a head in the coming year. After Christeen forced Theodore to leave in 1960, he found a house a few streets from the former chicken ranch.

Even after his eviction, Theodore continued to see his two children. Christeen allowed Bonnie to sleep overnight at her father's house, as long as she took along a girlfriend as insurance against further molestations. Philip, meanwhile, saw his father every day on the job. Theodore never had any interest in poultry farming, and long before he was expelled from the house, he became the owner and operator of True's Atlantic Richfield service station in town. Once he was old enough to handle the pumps and repair tires, Philip went to work there to help with his mother's expenses and to earn a little spending money. The young boy must have made an excellent worker. Nothing he did, however, led his absentee father to reach out emotionally to his only son.

As soon as the divorce was final, Theodore married a woman the children called Stepmom Ruth. Bonnie didn't mind Ruth, knowing she was protection. "We had some good times with Ruth over there. I hate to admit it, but we did," she said. "When Phil and I would spend the night there and we were still little, we'd climb into bed with Ruth, and my Dad would come in and pretend he was a waiter to take our dessert order. He'd have a white towel over his bent arm and he'd speak in a British accent and we'd order ice cream.

"Ruth bought me dolls as a kid, and one of them was this big three-foot doll. I loved it, but I always left it there so I wouldn't hurt my mom's feelings because she didn't have any money to buy me things like dolls. Did I mention to you that Ruth was Walt Disney's secretary? Well, she was or said she was, and when she retired she moved to San Luis Obispo. One day, years after the funeral, she called and said she was on a senior citizen's bus that was coming through Reno and she wanted to meet my kids. It was one of the worst visits I ever had with her. I had been through a lot in my life, there was a lot of muddy water under the bridge, and I didn't want to see her anymore. She was just some old lady."

Christeen, never discreet in front of the children, shared other family secrets with her young daughter. "My mom later told me about the time she walked in on Theodore and one of his male friends doing it right there in my mom and dad's bedroom," Bonnie recalled. "After that, the guy wasn't allowed over at our house anymore."

Father and mother each traded on their young daughter's lost innocence to undermine the other. "One time when I was in junior high school I was over there and my dad told me he and my mom used to be into wife swapping in the 1950s," Bonnie recalled, a topic of conversation that suggested her father still nursed sexual impulses toward his daughter even if the physical molestation had stopped.

"My mom just about had a cow when I came home and told her about it," Bonnie said. "She did it, she told me, because she was forced to do it, because he made her. She made an immediate phone call to him, lots of hollering. I never told Philip about that and I know my mom never did, either."

After the memorial service, Bonnie raised the issue of her father's sexuality with Ruth. "She told me she loved him, but that he had weird sexual habits. He was bisexual and liked kinky things, and she said she just couldn't handle it."

Not long after Theodore left the chicken ranch, another man took his place. Jerry Gunderson, the local minister at the nondenominational Christian church that Christeen and the children attended on Sunday mornings, began to frequent the True household. He came, he told the children, to minister to Christeen in her time of need.

"My mom was real gullible, especially after years and years of hearing my father tell her how stupid and worthless she was," Bonnie said. "The minister told my mom that he wanted to comfort her and give her the company she deserved. He let it drop that he was separated from his own wife and really understood what she was going through—at least that's what he was telling her."

Gunderson might have been a man of the cloth, but he also was an alcoholic and a predator, often arriving at the Trues' doorstep at 2:00 A.M., banging on the door, drunk and belligerent one moment, tearful and pleading the next for Christeen to open up.

"She'd be too scared, so my mom would yell in to Phil to get up and go to the door to face him down, make him go away," Bonnie said. "Phil told me later that having to get up at age 12, dressed only in his underpants, to run off a drunk man in the dark made him grow up real fast."

Joe Vasquez and True first met as teammates on the school's gymnastics team. "We met in our first year at San Fernando High, we started talking, and suddenly we were like brothers from the first day," Vasquez said. "We just kept talking about everything; he liked talking, even if he didn't agree with you."

And they talked about True's mother and the men she brought home. "I remember talking about religion with Phil; it was 2:00 A.M. and we were out cruising the LA freeways and he told me his mother had been messing around with the minister from church," Vasquez said. "That was the end of organized religion for him. He thought it all was a big pile. Being forced to take on household responsibilities so young made him cynical about institutions, about marriage, holding a normal job, going after material things or setting goals. He often used the phrase 'drop out' with me. That was his goal, to get out of school, get out of town, and drop out."

"I don't believe in God because I caught the minister with my mom," True remarked to various friends over the years.

The six-month affair with the reverend ended badly for Christeen and the children when Gunderson reconciled with his wife. News of the affair spread quickly through the small-town congregation, and the minister and his wife did nothing to dampen Sunday gossip that labeled Christeen a loose, conniving woman who had ensnared one of the Lord's servants in his moment of vulnerability. It was a truly sinful act by a local Jezebel doing the devil's work. The Trues were stared at, humiliated, and ostracized by their fellow worshipers. Soon after they stopped attending services.

"Never mind that he was the one coming on to her, showing up drunk in the middle of the night," Bonnie said. "To me, many of the people who are real strong churchgoers are hypocrites, so I understand where Phil was coming from. I still believe in God, but I don't go to church."

For Philip, it was a traumatic episode, coming so soon after his dad's abrupt departure and remarriage. He resented his mom's willingness to make herself available so easily to other men. That didn't stop her. Christeen put the minister in her past and began pouring coffee at her table for the neighborhood mailman, Steve Vadovich, whose deliveries began keeping him at the True house all afternoon, usually until the kids came home from school. "My mom was a sucker for whoever came along and treated her nice. She had such a low opinion of herself," Bonnie said. "It wasn't long before Steve was coming over for more than coffee."

Philip was fourteen now, and with the Reverend Gunderson affair still fresh, he allowed his feelings about his mom's choice of male company to show through loud and clear. "Phil didn't think we needed another jerk in the house and he was right," Bonnie said. "Steve picked up on that and made it real clear he was going to be the man in the family and Phil was just a kid and could go back to acting like it."

Christeen and Steve were married in 1962. Shortly afterward, Philip and Bonnie were told to pack their bags. They were leaving what was left of the chicken ranch, the only home they had ever known, and moving to the more comfortable and spacious Vadovich household.

"When we moved to the new house, Steve turned around and

announced there was no room for Phil inside the house," Bonnie said. "Phil was given a room in a back building, not a garage or anything, sort of a game room. It wasn't a bad room, necessarily, but it wasn't in the house and the message was pretty clear: Phil wasn't welcome in the new family."

Steve locked the house each evening and would not give Philip his own key. "He was locked outside at night and couldn't get back in, and there was nothing my mom could do about it," Bonnie said. "She tried to fight Steve but gave up. Phil ended up outside, sleeping by himself."

Christeen endured the tension for a little more than a year. By early 1964, her second marriage clearly was a failure. Bonnie and Philip were watching the Beatles make their historic appearance on the *Ed Sullivan Show* on February 9, 1964, when Christeen came in to tell them she was leaving Steve.

"My mom finally left him because of the way he treated Phil," Bonnie said. "He never hit him, but mentally he mistreated him day and night. Steve would cuss him out, and just kind of pick at him. Phil was like any other teenager, an hour after supper he'd be standing in front of an open refrigerator, holding the door open and looking in. Steve would come in and slam the fridge door and tell him he didn't need to eat again."

Christeen found a two-bedroom apartment in a nearby complex. Phil had his own bedroom and Christeen and Bonnie shared the other. Money was tight. Theodore often failed to make his child support payments, straining Christeen's ability to provide for her two growing children.

"My dad missed his child support payments not because he didn't have income, but he blamed our stepmom, Ruth, who ran though a lot of his money," Bonnie said. "I remember there was a time when we were really wanting for food, and I told my dad so, and he told me Ruth needed a new white carpet for her living room that she had been wanting. He gave my mom the same excuse. So we went without, and the next time I went over there, ol' Ruth had her nice new white carpet."

Soon afterward, Theodore sold the service station. Philip found a new job as a busboy at a Jolly Rogers fast food franchise. To Christeen and the kids, however, the sale of the family business was bad news. Ruth now controlled Theodore and his finances. Theodore's first wife and the children were on their own.

Whatever else happened, True had his best friend. When they were together, Phil's problems vanished. Vasquez recalls a happier, more carefree True, a teenager who talked some about his turbulent home life but cared a lot more about meeting girls, getting a driver's license, and debating politics and the Vietnam War. At times Philip and his father even seemed to have a normal relationship. Before True and Vasquez were old enough to drive, Theodore took them camping upstate in the Sequoia National Forest. Theodore had a small tow-trailer, and both boys spent the night at Theodore and Ruth's house so they could leave early the next morning. True's father served up a big breakfast of pancakes and eggs. Afterward, as they were getting ready to walk out of the house, Ruth suddenly attacked her husband.

"Whatever his father did to Phil's family, he got it back when he remarried because she was a lot tougher than him," Vasquez said. "I had never seen two adults, a husband and wife, fight, and basically there was this woman tossing him out on his ear. She was physical, and he was acting defensively. She just pushed him out that door.

"His dad was embarrassed," Vasquez said. "Phil was too, but we didn't talk about it then and we didn't talk about it later."

Once camping, the three had a good time. Neither boy knew much about the outdoors. "It was my first camping trip, and it changed my life," he said. "It was a big thing for both of us. It wasn't Phil's first trip, but he liked doing it and decided he wanted to spend more time out there."

Soon afterward, with driver's licenses in hand, they didn't need their parents to get around. "We lived in the valley in the dream years when it wasn't all asphalt and smog," Vasquez said. "Everything was new, it was suburbia, but there was still livestock and lots of orchards, and you could drive from one end of LA to the other without a traffic jam, just as those freeways were built for. Gas was cheap. The music was good. We could cruise until the wheels fell off."

Theodore gave his son his first car right after he got his license. "Phil still had illusions about his dad while he was in high school, especially after his dad gave him his first car," Vasquez said. "It was a '56 Ford, the model with the bigger engine. His dad arranged with a friend of his who owned a body shop to paint the car and metal flake the top. The lights made it glitter."

Vasquez said he watched with amazement and some envy as True approached girls they didn't even know and struck up conversations. "He was the master, just fearless, so he was dating all through high school, a lot earlier than I dated," Vasquez said.

The family hung together for a few more years and then came apart for good.

Philip graduated from San Fernando High School, a tough school with growing racial and ethnic tensions, in 1966. As middle-class suburbs developed in one place, older neighborhoods declined and became home to a wave of new migrants and minority families fleeing the city. San Fernando, Bonnie said, had become "rough." While the newer valley suburbs were overwhelmingly white and middle-class, San Fernando was working class, with a high school student body that was 50 percent black, 40 percent Mexican, and 10 percent white.

"It seemed like there were fights between gangs and ethnic groups just because the school year was ending, or the semester was ending, some ridiculous reason," Vasquez said. "Black and whites would gang up on Mexicans, or some Mexicans would join up with some whites and attack the blacks. Fights just broke out spontaneously."

The Watts riots, only miles away, unnerved Christeen. She moved her two teenagers to Reseda, farther out in the valley, where Bonnie could attend a better and safer high school. Philip's good grades and varsity gymnastics earned him a scholarship at Los Angeles Valley Junior College in Van Nuys. He didn't stay in Reseda long.

Christeen soon met "Leonard the truck driver," who, according to Bonnie, rolled into their lives and three weeks later proposed marriage. Christeen happily accepted. "My mom knew him three weeks, and she was married to him for three weeks, start to finish," Bonnie said. The only upside for Bonnie was that Leonard had a son her age who had made the high school football team and struck up a relationship with his new stepsister.

Vasquez remembers Philip's reaction on learning of his mom's third marriage. "Phil told me he came home from classes one day and found out his mother had gotten married again, so he just walked into his room without saying anything, packed his stuff, and walked out. He just left."

Bonnie said her brother's departure was the turning point, the moment when Philip cut ties with his mother and sister. True, 19, earned enough money to support himself, first as a busboy, then as a waiter. He wasn't going to wait around to find out what the new man in the family had in mind.

"Back in those days, Phil and I didn't get along too well, we didn't talk too much," she said. "We had fought a lot as kids, and now he was hitting me a lot, taking out all his built-up frustrations, I guess."

Young Bonnie, now a sixteen-year-old sophomore and unwise in the ways of relationships, also ended up disappointed. Leonard's son had shaved his head for the start of the football season and suddenly seemed to become someone else. He dumped Bonnie. Weeks later, things ended for Christeen too.

"Leonard was a dumb truck driver who couldn't pronounce three-quarters of the cities he had to deliver to," Bonnie said. "My mom and I were laughing one night at the ignorant way he talked, kind of imitating him, me doing it, then she doing it, both of us laughing real hard, not thinking he was in the house. Well, he was in there and he heard it all. He just walked in, looked at us, and without saying a word, started packing his stuff. My mom asked him where he was going. He never answered, and we never saw him again."

Christeen would wait eight years, until 1975, long after she was living alone, before she married for a fourth and final time. Bonnie can't even remember the fourth husband's name, or if Philip ever met him. It was someone her mom had known for years who had a long-running crush on her. Christeen finally agreed to go out on a date with the man and then promptly agreed to marry him.

"All I remember is that it lasted longer than three weeks, but not much, maybe a couple of months," Bonnie said. "I think after that, my mom decided to give up on men, to stay away from them."

All four men are now dead.

True eventually escaped his troubled childhood by doing something no one else in his family had ever done: he enrolled in a four-year college. Theodore had finished high school, a modest enough achievement. He nevertheless used to belittle Christeen, a middle school dropout, never failing to announce plans to attend his annual high school reunion. Philip finished his first two years at Los Angeles Valley Junior College and then transferred in the spring of 1968 to the recently opened UC–Irvine, south of Los Angeles in Orange County. "It was good, it was close, and it was free, or almost free. You could pay for college with a part-time job," Vasquez said.

That UC–Irvine experience exposed True to a bigger world and new friends, and it eventually led to a new life across the country on the East Coast, far away from San Fernando and the shards of his broken family.

One mystery is whether Philip ever confronted his father about the incest. He did tell his mother she was not welcome to visit him back East unless she would face up to having sexually abused him. She never did. Bonnie never challenged her father, either. It's one of her few regrets in life, she said, as we sat at her kitchen table inside her modest home set in the sparse foothills outside Reno. Outside, dogs barked and a pair of pet donkeys brayed.

"I wish I could have found a way to confront my dad, just to ask him why: 'Why was it necessary to do such things to me?' I'm just fortunate I finally found Stan [Biggs], and through him, the family I never had, just like Philip found Martha and, through her, the family he never had. I think I came out normal. I think my brother was affected more than I was. I never went through counseling."

Bonnie, less given to introspection than her brother, retains a surprisingly sturdy sense of humor and warmth for someone who endured early abuse and a bad first marriage. She has been married for more than twenty-one years now to Biggs, ten years older and twice-divorced, a former long-haul truck driver who dead-ends trailers near Reno and has provided the love, companionship, and stability that previously eluded her.

Bonnie works at the nearby JC Penney catalog fulfillment center in Reno. Now a grandmother, she also labors as a full-time caregiver, helping raise grandchildren on a fixed budget, shuttling them to and from school and appointments, while providing support for her two single daughters, both struggling with their own broken marriages, reduced economic circumstances, and bad choices in life.

"No, I'm not sorry I didn't go to college, even though in high school all my courses were college prep," Bonnie answered. "I decided I wanted to get out of my home and get married. It just so happens I picked a jerk the first time around and it took me a long time to do something about it."

Money might be tight, she said, "but we have other things."

Tragedy travels like a narrative thread through the extended True family.

While Bonnie's first marriage to Tom Erwin lasted a decade, her oldest daughter, Tabitha, was married for less than year while still a teenager. Today she is the mother of a young girl she conceived after being raped in a Las Vegas bus station. Tabitha is a good mother,

Bonnie added, despite her struggle with a drug habit. "Sometimes things disappear around here after Tabitha's been here," she said after failing to locate a particular family heirloom.

Bonnie's younger daughter, Kim, married an African American man named Shaun Vockel, now known within the Biggs family as "the idiot." Together they had two daughters, Brianna and Brittany. Vockel is now serving a lengthy prison term after pleading guilty to sexually abusing both girls when they were seven and four years old. Kim says she plans to divorce him someday. "Once I get a hold of $150, or if I don't do it myself, I'll need $500 for a lawyer to file the papers."

4

On the Road

Thus, as 1968 began, these were some of the sources of the malaise gnawing away at many of the six million draft-age students in college, the largest group of undergraduates in American history: an absence of religious conviction; an unwanted intimacy with the nuclear void; an unexpected familiarity with political assassination—Malcolm X in 1965, as well as John Kennedy's in 1963—and a yearning for the idealism that was the most evocative part of Kennedy's presidency. Together these disparate impulses: the desire to create our own culture, a world of our own where we could retreat from the world of our parents; and the need to embrace causes larger than ourselves, crusades that would give us the chance to define ourselves as moral people.

—Charles Kaiser, *1968 in America*

Standing there, gaping at this monstrous and inhuman spectacle of rock and cloud and sky and space, I feel a ridiculous greed and possessiveness come over me. I want to know it all, possess it all, embrace the entire scene intimately, deeply, totally, as a man desires a beautiful woman. An insane wish? Perhaps not—at least there's nothing else, no one human, to dispute possession with me.

—Edward Abbey, *Desert Solitaire*

True left the San Fernando Valley and drove south, right into a revolution. It was exactly what a repressed teenager from a broken family was looking for, a movement that put his feelings to words and music and told him that he wasn't alone. His new life in Orange County was less than two hours by car from the former chicken ranch in Pacoima, but True now lived in another world.

UC–Irvine, only three years old, was one of two new campuses in the state's vaunted higher education system. Only a few thousand students were enrolled, and the school still had the feel of a small college. The campus was established on lands that once belonged to the Irvine Ranch Company, three miles inland from Newport Beach. Fields of tall grass and miles of orange orchards surrounded the campus. Horse stables, cattle herds, and family farms dotted the landscape. Such bucolic calm belied the times.

UC–Irvine was a school just beginning to define itself. The students passed a resolution banning fraternities and sororities. There was no football team. It was perfect for True, who was just beginning to define himself. It was 1968, and a cultural and political firestorm was engulfing the country: the Tet offensive in Vietnam, antiwar protests on college campuses, the assassination of Robert Kennedy and Martin Luther King, urban race riots, and rampant police brutality in Chicago at the Democratic National Convention. True grew his hair to his shoulders and started smoking pot. Before leaving for college, he and Joe Vasquez went to LA's Griffith Park for the heavily publicized love-in.

"The police went berserk," Vasquez said. "We got to kiss some women we hadn't been dating before, some we didn't know. People were singing, dancing, stringing beads together, it was a big outdoors '60s party."

True tooled around in a 1968 blue Volvo, a gift from his mother after the last of the chicken farm was sold. Alice, a terrier-dachshund mongrel, and her pup, Skunk, became his inseparable campus sidekicks.

One day True emerged from classes to find that Alice and Skunk had been rounded up by workers from the Orange County Animal Shelter at the behest of university officials. Phil True, as he then was known, wrote a scathing letter to the editor decrying the seldom enforced leash law that was published in the campus newspaper. "Protect your dog, watch the cops," True ominously warned fellow students.

Millions of mostly white, middle-class men enjoyed student deferments that exempted them from military service. Women were exempt, period. Free to protest, they challenged just about every traditional social convention—marriage, career, church, politicians, military service, campus authority—held sacred by the patriotic generation that had emerged victorious from World War II.

The more conservative Vasquez, the grandson of Mexican immigrants and the son of a World War II veteran, was drawn to service rather than protest. He left junior college after one year and enlisted in the navy for a six-year stint. His math skills won him a slot as an electronic technician, training that later served him well in civilian life.

True, meanwhile, fell into a relationship with Kathleen Sullivan right after arriving on campus. "I think it was true love the minute I saw him. He just came up talking to me like I had always known him," Sullivan said. "He was handsome, delicate, and macho, what a combo, and smart and regular and nice and he seemed sure of himself. He wasn't afraid of anything."

"True love" in Southern California in the 1960s was a relative thing. The sexual revolution was well under way, and True and Sullivan took separate paths while staying close friends. He wrote to Sullivan for years: postcards from road trips, letters from Long Island. It was a pattern that True would repeat with other women along the way.

"I think you said it right—I'm in love with your ass, too, and that's how come we still come to be in touch," True wrote Sullivan in 1980 while he was in a relationship with Annette Fuentes.

"Both currently hooked up, we are, but here we are, still meaningful to each other. Very special and very precious, we for each other at Irvine. Very different—no firm type of conventional relationship, but strong and apparently long lasting."

True earned his first newspaper byline after he and ten other students traveled north to an antiwar rally in Berkeley's Peace Park. His account appeared in the May 29, 1969, edition of the school's unofficial newspaper, the *New University*. It was headlined, "Twenty-six hours in Santa Rita." True was more activist than budding journalist, but if one were looking for the seed of a future newspaper career, this is it, his first newspaper story.

True wrote that the Berkeley City police treated the protestors politely as they were detained in front of the national media. "All right, sir, please step this way," police told True and more than five hundred other students arrested that day for unlawful assembly and failure to disperse.

After a ride in the paddy wagon to the nearby Santa Rita jail beyond media scrutiny, police adopted a more belligerent posture: "All right, assholes, move! Down on the ground, face down. Anyone who moves gets their head split."

Those who responded slowly were prodded with riot sticks. "We were subjected to the full wrath of a band of sadistic guards, secure in the knowledge that there was no one around to whom they were responsible," True wrote.

He and the other men were made to lie face down in an open courtyard, some for more than five hours, before they were booked. During the booking process, they were struck with blackjacks, kicked, and thrown against walls. The rest of the long day and night in lockup was spent waiting in barracks for a bologna sandwich, getting finger-printed and photographed, and watching jail guards rough up detainees for sport.

University officials bailed out the Irvine Eleven and they came home to a warm welcome. The school held a student assembly to dis-cuss the arrest of the students and True was among those who stepped up to the microphone. His extemporaneous remarks made the *CBS Nightly News* and the *Orange County Register*.

True gained his first sense of the power of the media, and he con-nected with Cathy Bell, a fellow comparative cultures major with the same faculty adviser. "Philip and I kind of clicked on that trip," she said. "We were walking down the street and we could see helicopters and these tanks going down the street, and we came around a corner and here were all these tanks and guns, people marching, all coming toward us. We tried to get away but we were swept up."

True also met Peter Harris in 1969, a kindred spirit who similarly came to Irvine, in part, to distance himself from family. "I was looking for a place to live, and he was looking for a roommate," Harris said.

"There was this fourplex, two ramshackle duplexes in a little section of unincorporated county just west of the Orange County Airport, which at the time was still new and pretty small. The place was right under the flight pattern."

True had seniority, and he claimed the one bedroom. Harris settled for a makeshift loft in the living room. It hardly mattered, though, since so many people came and went, some for a visit, some for the night. Harris said the two talked New Left politics, got high, and lived the "garret phase" lifestyle common to students in the 1960s.

"He was proud of being working class, but we were really hippies," Harris recalled. "I remember driving down the freeway one day, debating him, and I told him we weren't really oppressed people, regardless of our political beliefs of the time. He didn't disagree with me."

During that same time period, True and Harris experimented with psychedelic drugs, including an acid trip taken one memorable overnight visit to Joshua Tree National Monument, where True discovered what Martha later called "his love for the dirt and rocks of the desert."

Now a national park, Joshua Tree, located a few hours inland from Irvine, is a wildscape of sand, stone, and the strange-looking Joshua trees, a place dotted with hundreds of prehistoric campsites. The two roommates dropped tabs of LSD and spent the night talking and wandering amid the rocks and under the stars.

True, sporting a shorter haircut, had lately taken to wearing a red bandana around his head and hiking boots on his feet as he began to move out of his hippie phase and into an outdoors ethos. Harris said the more True experienced solitude in nature, the less he resembled a dropout from society and the more he evolved into a wilderness sojourner. "If I had to put Philip in an ethos, it would be in the West of John Muir and his love of nature, and Mark Twain and his skepticism and story and truth telling," Harris said. "Philip was a hippie, but he wasn't a mystic."

The two roommates shared many epic travel and outdoors adventures, including several trips to Sequoia and scenic Mineral King. "It is a beautiful valley, and we backpacked a couple of times into the park, and once we did a longer trip," Harris said. "He told me the first time he went out there he didn't know much about camping and he brought a Coleman stove, lots of canned peas and chili, and lugged it all up to the top."

Later, in the summer 1971, True and Harris hitchhiked from Irvine up to Waldo Lake, near the Three Sisters Mountains east of Eugene, Oregon. Once again they relied on True's system of roadside camping, bologna sandwiches, and the kindness of strangers. "Hitchhiking was a big part of it, meeting people along the way, no schedule, getting lost, finding our way," Harris said.

Cathy Bell was the first woman to share wilderness experiences with True. The couple went on regular camping trips to Death Valley, Glacier Point, and Sequoia. They drove True's new Volvo to Vancouver and back to break it in, making a ritual stop at REI outside Seattle to check out the latest camping gear and meet like-minded outdoors enthusiasts.

"We never stayed in motels," she said. "Philip had this belief that you could always find people along the way to put you up, or we camped along the roadside."

Bell said they made friends with some people in Eugene, Oregon, who actually took them home. "Philip used to tell me, 'You're too paranoid, you need to trust people. You can always work things out.' I was less adventurous in that regard."

Bell and True graduated in June 1970 and found jobs working as assistants to a faculty sociologist who was conducting off-campus alpha wave experiments on the human brain. They wired up the subjects and helped the researcher record the results in his computer.

Bell was accepted at the State University of New York for the fall semester to begin her graduate work at the Stony Brook, Long Island campus. True drove there with her before returning to Irvine. "I was heartbroken, living there alone, but he wrote me really nice letters, which my mother threw away after I got married," Bell said.

A different kind of distance arose between True and Harris. "He could be a little prideful, or defensive, about being working class, kind of, 'How dare anyone suggest that one way of making money, as a professional, was better than another?'" Harris said, remembering his own path toward a career in academia. True left the laboratory job and went to work as a house painter.

Harris married his girlfriend, Grace, and began contemplating life as a college professor as the couple made plans to relocate to the East Coast to attend graduate school. True, meanwhile, seemed "kind of directionless." He had met Bronwen Heuer, a campus sophomore whom Harris described as "tall and lanky, charming, smart, someone who could keep up with Philip and his talk, and keep him honest."

True was still in a relationship with Bell, who soon heard about Heuer from friends. He told Bell he wanted to move to Stony Brook and into the house she shared with three roommates. She welcomed him but later said that True "upset the apple cart" when he moved there in January 1971, forcing her to find a new place to live.

"He didn't have a job, and I was trying to focus on my studies. It wasn't easy," Bell said. "He eventually found work unloading trucks at Academy Broadway, which made sports bags. He decided that his new thing was that he was going to become a union organizer. I thought he was being a bit idealistic, but he wanted to change the world."

They returned to the Irvine area in August, but there Bell learned that True and Heuer had stayed in touch during True's Long Island stay. Bell wanted a future that included marriage and children. True did not. "When it came down to committing, it wasn't happening with Philip," she said. "I wanted the house, the picket fence, a good provider, someone who would be around, a father for my children. I didn't want to be forty years old, hitchhiking across the country with our dogs."

Bell moved back in with her parents and she and True broke up in early 1972. She later returned to UC–Irvine to obtain an advanced engineering degree, where she met her husband. They are now happily married and live in Huntington Beach not far from the campus.

Still, her last comment to me was wistful one. "You don't meet many people like Philip in life. He was unforgettable."

When True broke up with Bell, Bronwen Heuer moved in. She continued her studies while True painted houses. Whenever possible, True hit the road, sometimes on spur-of-the-moment hitchhiking adventures that included Alice, his mutt, other times into the desert with his girlfriend. They spent two Thanksgiving holidays camping in Death Valley.

Peter and Grace Harris left for New Haven in the summer of 1973 so he could pursue a Ph.D. in sociology at Yale. True, meanwhile, seemed to put his own postgraduate plans for the future on hold, turning down a teaching job he applied for after he was told to get a haircut.

That September, True and Heuer went to see *Heavy Traffic,* a popular underground animated film. Something in the movie set off a switch in True's brain. "The next morning he got up and just announced, 'I'm going to New York,' and he pretty much meant right away," Heuer said. "Within a week I dropped Philip off on the entrance ramp to the San Diego Freeway and he hitchhiked to New York."

For the second time, someone important to him had moved east, and True once again was ready to follow. Union officials welcomed him back to the job he had held during his stint living with Cathy Bell. True returned to Irvine a few weeks later, packed his bags, and moved to New York in February 1974. "I was trying very hard to be a feminist, so I didn't leave until April," Heuer said.

They settled in the town of Melville on Long Island, sharing an apartment with two guys True had met, a window washer and an amateur photographer. "It was totally different culture," Heuer said. "We went from West Coast, college-educated people to East Coast working-class people. It was a big switch."

They tried to rekindle their friendship with Peter and Grace. "We spent weekends visiting, watching football games, drinking beer, telling stories, talking about Philip's new interest in the touch football league he had joined," Harris said. "But I was trying to start my academic career and he was trying to be a working-class man."

True was about to turn twenty-six. For the next fifteen years, he stayed on Long Island, held a succession of blue-collar jobs, lived in a succession of towns with an ever changing cast of roommates, and built and broke relationships with a number of women, wandering aimlessly without ever venturing far. When things got to be too much, he would take off hitchhiking or head for the wilderness. He accomplished little during these years as he struggled to find his place in the world. He drove a forklift at Brentano's warehouse, became involved in union organizing, and helped lead a strike against one of his employer's bookstores. But he also smoked pot every day, developed a compulsive appetite for ice cream, and seemed unable to fashion a long-term plan for his life. Not long after his father's funeral, True finally broke up with Heuer. Her frustrations with True's emotional walls were more than the couple could overcome. True soon found new roommates on Long Island and, in between jobs, hit the road again.

That same year after his father's death, True spent eight days in the winter of 1978 hitchhiking with Alice through Appalachia and on to Tennessee, pitching his one-man tent along the interstates, rapping for hours with various drivers about his Marxist philosophy.

True kept a journal as he made his way south, and once home, typed it out on the backside of ballots the bookstore workers had used for the strike vote. Most of his notes list pickup and dropoff points, the weather, and the names of drivers and their vehicles.

It was True's first look at the coal mining region, and it made an impression. He was appalled by the third world living conditions in some places and wondered why nonunion miners willingly descended into unsafe mines.

"For $110 a day, is why," one miner who gave him a lift in Harlan, Kentucky, said with little patience.

"Old people around here look like poorly preserved mummies," True wrote.

Joe Dalton, a one-armed farmer and cattle rancher from Rutledge,

Tennessee, took True over Clinch Mountain. "He showed me more beauty than I've seen since the Sierras," True wrote. "Mountain after valley after mountain after valley till you hit the Smokies and Carolinas way off in the distance. It's the stuff of epic dreams."

True lost Alice in a rainstorm one night along the interstate. Finding her hours later in the dark, he sat inside his small tent, crying and holding on to his shivering best friend.

True returned to Long Island and soon met Annette Fuentes, ten years younger than he and a recent American studies graduate of the State University of New York's Westbury campus. Shortly after they met in late 1979, Fuentes and her sister left for a two-month trip to Central America organized by CISPES, a Central America refugee solidarity group with close ties to revolutionary forces seeking to topple the military in El Salvador.

Fuentes came home and found work at *Ms.* magazine in the city, first as a freelance researcher and then as an editorial assistant. On her first day on the job, December 8, 1980, John Lennon was killed outside his home at the Dakota.

True continued to drive a forklift in a warehouse while he did organizing work for Teamsters for a Democratic Union, a radical offshoot of the powerful Teamsters Union. He still hoped to win a permanent position as a salaried organizer, but he was an outsider with an attitude toward authority, and he ended up on the wrong side of the shop steward after back-talking one too many times.

Fuentes was a longtime cyclist, and True decided to take up competitive cycling in 1980. But the thirty-two-year-old ex-smoker could not compete with more accomplished riders, and he began pedaling long-distance, discovering a new way to pursue solitude while heading off into parts unknown. With each passing year since that first camping trip with his father into Sequoia, pursuing solitude had become a more and more important element in True's life, as if everything else—urban life, jobs, friends, politics—merely filled in the weeks and months between these liberating sojourns.

On one occasion he and Fuentes drove to West Virginia with a canoe tied to her car roof. They camped on a farm with great scenic views, a place True had previously visited that probably was owned by Minears, relatives of his mother. After a few days sharing a tent, Fuentes drove back to Long Island while True set out on his bike. It took him more than a week to get home, his first long-distance solo trip. He was hooked.

His next long cycling trip took him to Bangor, Maine, and on to Quebec City. Riding home to Long Island, he lost his travelers checks and suffered a minor crash. Nothing deterred him. In a letter to Kathleen Sullivan, his first love interest at UC–Irvine, he wrote of his plan to bike the length of the United States and then Latin America, even though he had owned a bicycle for only a year. Sullivan wrote back, concerned that True might run into trouble while going it alone on such long journeys.

"Your response to my travel plans is a completely recognizable K.S. response," True wrote in a March 18, 1981, letter. "All I can say is that death is somewhere along the road and that I will find it someday."

Work for True was a means to pay the rent and save pocket cash for the next trip. He traveled with little money and a lot of optimism, meeting people along the way, depending on the kindness of strangers and his own infectious gift of gab to take care of food, shelter, and the other basics. He liked not knowing what came next.

He became friends with a house painter named Mike Collins, who had enjoyed some wild times of his own on the West Coast in the 1960s, grooving in the Haight Ashbury scene and tripping through a Cream concert at Golden Gate Bridge. Collins told True he once bought a car for $100 and drove it from San Francisco to Mexico, where he had enrolled in a university to learn Spanish. He eventually sold the car and came home but since then had returned several times to Mexico. The school part of the plan fell through, but his road stories sparked True's interest in a cross-border adventure.

True needed work, and Collins convinced him there was good money in hanging wallpaper. He borrowed $400 from Fuentes to attend a trade school in North Carolina for a month. "I told him about

the school, he looked into it, and damned if he didn't go off and do it,"
Collins said. "He was a rookie, but you wouldn't know it when he
came back. He was good, very meticulous."

If True showed any interest in journalism at that point in his life,
Fuentes did not detect it. She described him as a chronic pot smoker
who spent little time reading, someone who seemed largely indifferent to her career goals and the work of a more accomplished writer,
Barbara Ehrenreich, who rented True a room in her finished basement. At the time, Ehrenreich, who worked at *Ms.* magazine, was
building herself a name as a feminist and a writer. Later books met
with critical acclaim, most recently *Nickel and Dimed* (2001), a best-
selling account of her experiences as a low-wage laborer.

Fuentes, fresh out of college, had worked as a researcher for
Ehrenreich on a study of workplace conditions for women in the third
world. Ehrenreich and her then husband, political activist and organizer Gary Stevenson, hosted a Marxist study group in their home,
where True and Fuentes first met.

Brian Donavan, a Pulitzer Prize–winning reporter for *Newsday* on
Long Island, hired True to hang wallpaper in 1984. "He was a real
craftsman with an artistic sense, but he wasn't talking about becoming a newspaper reporter in those days," Donavan said. "He knew I
was a reporter and was very curious about my office at home. We
talked about my work, and I'd like to think I played some small role in
his life change."

Surely being in such close proximity to Ehrenreich and Fuentes
had the same effect.

True set out on his biking trip—intended to take him through the
United States, Mexico, and Central America—in October 1981, his
biggest challenge to date. It was a naive undertaking. Civil wars were
raging in El Salvador and Guatemala, where repressive security forces
treated unknown foreigners as guerrilla sympathizers and often shot
first and worried about the consequences later.

Fuentes trained for the trip alongside True. She was game for such a
young woman, especially given her older boyfriend's lack of encourage-

ment. True decided to cycle alone across the country and then meet her on the West Coast, where she would join him on her bike. She recruited a friend for the cross-country road trip in her car from Long Island to Los Angeles, and they arrived soon after True cycled down from San Francisco, where he rested and visited friends. Fuentes left her car in LA, and she and True took off for the border, intending to travel through Mexico and beyond. They'd take it as far as they could.

"We each had sixty pounds on our bikes, so it was hard work, but I kept up," Fuentes said. "I remember the first night we camped out along this concrete canal, and he wasn't a nice person. I needed some nurturing and he couldn't give it to me. I started crying, wondering what I had done, and his attitude was I shouldn't be there if I didn't want to do it his way."

She had already been to Mexico. True, who grew up only hours from the border, was making his first crossing. For the next two months, they braved high winds and dust storms, exhaust-belching buses and trucks, and impossibly steep hills. They cycled the length of Baja California and then boarded the ferry for the ride across the Sea of Cortez to Mazatlán.

Fuentes didn't eat meat, which made meals a bit more complicated and annoyed True. He wanted to spend each night in a tent along the roadside, and Fuentes had to coax him into stopping at a *pension* every few days so they could shower and enjoy a sit-down meal.

They steadily made their way south toward Guadalajara, True pushing Fuentes, still in her early twenties, at a testing pace. She found it difficult to get him to slow down enough to enjoy the journey. "We didn't stop to smell the roses along the way. It was more about accomplishing the task," she said. "There was not a lot of flexibility. He had a set route and he would not deviate from it."

By the time they reached Guadalajara, Fuentes was ill. "It was a hot day and we were out of water," she said. "When we got there I collapsed from heat exhaustion. My vision was fading, my ears were ringing. I just lay on the bed and felt like I was dying. Not only was Philip unable to comfort me, he wanted to be sexual with me.

"I couldn't even get up, so what did he do?" she continued. "He said he was going to go get dinner, and he ended up touring around for two hours while I just lay there. It was amazing what I put up with . . . so when I read that he went off on a hundred-mile trip and left a wife five months pregnant I thought, 'This is the same guy.' You just don't do that."

Any romance to the trip had long ago vanished, and they agreed to ride to Mexico City and call it quits. They'd go as far south as the Yucatán and Chiapas, but they'd go by bus.

Fuentes is True's toughest critic among the women who knew him intimately, and he is not here to defend himself. But with detailed memory and dormant anger she sounded convincing more than twenty years later.

The Guadalajara stage of the trip gave True his first glimpse of the Huichol Indians. He bought a piece of traditional woven yarn art depicting the Huichol "eye of god" as a gift for Bronwen Heuer. It had been three years since their breakup, but they had continued to exchange long letters and postcards, correspondence that covered True's developments in life along with introspective, pot-fueled ramblings about his psyche and unresolved feelings toward her.

Heuer made an extended trip to Colombia after she and True broke up, and later went to Nicaragua to experience the post-Sandinista revolution as a *brigadista,* one of thousands of solidarity volunteers welcomed by the regime to help build rural schools and clinics. When she returned, Heuer urged True to go as well. "When Philip came home from Nicaragua in 1981, it was the only time he ever gave me flowers. He showed up at my front door with flowers and a note that said, 'This is the best thing you've ever done for me.' We lived together for six years and I can't remember a single time when he told me he loved me, although I know he did," Heuer said.

When True set out on his cross-country bike trip, Heuer readily agreed to care for his aging dog, Alice. The former couple still turned to each other for support. "I had more time to work through a lot of the pain and hurt and regain Philip as my friend," she later said. "We spent many years after breaking up meeting on a regular basis, and whenever we got back together we would be seeking each other's approval—comparing our adventures, our accomplishments, our ability to speak Spanish, and on and on and on. Even our capacity for aloneness: we both took off traveling alone, trying to prove things."

Fuentes had a freelance assignment to write about the Guatemalan refugees who fled military repression and were living in camps in southern Mexico. After taking a bus down to the border, she and True hitched a ride with a farmer, sharing the back of his pickup truck with a hog, into a deeply wooded area where they found the camps.

True watched as Fuentes interviewed refugees about their experiences. The work piqued his interest, and he asked her to explain how she intended to turn her reporting notes into a written story. Years later, in 1989, when Fuentes was metro editor at the *Village Voice*, True called to see if she would publish one of his stories. "I admit I wasn't out to do him any favors, and I passed on the story," she said. "I never heard from him again."

After their trip to the Guatemalan border, True and Fuentes returned to Mexico City, collected their bikes, and flew to Los Angeles. They drove back east in Fuentes's car, but it was obvious long before they got there that the stresses of the four-month journey had frayed the bonds of their four-year relationship. By 1984 their relationship was all but over. Fuentes finally took the initiative and ended it. "He freaked out and basically kicked me out of the house," Fuentes said.

She returned days later to collect her belongings. "When I came back he had emptied out all of my clothes from the closet and thrown them in a heap in another room," she said. "He took a record he had given me and cracked it in half, and shredded all the photos of us together, and left a note on top of the pile: 'Here is a memento of our love.' I just left."

True took up almost immediately with Sandy Weber, a woman even younger than Fuentes whom he had met through her.

Weber too liked to camp, though she was more vocal about True's risk taking. But he didn't see himself as someone who took undue risks. He simply believed most people had little outdoors experience and were afraid of anything that took them outside their comfort zone or routine. That interpretation was somewhat self-serving, however. As Weber knew from personal experience, True had experienced close calls on the road over the years that he was fortunate to escape.

True first experienced trouble on the trail in the early 1970s, when he and Heuer hitchhiked from UC–Irvine to Alaska, to backpack the challenging, thirty-three-mile long Chilkoot Trail, the route to the Klondike gold rush. The first night, as she and True slept in their domed tent, someone stole their backpack holding their cold weather gear, food, and supplies. Dispirited, Heuer suggested they turn back and head home. True insisted they press on, and somehow they did. True came home, glowing with accomplishment, despite the discomfort.

He later told Heuer about an incident on his cross-country biking trip when he was crossing a high mountain pass in Colorado in late October, when temperatures routinely fall below freezing. As True pushed to reach his destination point before sunset, he was caught in a freezing downpour after ignoring approaching storm clouds. He spent a sleepless night in his tent, soaked and shaking so badly he couldn't undress. He wasn't sure he would wake up alive in the morning.

Such scrapes were worth it, True later said, even though testing his mettle on such outings occasionally brought him into contact with people unfriendly to outsiders, even some whose intentions were not good.

Sandy Weber remembered one trip in particular, when the couple drove to Canada in True's aging 1968 Volvo, camping along the highway at night on their way to Nova Scotia. Typical of True, she said, they had no final destination or set plan. "He was so committed to just going that we ended up driving hours more than necessary because we didn't know about the ferry from Maine," she said. "He just wanted to drive until it was time to pull over and sleep wherever we stopped."

As they were sightseeing along the scenic Nova Scotia coast, True turned into a private property, drawn by a picturesque farmhouse situated on a distant spit of land jutting into the bay. It was a spectacular vista, Weber said, and a captivated True ignored her concerns about trespassing. They parked the car and set out hiking along the land's edge.

"Within minutes the farmer emerged from the house, shouting, demanding to know who we are and what we are doing," she said. "Within minutes, Philip had talked his way out of the situation and before I know it I'm listening to the farmer tell us his wife just churned some butter and baked fresh bread that morning and we ought to come inside and try it."

Once they were settled in the kitchen, True tested his welcome and asked the farmer if he and Sandy could make camp near the water for a few nights. The farmer welcomed them to pitch their tent and enjoy the scenery. Unfortunately for the campers, he apparently paid a visit to the village tavern that evening and, loosened up by a few drinks, shared the big news that two American hippies were camped on his land.

Late that night, a truckload of drunken locals roared up to the tent, shining the truck's headlights through the tent wall as a panicked Weber rose naked from her sleeping bag to retrieve her clothes. As the truck slowly edged within feet of the tent, the boys in the back loudly egged the driver on, daring him to push the tent off the land and into the bay. It was the most frightening moment of Weber's life.

True pulled on his jeans and went outside to reason with the men. At first they shouted him down, but True stood his ground and patiently let the men whoop it up before he continued. Eventually, Weber said, they quieted down and listened as True reminded the men that everyone would regret it in the morning if events got out of hand that night. "You've had your fun, now please leave us alone," True told them. "We're not hurting anybody."

The drunks, spoiling for a fight minutes earlier, piled back into the truck and left. True watched them leave, then came back into the tent where a half-dressed Weber was shaking with fear. "You get me out of here five minutes after dawn," she demanded.

True look surprised. "The farmer said we could stay two nights," he said. "Why leave now?"

Weber looked at him with disbelief. "Are you insane? A truckload of men almost rape me and run us over and you want to stay and enjoy a second night? Get me out of here."

They broke camp and left at daylight. Weber says she can't remember a single thing about the trip home.

As months passed, Weber grew impatient with their relationship. She was close to her family, and it bothered her that True had so much trouble connecting with her parents or talking about commitment, especially the possibility of marriage and children one day. She loved True, found him different and more interesting than anyone else she had dated: smart, well read, a great conversationalist, and the most self-reliant person she had ever met. But Weber wanted a family and True was unwilling to fulfill those desires. One year after they began dating, they broke up. Weber told True what he had heard before from Heuer and Fuentes: if he was ever going to achieve his potential and sustain a relationship, he needed to get into therapy and deal with his past.

This time he listened. True began to see a therapist, something he told few people. In fact, he did not disclose the therapist's name to any of his friends. Whoever he was, he was able to help True deal with his past and imagine a more fulfilling future. There were no instant miracles, but the change in True and his motivation to pursue new challenges was obvious to friends. His weariness with blue-collar work and his growing interest in Mexico developed as he continued therapy.

Joe Vasquez, True's high school friend, had a reunion with True in the mid-1980s, years after their lives had taken different paths and both were approaching their fortieth birthday.

Vasquez's wife, Rita, was happy to meet Joe's long lost "best friend," but that soon changed. Even as True made himself comfortable in the couple's spacious, well-furnished Sacramento home, he launched into a critical commentary on organized religion, middle-class family life with children, and other mainstream values. True told Joe and Rita that he would never father children and had no interest in women unwilling to accept that reality. Rita quickly tired of his "class rant," although True seemed unaware of her feelings.

More than fifteen years had passed since their last real visit. Vasquez had made the most of his military service, returning to college to earn an engineering degree, courtesy of Uncle Sam. His telecommunications consulting business for Central Coast businesses was thriving. True, despite having a college degree, was still hanging wallpaper. He was still a protestor, still "dropped out."

After a few days in Sacramento, the two piled gear into Joe's old Blazer and drove over the mountains to Eagle Lake, a state park that occupied the highest point in the Sierra on the highway from Sacramento to Reno. Vasquez had selected an area accessible only by four-wheel drive. A state policeman suspicious of their presence in the otherwise empty high country stopped Vasquez and subjected the two to a lengthy search, finally allowing them to proceed after he failed to turn up any illegal substances. True and Vasquez, both sporting much shorter haircuts by now, shared a laugh over how they still seemed to attract trouble.

They were the only campers at the park. None of the other seven remote campsites were occupied. Vasquez thought they were in heaven. "Phil looked at me after we got there and said, 'This really isn't wilderness camping if you can drive to it, Joe. You've got to walk in, backpack in; it has to be a challenge, if you want a genuine wilderness experience.' I just looked at him, not knowing what to say."

Afterward, they drove down to Reno and visited True's mother. "She came out of her trailer and gave me a great big bear hug, and they didn't even embrace," Vasquez said. "It was awkward, Phil just standing off to the side."

Christeen was apparently married at the time to her fourth and last husband, and the four of them had dinner at a local fast food diner. "His mother asked about my life and then she'd ask about his life, but she did it in a very unflattering way, in a way that put him on the spot," Vasquez said. "She'd ask me about my family or my business success and then she'd look over at Phil, who was close to forty and didn't have those things. He still hadn't settled, didn't have a family, didn't own a home; he was still looking at what he was going to do. I was very uncomfortable."

True and Vasquez were parting ways in Reno. True planned to fly home to Long Island, while Vasquez was driving back over the Sierra to Sacramento. "That was the last time we saw each other, and as we shook hands, I'll never forget the look on his face," Vasquez said. "He looked like a child who looked at me like I was leaving him behind."

Back on Long Island, True continued to hang wallpaper, but he also returned to school, enrolling in night classes to study writing and photography. He began telling friends that he was going to become a journalist.

Fuentes, whose own career was developing nicely, undoubtedly influenced his new direction. True met others who shared his political interests at the New School in the Village. He spoke Spanish at every opportunity.

The community of Central American refugees on Long Island, mostly Salvadorans, had grown rapidly throughout the 1980s as peasants and urban poor fled the violence and economic chaos. Even after the region's civil wars subsided, the refugees kept coming in search of steady work. True met some of the journalists contributing to *La Tribuna Hispana,* a local Spanish-language weekly that served the area's migrant and refugee community. He soon won assignments to cover local events, including political rallies protesting Reagan administration policies in Central America.

He was still more of an activist than journalist, but he was developing new skills. He and Fred Chase, another budding photographer he met at one such political rally, became friends. Both were antiwar activists and both later traveled to Central America, principally to Nicaragua to follow in Heuer's footsteps as *brigadistas.*

True used his Salvadoran contacts to arrange a visit to guerrilla territory in northern El Salvador and then persuaded the editors at *La Tribuna* to help with his travel expenses in return for the stories and photographs he promised he would bring back for their readers. By now, in the late 1980s, the war was winding down, although there was still sporadic fighting, and even one more major push by the guerrillas into the capital. True's account of his stay in a "model community" in rebel-controlled territory filled an entire page of *La Tribuna*.

On the way home, he traveled through Mexico and across the border into Texas and the Rio Grande Valley, where a wave of Central American refugees had overwhelmed federal and local agencies. While working a story there, he got his first good look at life on the border. He also met Rebecca Thatcher, a newspaper reporter who suggested he apply for a job at the *Brownsville Herald*. Nothing was open at the moment, and True headed back to Long Island to file his stories. He and Thatcher agreed to stay in touch, and she promised to put in a good word with Lavis Laney, the editor.

When Thatcher called in 1989 with news of a job, he didn't take long to decide. True, 41, packed his bags, sold his ladder to his volleyball buddy, Bob Horchler, and headed south to Brownsville. The wallpaper hanger had become a journalist.

5

A New Life on the Border

As I held her close to me I could see the big steel span across the river, and I could see the people crossing the bridge between the two nations... She was born in Mexico. And even though we held each other in a tight embrace, a river flowed between us.

—Hart Stilwell, *Border City*

Almost all the literature about the border stresses the illegal, the vile, and the violent. My purpose here is to show instead the wide range of activity and attitudes among its people, to illuminate their day-to-day struggles and pleasures.

—Tom Miller, *On the Border*

Martha's parents, Roberto Perez and Concepción Gonzalez, worried about their daughter's future. They knew her former boyfriend, the surgeon, and his well-respected family. Marriage to him would solidify Martha's place in Matamoros society and guarantee a secure and prosperous future. On the other hand, Roberto and Concepción had raised their daughter to think for herself.

Roberto, a retired property manager for the state of Tamaulipas, and Concepción, Martha's selfless mother, gave Martha and her three younger sisters, Oralia, Yolanda, and Issa, a stable, nurturing upbringing, seeing to their education, moral development, and belief in their own self-worth. All three younger sisters married Mexican men, but Martha chose to forestall marriage to attend the Universidad del Noreste in Matamoros, graduating with a degree in social work.

Now she was serious about a *norteamericano*, a stranger from California who didn't seem to have a family of his own or much of a past. He was a nice enough man, *un periodista*, who spoke Spanish and displayed a clear passion and respect for Mexico. But he was older, rootless, hard to read.

¿Quién es este otro? Who is this other guy, really, they wondered?

But as time passed, it seemed equally clear that "Felipe," as he was known in the family, truly loved Martha, their only unmarried daughter. Mexicans worry about unmarried daughters who turn thirty. And Martha's parents, like just everyone else who happened into True's life, couldn't help but like him. "I guess the only one uncomfortable in the end was his parrot Fidel," Martha said.

Philip Theodore True and Martha Patricia Perez Gonzalez were married on June 6, 1992, at the Catedral de Nuestra Señora de Refugio across the river from Brownsville in Matamoros. However joyous the occasion, it must have been somewhat uncomfortable for Martha's parents to learn that Felipe, a self-declared agnostic, refused to be married at a mass inside the cathedral. His rejection of organized religion would strike most Mexican families as extreme. Tens of millions of Mexicans consider themselves Catholics, although they do not attend weekly mass or regularly take the sacraments. Most maintain a parish connection and would consider it unthinkable to forgo a church baptism, marriage, or funeral.

True did agree to be married by the family's priest, Padre Ruperto Ayala, the same Catholic priest who years earlier had organized the summer camp where Martha first met her friend Juanita Serrano. Philip wore a white *guayabera* and Martha wore a white dress. They exchanged vows in the uninspiring confines of the cathedral office.

While Philip seemed indifferent to his lack of family ties, he confided to Martha that he wanted to be married on June 6 because his estranged father, Theodore, died on that date in 1977, thus tying their own wedding day to the memory of his lost father.

Martha was two weeks shy of her thirty-first birthday, which fell on June 13. Philip would turn forty-four days later, on June 18. Now with a wedding anniversary to celebrate each year, June became their special month.

All the guests came from Martha's family and circle of friends. True didn't even recruit a best man to stand at his side. After the ceremony, the wedding party gathered on Martha's parents' back patio for a modest reception. The honeymoon was in the old colonial silver mining city of Zacatecas. Then Philip and Martha came home and were married again in a brief civil ceremony in Brownsville.

They set out that September in their two-door Hyundai on a road trip to the West Coast. Philip was ready for Martha to meet his mother and sister. After a short stay in Reno, they would drive to the San Fernando Valley to visit the site where the family chicken farm once stood and then up the scenic California coast for a second honeymoon in San Francisco.

Philip's mother and sister, both divorced, were living together again, sharing a trailer home with Bonnie's two children on the sagebrush outskirts of Reno. The unspoken tension among the Trues was palpable, Bonnie remembered, and Martha said she could see the hurt on Christeen's face when Philip casually dismissed his mother's protests at not having been invited to the wedding.

Christeen and Bonnie, barely able to pay the bills and find extra money for the kids, had sent Philip and Martha a $100 gift certificate to JC Penney, where Bonnie worked in the catalog fulfillment center.

"It was just a small, informal service in Mexico without family or friends," Philip told them, perhaps believing the truth would hurt their feelings.

It was a bittersweet visit. Theodore was long dead, but the three remaining Trues were in one place again, if only for a day. In one place, but hardly reunited or reconciled. No one dared revisit the family's painful past and disintegration. Christeen enjoyed more conversation with her new daughter-in-law than she could coax from her son.

Martha's presence did little to change the family dynamic. Bonnie said she and her mother yearned to grow close again with Philip, but he had told his sister he had no feelings, good or bad, toward his mother. The younger sister doubted her brother's claim. While lacking his formal education and worldliness, she had good instincts and believed the need to reconnect was mutual. But no one seemed to know how to take the first step.

"I asked Phil if he would consent to a family portrait and he said okay," Bonnie said, recovering the framed photograph from its nook in her living room where Philip and Martha had sat. "I'm so glad he said yes. For all our lives, it was the only family portrait we've ever had done, ever. Then he was gone. We knew before he came out he wouldn't stay for very long."

True never saw his mother again.

Toward the end of their West Coast road trip, Philip pulled over to call Fred Bonavita, soon to be his new editor, to make sure there were no hitches with his start date on his new job as a border reporter at the *Express-News*. He emerged from the phone booth, visibly rattled by his conversation.

"It's a good thing we took the job with the *Express-News* instead of the *Light*," he said. "They just announced the *Light* is going to close. If I had taken the *Light's* offer I'd be out of a job right now."

What Philip told Martha, in so many words that October day in San Francisco, was, "It's a good thing I didn't listen to Bob Rivard."

While Philip was courting Martha in Brownsville, his work as a border reporter for the *Brownsville Herald* caught my attention. The city's poverty and the newspaper's tiny circulation belied the borderland's hold on aspiring journalists. Life along the border is different— less developed, more lawless, a place that is neither the United States nor Mexico, existentially speaking, but a world of its own that lies between the two, even if it doesn't appear that way on any map. Once every few years, a budding journalist with genuine potential will turn up at a border newspaper like the *Herald,* and after a few years spent perfecting Spanish and exploring the region and its culture, seek to move on to a bigger, better newspaper.

Mutual friends in the Rio Grande Valley had urged True to look me up in San Antonio. There were similarities in our two lives that were apparent to those who knew us both. We were restless gringos from dysfunctional families who had led underachieving, blue-collar lives as young men before finding our calling as newspapermen. And we both had found strong, healthy women who brought new balance and possibilities into our lives. Philip had Martha. I had Monika, the daughter of German immigrants, whose first admonishment to me had been to pay off my long-neglected college tuition loans if I wanted to date her. I took that advice and a lot more in the ensuing years and the payoff for a college dropout was evident.

I was a senior editor at the *San Antonio Light,* the underdog daily in the newspaper war of the 1980s. We competed fiercely with the rival *Express-News* for the best of the bilingual reporters working their way north from the border. True, however, already knew Bonavita, and the *Express-News* enjoyed the upper hand in the bitter circulation war. Most journalists regarded the newspaper as less ambitious journalistically than the *Light,* but the *Express-News* owned the morning market and the majority of the advertisers and the loyalty of the establishment; even after the afternoon *Light* switched to morning publication, it was unable to catch its bigger rival.

No one wants to be at a newspaper when it closes. The decades of the 1970s and 1980s had seen one U.S. city after another lose its second daily; now with the advent of the 1990s, the last holdouts in Texas—in Dallas, San Antonio, and Houston—followed suit.

Competition between the two San Antonio newspapers was cut-throat. There was little social contact among working journalists in the two newsrooms, and the editors at both newspapers competed to hire the best talent coming out of the smaller Texas markets. Each side tended to exaggerate the shortcomings of the competition, while inflating its own accomplishments. At the time, the Hearst Corporation owned the *Light,* while Australian publishing tycoon Rupert Murdoch's NewsCorp owned the *Express-News.*

Months earlier, Bonavita had offered True an opportunity to earn extra money and build his résumé by freelancing articles from the border. True's editor nixed the proposition. The *Herald* prohibited staff members from working for the regional newspapers, considered competitors along the border.

"I then countered that we'd be willing to publish his stories and not use his name, to protect him from any recriminations down there," Bonavita recalled, "and to his credit, he told me, 'No, that wouldn't be honest or ethical. I'll just have to wait until I can get a job there someday.' From that moment on, I knew I wanted to hire Philip True."

True and I met in my office at the *Light,* located only one block from the *Express-News.* Our scheduled half-hour interview lasted hours. We had a lot to talk about as two reporters who had remade their lives on the border. Each of us won our start in the business with backdoor entrée into a small newsroom where editors with few other choices were willing to take a chance on unproven walk-ins. I gained my foothold at an earlier age than True, but I, unlike him, was a college dropout who did not earn my degree until I turned forty-four.

We talked about our blue-collar backgrounds. True had painted houses and hung wallpaper. I had worked the brutal overnight shift in a Kansas slaughterhouse, in various states as a Volkswagen mechanic, and in one particularly desperate period of unemployment on the border as a door-to-door vacuum cleaner salesman. It's an easy laugh line, but journalists with blue-collar backgrounds bring a perspective to our work that white-collar reporters who have never labored with their hands cannot match.

True would be happier working with a kindred spirit, an editor who shared his love of the border and Mexico, I told him. True was tempted but expressed reservations about the *Light's* future. He didn't want to sign on to a dying newspaper.

"Hearst is here for the long run," I assured him. "Frank Bennack, the CEO of Hearst in New York, is a San Antonio native. He'll win the war."

We talked career trajectories for a while. True wanted to know how I had moved from a reporting job in Brownsville to an assignment covering civil wars and living in Central America in only four and a half years. Could I offer him a similar opportunity?

No, I couldn't, but I wanted him to come to San Antonio. True hedged. We said good-bye and he headed over to keep his appointment with editors at the *Express-News*.

What True and I did not know then is that he, too, would enjoy remarkable success in a short span of time. Within five years of the day he walked into his first full-time newspaper job, True would be posted south of the border for a major Texas newspaper, almost exactly as things had worked out for me. It was one more intriguing parallel in our lives.

My connection with True proved fleeting. He called the next day to say he had accepted a job with the *Express-News,* where editors had offered a coveted reporting job on the border in Laredo. It was an opportunity the struggling *Light* could not match.

Sometime after Philip and Martha had settled into their new life in Laredo, Philip introduced Martha to the great outdoors. They drove several hours south into the state of Tamaulipas, a harsh desert environment of cacti, dry creek beds, and arroyos—steep, rocky canyons. The land seems uninhabitable at first sight, but the dense brush is ideal for wildlife: deer, coyote, javelina, rattlesnakes, jackrabbits, quail, and dove abound.

It is not uncommon to see impoverished peasants, burros in tow, standing on the edge of busy highways, braving the roar of speeding trucks and cross-border traffic, offering tethered fawns, live armadillos on a string, even rattlesnakes for sale. If there is a closed season to hunters in this stretch of Mexico, few heed it.

Into this environment Philip guided Martha, newly outfitted with hiking boots and outdoor apparel, for their first shared hike. Martha struggled to keep up with her taller, fitter husband, despite her eleven-year age advantage. Miles away from their parked car, she fell into a patch of *nopales*, prickly pear cactus. "I couldn't even get myself up I was hurting so badly," she remembered. "Philip had to pull out as many of the *espinas* in my backside as he could, and then carry me on his back all the way to the car. That was our first and last outdoor trip together. After that, I said, 'Vete. Go by yourself from now on. I'm staying at home.'"

While Martha was adjusting to life apart from family and friends, Philip's new job brought him three hours closer to Big Bend National Park in West Texas. "Philip was a desert and rocks guy, not a beach or a mountains and forest guy," Martha said. "He found some kind of peace of mind in that kind of country. He was happy we were there."

For the three years they lived in Laredo, Philip went on solo camping trips into the Tamaulipas desert and out to Big Bend. On one occasion, he set out on a forty-five-hour canoe trip down the Rio Grande. Martha stayed home, working on her degree in psychology and preparing for the state exam to obtain her social worker's license.

"I remember Philip telling us such journeys were where he found himself," Juanita Serrano, Martha's best friend, said. "We just knew he had to go off alone, something he had been doing since an early age when he was left alone by his family."

The San Antonio newspapers, meanwhile, went from publishing the news to making news. After losing $1 million a month for five years, Hearst was ready to give up on the Light. Bennack, however, was not about to lose the market. He negotiated an unprecedented deal with Murdoch, whose broadcast investments in Europe had left him dangerously overloaded with debt. Murdoch reluctantly agreed to part with his San Antonio newspaper, but the deal was bittersweet for both men. The Express and News, separate morning and afternoon newspapers when Murdoch acquired them in the early 1970s, were his first acquisitions outside Australia after inheriting the company from his father. But the cash he gained in the sale helped stave off his bankers. In the ensuing decade his businesses thrived. Bennack, the up-by-his-own bootstraps product of a working-class south side San Antonio family, won the market, but at the cost of folding the Light and parting ways with many of the stunned employees.

Bennack and his New York team arrived in the Light offices on October 6, 1992, to make the announcement. Under the terms of the deal, *Express-News* employees were guaranteed jobs for two years while *Light* employees not hired by the *Express-News* would receive severance packages. Hearst kept the name of the dominant paper, the *Express-News*, while the *Light's* last front page featured a cartoon showing a hand pulling a chain to extinguish a dangling lightbulb.

Senior management at the *Light* would stay on the payroll for one year or until they found new employment. The prospects for most *Light* journalists going to the *Express-News* were dim. A handful were offered work, but the acrimonious nature of the newspaper war meant that *Express-News* editors were reluctant to make room for their longtime adversaries. Hearst executives deferred to local management in deciding who made the one-block walk from the *Light* to the *Express-News*.

Three years earlier, I had left a better-paying, higher-profile job at *Newsweek* in New York, where I worked as a senior editor and chief of correspondents, overseeing the magazine's domestic and foreign bureaus. It was a position that included world travel, a spacious office on Madison Avenue, and entrée into the intense media world of Manhattan. It also was a job that forced me to travel while my wife, Monika, stayed at home, caring for our two infant sons. After nearly a decade outside Texas, half spent as a foreign correspondent in Central American war zones and the rest as a traveling editor based in New York, it was Monika's turn to set our course, which meant coming home to Texas to raise our sons. She had endured more than her fair share of a rootless, uncertain, sometimes unsafe life in our first years of marriage.

Weeks after our marriage and brief honeymoon in Cancún, then a one-hotel beach resort, we packed up our belongings and moved to San Jose, Costa Rica, where I had rented a home to serve as our base while I covered the region's civil wars. Days later I left for El Salvador, leaving Monika, who spoke no Spanish, to enroll in an intensive language school and fend for herself. I'll never forget her lonely voice in those first few weeks when she called me in San Salvador to complain that Costa Rican customs officials wouldn't release our household goods until she paid a hefty bribe, something she didn't know how to do. It wasn't the only time I wasn't there for her. It was an inauspicious start to a marriage. Not many wives tolerate husbands for very long who cover war during the week and arrive home for the weekend, news permitting.

For all that, we also shared indelible memories as young newlyweds, climbing volcanoes, exploring cloud forests, fishing for tarpon in jungle canals, picking mangoes from the tall tree in our yard, roasting freshly harvested coffee beans bought in the market that morning, and walking through abandoned, vine-choked Mayan ruins. We knew we were living an extended honeymoon and would forever look back with longing to experience something that one day would no longer exist.

Now, three years after our Texas homecoming, I found myself on the telephone, telling her I had just lost my job. Many of my fellow journalists in the newsroom wasted no time in leaving, choosing the certainty of an available job over the promise of a future severance check. The *Light* published until January 27, 1993, while Justice Department officials reviewed the deal and would-be purchasers looked at the books. Nearly half the newsroom staff left before the *Light* actually folded some three and half months after the announced sale.

Ed Rademaeckers, the last executive editor of the *Light,* said there was no chance the *Express-News* would hire me. "You need to disabuse yourself of the notion that you are going to walk over there, ever," he told me, waving his cigarette at me, the shutdown bringing his eight-month abstinence from smoking to an end.

I was miserable as the writing on the wall came into focus. In the space of three years, I had gone from senior editor at a magazine whose name opened doors around the world to an unemployed senior editor at a shuttered San Antonio newspaper.

After the closure, managing editor Jeff Cohen and I were assigned the task of helping to find jobs for unemployed staff members. A team of workers from a job placement agency moved into the empty newsroom and offered counseling, gave résumé advice, and coached people who hadn't interviewed for a job in years. We spent our days working the telephones, calling other editors in other newsrooms, looking for work for those on our staff who were willing to relocate. It was a sobering experience.

As our work wound down in the vacant *Light* newsroom, I sent a letter to Larry Walker, the *Express-News* publisher, outlining why I would make a smart addition to the *Express-News*. A number of community leaders wrote letters or spoke up on my behalf.

With the support of George Irish, the former *Light* publisher who had been elevated to vice president of Hearst Newspapers, Walker invited me to lunch to talk about my proposal. Stubbornness in defense of the right cause can be a strength. Four months after the *Light* folded, I was hired as assistant managing editor, the third ranking editor at the *Express-News*.

True and I now worked at the same newspaper. It had happened in a way neither of us could have imagined.

True wasted no time in establishing himself with his new editors. Bonavita, a former UPI reporter, placed a high value on prolific reporters and Agent True answered the challenge. His byline appeared every few days with a dateline from Laredo, Brownsville, McAllen, Reynosa, or Nuevo Laredo. True assiduously worked both sides of the border, always ready to pursue a story on either side of the river. Working alongside more experienced journalists, the former wallpaper hanger quickly improved.

In 1993, his first year at the *Express-News*, True's byline appeared on 177 published stories. Even later, when True's job in Mexico made it possible to spend more time on reporting and writing, his output was high. He averaged more than 135 stories a year through 1998, an especially impressive output from 1995 on when he lived in Mexico City.

A peso devaluation took place as President Carlos Salinas de Gortari handed power to President-elect Ernesto Zedillo in 1994, crippling Mexico's emerging middle class and devastating the border economy.

Mexican business owners and workers more than ever feared the implications of unprotected domestic markets and the enveloping global economy. Mexicans were growing increasingly impatient with one-party rule, deeply rooted official corruption, and the lack of real political reform. True covered the serious big picture story, while developing a good eye for the offbeat story that readers enjoy.

For example, as more Americans crossed the border to buy cheaper prescription drugs, True wrote about two Dallas women, one six months pregnant and the other wearing a double girdle, who were stopped at the border by U.S. customs inspectors as they tried to cross with nine thousand Valium tablets taped to their abdomens and buttocks.

True wasn't a golfer, but he was quick to appreciate the implications when cost-cutting Laredo officials replaced greens keepers at the local municipal course with county jail inmates, a move that made golfers uneasy as they teed it up amid watching prisoners.

My favorite was his description of a new Laredo police department policy restricting public access to headquarters. An excerpt:

> Laredo party animals will have to find a new spot to boogie now that the Laredo police have declared department headquarters off limits at night.
>
> No boys in blue nipping on the job with these folk, many of whom were civilians who simply wandered in off the streets looking for something to do, Assistant Chief Eliodoro Granados says. "You'd be surprised at who comes here to hang out," Granados said Thursday.
>
> During evening hours, the crowds got so thick and sometimes so rowdy, that the department last week closed the building to all but officers and those with official business between 5 p.m. and 8 a.m.
>
> "This place has been open to anybody who wanted to walk in, 24 hours a day," Granados said.
>
> That definitely isn't the way a police station should be run, he continued.

"If you go to any other station, they won't let you past the front desk," he explained.

Besides the drunks, the word apparently got around that the department was a soft touch for transients.

"We had homeless people who came here and showered up," the officer said.

And don't forget about domestic disputes, he said.

"Officers would go to a party or a family quarrel, arrest somebody and bring them in. And the whole group would follow along. Once inside, they kept right on fighting," Granados said.

There was plenty on the serious side to keep True busy too.

While President Clinton lobbied Congress to pass the North American Free Trade Agreement, True ventured beyond free trade to write about Mexican migrants, drug trafficking wars, money laundering prosecutions, Mexican fruit fly paranoia, even a controversial federal program to hunt rabid coyotes from helicopters.

One week, nearly two hundred students in the Laredo school district were set to be expelled after they were discovered crossing the bridge from their homes in Nuevo Laredo each morning to illegally attend classes. The border was a different world, not Mexico, not like the rest of the United States. True thrived.

Fred Chase, True's photographer friend from Long Island, had visited True in Brownsville in the summer of 1991, shortly after True began dating Martha. He was exiting his own unhappy relationship and considering a move of his own. Now a freelance book editor, Chase could work anywhere in the age of e-mail and overnight package delivery. As 1992 came to a close, he moved to Laredo. "I was attracted to Central America, Mexico, the border, the whole culture, the people," he said. "Here Philip was doing what I kind of wanted to do.

"I loved New York, but I didn't miss it," Chase recalled years later, sitting in the modest Laredo apartment he shares with his three adopted children, two brothers and a sister he met while doing volunteer work at a Nuevo Laredo orphanage. "At some point, New York had just become a place to live. The city is for rich people, young people, poor people. I was in my early forties, and I was none of those three. I'm very happy living on the border."

For True, Chase's arrival in time for New Year's Eve celebrations on the border as 1992 wound down cemented the kind of enduring friendship that had eluded him over the years. Chase, meanwhile, could see True's transformation since meeting Martha. She had sparked something deeper and more real in True, helping him achieve new levels of commitment in his personal life and accomplishment as a reporter.

Off duty, however, True had no better luck recruiting Chase for his forays into the wild than he had Martha. "Hiking into a desert where you won't see water for three days is not my idea of a good time," Chase said.

A little more than a year after arriving in Laredo, True won his first major assignment in Mexico. Editors awoke him early New Year's Day 1994 after self-described revolutionaries poured into the plaza of San Cristobal de las Casas in Chiapas state where True had gone with Annette Fuentes a decade earlier. Some of the so-called Zapatistas were armed only with machetes or sticks, but the guerrillas succeeded in occupying the municipal offices, driving away the few soldiers and police in the city, and declaring war against the Salinas administration. Could True head down there as soon as possible? Bonavita knew the answer even before he asked. Later that day True, accompanied by Chase and his cameras, crossed the bridge into Nuevo Laredo to catch a flight to Chiapas. Less than five years after winning his first job as a newspaper reporter, True was on his way to cover a guerrilla uprising in Mexico.

I was promoted to managing editor in the summer of 1994, the number two position in the newsroom. Now I reported directly to long-time executive editor Jim Moss, who intended to retire in a few years to his Hill Country river ranch with his wife, Adele, to tinker with his antique cars and watch over his growing herd of longhorn cattle.

As my own vision took shape for how we could transform the

Express-News into a regional newspaper, coverage south of San Antonio became increasingly important. Moving True to a full-time position in Mexico was an obvious move once Carmina Danini, a Laredo native who worked for us in Mexico City, asked to return to San Antonio to care for her ailing parents.

Monika and I, along with our two sons, Nick and Alex, traveled down to Laredo to celebrate True's year-end promotion. We walked across the international bridge to dine at one of True's favorite Nuevo Laredo restaurants, Victoria 3020. It was a relaxed, comfortable evening, and I regretted not getting to meet Martha earlier as the conversation developed.

True looked like he had hit the lottery, and Martha seemed excited, too. Monika and I felt we were reliving our own assignment to Central America fifteen years earlier when we'd been newlyweds in Dallas. True and I relived our near miss two years ago at the *Light,* and True gleefully reminded me of my claim that the *Light* would not close. I had made a similar claim, he had learned, when the Dallas *Times Herald* closed and I made an unsuccessful attempt to recruit MacCormack, the paper's former San Antonio correspondent. He too chose the *Express-News* over the *Light.*

"Well, I was actually right," I told True. "Frank Bennack won the market, didn't he?"

We talked more about our shared ambitions for the *Express-News* in the years ahead. It was a promising time. The newspaper was improving in visible ways: an eye-catching redesign, state-of-the-art printing presses, new computer systems, a remodeled newsroom, and, most importantly, a growing staff of talented journalists.

Nick, our oldest son, was celebrating his tenth birthday that day, November 6, 1994, and we arranged for a birthday cake topped with sparklers to arrive at the end of the meal. At this age he no longer wanted to be treated like a child, and Nick frowned when Martha summoned a band of roving mariachi to play "Las Mañanitas," the traditional Mexican birthday song. In those days, Nick knew little Spanish. He glowered in his chair while the adults sang along.

After leaving the restaurant and saying good night to the Trues, we wandered the streets, window-shopping. Nick's dark mood lifted when we let him purchase a cheap pocketknife from a street vendor posted on the small plaza. Past experience told me the knife would cease to function within days and then be forgotten. For now, indulging an American boy's urge to barter with a street vendor got the better of me.

We parted ways with Philip and Martha that evening, invigorated by the good meal and company, the balmy November evening, and, above all, what lay ahead for us. The Trues were heading south to Mexico City in December. I was closing the year as the managing editor of a newspaper on the move. Life was good.

Road trips became a hallmark of Philip and Martha's relationship. Even after they had established new lives and jobs in Mexico City, they continued to plan trips to other destinations. Staying put didn't seem to be an option for True, and his wanderlust gave Martha a whole new view of the United States. After upgrading from the old blue Hyundai to a small red Honda, they set out for Minneapolis on a visit to Stewart Selman and his family, old friends from True's Long Island days. True spoke weekly with Chase, now his best friend; as he realized more professional success, he seemed interested in rekindling friendships that had gone cold. Philip and Martha drove on from the Twin Cities to Niagara Falls and then headed downstate to reconnect with some of his contractor friends on Long Island.

Near the end of their first year in Mexico City they set out for Seattle to renew True's long dormant friendship with his former college roommate, Peter Harris, and his wife, Grace. The Harrises had moved there years earlier after Peter completed his Ph.D. at Yale. Philip and Martha also planned on making a subsequent side trip to San Francisco.

The journey introduced Martha to someone who had been important to True in his years as a university student, and Philip got to meet the Harris's two adopted children, Alexandra (who enrolled at UC–Irvine in fall 2004) and Edward, three years her junior. Peter and Grace adopted each child from Korea at the age of about six months.

Philip and Peter had not seen each other since 1980, when the Harrises lived in Connecticut and True lived on Long Island. It was one more relationship in True's life that seemed suspended in time, disconnected and untended.

Grace later explained why the friendship cooled. "My take on the relationship was that Peter and I were kind of like Phil's parents in college, despite our similar ages, and in 1971 we decided to get married at a time when people our age were not getting married, and Philip and everyone else were putting down marriage," Grace said. "So Peter chose to ask someone else, a professor friend, to be his best man. I know that really hurt Philip. It took him by surprise, but there was nothing we could do about that at the time. Philip was really wounded by that. They never, ever talked about it."

Philip did not invite Peter and Grace to his wedding either. "Phil just called out of the blue to say he was coming up here to introduce us to Martha," Grace said. "I told Peter, 'The son is coming home to get approval from his parents for his new wife.' They stayed for four or five days, and we had a blast together."

By then Peter and Grace had carved out successful careers in city government, he as a policy analyst and she as the budget director for the parks and recreation department. They live in a postcard setting on Bainbridge Island, west of Seattle, connected by a bridge to Kitsap Peninsula on Puget Sound. On a clear day, you can see 14,000-foot Mount Rainier. The heavily wooded island is the size of Manhattan yet there are only 20,000 year-round residents, most of them commuters who board the ferry each day for the ride to the city.

"He and Peter yukked it up like they had never stopped seeing each other," Grace said. "They went off to REI like they did when they were nineteen to buy camping equipment."

Martha and Philip were conservative with money. She was taken aback when her husband went on a spending spree at the outfitters store. "I had never, ever seen Philip spend money like that," Martha said. "I wasn't sure how we were going to fit everything he bought—a tent, a backpack, and new hiking boots—in our little car. I think he spent thousands of dollars. I was in shock."

Harris said the bill that day was actually in the hundreds of dollars but agreed that True always coveted the latest outdoor gear and always kept abreast of technical advances in equipment design.

More than one friend of True's remembers the pride he took in his low REI membership number, 110-399, issued in 1969. Peter, who signed up in 1965, had an even lower number, 47-523. The numbers represent the customer's rank since the company's founding in 1938. Today a new member would get a number close to 7 million. REI members share an almost fanatical loyalty to the company and its values. For Martha, who had never heard of REI, it was further evidence of Philip's almost religious devotion to the outdoors.

"Philip was like this person who had drifted off and had come back to life," Grace said. "He was proud of himself. He seemed very anchored, very settled. He was grown up. He didn't have to have funky long hair anymore. It was as if all those years of separation had never happened. Everyone was relaxed, and we loved Martha. She was smart, had a good sense of humor, and Philip was obviously proud of her. It was clear they were made for each other."

True, the prodigal son, had revealed little about his and Martha's new life during his earlier visit to Reno and had shown no interest in rebuilding family ties or seeking his mother's approval, even as Bonnie all but begged her brother to open up. But his close relationship with Chase in Laredo and his trips to Minneapolis and Seattle with Martha showed he had finally developed an appreciation and need for other long-term relationships in his life.

True was well established in the Mexico City press corps after three years. Story assignments had taken him into every corner of the republic. As he gained a deeper appreciation for the country, he was drawn with increasing frequency to write about the two conflicting Mexicos that existed as a single country.

Old Mexico, so often romanticized in the minds of travel writers and wandering American *turistas*, was a harsher landscape in reality: the rural, agrarian countryside was underdeveloped and peasants had little access to education, economic resources, or political power. For the millions of Mexicans trying to eke out a meager living from the land, there were two alternatives to poverty at home. One was an uncertain life in the urban slums, the other an expensive and risky exodus across the Rio Bravo to find work in the United States.

Al otro lado (on the other side), as every Mexican knows, better wages await—if you can make it past the people smugglers, the corrupt police, and *la migra*, the green-uniformed U.S. Border Patrol agents whose border town blockades were driving desperate migrants to risk dangerous desert crossings.

Urban, educated Mexicans fared far better, benefiting from rising social freedom and new economic opportunities. This new Mexico, the Mexico of open markets, multiparty elections, and a more independent media, offered a glimpse of Mexico's potential as a full democracy.

On closer examination, however, Mexico still fell short. One party controlled the presidency, each president handpicking his successor, who was then "elected" even if it meant rigging the vote, which it usually did. Corruption was endemic. Networks of drug traffickers operated beyond government reach. The rule of law existed only for those with the money or power to afford it.

True was not interested in the latest Wal-Mart opening, the growing use of cell phones in a country where many could not get a land line installed in their homes, or the Bolsa, the increasingly active and growing Mexican stock exchange. He pushed editors to give him the time and freedom to write penetrating stories about the more timeless Mexican condition. "He was the Jack Kerouac of the Mexico City press corps," said Tim Padgett, then the Mexico City bureau chief for *Newsweek* magazine.

True often joined other foreign correspondents for drinks and shop talk at *Cantina*, the ritual Friday evening gathering held at the Bar Nuevo Leon in Colonia Condesa. "Philip and I first met at the *cantina*," said Joel Simon, a freelance journalist writing a book about Mexico's environment and now the deputy director of the New York–based Committee to Protect Journalists. "It was a fairly big group, the regular correspondents, the wire reporters, freelancers, and people working on books. People would have a couple of drinks after work each Friday and then go their own way. Philip and I had a number of long conversations because we both cared about environmental reporting."

Simon told True about his experiences visiting the Tarahumara Indians in the remote canyon country of Chihuahua state, where he was documenting environmental degradation. Living off a modest book advance, Simon traveled only with local guides, unable to afford a photographer as a traveling companion.

"You could also say I was young and foolish," he said. "These places are some of the most remarkable, beautiful, enchanting places that I've ever seen, and not everyone is interested in pushing themselves that way. It's hard to find people who are willing to go on these trips."

Simon survived one frightening episode with the Tarahumara, when he was obliged to join the Indians drinking a ceremonial beverage called *tejuino*, which is brewed from maize and is similar to beer, except it continues to ferment in your stomach.

Several of the Tarahumara grew violent under the influence and one barged into Simon's room, armed with a pistol. A groggy Simon sprang from bed and talked the Indian into leaving, but he knew the culture viewed any violent act committed under the influence as an accident rather than a punishable crime. The next morning the Indian acted as if nothing had happened.

Simon's account made an impression on True, who decided to telephone Jerry Lara, an *Express-News* photographer he knew and trusted. Lara, a border native, was fluent in Spanish and cool under fire. He had followed True down to Chiapas after the guerrilla uprising, and the two had enjoyed working together. Now True gave Lara the outlines of his planned trek into the Sierra Madre in pursuit of a story about the reclusive Huichols. Was Lara interested? "Sure, count me in," Lara told him. "Call me when you're ready to go."

A few months into the new year, True wrote his proposal for traveling to the Huichol sierra. "Then I forgot all about it when I didn't hear anything more about the trip," Lara said. "I didn't know that he finally decided to go until after he had left. He never called me back."

True ordered a special tent and topographical maps, and as October gave way to November, his daily seven-mile jogs turned into ten-mile walking marathons with his rock-filled backpack. Martha accompanied him one day as he drove their car around La Lomas and up and down Avenida Reforma to carefully measure his training route. He also bought a compass and a book on orienteering to teach himself to read his new topo maps. He didn't want to lose his way. Unlike his many stateside treks, this one would include no national park signage and there would be no fellow hikers to consult. He would be days away from the closest food supply, telephone, or medical facility. He would be in another world that differed in almost every way from the place he was leaving.

6

Desaparecido

The longest journey begins with a single step, not with a turn of the ignition key. That's the best thing about walking, the journey itself. It doesn't much matter whether you get where you're going or not. You'll get there anyway. Every good hike brings you eventually back home. Right where you started.

—Edward Abbey, *The Journey Home*

It's probably sensible, at least in some cases, to leave a map marked with your proposed route—if you have a route. And even if you're simply going to wander and have no idea where you'll end up, state a date and hour by which you'll return—or will emerge somewhere and immediately check back by phone. Let it be clearly understood that if you haven't reported back by the time specified, then you're in trouble. In fixing the deadline, allow yourself a little leeway. And once you've fixed it, make hell-or-high-water sure you meet it. I repeat: make hell-or-high-water sure you meet it.

—Colin Fletcher and Chip Rawlins, *The Complete Walker*

Martha awoke Thursday morning, December 10, with a sense of dread. Something was wrong. She had waited stoically as the days passed, one after another, without a telephone call from Philip. More than once over that seemingly interminable ten-day period Martha had turned to her copy of the map and wondered where, on the wandering line her husband had penned, he might be walking at that moment. Which villages had he passed through, and where was he going next?

Nearly two weeks had passed since Philip left in a taxi for the Mexico City airport. Was the radiotelephone in San Miguel out of service? Had he lost his way?

Philip never lost his way, she told herself. Doubt began to creep in as the first week passed without a word. By the second week, doubt had turned into foreboding. One night during that time alone Martha dreamed that she was giving birth to her baby while someone else was dying. Her therapist, Sara Rojas, told her not to worry; she was just anxious about the baby's imminent arrival. She tried to lose herself in her job as the executive director of a nonprofit environmental organization. Her building anxiety made it impossible to concentrate.

Philip had left on Friday, November 27. He had called her Sunday night, November 29, from the town of Tlaltenango, frustrated that the Sunday second-class bus to Tuxpan de Bolanos had never come. Perhaps it broke down or maybe the driver had a long night and failed to come to work.

The historic old town was getting ready for its annual *fiesta* honoring the Virgin of Guadalupe on December 12. The feast day celebrations would start December 2 and last ten days. People were pouring in from surrounding communities and places as far away as California. Philip wanted Martha to know before he got out of range that he would arrive at the trailhead at least one day behind schedule. He still planned to call her when he reached the radiotelephone in San Miguel. Meanwhile, he was killing time working with his new Canon 35 mm. After shooting a few rolls, he thought he had the hang of it.

Thanksgiving Day had been almost two weeks ago.

That evening, after returning home from work, Martha broke her nervous silence and reached out for help. She called Sara again. "I remember she told me, 'Don't worry, he's probably late. You should write down your feelings to collect your thoughts,'" Martha said.

Her next call was to Juanita Serrano in Matamoros. "Philip has not returned," she told her.

"What did Philip tell you before he left?" Juanita asked.

"He told me to come looking for him if he wasn't home in ten days," Martha said.

"If that's what he told you, then you should start immediately," she said.

Juanita asked Martha if she had notified Philip's editors, and when Martha said no, she urged her to call San Antonio. "She sounded okay," Juanita said, "but when she called back the next morning she was pretty anguished. I told my husband I had to go to Mexico City. I arrived Saturday, December 12."

Juanita's advice inspired a sense of urgency in Martha, not unlike a slap in the face. In quick succession, she telephoned her brother-in-law, Manuel Obaya, an engineer who lived in Monterrey, and Fred Chase in Laredo.

Obaya agreed that Martha should call the editors in San Antonio first thing in the morning and ask for their help. Meanwhile, family and friends should launch an immediate search, he said. If True had been gone this long, Obaya reasoned, he must be at or near his final destination along his planned hundred-mile route. It made sense to start at the end of his trail rather than at the beginning.

He, too, made arrangements to fly to Mexico City to meet with Martha, and then he intended to fly to Tepic. Martha had wisely noted the name and telephone number of the charter service and pilot, Chuy López. Once there, Obaya would board the same small aircraft scheduled to carry True out of Huichol territory. Even before Obaya could reach Tepic, López and his single-engine Cessna were ready, waiting to fly in a search team.

Friday morning, Juanita carefully packed her hiking boots, warm clothing, and a supply of energy bars. Then she boarded a bus bound for Monterrey, four hours south of the border, where she connected with Obaya and flew to Mexico City.

Chase crossed the border into Nuevo Laredo that same day and caught a flight south to Guadalajara and then another to Tepic, where he would meet Obaya.

Friday morning Martha called Bonavita. "Something's wrong and I need your help," Martha told him. "Philip was supposed to call and be home in ten days, and I haven't heard from him. I think something bad has happened. What should I do?"

Bonavita heard desperation in Martha's voice. He quickly debriefed Martha on the details of True's planned trek and then huddled with fellow editors to assess the situation. All agreed to send

Susana Hayward, a bilingual reporter and former Associated Press correspondent in Mexico, to join the search.

Bonavita called back and advised Martha to alert U.S. embassy and Mexican government officials, as well as the Foreign Correspondents Association. A missing member was highly unusual. Any official help would be invaluable.

He offered encouraging words, reminding her of Philip's considerable experience in the backcountry. Later, however, Bonavita and others couldn't help thinking the obvious: Martha had waited a long time to share the bad news. True's trail would be hard to pick up in such a big, unfamiliar wilderness.

Martha called the embassy but hung up a few minutes later, thinking officials there did not seem particularly concerned.

Within minutes that Friday morning, Bonavita and a group of editors were standing at my office door. "We need to see you right away," said Bonavita, walking in. "Philip True has disappeared."

I slowly looked up to meet his eye as his words sank in. "What do you mean 'disappeared'?" I asked.

Disappeared, *desaparecido*.

The word carries a singularly intimidating meaning for anyone who lived in Latin America in the 1970s and 1980s. "Disappeared" people were never seen again. Throughout the Americas, repressive regimes from Argentina and Chile to El Salvador and Guatemala carried out ruthless campaigns of violence against anyone even suspected of supporting or sympathizing with revolutionary movements.

"He hasn't been heard from for at least ten days," Bonavita said. "He was supposed to call Martha and he hasn't called."

"You mean he is missing? I didn't even know he was gone from Mexico City," I said. "Where exactly is he? Is he with a photographer?"

Silence ensued. No one was eager to be the first to speak.

Bonavita cleared his throat and summarized the history of True's earlier story proposal, his frustration with senior editors, and his decision to use vacation days to proceed on his own. He handed me a copy of True's story proposal, but now it was too late to address True's growing discontent or challenge his decision to embark on a solitary trip.

"Alone, without a buddy?" I asked. "Why wasn't I consulted? You don't just go off alone in the wilds in Mexico. Did any of you know?"

The editors were taken aback, probably thinking I was laying blame, but I was really venting my own fears. How could I, the editor, not know that the newspaper's Mexico correspondent had left for a ten-day solo hike into the Huichol wilderness?

None of the other editors had worked in a foreign country. They didn't know the rules, and one rule is that there is strength in numbers. Off the beaten path, a buddy, a fellow journalist, always has your back, always serves as a witness to any trouble. People with bad intentions are less likely to act against a pair or groups than an unwary individual.

I sent True to live and work in Mexico. I knew what living and working in Latin America entailed, and now I realized how disconnected from him I had become in my job as editor over the past sixteen months. Four years had elapsed since we celebrated his promotion to Mexico City bureau chief at the restaurant in Nuevo Laredo.

True, I thought, hadn't wanted me to know he was going. He knew I would challenge him. Now he was missing.

From my office window, I could see the outer wall of the Alamo and, beyond it, the six flags of Texas held up by actors dressed as soldiers reenacting the shrine's history, especially the defense of the mission turned military outpost. A young couple dressed in shorts and T-shirts pushed a stroller and walked slowly in the company of their toddler, passing by the same stretch of historic wall. It was a scene I could watch any day, and often did as I paused to think.

Turning back to the editors, I suggested we send someone down right away and start calling every official we knew in Mexico City and Washington. They were ahead of me. We agreed the *Express-News* would pay for the chartered airplane and any other costs associated with the search. True was our reporter. Vacation or not, authorized or not, he was in Mexico as a member of the *Express-News* team, and we would take responsibility for finding him. "We need to take charge of the search," I told Bonavita.

"Search and rescue," he added.

"Search and rescue," I agreed.

After a restless night, Martha remained outwardly calm, but feelings of despair engulfed her as she left for work on Friday morning. Inside her office, she recalled the advice her therapist had given her: "Write down your thoughts as a way of collecting yourself."

She sat down at her computer and stared at the blank screen, then typed out a single sentence: "Philip is dead."

7

Out There Somewhere

I sleep uneasily, waking often in order to worry. And my dreams are complex, anxious, in no way satisfying. The night is cold and very long.

—Edward Abbey, *Beyond the Wall*

True was missing, out there somewhere. I slept in fits Friday night, dreaming of a *Newsweek* photographer, John Hoagland, who was killed in a crossfire in 1983 when we worked together in El Salvador. It was an old dream, put away and long forgotten.

Earlier in the day, I delivered the news that True was missing to Larry Walker, my boss, and Tom Stephenson, general manager. Neither man knew any of the details surrounding True's trek through the wilderness of western Mexico, so they weren't overly concerned at first. "Do you think he's lost or hurt somewhere?" Walker asked.

"We hope he's sitting in some hut at the bottom of a canyon with a sprained ankle and no way to get out or call us," I said. "But there's always a chance the news won't be good."

Stephenson mentioned that he had never been to Mexico, except for a single visit across the border to Tijuana years earlier. He asked me if True could have run into drug traffickers. "Anything is possible," I said, realizing that Stephenson has just raised a disturbing possibility not yet considered. A number of Mexican reporters have been assassinated by drug traffickers in recent years, but none of the cases had led to credible investigations or convictions.

Walker telephoned George Irish, the former *Light* publisher and now the president of Hearst Newspapers in New York, to alert him to True's disappearance. The news would move quickly once the wire services were alerted, and we didn't want corporate headquarters to learn about it elsewhere.

One of Walker's dictates was, "Don't surprise me." It was his way of making sure he stayed in the loop. I expected the same from my senior editors. Obviously the system had broken down over the previous months as tensions built between some of the bureau reporters and the editors making page one decisions in San Antonio. But there was no sense in revisiting past events now.

"There is a possibility that I will go down there and join the search," I said. Both seemed surprised and asked why. It was simple: I had more south of the border experience than anyone else in the newsroom. I had met every Mexican president going back two decades. Finding True might come down to how much official help we could muster. "I'm not going to send anyone on the staff into a situation where I wouldn't send myself," I added.

"Let's make up our minds after we see how things develop," Walker said. "Let's not turn one person in trouble into two people in trouble."

Walker and I were both members of Los Compadres, a tightly knit group of ten San Antonio men who rode Harleys and came together during the summer for one epic ride. Two years earlier, we had spent two weeks riding the back roads of Mexico, a trip that skirted Huichol territory as we rode through Zacatecas and into Jalisco. Walker, in other words, knew enough about Mexico to worry about my following True into the backcountry. "I'll have to talk with George about your going," he said. "You know your way around down there, but like it or not, you are an executive of the company and that has to be considered."

We agreed to regroup the next day and review developments.

Saturday morning, Manuel Obaya and Juanita Serrano met Martha at the Mexico City airport. Martha gave her brother-in-law a copy of True's map, along with a stack of fliers that included a press photograph of a smiling True, a description of his intended route, and a reward offer. The flier also listed the villages that True intended to visit.

The editors had settled on a 10,000 peso cash reward for information leading to True's whereabouts. The sum, equal to US$1,000 at the going exchange rate, represented a significant sum in Huichol territory. Officials in Mexico cautioned us not to offer a larger sum, fearing con artists would overwhelm us with false leads.

"He left Tuxpan de Bolaños on Dec. 1, on a walking excursion . . . and should have arrived in Santa María de Huazamota on Dec. 10th. He might need medical attention," the flier advised.

Chuy López, the charter pilot awaiting True's call at the end of his trail, told Martha that her husband never called. López was standing by now, ready to fly Obaya and any other searchers into the sierra. Obaya caught the next flight to Tepic on the Pacific coast, but Martha asked Juanita to stay behind and remain in Mexico City. She needed help handling the telephones. Friends, reporters, officials—everyone was calling, overwhelming her as she tried to juggle her husband's cell phone and the office and home lines. Even more, she needed emotional support from her best friend.

"It was nonstop, the calls and people coming to the house," Juanita said. "We were so busy, at least Martha didn't have much time to stop and worry."

As dawn approached that same day in San Antonio, I logged on to my home computer and searched for news. No e-mail, nothing on the wires, nothing on Mexican newspaper websites about True. News of his disappearance was still limited to Texas newspapers and brief wire service reports. I drove downtown to the *Express-News* offices to check on the next day's edition and finish my Sunday column.

Editors had used ATM cards to accumulate enough cash for Susana Hayward to pay López for the charter service, cover the reward payment in the event True was located, and otherwise maneuver in circumstances where credit cards were useless. She also carried a thick stack of photographs of True for distribution throughout the search area.

Hayward arrived at the True home in Mexico City that afternoon and took charge of the time-consuming and often frustrating task of calling officials in Mexico City, Guadalajara, and Tepic to sound the alarm and press for official help as our search effort started to take shape. Calls also were placed to regional newspapers and radio stations in an effort to get out word of True's disappearance and the reward. Arrangements were made for regional radio broadcasts in Spanish and Huichol offering a reward to anyone with information about True.

Our strategy was to envelop the vast region with news of the missing American journalist, hoping the reward money would spur individual Huichols and even whole villages to search for our missing reporter along his hundred-mile route, or at least bring forward someone who had sighted True along the trail. Any confirmed sightings would reduce the search area and increase the odds of finding him quickly.

Obaya and Fred Chase arrived in Tepic Saturday evening. They checked into a local hotel and then went straight to López's home. Within minutes of their arrival they were studying True's route map placed over a larger, more detailed topographical map provided by López. Obaya, who had never been to that part of Mexico, was struck by what the big map showed—mostly vast empty spaces.

López noted the dirt landing strips closest to the villages along True's route, and the group settled on their Sunday flight plan. They would hopscotch from one distant village to the next, stopping at each point to meet with village elders and ask if anyone had seen or heard about a gringo backpacker walking alone through the sierra. Three men in one small plane would be searching for the proverbial needle in a haystack thousands of square miles in size. They could only trace True's actual route overhead, since several of the villages were not located near landing strips. Where they could land, López cautioned Obaya and Chase about the welcome they might receive. They would be arriving unannounced, quizzing reclusive Huichols wary of outsiders, and many of the elders spoke little or no Spanish. It was a daunting task, but there were no other options. Obaya and Chase returned to their hotel to grab a quick bite of supper and catch some sleep. It might be a while before they returned.

We spoke with Hayward and Martha in Mexico City Saturday night as the day came to a close, fifteen days since True had left home. We had contacted virtually everyone who might be of help. Most of our conversation that evening was to keep the faith, to stay busy and focused on the search.

Friends filled the True home, many bringing food. Despite all the support and activity, Martha's intuition told her bad news was coming, sooner or later. Outwardly she said nothing, grateful for the support and the buzz of distracting activity. Being alone was much harder.

Morale also ebbed in San Antonio. Saturdays are busy times at daily newspapers as the big Sunday edition is put to bed. Reporters and photographers came and went, stopping by the city desk to ask for the latest news. Many had worked with True before, and many had worked in Mexico. They knew December nights in the sierra were cold, with temperatures often falling below freezing. True had packed enough food and water for only ten days.

As I stayed on at the newspaper into the late evening, bits of newsroom chatter drifted my way around the city desk. In some corners, second-guessing had set in: Why did editors let him go alone? Was the company trying to save money by not assigning a photographer to accompany him? News organizations in both countries, meanwhile, were calling Martha and the *Express-News,* speculating, pushing for statements. Did we think True was dead?

That night in Mexico City, Martha and Juanita shared a bed. Juanita lay awake as Martha tossed and turned. Just as the two would drift off to sleep, they would be awakened by the ringing of the telephone. Around 4:00 A.M. Martha quietly turned toward Juanita, their faces separated by inches.

"I know Philip is dead," Martha said in a flat voice.

Juanita just hugged her.

Martha then told Juanita about her recent dream, the terrible sensation of giving birth and sensing death all at once. For both women, the dream was a telling omen.

Sunday morning was a perfect South Texas winter day, the kind of weather that brings droves of northern retirees, "snowbirds," into the Sunbelt. As I headed north on the expressway, a caravan of recreational vehicles with out-of-state license plates came the other way, headed south to the Rio Grande Valley and the border. RV and trailer parks, landscaped with graceful rows of tall palms and citrus trees, spring to life in winter as migrating seniors arrive in flocks to enjoy the climate and low cost of living.

Walker, Stephenson, and I were participating in an all-day golf clinic at the Westin la Cantera, home of the Texas Open, a September stop on the PGA Tour. Months earlier, we had booked a group lesson with Bryan Gathright, rated one of the hundred best teaching pros in the country and director of the golf academy there. Now I found myself too distracted to enjoy the opportunity, especially after spending two restless nights worrying.

Editors, with a few notable exceptions, make lousy golfers. As a teenager, I earned money caddying at the local country club, where I observed a new world of successful people who worked hard and enjoyed choices in life. Golf is a sport that only now is atoning for its past sins of exclusion, and many still view it through a class and race prism. At any rate, despite my best intentions, I seldom played or practiced.

Stephenson, on the other hand, maintains a single-digit handicap and always seems to win money on the course. He came to the game relatively late in life and has been making up for lost time ever since. His home backs up to a golf course. He plays several rounds each weekend and usually works in a weekday practice. An avid runner, Stephenson once ran a marathon—26.2 miles—then went home and played 18 holes of golf without a cart or caddy. Walker, a onetime minor league baseball player, also plays regularly.

It was not a good day for golf. By the end of my lesson, I could hardly strike the ball. Out on the course things only got worse. I thought about stopping at the turn, but it was against my nature to quit. I didn't want to be a bad sport, even though I was paying more attention to my cell phone than my swing.

Walker and I were riding in one golf cart, while Stephenson and Walker's son, Lawrence, were in another. A call came in from the newsroom, but it was just the weekend editor manning the city desk calling to say there was no news from Mexico City or the sierra. Three days had passed, and still nothing to go on. Before the round ended, I had made up my mind. It was time to join the search.

"Larry, there is no good news about Philip," I said. "I've got to get down there as soon as possible. I'm booking the first flight in the morning."

"What can you do that we're not already doing?" he asked.

I knew it was his job to make sure I didn't take off on a wild goose chase, but a plan was already forming in my mind.

"I'm not going to do anything crazy," I said. "I'm going to try and see President Zedillo and ask him for help."

Walker gave the trip his blessing and told me to be careful and stay in touch.

I raced out of the parking lot to make the twenty-five-mile drive home, beating myself up along the way. What the hell was an editor doing on a golf course when a reporter was missing in Mexico? I should have left two days earlier.

Once at home I sat down with Monika and shared my frustrations, unable to contribute to the search efforts, which somehow needed to be broadened. Monika had her own busy career as the Texas regional manager for *Business Wire,* a San Francisco-based commercial wire service. A prolonged absence on my part would be an added burden as she watched over our sons and the household, while keeping up with her own work. I did everything except come out and state my desire to head south, instead searching for some way to infer what already must have been obvious to her. After a few minutes she cut me off.

"You have to go," she said.

The search party met early Sunday morning at the Tepic airport. López was waiting beside his aging, single-engine, four-seat Cessna, ready to roll. Obaya, ever the engineer attentive to detail, paused at seeing the aircraft he and Chase were about to board. "*¡Híjole!* I was taken aback when I first saw that old airplane," Obaya said. "I was expecting something a lot more modern."

López assured them the vintage aircraft was safe. Minutes later they were in the air, gaining altitude quickly as they left behind the small state capital and took aim at the approaching mountains. Despite the nature of their journey, True's best friend and his brother-in-law marveled at the bird's-eye view of the verdant, canopied sierra rising above the Pacific coast.

Americans might not know the state of Nayarit by name, but many know the famous beach resort, just over the Jalisco border, Puerto Vallarta, where Richard Burton and Ava Gardner fell in love and filmed Tennessee Williams's *Night of the Iguana* in 1963. John Huston, whom True evoked in his story proposal, directed the film. Much has changed since then. The mythical gold sought by Huston's American prospectors in *The Treasure of the Sierra Madre,* filmed in 1948, had been replaced by poppy and marijuana cultivation fed by an ample rainy season, year-around sun, and the region's remoteness and poverty.

As López crossed the line of mountains into Jalisco, the landscape changed from green to brown, evidence of the reduced annual rainfall on the landlocked side of the sierra. Trees were stunted, the vegetation sparse. The land appears drought stricken with only patchwork fields. Illicit drug cultivation also declines, according to anthropologists, the state cops, and others familiar with the region, but it still exists, an irresistible cash crop.

López's first stop on his flight plan was San Miguel Huaixtita. True had to pass through this village of several hundred Huichols once he ascended out of the Chapalagana and crossed the river to continue on his route, López explained. It also was the place True intended to call Martha via radiotelephone. If True had not reached San Miguel, López said, it was doubtful they would locate him farther along his intended route. Still, they had no choice; they would check everywhere. López knew every village and airstrip in the region and had contacts throughout the sierra. Any doubts about his skills as a pilot were dispelled, Obaya said, when they touched down in San Miguel.

"He landed on a very short and bumpy dirt airstrip," Obaya said. "There were cows grazing all around the landing strip, and it seemed to disappear into the big canyon. It was exceptional the way he handled that unforgettable landing."

A knot of villagers assembled excitedly along the landing strip at the first sound of the approaching aircraft, most dressed in traditional Huichol embroidered white cotton trousers and blouses.

As the three men climbed out, they were warmly greeted by *el anciano*, the village governor. He listened as López and his two passengers explained the nature of their mission. Fliers were passed among the villagers and studied, but True had not passed through San Miguel. No one knew of his presence in the sierra.

After bidding farewell to the Huichols, the search party boarded the plane for the takeoff facing the canyon, an even more dramatic moment as López turned northwest in the direction of Santa María de Huazamota, the planned exit point for True, the place he should have called López on December 10 for his lift to Tepic.

Santa María is a town rather than a village, populated by Huichols and mestizos. There were automobiles, some paved roads, a plaza with a church, and a variety of storefronts. After landing, López led them on foot to the small hospital to see if any foreigners had sought treatment. Once again, no one had seen True or anyone matching his description. López knew most of the merchants by name, and while they treated Obaya and Chase with courtesy, the answer was always the same when they were shown the flier. No one had seen True or even heard about a gringo backpacker. Several of the townspeople suggested López backtrack on True's map to San Andrés Cohamiata, where the Huichols maintained a jail.

Traditional Huichol jails are crude, open-air cages made with saplings bound together, resembling an animal cage from a nineteenth-century circus. Huichols also employ wooden stockades to restrain individuals. One ethnographic study of Mexico's indigenous groups contains a photograph of forlorn Huichol children locked up by their ankles for unknown transgressions. One human rights investigator from Guadalajara told me she witnessed the same kind of restraints in use during a recent visit to the sierra. The San Andrés jail, however, was a more modern affair built of concrete and steel bars.

"We decided to fly there next," Obaya said. "They told us in Santa María that it's very common for Huichols to arrest trespassers, often uninvited tourists, and hold them for a weekend before expelling them."

The search team made its third landing of the day without incident in San Andrés. The three men were met by several Huichol and escorted into the village, where the annual feast day celebration was well under way.

"The traditional governor came out to meet us and told us Philip wasn't in their jail," Obaya said. "They hadn't seen him, either."

Obaya and Chase were wary, sensing that they were the objects of scrutiny. Many of the village men were staggeringly drunk, some sprawled in the dirt, others sitting in small groups. A pack of loud revelers moved toward the visitors, a Huichol string band playing folkloric music following them, and other villagers trailing behind.

Obaya, who collects Mexican folkloric music, felt increasingly threatened by the loud music and the drunken atmosphere. Just then a young Huichol man thrust himself into Obaya's face and began questioning him aggressively.

The governor told the younger Huichol to leave.

"Okay, then I want him to drink with me now," the younger man insisted, waving a bottle at Obaya.

"We don't want anything to drink; that is not why we are here," Obaya told him.

"I told you to leave him alone and get out of here," the governor demanded. "These men are my friends and I am talking with them. Go away."

The young Huichol reluctantly backed off, waving his bottle in defiance.

It was past noon, and López suggested they move on.

"The governor was very good about taking care of us," Obaya said, "but we weren't going to stay and eat, that's for sure."

They next visited San Juan Peyotán, another village located near the end of True's route, where they picked up a promising thirdhand report of a passing backpacker. Chase used the only telephone in the village to report the promising news to Mexico City, and the group then spent hours tracking down the Huichol who purportedly saw the backpacker. When they showed him True's photo, however, he shook his head. He had not seen True, he was certain.

López took the Cessna back up and flew the short distance to the edge of Chapalagana Canyon. He had no set destination at that point and instead seemed to be considering options beyond the flight plan agreed on the previous night.

He flew low along the line True would have taken out of the canyon and up to San Miguel, low enough that Obaya and Chase actually watched from their rear seats, eager to spot a hiker carrying a red backpack.

As they overflew the canyon, López turned to them and said, "On the other side of the river there is a small settlement, just a few houses, called Amoltita, and there is an old landing strip there. Why don't we try there?"

López banked the airplane and flew his passengers over the small collection of huts so they could take a look for themselves. The winding river sparkled in the sunlight below them.

"Señor True would have had to cross through this place before he entered the canyon to go down to the river," López said. He turned back to take a closer look at the runway, which was only partially visible through the undergrowth.

Chase remembers the pilot expressing serious reservations about landing in Amoltita, as if the people there were known to be hostile to outsiders. "I recall the pilot warning us ahead of time, 'You don't want to go to Amoltita if you don't have to go,'" Chase said. "His thought was that people there were not good."

Obaya recalls the pilot's reluctance having more to do with the overgrown condition of the runway. "He told us the grass could easily obscure a pothole big enough to flip us," Obaya said. "Whether we landed was our decision. He would try a landing if we wanted him to."

They had few other options. They had landed in four different settlements along True's route, covering territory that an experienced walker would take less than two weeks to traverse, yet they had not turned up a single sighting of True. Now, as they overflew Amoltita, they were approaching the point that True should have reached within four or five days, at most, after leaving Tuxpan de Bolanos.

The landing was routine, but as López taxied to a stop, a group of fifteen men quickly approached. Some brandished machetes.

"Hombres sin ojos buenos," Obaya said, referring to the unwelcoming faces coming toward them. "Men with a bad look in their eyes."

The Huichols demanded to see written permission for the group to use the airstrip. They complained about foreigners entering their county without written permission from the proper Huichol authorities. They told López they had not seen True and that he should not have come.

López knew some of the men and tried to defuse the tension with small talk, pointing out that they were searching for an important journalist who respected the Huichols and their culture. As the men were escorted into the village center, Chase noticed several of the Amoltita men were drunk and noticeably more sullen than the men they had encountered in San Andrés. "These guys had all been drinking, and some of them just stared at us," Chase said. "No one offered us a drink of water or seemed concerned that our friend might be missing and in trouble."

As the search team tried to interest the unresponsive villagers in their fliers, the Huichols suddenly changed their story, stunning Chase and Obaya as they admitted they had seen True.

True had hiked through their village on Saturday, December 5, five or six days after he left Tuxpan de Bolanos. That would have put him behind schedule at least two days, but here was their first evidence he actually had entered Huichol territory and appeared to be on course.

The Huichols told Chase that True was bleeding from his legs after being attacked by wild dogs before reaching Amoltita. He had passed through the village without much contact, other than to confirm the direction of his path to the canyon and across the river, the Huichols claimed.

That scenario did not explain how the villagers knew about the supposed wild dog attack, and it seemed strange that the villagers failed to offer True first aid or even water. One Huichol man mumbled under his breath, loud enough for Chase to hear, that True deserved whatever befell him.

The three outsiders pressed for more details, each firing questions intended to resolve discrepancies in the story told by the Huichols. Why did they say they had not seen him at first and then change their story? Why didn't they help him?

The Huichols grew tense and repeated their complaint that the foreigners were trespassing and had to leave immediately and never return. They grew more agitated by the minute. Obaya began to fear the men wielding machetes might turn on the small, unarmed search party. "Some of the younger men were looking at us with angry faces," he said. "We were unarmed and scared."

It was courageous of the three men to venture even as far as they did, given the hostile welcome they received. Had they not ventured into Amoltita, chances are the Huichols would never have come forward to admit they had seen True.

"Curious," Chase said. "They were dirt poor, and yet not one of them showed the slightest interest in the reward, even though they claimed he had passed through and was injured. You'd think they would have set out to search for him."

López wasted no time in getting airborne, the cluster of Huichol men with machetes growing smaller and less threatening as the plane gained altitude. There was little conversation as they flew back to Tepic, each man lost in his own thoughts. The news from Amoltita was somewhat encouraging, in the sense they now had a confirmed sighting of True. If there were any truth to the account offered by the villagers, eight days had passed since True reached Amoltita on December 5. Yet he had failed to emerge from the canyon or reach San Miguel.

The most foreboding aspect of the afternoon, however, was the hostile reception in Amoltita and the inconsistencies in the villagers' accounts of True's passage. The men were hiding something.

After landing back in Tepic, López took Chase and Obaya to his home to discuss the next morning's flight plan. They agreed there was no sense in backtracking any farther along True's route. "Something happened there in Amoltita, I am convinced," López told Chase and Obaya. "Philip was definitely there, but there is more to the story than they are telling us."

Chase and Obaya agreed. "We decided to return to San Miguel," Obaya said. "We knew he went into that canyon and we knew he didn't come out the other side, at least not in San Miguel. Perhaps there was one other possibility, that he accidentally turned in another direction and got lost, but they told us in San Miguel he had to come out of the canyon through there. It was the only way out. The pilot said the same thing."

Chase and Obaya returned to their hotel and called Martha in Mexico City. Any hope of promising news was dashed as the fatigued men recounted the long day's events. Neither had eaten a full meal that day, and their tense visit to Amoltita had been more emotionally draining than either at first realized. Later, in the comfort and safety of their hotel room, as the adrenaline wore off, both men felt shaken by the encounter.

Martha sensed the pessimism in their voices. She agreed to relay the news to San Antonio and asked them to call as soon as they returned from their Monday search. Susana Hayward, she told them, was arriving in Tepic that evening to join the search party.

Hayward and I had spoken by telephone Sunday afternoon after my ill-advised golf outing. I explained my decision to fly to Mexico City. We needed to deploy ourselves as intelligently as possible, I explained. There was no sense in both of us working official sources. Officials in the Zedillo administration and at the U.S. embassy, as well as members of the Mexican press corps, would be more attentive to the newspaper's editor than a reporter. Hayward, meanwhile, could really contribute in the sierra, where we were woefully thin.

López was ready to go when Chase, Obaya, and Hayward arrived at the airport the next morning at 7:00 A.M. With Hayward in the copilot's seat, they took off and headed back to San Miguel.

"We wanted to go back there, this time with the information from Amoltita that Philip had definitely reached the other side of the river," Obaya said. "Our image was that Philip had fallen off a ledge and broken a leg or been attacked by wild animals and was fading fast. We wanted as many Huichols in the hills and down in the canyon looking for him as we could find."

This time they met a young physician from Guadalajara, Dr. Sergio Ramirez, who was serving a one-year residency in the village. Ramirez, nearing the end of his stay there, provided free medical services to the region's Huichols. He worked out of a simple clinic in San Miguel and often spent days hiking to remote settlements in the company of one or two Huichol family members to deliver a breached baby or treat a sick or injured relative. He enjoyed considerable stature throughout the region, a standing that would prove invaluable in the days ahead.

López and Obaya recounted their previous day's experiences in Amoltita across the canyon. Ramirez seemed genuinely surprised by the hostile reception. He had never been subjected to such treatment, and he pointed out that he often worked with another Guadalajara medical resident, a young female doctor, who traveled to outlying settlements in the company of local Huichols to treat patients. She had never been threatened or assaulted, Ramirez said.

"The people here are peaceful," he told the search party. "Not too many weeks ago, another hiker, an Italian tourist carrying a big backpack, came though, and he didn't have any trouble."

Ramirez agreed to organize a search party of Huichol men from San Miguel. He and the village governor accepted money from the group to pay each of the men. What the search party most wanted, Obaya explained to Ramirez and the governor, in addition to a diligent search of the Chapalagana, was for the Huichols to press the inhabitants of Amoltita for more details about their contact with True. Perhaps the villagers who greeted the search party with hostility would be more forthcoming with Huichols seeking information. Ramirez and the governor agreed to do all they could.

The search party had been in San Miguel for three hours, Obaya said, yet this time they were in no hurry to move on. There were no other places to visit, nowhere else to fly. Somewhere in the great chasm of the Chapalagana, they sensed, lay the answer to the mystery. True had left Amoltita, descended into the canyon, and never come out.

Obaya and Chase and Hayward gazed at the vastness of the Chapalagana, all but indescribable to someone who has not experienced its depth and breadth. It was so big, and they were so few. It was like another world, even to a Mexican. The place seemed beyond their reach.

That evening Manuel reluctantly called Martha. "Philip is somewhere in this triangle of Amoltita, the Chapalagana, and San Miguel," he said. "But we can't do much else. Fred and I are not enough. You need something more, Martha, much more help."

Obaya had to return Tuesday to his work as a chemical engineer. He flew from Tepic straight to Monterrey, leaving Chase and Hayward to keep up the search. He hated to leave the job unfinished, but instinct told him Martha's husband was not out there somewhere, waiting for his rescuers. If he were still alive, Obaya told himself, someone would have found him by now.

The next morning López took Chase and Hayward back into San Miguel.

One Huichol shared a vision that True would be found along a river, alive. He urged them to go there.

8

Five Extra Letters

Mexico, grail to generations of artists, site of primordial revelation—
Mayan temples, *brujos,* muralists, hallucinatory mushrooms—has fallen
off the map. This whorled, ornate neighbor civilization, secretly and
essentially entwined with ours, is invisible, its people among us silent,
nameless wraiths who clip lawns and clear tables.

—Tony Cohan, *On Mexican Time*

The view from my window seat at 20,000 feet seemed infinite and
timeless. The bright azure sky spread over South Texas and northern
Mexico, land untouched by negotiated lines on a map. A few wispy
clouds drifted along the horizon. The Gulf of Mexico, a darker midnight blue, was barely visible to the east, where the unbroken land
gave way to a serrated coast cut by inlets and shallow salt flats.
Sorghum and sugar cane fields, irrigated with water drawn from the
river, stood out from the semiarid ranchlands. The shadow of the airplane raced across the Rio Grande, signaling our entry into Mexican
airspace.

I had checked two pieces of luggage. A conventional suit bag contained everything I needed for a working business trip in Mexico City.
The second was a diver's duffel with hiking boots, daypack, water

bottle, warm weather clothing, a global positioning device, binoculars, just about anything that might be useful if events took me into the sierra.

The same morning, an Aeromexico flight from Tepic landed in Monterrey, a few hundred nautical miles south of the border, bringing home a doubtful and weary Obaya. In his mind's eye he still saw the canyon, a beautiful yet forbidding place, unlike anywhere else he had been in Mexico. He had felt like a foreigner looking down into the Chapalagana, as if he were standing in a country that was not his own. He was sorry to leave the others behind. They had picked up True's footsteps and then lost them. Someone would have to go down into the Chapalagana to find Philip. "I lost eight pounds in that short time from a lack of sleep, a lack of food, and the pressure," Obaya later said. "I left knowing there was nothing more I could do. That is a feeling of helplessness."

My own flight, Mexicana 831, passed over industrial Monterrey, climbed over the sharply creased mountains of the Sierra Madre Oriental, and then descended into the Valley of Mexico. Snow capped the top of Popocatépetl, its majestic volcanic cone rising high above the valley floor.

I felt a sense of relief after I cleared customs and headed toward a waiting car. It was good to be on the move, no longer sitting in San Antonio, hostage to a telephone. We needed the Mexican government to mount a major search and rescue operation. We could do that if we could get in front of the right people in the Zedillo administration, who worked inside Los Pinos, the sprawling, park-like presidential palace on the edge of Chapultepec Park, named for its tall pines. It was not far from our missing reporter's training route.

I was counting on two things. First, the Mexican government would not allow an accredited U.S. correspondent to simply disappear, an event that would fuel rumors and speculation that True was the victim of drug traffickers or other criminal elements, with the government helpless to act.

Second, I had spent years building friendships and cultivating contacts in Mexico. My appreciation for the country and its people had given me a greater sensitivity to how Mexicans see the United States and the world. That sensitivity was not lost on Mexicans who knew me.

The average American's image of Mexicans is sadly limited to stereotypical views of "illegal aliens," the phrase itself a dehumanizing description of the workers who toil in America's restaurant kitchens, construction sites, and landscaping businesses. Millions of determined, hard-working Mexicans have risked their lives to cross the border in search of economic opportunity. In the process, this invisible community holding up the American economy from the bottom has become the single biggest force in the Mexican economy. Workers here send home billions of dollars to support their extended families. They are everywhere, yet they are invisible: Spanish speakers humbly passing by us with mops and brooms in hand, refilling our water glasses in restaurants, taking away our plates when we finish eating, mowing our yards.

Yet there are other, different Mexicans whom few Americans ever meet. These are Mexicans who enjoy low-cost university education, who are steeped in their own culture and history, who speak fluent English and display an understanding of the United States, its history and politics that goes far beyond what Americans know about Mexico.

An American tourist can easily find someone who speaks passing English in virtually every town and city in Mexico, while the number of non-Hispanic Americans who speak Spanish remains comparatively small. Mexicans invariably shower praise on U.S. citizens just for trying to speak Spanish, being more accustomed to insensitive tourists who raise their voices when they cannot communicate effectively.

I had met every president since Jóse López Portillo, who held office when I made my first extended reporting trip to Mexico in 1979 to cover the historic visit of Pope John Paul II. Ernesto Zedillo began his six-year term in 1994, and as president-elect, he granted his first sit-down interview with the foreign press to the *Express-News*. Interest in Mexican politics is strong in South Texas, leading editors to cover the candidates there just as we cover campaigns on our own side of the border. After the interview, we presented Zedillo with a copy of a photograph taken the previous day by Robert Owen, the newspaper's chief photographer. It showed Zedillo using his son's head as a table as he marked his paper ballot. The image had been published widely. "So this is where that photograph came from," Zedillo exclaimed that day, having seen it in newspapers. "I will treasure it."

It was my first opportunity to meet the "accidental candidate," a Yale-educated economist and technocrat who had never run for public office. He was thrust into the presidential campaign after Luis Donaldo Colosio, Salinas's handpicked choice, was assassinated at a Tijuana political rally, supposedly by a lone gunman. Mexicans remain as divided and uncertain about the killing as Americans are about the Kennedy assassination.

Zedillo, then a youthful 42, told us something in that first interview that would resurface in my memory years later. "There's a sense among Mexican citizens that our legal system leaves much to be desired, and I agree with them," Zedillo said.

Now, four years after that interview, I was back in Mexico City. Once upon a time I would have hailed a street cab at the airport. No longer. I had arranged in advance for the hotel to send a driver and car that would remain available throughout my stay in Mexico City. The luxury of such service made me self-conscious, but I was no longer a twenty-something street reporter. I was an inviting, forty-six-year-old target in a dark suit with a briefcase and a wallet full of pesos and credit cards.

My room at the Four Seasons overlooked the hotel's elegant garden, abloom with flowers and alive with the music of caged songbirds. Small groups of people sat along the patio, conversing in the shade of graceful arches. There would be no time to enjoy the city's charms. I quickly unpacked and headed downstairs. It was time to go see Martha.

*

The hotel driver stopped twice to ask directions as we sought out the little-known side street of Sierra Amatepec, number 289. We pulled up to the nondescript wall that concealed the True residence from the outer street. Martha met me at the door and we embraced. We had made arrangements before my departure for Martha to host a meeting of key individuals and organizations as we sought to intensify the search. As I stepped into her cozy living room, decorated with Mexican folk art, including a wildly colored beaded Huichol animal, that group was waiting.

Eloy Aguilar, the AP bureau chief and the dean of foreign correspondents, was there, along with David Nájera, Zedillo's liaison with the foreign press. Anne Eaton, then the wife of Tracey Eaton, the *Dallas Morning News* bureau chief, also was on hand. The Eatons and Trues, I learned, were good friends.

Two officials from the U.S. embassy were there as well. I was disappointed to learn that Don Hamilton, the chief press officer at the embassy and a friend from my years in El Salvador, was in Washington with then-U.S. Ambassador to Mexico Jeffrey Davidow.

Martha introduced me to Juanita Serrano, who had been there since Sunday.

For an hour or so we reviewed events of the past few days. Martha showed me the map and the reward flier. We studied a larger map from the embassy that gave me a better sense of the region and terrain.

Coffee was served, but a large tray of *tortas y galletas,* Mexican sandwiches and cookies, went untouched. No one seemed hungry.

Martha summarized her conversations with Fred Chase and Manuel Obaya, adding that her brother-in-law had returned to Monterrey while Chase and Susana Hayward were back out in the sierra for a third day with Chuy López, hoping to get more Huichols involved in the search. We would wait for their update later that evening.

The most significant information gleaned from their search came from the tense Sunday visit to Amoltita. No one doubted True had passed through the small hamlet, but the villagers' version of events was highly suspect. The claims of a wild dog attack seemed contrived. Every third world village has its snapping mongrels, until you offer them a scrap or bone to fight over. Wild dogs? I had lived and worked in Central America and Mexico for many years. Packs of man-attacking wild dogs roaming the wilderness did not exist.

I turned to Nájera, a handsome, well-dressed young man who occasionally stood up and left the room to take a call on the smallest cell phone I had ever seen. A diplomat by training, Nájera was the prototypical new Mexican, educated at home and abroad, well-spoken in several languages, uncorrupted and competent. He said a few army ground troops had been deployed into the area to search for True.

"The Mexican army has received great press in Texas and elsewhere for its recent search and rescue efforts in Honduras after the hurricane," I said. Hurricane Mitch had struck Central America with a fury in late October. Floods and mudslides had swept away entire villages. More than nine thousand Nicaraguans and Hondurans died in the storm. Mexico dispatched troops, helicopters, and truckloads of food and supplies to the region, taking on a major role in the humanitarian mission. "People aren't used to Mexico playing such a role. We are hoping you will do the same for us. We can't find Philip without your help."

I asked Nájera if he could arrange an audience for me with Zedillo, reminding him of my first meeting with the president four years earlier. "President Zedillo is not in Mexico City, but I will ask if you can see my boss tomorrow morning," Nájera told me. "You can make your request directly to him, and he will have the authority to act for the president. I will talk to him first, and I can tell you, I believe we will give you the help you need."

Nájera worked for Fernando Lerdo de Tejada, the director of social communications. Lerdo de Tejada was Zedillo's official spokesperson. Unlike his counterpart in the White House, however, he held cabinet rank and was a member of the president's inner working circle.

Nájera got up to leave, promising to call me once he confirmed my appointment at Los Pinos. "One more thing, David," I said as he turned back, halfway out the door. "I want to join the search. Please tell the minister that when the military goes, I want them to take me with them."

Nájera looked doubtful but nodded and left. The embassy officials left soon afterward, followed by the others.

Martha and Juanita asked me to stay for dinner. No one was in the mood to go out for dinner, and I wanted to wait with Martha for news rather than return to my empty hotel room. Well-wishers had left plenty of comfort food.

After supper, Nájera called to say I had a 10:00 A.M. appointment at Los Pinos with Lerdo de Tejada. Everything seemed to be moving in a positive direction and, as we chatted about Philip and his considerable experience hiking and camping—something I had not previously known—we convinced ourselves that good news might be forthcoming.

Later that evening, as Martha, Juanita, and I sat talking, Nájera called again. I could hardly believe what I heard him say. "Philip has been found alive," I joyfully repeated his words.

Martha and Juanita raced into the kitchen, shouting, laughing, and embracing. Our search was over.

True was in an army helicopter bound for a military base in Guadalajara, Nájera jubilantly reported. He was hungry and disoriented, but alive and well after being found in a village far south of his planned route. As soon as there were more details, he would call back.

"Leave a line open at the house for me," he asked.

We hung up, hugging, talking all at once, and sharing our disbelief as we gave thanks for the good news.

True, we assured one another, had lost his way and stumbled south through the sierra instead of west. He also had worried us half to death. Now we were euphoric. I called the newsroom in San Antonio and Bonavita answered.

"Philip has been found. He's okay."

Fred Bonavita covered his mouthpiece. I could hear his muffled shout as he relayed the news to the reporters and editors nearby. That was followed by the sound of journalists erupting with applause and cheers. Bonavita passed the phone to Carolina Garcia, the managing editor, and I repeated what little we knew.

"Please call Monika at home and give her the news," I asked. "Let her know everything is okay and I'll be coming home as soon as I can meet with Philip here."

Garcia and I discussed our next steps. She would call everyone together to share the few details in hand, and then call Larry Walker and Tom Stephenson to give them the welcome news. Meanwhile, Bonavita would try to reach Fred Chase and Susana Hayward in Tepic. I promised to call back as soon as I could scribble a few paragraphs to contribute to the morning story that would announce True's return, safe and sound.

Martha and Juanita were in a state of happy shock. It was such a sudden change in fortune. Martha used the second telephone to share the news with friends. I sat at the kitchen table, writing into my notebook. Minutes later I called the newsroom again and dictated a few sentences.

Now it was time to await Nájera's next call. Garcia made the announcement to a gathering in the newsroom, presciently stressing that what we knew came from "uncorroborated reports."

Nájera had promised us that True would call in twenty minutes, as soon as the army helicopter set down at the base and he reached a ground telephone. The occasion, I announced, merited a cold, celebratory beer.

The three of us sat and chatted, but time passed and we began to watch the clock. An hour ticked slowly by, and still we waited. I began to pace impatiently. The phone finally rang just before 8:00 P.M., two hours after we had been told True had been found and was en route to the base. I hurried to answer it, but it was only Nájera again.

"Bob, can you speak privately?" he asked.

"Yes, I can, but why?" I asked.

"Did Philip abuse drugs such as peyote?" Nájera asked.

"What?" The question unsettled me.

"He says he doesn't want to talk to Martha, that she isn't his wife," Nájera replied. "He's incoherent. Is there something you haven't been telling me about their relationship? Could he have been running away from her?"

I was stunned. Nájera's questions didn't make any sense. What was he saying? True was a moderate drinker. He didn't use drugs, to the best of my knowledge, and seemed to have a storybook marriage with Martha. I thought of the baby growing in her belly.

Despite my best efforts to keep my voice down and the conversation private, Martha and Juanita sensed trouble. They drew closer and began to fire questions at me as I listened to Nájera promise to find out more and call me back.

I hung up and lied.

"Nothing really to report," I mumbled. "Sounds like he's really out of it. I don't know if he's just exhausted or sick or what. Let him rest and we will wait for his call."

Military commanders, Nájera had told me, would work with True to sober him up so he could talk later that night.

Time passed like a prison sentence. The air of celebration had given way to growing discomfort. Martha grew irritable, then angry. She suspected I knew more than I was admitting.

Finally the phone rang. It was Nájera again.

This time he was the one who sounded stunned. He informed me that the U.S. consul general in Guadalajara had arrived at the base and interviewed True. Only it wasn't True.

"What?" I felt myself shaking. "What do you mean, it's not True?"

"He's tall like Philip," Nájera said, his own voice trembling. "But he's got blond hair, dreadlocks."

True had dark, clipped hair and a mustache.

"He speaks English with an accent and has a Swiss passport," Nájera said. "You won't believe what I am about to tell you, Bob. The name on his passport is Philip Truempler."

Five extra letters in the last name, a different nationality, and the wrong person.

Nájera continued. Truempler was a Swiss anthropologist, apparently encountered by a small army search team in Guadalupe de Ocatán, a village located due south of San Miguel, well away from the Chapalagana.

Truempler was there researching Huichol peyote rituals, Nájera said, which apparently explained his incoherence. It also explained his resistance to boarding a military chopper for a ride to an army base and his insistent claim that he was not married to a Mexican woman named Martha.

I will never forget the look on Martha's face as she and Juanita listened, both standing still as statues.

Shaken, I asked to be patched through to the military base so I could speak to Truempler. I no longer trusted anyone or anything and needed to know for myself.

Through the distant echo of the telephone line, I heard an unmistakable French accent as Truempler answered me in English.

"Would you mind slowly spelling your last name for me?" I asked.

"My name is Philip Truempler, T-r-u-e-m-p-l-e-r," he answered.

Desperate for something, anything, before I turned back to Martha, I asked if he had seen True, or whether any Huichols had mentioned seeing him.

"I can't help you," Truempler replied. "I am sorry."

I hung up and turned to share the bitter news, but there was nothing to share or to say. Martha had collapsed face down on a nearby sofa. "He's dead, I knew it. Philip is dead. He is never coming home," she sobbed.

Night had fallen, and a single dim lamp glowed in the corner of the room. For what seemed an interminable time, Juanita and I sat silently in the gloom, listening to Martha weep, neither of us able to move or speak.

In a city of monuments ranging from Aztec pyramids to sixteenth-century churches to a nineteenth-century golden angel, the president of

Mexico lives and works in a complex of nondescript modernist buildings. Los Pinos, as its name implies, is a green expanse of stately pine
trees and well-tended gardens. Tropical birds flit though the air, giving
the space the feel of a country estate, far from the hustle of Mexico
City.

Ordinary citizens will never see Los Pinos, except in the distance
from a busy thoroughfare skirting Chapultepec Park. Soldiers in army
uniforms toting automatic weapons guard the walled perimeter and
entryway. Mexicans could once point with pride to the lack of political violence in their society, in contrast to the United States. That
changed as the *sexenio*, the six-year term of President Salinas, wound
down in 1994.

In the space of a few years, Mexico was rocked by a rash of
unsolved killings and political assassinations. A DEA agent was kidnapped, tortured, and executed by drug lords in Guadalajara, a
Catholic cardinal died in a hail of bullets at the Guadalajara airport, a
political figure close to the Salinas family dynasty was shot at close
range in his own car on a Mexico City street, and finally Salinas's own
handpicked candidate to succeed him as president was gunned down
on the campaign trail in Tijuana.

My first visit to Los Pinos was in 1979, during the López Portillo
administration. As a twenty-five-year-old reporter at the *Corpus
Christi Caller*, I had convinced my editor, an affable man with a pronounced New Jersey accent named Robert Rhodes, to let me report
on the historic visit of newly-elected Pope John Paul II.

With some luck, I joined a large group of Mexican reporters at the
front gate and accompanied them into a salon already packed with
Mexican newspaper and television reporters. All were eager to question the president about the country's preparations for the pope's
visit.

The Roman Catholic Church and the Institutional Revolutionary
Party (PRI), Mexico's ruling party from the early twentieth century to
the year 2000, have maintained an uneasy accommodation since the
Mexican Revolution, when Catholic bishops saw their political power

all but destroyed. Church lands and estates were seized and divided into *ejidos*, peasant agrarian collectives. The clergy were banned from political activism and public life.

López Portillo walked into the salon, trailed by aides and his translator. He was met with a barrage of shouted questions. Tall, balding, and regal, López Portillo held up his hands and silenced the reporters. He then patiently called on one reporter after another, each time offering a brief answer.

Yes, the massive cleanup and facelift undertaken in Mexico City and the other cities on the pope's itinerary would be completed before his visit. No, he was not worried about security arrangements or the task of handling the vast crowds expected to attend the public masses. Yes, it was special honor for all Mexicans that the pope had chosen the Virgin of Guadalupe as the object of his journey and veneration.

The translator looked at me with anticipation and smiled. I was next. My knees were shaking, and my throat suddenly felt hoarse. I had been a reporter for only two years and had never spoken with the president of any country, and the question I had in mind was less obsequious than those the Mexican reporters were asking.

"*Señor presidente,*" I began, "is it true that Mexico's constitution forbids priests and nuns to dress in clerical garb in public? Will you enforce that law during the pope's visit?"

An eternity passed as I stumbled along in Spanish. The president's eyes narrowed as he took in my words. The Mexican reporters all seemed to turn and see me for the first time. Given that reporters ask questions designed to elicit responses that make news, it was a naive question. What did I expect him to tell an American reporter?

López Portillo leaned toward his interpreter, whispered something into her ear, and then turned back to the reporters. Without a word, he nodded at the next reporter and left me standing there, my question unanswered, my face burning with embarrassment.

In the intervening twenty years, I had been back to Los Pinos a number of times under less intimidating circumstances, with improved Spanish and greater self-confidence. Now I was here again, this time not to ask a question but to ask for help.

I waited patiently in a downstairs salon, admiring a Rufino Tamayo oil and other works by some of Mexico's greatest artists. A trio of volcano drawings by the well-known early-twentieth-century artist and radical Dr. Atl, whose real name was Gerald Murillo, hung along the wall above the banister of the curving staircase.

Nájera came down the stairs to welcome me, but this time we embraced in an *abrazo*, the traditional Mexican greeting of trust and respect. We were both shaken by the Philip Truempler incident the previous evening. A good novelist would never employ such a trick with the reader. Some Mexican newspapers that morning carried "believe it or not" accounts of the false report of True's rescue and the eerie similarity of the Swiss man's name.

Nájera felt crushed and asked about Martha. There was no way he was to blame for what happened. Actually, the extraordinary coincidence served to elevate the True case in the public consciousness, which was good for those of us searching. Mexican administration officials, Nájera later told me, worried that the story might spin out of control and become an issue of contention between the two countries.

"We, too, want to find Philip True," he assured me.

Nájera led me to Lerdo de Tejada's suite, and after a brief wait, brought me into his private office for introductions. We had never met, but I immediately liked Zedillo's social communication secretary. Like True, I thought, he didn't wear a suit and tie, at least not when the boss was out of town. He sported a neatly trimmed beard and was wearing hand-tooled cowboy boots and a stylish leather jacket over an open-collared dress shirt.

Coffee was served, and Lerdo de Tejada invited me to update him. In retrospect, he probably knew everything I was telling him, but it gave me the chance to connect with him.

"What exactly do you want us to do?" he asked.

I repeated my praise for the Mexican military's lead role in the humanitarian efforts after Hurricane Mitch. "We'd like to see the mil-

itary devote the same energy to helping us find Philip," I said. "We
want the Mexican government to mount a major search and rescue
operation with the army, helicopters, ground troops, whatever they
can do," I said. "We want you to treat this case the same as if the son
of a Kennedy turned up missing."

He stared at me without speaking. I wondered if I had asked for
too much or offended him by implying that very important people are
treated differently than everyone else in Mexico. Of course they are,
in Mexico and everywhere else.

"We are asking for a lot, but here I am, I am asking," I added, trying to fill up the silence, hoping it didn't sound like I was begging.
"The truth is we've done all we can on our own. We need your help."

Lerdo de Tejada uncradled a nearby telephone and spoke into the
receiver without breaking eye contact with me. "Get me the minister
of defense," he said, waiting on the line.

It was a melodramatic moment, but one I greatly appreciated. I
heard myself exhale and felt my face flush with relief. What would we
have done if he had said the government could not help us?

Minutes later the request was granted. Some troops were already
searching the zone, he reminded me. Now the search would be inten-
sified: more helicopters, more ground troops. I started to thank him
profusely as we stood up to part ways. He asked me to convey the
administration's commitment to Martha.

"We will find Philip True," he said.

"You need to get to Guadalajara as soon as you can," Nájera told
me a few hours later. "The commanding general of the Fifth Military
Base, who is leading the search, will be waiting. You leave with him
tomorrow for the sierra."

9

Trail of Feathers

The Mexican's indifference toward death is fostered by his indifference toward life. He views not only death but also life as nontranscendent. Our songs, proverbs, fiestas and popular beliefs show very clearly that the reason death cannot frighten us is that "life has cured us of fear." It is natural, even desirable, to die, and the sooner the better. We kill because life—our own or another's—is of no value. Life and death are inseparable, and when the former lacks meaning, the later becomes equally meaningless. Mexican death is the mirror of Mexican life. And the Mexican shuts himself away and ignores both of them.

—Octavio Paz, *The Labyrinth of Solitude*

After racing back to the hotel and exchanging my business suit for blue jeans, hiking boots, and a lightweight jacket, I was back in the car and headed for the airport. The backpack I had prepared earlier was next to me.

The driver, an elderly man with a neatly trimmed mustache, was visibly excited. He had read the newspapers and overheard my cell phone conversations.

"I wish I would join you your search, *señor*," he said. "I hope you find your reporter."

He must have been seventy years old, a slow, overly cautious driver in a city that placed no value on responsible, courteous driving. He had worked for me on previous trips, and I often wondered why I didn't look for someone else, but he was a gentleman and always reliable.

I reached the restricted sector of the Guadalajara international airport early the next day. Hayward soon followed, having returned from Tepic to meet me there and join our search party. We embraced and filled the time talking about the search and what she had gleaned from her time in the sierra. Anthony Giovanelli, a local U.S. consular official, also materialized. The presence of a consular official surprised me, and I wondered whether he was an intelligence operative with diplomatic cover. I had never known a U.S. consular official to venture afield during my years in Central America.

An eight-seat civilian Bell transport helicopter was parked nearby. The waiting military pilot said it was on loan from the governor's office in Nayarit and was the only available craft big enough to carry our group.

General Eulalio Fonseca Orozco, commander of the Fifth Military Zone, taut, wiry, bespectacled, appeared without warning from inside the hangar. He strode toward us, dressed in sharply creased, starched olive drab trousers tucked into polished black jump boots.

Behind us, the military pilot fired the helicopter's ignition.

You can serve an entire tour of duty as a foreign correspondent in Mexico and never spend time with a ranking military commander. I extended my hand to greet him. "Buenos días, general. Soy Robert ..."

The general strode past me without saying a word, ignoring my outstretched hand, not even making eye contact. He was not happy to see us, but was under orders from the minister of defense that had been handed down from the presidential staff at Los Pinos. Fonseca was not particularly interested in a humanitarian mission. What was one missing reporter who should not have walked into the Sierra Madre in the first place?

Determined to engage him, I waved Hayward over and introduced her. The general stood at the door of the helicopter. "No, mujeres, no," he said, wagging his index finger back and forth through the air. No women. He seemed astonished I would propose such a thing.

"She's a journalist," I said, "and she is a close friend of our reporter and has been up in the sierra searching for him."

"It's a question of weight," Fonseca countered, intent on leaving Hayward behind. "We are overweight. Do you want me to give orders for an overweight helicopter to take off?"

Hayward was ready to go ballistic. She was operating on little sleep. It's impossible to be a dispassionate reporter when a friend from the same newsroom goes missing. She let loose a stream of Spanish, an expression of her frazzled nerves and pent-up anger. If she didn't stop, I feared, the general would kick both of us off the chopper.

We walked toward the hangar and away from the general. "How much will it cost for you to go back into the terminal and charter a plane?" I asked

"By myself, a whole plane?" She seemed doubtful I would continue with my plan once I had heard the price.

"Just go do it," I said, handing her $500. "If you're lucky, you'll beat us to San Miguel."

Hayward would have preferred to ride in the chopper and was still inclined to give Fonseca a piece of her mind. I didn't blame her. The general was a dinosaur, but right now he was our dinosaur, the only chance we had, and it was my job to make sure the search moved forward. She turned and left. She didn't seem happy with me either and probably thought I should have put up more of a fight.

Fonseca motioned me toward the chopper door and I climbed in behind him. Captain Jorge Alberto Sanchez Salvator, an officer in the state police, also was on board. He wore a .45-caliber semiautomatic pistol on his belt and bore an uncanny resemblance to ranchero singing idol Vicente Fernandez.

I strapped in next to the general's aide, and we prepared to lift off. "I think we will recover your reporter somewhere across the state line in Nayarit," the general's aide said, turning my way as the pilots revved the engines.

I stared at him for a moment, wondering if he knew something we did not know.

"I'm sorry," he said, reading my face. "We could find him anywhere out there, maybe hurt, maybe not."

The noise after takeoff discouraged conversation, and everyone took in the bird's-eye view of the city as the pilots followed an undulating ravine below that divided Guadalajara in two—modern, bustling commercialism on one side, shantytowns on the other.

We flew over the old colonial capital of the central city with its pink domes and arches and long, descending plazas. I gazed down at familiar landmarks, trying to steady my binoculars, remembering places I had visited with Monika and the boys several summers earlier. Nick had come to attend a youth soccer camp run by Club Atlas, one of the city's two professional clubs. Afterward, we spent a week in the old city before driving back to San Antonio.

The general's aide spread out a topo map and began punching coordinates into his handheld global positioning system. I brought mine out, a later model purchased days earlier, and started copying his numbers. He looked on with undisguised interest and asked to see it.

"Help me find our guy and it's yours," I told him. "I won't be needing it anymore."

The aide's face brightened, and he moved the map closer so we could read it together.

A small circle was drawn around San Miguel, across the Chapalagana from Amoltita, the settlement where Fred Chase and Manuel Obaya had encountered the hostile Huichols. Fonseca noticed us and swiveled in his chair. He tapped his finger on the circle. "San Miguel will serve as our base of operations for the ground and air search," he said over the loud thudding of the rotors. He borrowed the aide's pencil and drew a triangle on the map around the San Miguel area reaching out toward Amoltita.

"This is where I expect we will find him, according to our intelligence," he said, tapping the map with his pen for emphasis and looking at me. Fonseca did not mention that his "intelligence" came from what Chase and Obaya had passed on to the government. I wasn't about to remind him.

The shabby outskirts of the city gave way to tin-roofed shacks and narrow dirt roads and then all signs of life disappeared into the steep folds of the foothills. It seemed like a good time to engage the general. "Is there a lot of poppy and marijuana cultivation down there?" I asked. The more time passed without any word, the more we wondered if True had run afoul of drug traffickers.

"No marijuana or poppies, zero," the general emphatically declared. "On the other side of the sierra, in Nayarit, yes, where there is much more rainfall, but here on the side of Jalisco, there is little rain and you can see how dry it is, so there is nothing."

Pausing for a moment, Fonseca looked back at me. "No, *señor,* I see what you are thinking. Your reporter did not cross paths with *narcotraficantes* or their people," he said, watching to see if I believed him.

He seemed too sure of himself.

Less than an hour after we left Guadalajara, we were hovering over a dirt soccer field on the edge of San Miguel. A cluster of locals, dressed in baggy, embroidered white cotton garments, walked toward the helicopter while children raced excitedly ahead of the elders. Some Huichols waved at us. Others held their hats and lifted bandanas to mask their faces against the dust cloud. The arrival of a helicopter with soldiers aboard is not an ordinary thing.

We jumped down and ducked under the still rotating blades. The mountain air was noticeably cooler than Guadalajara. A short, intense-looking American with thinning, sandy hair and wire rim glasses approached me. Putting his face close to mine, he shouted over the rotor wash, "They found Philip. He's dead."

I just stared for a moment, processing his words. We were there to launch our search. We shook hands. It was Chase, True's best friend from Laredo. He had been in the sierra since Saturday and he looked frazzled. "A Huichol hunter found him. He died in a hiking accident," Chase shouted. "He fell off a cliff."

I thought of Martha and her premonitions and was relieved she was back in Mexico City. Fonseca jumped down, and I repeated the news. Chase introduced us to Dr. Sergio Ramirez, standing next to a short, barefoot Huichol man wearing a straw sombrero edged with blue ribbon and decorated with small ornaments that hung from the edge of the brim.

Margarito Díaz Martinez, a wizened, white-haired hunter from Popotito, a village along True's route that was a two-day walk away, had come across True's body lying in the wilds, his backpack next to him, as a flock of turkey vultures fed on his decomposing body. Horrified, Díaz had returned to his village and then walked to San Miguel to deliver the news to his nephew, who worked in Ramirez's modest clinic.

Díaz and the other Huichols I met that day knew all about True's disappearance. Many had been searching for him, spurred by the reward money. The *Express-News* had become a welcome employer in the village. Díaz, however, had been hunting wild pigs, not True. He came across the body while walking along the canyon rim, preparing to descend to the bottom to fish in the river if he failed to track a pig. We walked away from the helicopter to talk. Díaz, his Spanish somewhat limited, said he found True at the base of a steep, rocky ravine.

"He fell off a cliff and died," Díaz told us. "He still sits, next to his backpack."

"How far from here?" Fonseca asked him.

"One day or more, very difficult," Díaz said, looking us over.

The general listened and then turned toward the helicopter and circled a finger in the air several times, signaling the pilots to rev up the engines.

"*Vámanos.* Back in the helicopter, everyone," he said, turning to Dr. Ramirez and Díaz and waving them forward too.

Chase looked at me with pleading eyes.

"I have to be on this chopper, I was his best friend," he said. "I need to be there for Martha."

Something about Chase's intensity told me he would grab the landing struts and hang from them if we left without him. After all, how many people would leave their homes and jobs and head off into an unknown wilderness in another country to search for a missing friend? Many might say they would go, but few would do it.

I turned to Fonseca and pointed to Chase: "This is True's only brother," I said, "we can't leave him here."

Fonseca nodded his assent and ordered two of the soldiers off the helicopter to keep the load within the pilot's comfort zone. Then he turned to the doctor.

"Tell your Huichol friend that a two day-walk for him only takes a general fifteeen minutes," Fonseca said. "He's about to get his first helicopter ride."

Ramirez bent down to speak into Díaz's ear, whose eyes widened. They both looked back at the general.

"He said he has never even been in a car," the doctor said. "Of course," he quickly added, gazing up at the blade as it gained velocity, "I myself have never been in a helicopter, either."

Fonseca pointed to the entryway. One by one, we climbed aboard. A soldier leaned out to give Díaz a hand while another pushed from behind. I glanced at my watch and made a note. We had been on the ground in San Miguel for exactly fifteen minutes.

With the doctor, Díaz, and Chase aboard, we lifted off. I asked Chase if he had seen Hayward that morning, but her charter had not arrived. Once again, she would be left to sit and wait in San Miguel. I felt badly for her but also relieved that she was not going with us into the Chapalagana to retrieve True's remains.

The pilots gained altitude and then banked away from San Miguel. "That way," Díaz said, pointing east toward the late-morning sun, as he gazed out the helicopter window, seated next to the general.

Díaz was dressed in traditional clothing that seemed impossibly thin in this mountain climate. His trousers were cinched around the waist with a rope belt that held a square cloth bag, a sort of small hip purse. His skin had been baked by years under the sun and was the color of an old saddle. He had walked barefoot two days through the mountains to reach San Miguel. His callused feet were scaly and club-shaped from years of traversing the rocky terrain without san-dals. He stood less than five feet tall and seemed in good health, despite his weathered countenance. Mortality rates for children in indigenous societies are high, and life expectancy is far less than we enjoy. It is easy to romanticize the lives of Huichols when the truth is they live brutally hard and short lives, wed to the earth as subsistence farmers. Daily life is filled with privation. People always look older.

Díaz looked like a seventy-year-old man, perhaps older.

He smiled easily as our eyes met.

"How old are you, *señor*, if you don't mind me asking?" I asked as the doctor looked on.

"*Viejo*," he said, smiling. Old man. "Forty-eight."

Then, as he watched me writing in my notebook, he tapped Ramirez's shoulder and said something.

"He thinks he is forty-eight," Ramirez said, smiling. "It's not an exact thing."

We flew low across deep ravines, cut at the bottom by trickles of blue water that caught the sun. Terrain that looks parched from high up reveals fertile pockets nestled below the cliffs and hillsides. Great ochre and sand-colored rock domes rose up in the distance. The helicopter labored in the thinner air as we climbed above the formations ahead. Massive boulders and ledges came into view. Some rocks, stories high, appeared to balance on flat table rock. This was unfamiliar terrain. It didn't look like anywhere else in Mexico that I had seen.

Minutes later, the pilot began to circle as Díaz began speaking rapidly to the general and pointing toward a small hillside clearing. We dropped down, hovering one hundred feet above the treetops, but there were no signs of a body visible through the stunted trees. Fonseca ordered the pilots to land, but they were unable to find a safe landing zone. They flew wider and wider circles until we reached La Tortuga, a windswept village on a high plateau a few miles distant that was large enough to safely set down. Wind gusts off the cliff faces buffeted the craft. The pilots concentrated and slowly descended.

A cluster of adobe brick huts appeared to be deserted. Then several small figures emerged as we landed, the men holding their straw hats, the women clutching their white skirts. The pilot pointed toward the area where Díaz had spotted the body, but Díaz and a handful of other Huichols from the huts had already set off in the same direction.

We quickly followed, the general and his small retinue in front, Dr. Ramirez, Chase, Giovanelli, and I bringing up the rear. I threw on my backpack, tried to punch in a GPS reading of our landing zone, and slipped an inexpensive, throwaway camera into my pocket.

The path leading away from the plateau was narrow and flat, chiseled out of the side of the mountain, the land falling away below. Such man-made paths in remote, challenging terrain are a mystery. How do people without modern tools or machinery carve out such efficient pathways, and also tend crops, hunt, and fish, make their own clothes, and secure their survival? We headed into dense scrub brush and a grove of trees.

The December chill had evaporated as the sun rose above the peaks to the east. It was afternoon now and we would soon be sweating. The path twisted around dead-end rock walls, skirted sudden drop-offs, and led through thick foliage that shaded us.

The Huichols accompanying our party seemed shy and uninterested in conversation. We passed others on the path going the other way, and while some exchanged greetings in Spanish, others simply averted their gaze. They seemed reclusive rather than hostile. We were foreigners. Even the Mexicans were foreigners, especially the rifle-toting soldiers.

The path eventually veered sharply up and to the right. A switchback brought us around a protruding rock formation and we disappeared into a grove of scrub oaks at the base of a steep ravine. A Huichol pointed to an even narrower path above us, perhaps 150 feet higher, that ran like a beaded seam along the steep side of the ravine. A goat path, I told myself, hoping the Huichol was not suggesting our destination.

One hour after departing our landing zone, we came to the spot where Díaz said he had found the dead backpacker. One by one, we collected ourselves into a group and listened as he spoke. He pointed to a nearby rotting log.

"That's where the man sat," he said, mimicking a slumped over corpse. "*Los zopilotes* were on him." As Díaz spoke, as if on cue, a flock of vultures roosting in the nearby stand of trees flapped their wings in protest, emitting a guttural coughing sound. Díaz pointed upward and we followed his gaze to a point on the narrow seam, perhaps ten yards long, that appeared to be an all but impassable rock bridge for a man burdened with a heavy backpack.

A tumble of disturbed shale fell away from the narrow passage, cascading down to where we stood. A talus field of shattered rock that had broken off the ledge and tumbled down the ravine slope to a point just above the grassy clearing offered further proof of the uncertain footing.

"What in the hell would True be doing up there?" I asked no one in particular. "That doesn't look to me like it's a path to anywhere."

A slight breeze brought the stench of human death. It's an unmistakable odor, one you never forget, different somehow than the foul odor of a dead animal. You can go years without experiencing it, and then one day, it's there again, and you know it in an instant. There is nothing as uncivilized or repulsive as the corpse of man or woman left to the ravages of nature. The vultures flapped again in the trees, resigned to our presence. One or two lazily flew off their perch, only to circle and return.

Dr. Ramirez called out to the group. Down on his knees, he had found a rusting bloodstain in the dirt. He pulled a plastic specimen bag from his pocket, along with a pair of tweezers and swabs.

"Sangre," the young village doctor said. "Muchísima. Aquí alguien murió, seguro." Blood, he said, a lot of it. Someone died here, for sure.

"*Sí*, he was right here, in a sitting position," Díaz said. "It was terrible, doctor. I once saw a dead man when I was a small boy. I thought of that again. I saw the vultures eating his face and legs."

"It's obvious he died here," the general said. "Probably fell from up there and bled to death down here."

Sanchez, the state police investigator, agreed. He pointed up to the disturbed narrow ledge and the tumble of broken rock.

"Your *amigo* died in a hiking accident," he said, hunching his shoulders and spreading his palms outward. "He was, forgive me, foolish to be on a trail of this nature."

The doctor called me over, and I squatted down alongside him. He had donned a face mask now. As I watched, he held up his tweezers and a small shard of dessicated skin, then dropped it into his bag that held a few wet clumps of dark hair and other bits of curled skin. It was a dispiriting moment, watching a stranger, squatting low to the ground and awkwardly moving forward, picking at the earth and gathering minute, unrecognizable pieces of what had been True's body. Still, I was grateful the young physician had come so prepared.

The evidence, at first glance, seemed to point rather squarely at the scenario voiced by the general and the police captain. But where was the corpse and True's backpack? Díaz had been here only two days earlier. There were no obvious signs of activity: no footprints, no drag marks, no freshly turned earth. Had someone moved or buried the body? If so, why didn't they claim the 10,000-peso reward?

Fonseca ordered everyone to spread out and walk the area in circles. The doctor and I stayed and began to dig with our hands around the heavy concentration of blood. Perhaps True was buried right there. Inches down, we hit rock.

The doctor pointed to a small circle of ash and charcoal, the remnants of a small campfire a few feet from where True had reposed in death. A cigarette butt lay in the carbonized wood residue. Had True somehow survived his painful fall and managed to light a fire as night descended? He didn't smoke, I reminded myself.

We joined the others, wondering if wild animals had dragged True's remains into the underbrush. That seemed unlikely. Animals, if there were any left in the overhunted sierra big enough to drag a human corpse, would have left some sign. Animals don't drag off backpacks.

A Huichol cried out in his native language, and soon several of the men were talking excitedly. One of them approached us with a few small feathers in the palm of his hand.

"Mira, plumitas," he said. "Look, little feathers."

He handed them to us to examine. They looked like they were from a juvenile bird.

"Those are goose down feathers from Philip's sleeping bag," Chase declared.

We moved quickly toward the spot on the trail where the feathers had been found, but the Huichols were ahead of us, already tracking. A short way down the trail they cried out again. More feathers. Then, farther down, even more. The footsure Huichols moved quickly ahead of us through the thorny brush that tugged at our clothes and stung our faces as we struggled down the overgrown trail. We could hear the excitement in their voices as they lost the trail one minute, then found more feathers the next. It was like tracking a wounded deer.

Here and there, tiny wisps of feathers guided our way, some scattered in the dirt and grass, others clinging to ground brush. A trail of feathers led us down the steep slope and toward the canyon we could not see but knew lay somewhere just ahead.

As we descended toward the actual edge of the canyon, the brush and trees gave way to rock and dirt and a massive flat outcropping that reached beyond the slope and hung above the abyss. Row upon row of ancient, weathered mountains, flat and decapitated, lay before us, until the farthest disappeared in the cloudbank. Giant mesas and distant rock formations, shaped by eons of wind and moving water, stood out against the range. As we ventured onto the edge of the outcropping, we looked down. A thousand vertical feet below, the Chapalagana, a deep, snaking slash in the earth, cut through the rugged sierra.

Chase and I just stood there, in a vast and swallowing landscape. Díaz also stood there gaping. Even a lifetime in the sierra does not diminish the experience. Now I knew why True had come here, why he had refused to let us stop him.

True would have greeted the Chapalagana from the east looking west, opposite our vantage point. He had experienced it, of course, not as one person in a search party but in total solitude. At the approaching hour of sunset this world untouched by anything man-made must have appeared even more majestic, an unending vista curtained in a cloak of colors only the Huichols know.

One can imagine the inner joy that pulsed through True as he stood atop the Chapalagana, alone in his own wild universe. After months of waiting, the rejections from San Antonio, the weeks of training, the false starts, his long struggle to be there, he must have felt great accomplishment. This was how True found inner peace and, amid the natural splendor, put together the pieces of his broken soul.

However infinitesimally small he must have felt on the edge of such terra incognita, however overwhelmed by the grandeur and enormity of space, however weary after so many days on the trail, he knew he was just one day's walk from San Miguel and the sound of Martha's voice through the radiotelephone. It seemed to me impossible for True, in this solitude, not to have thought with deep emotion about Martha and the baby, about his own future as a father.

His odyssey now struck me in a very different way than when I first read his story proposal. Taking on this landscape, on foot, seemed impossible. Yet he did. He planned to move from village to village, sleeping under the stars or a thatched roof wherever he was welcome. He would cook his meals on a small propane stove and await the invitation of Huichols to join them in their own daily repasts. He would bathe in rivers and glory in the rise and setting of the sun. He would record the day's events in his pocket notebook and, before crawling into his narrow tent, witness a night sky known to only a few. The stars and planets must have seemed within his very reach.

I eased out farther onto the rock outcropping, fighting my aversion to heights, and snapped a photograph that now hangs outside my office. Then it was time to go.

The search party had broken into twos and threes as we struggled down the steep path, grasping at rocks and saplings and thorn bushes to break our momentum. Twice I turned around to climb down backwards, using my hands and feet. I was reassured to see one of the Huichols do the same. "Are all the paths between villages this bad?" I asked Díaz at one point along the way.

"This is a game trail, wild animals and hunters," he said, smiling. "No one else comes this way."

"It would be unusual that your friend chose this way to hike," the doctor added. "This is not the path to San Miguel or to anywhere else, for that matter."

We overtook the general and his troops. Fonseca was seated on a rock, perspiring heavily in his fatigues. A look of pain was visible on his face.

"*Mi general* has sprained his ankle," his lieutenant, standing at attention, formally informed us. "We will stay with him. Go on without us."

We continued downward, still finding scattered feathers, until the slope began to flatten out. The massive redoubt where we had stood to gaze down at the canyon loomed above us and seemed far off in the distance. For the first time I thought about the climb back out. It was going to be a long, testing day.

The sound of moving water told us we were nearing the canyon bottom, and moments later we emerged from a thicket and stood before a sheer rock face, dark with dripping water. Swallows disappeared into hidden crevices guarded by bright, hanging blooms.

"Where are we?" I asked Díaz.

"La Chapalagana," he answered. The Twisted Serpent.

Díaz said it was a spiritual place, named for the winding river that cut through the high-walled canyon. The specific place, he added, was called "la Casa del la Boa," the House of the Boa.

A mongrel belonging to one of the Indians sniffed at a sand bar fifty yards from where we stood, growling as it began to paw at the sand. Freshly cut river willows, still green, lay strewn about the spot. I ran to the place where the dog was standing and knelt down, placing my face close to the sand. Through the sand the stench of decomposition made me gag and burned my nose and throat. I began to dig with my bare hands. Chase found a stick and joined in. A few Huichols edged nearer, saying nothing, watching.

It isn't easy to unearth a corpse without tools. Sand slipped through our hands almost as fast as we scooped it, as we sweated through our shirts in the afternoon heat. Ramirez handed me a face mask. The soft walls of our growing hole caved in each time we gained a few inches of depth. Finally we began to paw sand though our legs like dogs. Chase, Dr. Ramirez, and I took turns, switching places every few minutes. Sweating and sickened by the stench, we dug down more than a foot before we hit a hard form wrapped in a blue plastic ground cloth identical to the one Martha had described. We had found True.

Now we dug more slowly, as if we didn't want to disturb him any more than he had already been disturbed. Yet we knew we were unearthing a corpse, that the spirit of Chase's best friend and my reporter was beyond our reach.

Seeing how little progress we were making, Díaz climbed into the sandpit to help. Together, we slowly exposed a mummylike form bent in a semifetal position, encased in True's sleeping bag and ground cloth. Feathers spilled out around us, sticking to our hands and clothes, identical to the plumes that had led us to this hidden grave.

Unearthing True with nothing but our hands was difficult. The corpse was in an advanced state of decomposition, swollen with gases and grotesquely enlarged. We could not stay in the sandpit more than a few minutes without stepping away to clear the contaminated air from our lungs. Even fresh water tasted putrid. As we struggled, unable to free the corpse from the sand, I found my anger growing. Who had done this to True?

Dr. Ramirez placed his hand on my shoulder and gently suggested we stop. Part of the blackened corpse was exposed, and he said he was worried about disease. We could do no more without spades.

I asked Chase to photograph me next to True's body. We needed physical proof of this scene, I said.

Indigenous people often are sensitive to camera-wielding foreigners. I asked Díaz if he would allow me to photograph him on the perimeter of True's grave, and he readily agreed. Most of the other Huichols, perhaps a dozen in all, had gathered far enough way to escape the foul air, around a tumble of large boulders that overlooked the clear pool of water.

They were seated, talking quietly among themselves. I resisted an impulse to photograph them too, something to help us remember who else was present this day. Later I stepped back and discreetly snapped a few frames. I finished taking photographs of the others standing around the grave. Whatever else happened, we were not going to allow anyone to dispute the day's events.

"This was not the act of a Good Samaritan," I said to Chase, neither of us quite comprehending the sequence of events that ended with True's burial in the sandbank.

"It's obvious someone wanted to conceal this grave," the doctor said, "or they would not have cut all these reeds and spread them around. Their work was hasty."

"You have to wonder if they know anything about who dragged True down here and dug this grave," I said to Chase, looking at the Huichols.

"Oh, they know all right," he said, tension in his voice. "There are no secrets up here in these villages."

The limping general and his troops dropped into the canyon bottom.

"How is your ankle?" I asked.

"There is nothing wrong with my ankle," he said. "We were just resting."

Then he seemed to relax as he regarded Chase and me with newfound respect.

"You did very well getting down here," he said. "This is some place, isn't it?"

"We found Philip True," I said, motioning to the nearby grave.

Fonseca had already tied a bandana around his nose and mouth and didn't need me to tell him about the remains. The general stood over the gravesite for a minute, then surveyed the narrow canyon walls.

"Give me the radio," he commanded his aide. He ordered the chopper pilots to descend to the bottom of the Chapalagana. He listened to the cackle of their voices in response, then answered, "You can make it if you are careful. Watch the rock wall."

"We are going to order a forensics team here to finish the work and remove the body," Fonseca told us. "I will fly to Tepic to see the civil authorities since we are in Nayarit. Some of you can come with me now; the others will have to stay here until we can send a helicopter big enough to transport the corpse and the rest of you."

"I'm not leaving the body," I announced, surprised at the aggression I heard in my own voice.

"Okay, you stay," he told me. The doctor and the state policeman also agreed to remain behind. Chase would return to San Miguel or Tepic. He volunteered to deliver the bad news to Martha.

"We will catch up to you," I said. "Please tell Martha how sorry I am, and tell her we are bringing Philip home and we will stay with him until then."

Minutes later, the thunder of the general's helicopter echoed around the canyon, the sound reaching us even before we could see the craft. The pilot circled the vertical flume, gauging his clearance and landing spot. He descended slowly, the canyon walls seemingly only feet away. We covered our ears against the deafening roar. Fonseca and the others climbed aboard and the white chopper disappeared quickly in the afternoon sky. The canyon was silent again.

Captain Sanchez had settled into some rocks near the seated Huichols, who were conversing in their language. He leaned back, tired, preparing to take a nap.

"If you don't mind me asking, is your pistol fully loaded?" I asked. Years ago, I had been told that poorly paid Mexican soldiers and police are required to purchase their own ammunition and thus carried firearms that were either empty or loaded with only a few rounds.

"Always ready," the captain said, patting the holster.

"Good," I said. "I'm armed with enough water for both of us."

Sanchez looked at me gratefully. I handed him an unopened bottle and watched as he took a small sip and handed it back.

"Drink it," I said. "It's all yours. I have one for myself."

"Mil gracias," he said.

"That's how I feel about you being here with your gun right now," I said.

"We aren't going to have any trouble," he said, lying back down and covering his face with his hat.

I stood up and walked toward the Huichols, but none would look at me, and their body language signaled that I was not welcome to join their conversation. Perhaps they did not feel comfortable speaking Spanish with a stranger.

I eyed their garb. Their sandals were cut from old tire treads. Loose-fitting trousers, spun from white cotton, ended at midcalf, revealing sinuous leg muscles. There wasn't an ounce of fat on any of them. With their black hair, sturdy frames, and wide eyes, they looked and dressed differently than any other indigenous people I had encountered in Mexico. All the men carried square woven bags, adorned with deer and other venerated figures. These small purses, made from coarse wool, appeared to be empty, making me wonder what they carried in them.

In the lengthening afternoon shadows, there was time to consider the facts. Had True been reckless enough to hazard a crossing on such a narrow path? If he had fallen to his death, as the general suggested, why did someone move his body down the treacherous path and then forfeit the reward? Why did it take so long for someone to come across his corpse? In the sun and heat, it takes only a few days for decomposition to set in, but True appeared to have been dead longer than that.

Perhaps robbery was the motive, I thought. The backpack and its contents remained missing. A camping stove, tent, rainproof garments, cash, the camera, binoculars—there were plenty of items in the pack that were beyond the reach of all but a few Huichols. But why would anyone risk his life to drag a badly decomposed body down such a steep canyon? It must have taken several strong Huichols who knew the land to accomplish the task. Why not steal his backpack and bury him on the mesa or leave the corpse for authorities to retrieve?

Then there was the telltale trail of feathers that led us to his hidden grave. Whoever moved the corpse must have done so under cover of darkness, stuffing the corpse inside the sleeping bag and then using the ground cloth to drag the heavy weight down into the canyon, unaware they were leaving behind a Hansel and Gretel trail of evidence. No, whoever brought True to the banks of the Chapalagana intended that his grave never be found.

If Díaz had not happened across the body on December 13, two days earlier, whoever moved True would have succeeded. There is little chance soldiers would have come across the spot where True allegedly fell or found the traces of blood and other evidence. Whoever did this almost got away with it.

We lingered three hours, waiting. There was plenty of time to think and take notes, but no simple answers to the questions materialized. I walked back over toward the grave, pulled on my face mask and checked on True, as if there were anything I could do. I bent down and rested my hand on the ground cloth for a moment and felt the corpse through the vinyl. It seemed important to touch True in this strange wilderness where he died alone. Reaching into my pack, I pulled out a small plastic film canister and filled it with sand and placed it carefully back in the bottom of my pack to give to Martha.

A loud splash followed by whooping and laughter startled me. A Huichol boy, perhaps 17, surfaced in the pool just as I turned, shaking the water from his long, slick hair. He beckoned to the others, assuring them the water was not so cold. Another Huichol finally stood up and dived in, surfacing in a howl of words and swimming quickly to the rocks to get out. All the Huichols laughed.

I was filthy and tired. My hands and clothes stank. I thought about stripping down for a swim. There was soap and a change of clothes inside my backpack. But I hesitated. Díaz had said the river was a well-known spiritual destination for the Huichols, and while the teenage swimmers weren't acting particularly spiritual, I refrained. It was their place, not mine. So far I hadn't done anything to offend them. Keep it that way, I told myself, wondering how much longer we would be together in the canyon.

As the afternoon advanced, a breeze brought a chill to the air. The sun was starting to dip below the mesas west of us. There was still plenty of daylight, but temperatures would drop quickly in the canyon. "We should have asked the general to let us keep the handheld radio," I said to the captain. "I hope they get back here soon. No pilot is going to descend in the dark, and I'd hate to spend the night here."

"*Hombre*, don't even say that," he said.

Not long after I spoke, we heard the faint sound of an approaching helicopter. Minutes passed, but it didn't seem to come any closer. We had the same look on our face: please don't pass us by.

Then three helicopters appeared as black dots in the sky. Two were small, but the third was a large, Soviet-built transport. It looked enormous. Setting it down in the canyon would test the crew's skill.

The choppers descended one by one, using a sandbar a hundred yards upstream where the canyon bottom widened. We watched as soldiers escorting a medical team headed toward us. The technicians were dressed in white jackets and carried medical bags and equipment. Soldiers hefted spades and a stretcher.

The Huichols remained knotted together on the rocks. They seemed as excited as us to watch the helicopters, but the presence of armed soldiers made them uneasy.

A young lieutenant had replaced the general as the ranking officer. He ordered a detail of three soldiers to begin digging and he dispatched others to scramble up the slope far enough to establish a perimeter guard. Working from three sides, the soldiers quickly exposed the entire corpse.

The chief pathologist of Nayarit, who was among those in the arriving helicopter, ordered a portion of the ground cloth and sleeping bag cut away so he could inspect the corpse.

I have seen many war dead, but what we saw shocked me, perhaps because this was my reporter and I would have to tell Martha about the condition of Philip's remains.

The corpse was black and bruised, and the swollen skin was split open at various points. It could have been anybody. There was no face, no eyes, no ears, only the black specter of a skull covered with rotting flesh. The vultures had ravaged every distinguishing feature. The outline of blackened nose cartilage was all that remained. The scalp was slick with leaking body fluids. Gas audibly escaped as the forensics team struggled with the ground cloth. A fluid-soaked bandana, its faded red color still visible, stretched tightly around the badly swollen throat.

"How tall was your reporter, about two meters?" the pathologist asked me.

I paged through my notes to confirm True's height and weight, 5′11″ and 165 pounds. This corpse looked like a giant.

"Just under that," I said. "This body looks a lot bigger than that."

"It's just the state of decomposition," he told me. "I would estimate he has been dead for eight to ten days."

"How can you tell that?" I asked, not believing True had been dead for so long. If the pathologist was right, True had been dead for four or five days before Martha sounded the alarm. Nothing we did would have made any difference.

"Look here," he said, drawing me closer.

I gagged as I saw maggots swarming inside his flesh.

"They appear after about eight days," he said, "but they don't appear to have been on the body for too many days."

As his assistants unrolled more of the ground cloth, they exposed True's extremities.

"His jeans are pulled down," I cried. "How did that happen in a hiking accident? His boots are missing, too."

"It probably happened when he was dragged down the canyon," the pathologist said. "That's probably how he got all these bruises and other injuries."

The police captain nodded in agreement. Dr. Ramirez stood by quietly, listening, his face as expressionless as the surrounding rocks.

I felt outnumbered. Everyone seemed to be trying awfully hard to rationalize True's death as a hiking accident. That might make life simpler, but it seemed increasingly doubtful.

The pathologist asked if I had any information that might help with a positive identification of True. I turned back to my notes. Martha said he was wearing a simple, inexpensive wedding band on his left hand, a second simple black ring on his right hand, and a Swiss Army watch with a cloth watchband on his right wrist. An assistant lifted his hand. An inexpensive wedding band, also blackened, was on his ring finger. One of the assistants wiped at the watch face, enough for everyone to see the telltale Swiss red cross.

"Everything matches, the rings, the watch, the sleeping bag and the ground cloth," I said. "Who else could it be?"

"I would say the presence of the watch and wedding band confirms he died in an accident and was buried here by locals," the pathologist said. "If they were robbers, why did they leave the watch?"

I looked at him and the police captain in disbelief. I was still furious at the condition of True's remains, which had lain in the wilds for days, unattended. "You haven't even seen the place where he died and you're calling this an accident," I argued. "There is no way someone would have dragged him this far down such a dangerous path. Where is his backpack, his camera, his money? Why didn't the people who buried him claim the reward money?"

I was confused. Seeing the ring and watch made me think robbery might not have been the motive. Could Huichols tell time? Did they wear jewelry? I didn't know anything about them, really. "What about all these Huichols over there?" I demanded, looking at the lieutenant. "Aren't you going to take their names and question them?"

"The investigation will come later," he answered. "Right now our orders are to remove the body and transport it to Tepic for autopsy."

The medical assistants wrapped the ground cloth loosely around the corpse and, with the help of several soldiers, lifted True into a body bag. They then sealed the corpse in large plastic garbage bags and wrapped it once more in a white cotton blanket, which they tightly taped.

I walked past the Huichols and climbed up the rocks to where two soldiers had been posted guard. They were sneaking a cigarette, keeping an eye out for the lieutenant. The pilots fired up the helicopters and the officer motioned everyone aboard. Soldiers ferried the enshrouded remains by stretcher to the transport chopper, ducking low as they reached the open doorway. I took more photographs.

There were two empty benches along each wall inside the large transport. Dr. Ramirez and I climbed in together. Two soldiers huddled near the front of the craft. True's bundled corpse lay on the metal floor at the rear. I sat down and buckled my seat belt, just as the lieutenant climbed aboard and sat down next to me.

I waved to the Huichols through the open entryway as we took off. They didn't wave back. It no longer mattered. We had found True and we were leaving the Chapalagana together. The drama of the Sierra Madre, which had enthralled me hours earlier, now held little appeal.

The lieutenant had reluctantly agreed to detour to San Miguel to drop off Dr. Ramirez and pick up Hayward before we flew on to Tepic, where I expected to find Chase. Dozens of Huichols were waiting as the pilot set down the helicopter on the same dirt field we had visited that morning, which now seemed a long time ago. The lieutenant jumped out with his rifle even before we settled to the ground. He waved at Hayward to hurriedly board, as Dr. Ramirez and I shook hands and said farewell. As she walked toward the helicopter, a tall, lanky young man with blond dreadlocks trailing below his shoulders gestured wildly at me as he tried to make his way around soldiers blocking his path.

"Take me with you, please," he shouted. "I am Philip Truempler, please don't leave me here."

It was the Swiss anthropologist, although he looked suspiciously more like a peyote-seeking hippie than a scientist to me, who had mistakenly been taken out of the sierra and brought to the military base in Guadalajara the previous evening. Apparently one of the military helicopters traveling from Guadalajara to San Miguel had brought him back. Unfortunately he was now a considerable distance from Guadalupe Ocatán, with no practical means of making his way back.

Hayward stood near the door, hesitating. "He will have to make his own way back," she said. "That seems cruel."

"I hope he doesn't have to pass by Amoltita," I said.

I gestured toward Truempler, feeling sorry for him, and pointed to the lieutenant, as if to signal that it was not my decision. The lieutenant looked at me and shook his head. The Mexican army had completed its mission as ordered by Los Pinos and was not doing the *Express-News* any more favors.

I reached out the open bay of the helicopter and extended my hand to Hayward, hoisting her into a seat on the hard, narrow bench of the troop transport. We were alone for the ride to Tepic, except for the same two soldiers seated near the flight crew.

Her face filled with horror as she looked down and saw our lifeless cargo. She began to sob. I put my arm around her shoulder. We were both tired, feeling the fatigue that sets in when all the possibilities are played out.

The chopper rose quickly. Truempler jumped up and down, waving his arms, his long, blond dreadlocks flying around his head, his shouts inaudible as he pleaded futilely for a ride out of San Miguel, his height and white skin causing him to stand out among a small sea of Huichol onlookers as we climbed and banked toward the west.

"We wouldn't have found Philip without all the hard work you and the others did," I said. "We're bringing him home to Martha."

For the rest of the ride back to Tepic, we sat together in silence, reality sinking in, True's corpse at our feet.

10

Two Autopsies

Look, I have been doing this a long time and the bodies of accident victims don't get moved with their *pantalones* around their knees.

—Dr. Mario Rivas Souza, coroner

I tell you, the order to have a second autopsy, to bring the remains to Mexico City, to bring in an FBI observer, that all happened without our involvement. We didn't know anything about that.

—David Nájera, President Zedillo's foreign press liaison

The early evening air was still warm and sticky at the small military installation in Tepic where we landed. Three young soldiers loaded True's remains into the back of a waiting truck, at first gagging, then laughing as they complained and wrestled with the awkward load. We were weary and I had to stop myself from snapping at them. They were young and the task was unpleasant. They meant no disrespect.

Hayward and I climbed into a second vehicle and followed the truck to an empty wooden barrack. A base officer suggested we make ourselves comfortable and then left, promising to return momentarily. Scattered pieces of office furniture were stacked against the walls. True's corpse was deposited on the cleanly swept wooden floor like one more piece of inventory. There was nowhere to sit, except on the front steps.

Fred Chase had been waiting there since departing with the general on the first helicopter out of the canyon. For the first time, the three of us were together. The intensity of the day was wearing off as we idled on the base. The long, challenging hike and canyon descent, the search for True's remains, and the removal of his corpse from the hidden grave had occupied my attention. Now we were left to brood, cranky with hunger and uncertainty as darkness settled in. We had been told there wasn't time to walk into town for a meal, but then we were left waiting for hours. Something was amiss.

We asked to speak with General Eulalio Fonseca Orozco, but were told he was unavailable. Another officer emerged to inform us that a review of the map coordinates confirmed True's gravesite was in the state of Jalisco, close to the Nayarit border. We were welcome to join a convoy of vehicles transporting the corpse to Guadalajara where civil authorities would conduct the autopsy. Fonseca, we were told, had left hours ago.

The road to Guadalajara was jammed with traffic. Our driver employed flashing lights and a siren to pass trucks and second-class buses slowly grinding up the steep inclines. As we reached the outskirts of the city, a television crew in a van pulled alongside and blinded us with a bright spotlight. A cameraman leaned out the rear window and began filming. Our midnight arrival would not be a quiet one.

The three-vehicle convoy maneuvered onto a secondary street and parked outside the nondescript state forensics laboratory. The press was waiting in force. Klieg lights snapped on and a camera crew surrounded us. A reporter thrust a long, foam-covered microphone in my face: "Was Philip True murdered, Señor Rivard?" she asked breathlessly. I wondered how she knew my name.

"We don't know what happened, so we will await the results of the autopsy," I said. "We do want to thank President Zedillo, the civil authorities in Nayarit and Jalisco, and the Mexican army for helping us find Philip and then bringing him out of the Chapalagana."

She said it was strange that True had been buried deep in the Chapalagana.

"We don't believe it was the act of a Good Samaritan," I answered.

"Do you blame the Huichols?" she asked.

I didn't answer.

Fatigue was setting in, but it was important to avoid a Mexican reporter's offer to point the finger of blame. We knew something bad had befallen True, but we couldn't sort it out yet. The specter of a U.S. newspaper editor appearing on Mexican television and leveling accusations could quickly turn the Mexican government and public against us. We wanted authorities to get to the bottom of True's death without distractions. I was aware that the traditional arm's length distance separating myself as a journalist from government officials had been breached. This was not the first or last time in the True case we would find ourselves asking the government for help even as we questioned its willingness or ability to win justice in the case.

True's corpse was unloaded from the ambulance truck and taken inside as cameras filmed the scene. I said a silent prayer that Martha was not watching television. We later found out that she first learned of Philip's death from a U.S. embassy official that afternoon even before Chase called.

To our surprise, no one tried to stop Chase or me as we followed the gurney with True's corpse into the examination room. A guard nonchalantly waved us through when I identified myself as True's editor.

While Hayward went off to finish filing the story she had written in San Miguel and Tepic, we descended into a large room below street level that smelled of formaldehyde. The door was open to let in the cool night air, but inside it was dank and foul. A dead man, the victim of a gunshot wound to the head, lay uncovered and face up on a steel table.

Medical staff summoned for the True autopsy milled around, oblivious to the naked corpse, gossiping, laying out instruments for the procedure. The room was crowded with police, drivers, hangers-on, and Mexican reporters. All seemed oblivious to the dead man lying there, a grotesque entry wound visible on his disfigured forehead. A wide seam of stitches ran down his torso where pathologists had sewn him closed after the routine examination. There was little doubt about cause of death.

"What happened to him?" I asked one of the medical staff, peering at the bullet hole just beneath a sweep of thick, wavy hair.

"Just a fight at a bar, and the other guy had a pistol," he said, shrugging. "One bullet. No name. No one has claimed him."

Surely our presence there violated all the rules, but we wanted to know the truth. If they let us stay, we intended to watch, if we could stomach it. Several young medical students lifted the mummy-shaped bundle off the gurney and onto the steel table under a bright overhead light.

The general commotion and chatter died down as a tall, white-haired man with heavy-rimmed eyeglasses and a trim mustache entered the room, the open tails of his lab coat trailing behind him. A medical technician holding a video camera began to record the scene, panning from the unwrapped corpse across the group of a several dozen forensics students. His camera came to rest on the older man who had taken his place next to the corpse and obviously was in charge.

Dr. Mario Rivas Souza was the venerable and sometimes controversial chief forensic pathologist for the state of Jalisco. Still tall and erect at age 72, he was an independent-minded, outspoken figure, not widely admired by authorities in the ruling party. Rivas Souza also held the title of senior forensics professor at the University of Guadalajara medical school and later told Hayward he had participated in more than 80,000 autopsies. Such a claim suggested hyperbole. He must have been a busy pathologist, performing approximately three autopsies every day of his seventy-two years. Anything, of course, is possible.

Rivas Souza was outspoken in a profession where discretion is rewarded and higher authorities decide what is divulged to the press and public. He had first gained attention five years earlier when Cardinal Juan Jesús Posadas Ocampo, the archbishop of Guadalajara, was killed in a hail of automatic weapon fire while seated in his chauffeured sedan at Guadalajara's international airport. Rivas Souza was called on to perform the autopsy in a tense, highly politicized atmosphere. The Vatican and governments around the world awaited developments with great interest.

The sensational murder of a cardinal threatened to undermine the international stature Salinas had labored to win as an advocate of free trade in the global marketplace. Political killings, especially unsolved killings, suggest an absence of the rule of law, which can lead foreign investors to flee with their badly needed investment capital.

Controversy surrounded the case from the outset. Federal authorities advanced the theory that Cardinal Posadas was caught in the crossfire between triggermen working for feuding drug lords. If the hitmen did target Posadas, they said, it was only because the prelate physically resembled their intended target.

Rivas Souza conducted his examination and dismissed the government's dubious scenario. The cardinal, he announced, was clearly the target, hit in the chest at close range by no less than fourteen bullets. His killers stood directly in front of him as they fired.

Guadalajara had become the undeclared drug capital of Mexico by the 1980s. The attendant turf wars, shootouts, and kidnappings transformed the city from a quiet, conservative state capital surrounded by small towns favored by foreign retirees to a place seemingly controlled by gangsters beyond the government's touch.

Rivas Souza also had autopsied slain DEA agent Enrique Camarena, whose decomposing remains were not recovered until long after he had been kidnapped, tortured, and executed in 1985. His murder was a brutal message from the cartels to U.S. law enforcement as well as the Mexican government, which allowed foreign agents to operate on Mexican soil. The maverick pathologist refused to downplay the horrible nature of Camarena's suffering during extended torture sessions. Later, captured tape recordings of the torture and interrogation sessions confirmed his findings.

Now, as we stood on the edge of the circle surrounding the examination table, Rivas Souza began speaking into a handheld microphone as the camera rolled. He introduced himself and his fellow pathologist, Dr. Luis Valtierra Estrada, who would actually take the lead in the autopsy.

We donned face masks as an assistant cut away the plastic ground cloth and sleeping bag. Rivas Souza and Valtierra drew close and examined the red bandana knotted tightly around True's neck. They cut if off, revealing a deep channel cut into True's neck. The bandana, a key piece of evidence, later disappeared.

True's denim jeans, pulled down around his knees and opened, drew considerable attention. As the last of his clothes were cut away, a number of students were enlisted to turn the corpse onto its back. The sight of an erect penis caused members of the forensics team to crowd around the body. I asked why everyone suddenly grew so interested. "The presence of an erection indicates possible sexual assault in the anus," one of them told me.

Rivas Souza called for a long swab. The anus protruded as if it had been pulled out forcibly.

"He's testing for sperm," the same man said.

Rivas Souza briefly eyed the withdrawn swab and then handed it to an assistant, who placed it a sample tube.

We watched as True's scalp was separated from his skull and his chest and abdominal cavity were opened to extract his organs. Rivas Souza spent some time studying True's extremities, which were covered with small bruises. His skin seemed to have been cut in numerous places.

As the procedure continued, local investigators appeared at my side and asked that I accompany them across the street to give a statement. For the next thirty minutes I sat next to a typist who pecked away at a manual typewriter while struggling to construct a narrative of the day's events. "Why don't you turn that typewriter around and let me write my statement and save us both time?" I suggested.

"That's prohibited, _señor_," he told me.

"Then read back to me what I just told you," I demanded.

It came as no surprise that what the clerk read aloud was nothing like what I had told him. Instead he had fashioned an inexact summary of events in the vernacular of the local police. I flinched as I heard him declare that I did not think a crime had been committed. "That's not what I said," I told him. "I said I wasn't going to make a final judgment until I knew the autopsy results."

We were at a standoff.

A supervisor happened to be passing by in the company of a prostitute. He was carrying an old six-shooter with a broken grip, dangling it from a single finger wrapped through the trigger guard, chatting casually with the woman, who greeted the clerk by first name and appeared to know everyone.

Both the clerk and I appealed to the supervisor. The clerk wanted to proceed according to custom. I refused to sign any statement that was not, word for word, what I had said. The supervisor mentioned that Chase had refused to cross the street to give a statement. If I spoke to Chase, he said, the clerk would start over.

As the clerk angrily sat back down at his typewriter, Chase appeared in the room. "Hey Fred, I know they are incompetent, but why don't you cooperate and give them a brief statement, just to keep the peace?" I asked.

Chase was ready to explode. "They don't want to hear what I have to say," he warned.

"What's wrong, Fred?"

"I'll tell you what was wrong: it wasn't a hiking accident. The doctor just told me Philip was murdered. He was strangled and sexually abused."

It was the second time in a day Chase's words had stopped me in my tracks. Our worst fears were true. I stood up to leave. As the clerk protested, I signed the sheet and told him the interview was over. "Give me a copy of that," I demanded, taking one of the thin copies of paper. I wanted to speak with Rivas Souza.

We raced back across the street. The room was nearly empty, save for a few medical students examining and weighing True's organs on a table. Rivas Souza was bent over a sink in the far corner, lathering his hands and forearms.

"Yes, I am sorry, your reporter's death is a homicide, no doubt," Rivas Souza said as I drew him aside. "Unofficially speaking, of course, because I have not filed my written report," he told me, "this is a clear homicide. It was evident from the outset."

"How can you be sure?" I asked.

"Look, I have been doing this a long time and the bodies of accident victims don't get moved with their *pantalones* around their knees," Rivas Souza said, in what I would come to appreciate was his famously blunt manner of speaking.

He also noted that the bandana was tied from behind in a tight double knot used by Huichols, which differs from a Western-style knot.

"Hay más," he told us as we followed him to the back corner where True's corpse lay, making space for the next arrival. There was more.

He peeled back the rotting scalp and exposed the bone-white skull. A harsh, circular red spot the size of a softball covered the back of the cranium. "He was struck very hard in the back of a skull, perhaps with a rock, perhaps with something else. The blood is an indication he was struck while still alive, but the bone is not broken so this probably is not why he died," Rivas Souza said. "Furthermore, he could not have died in a fall. If he had fallen while still alive, he would have broken bones, bruised organs, and internal bleeding. There is none of that. He was a dead man when he went over that cliff."

The team had carefully examined the inner lining of True's throat, Rivas Souza added, leading us back to the middle of the room toward the students. "Look at these lines," he said, unfolding the dissected throat tissue. Thin, bloody striations lined the interior flesh, telltale signs, according to Rivas Souza, that True had been strangled. His killers had done it with True's own bandana.

"There was no evidence of semen in the anus," Rivas Souza said. "They could have violated him with a stick after he was unconscious or dead."

"Is it possible all these cuts and bruises are the result of torture?" I asked.

"It is possible, but it also could be defensive wounds and also the result of dragging the body in its decomposed state for such a long distance," he said.

We nodded and thanked Rivas Souza for his work. "We especially appreciate your honesty," I said as we shook hands.

"I am not going to lie," Rivas Souza said. "I am sorry about your friend the journalist." He would await the lab tests and issue his report within a week.

Chase and I walked out, numbed by the news and the specter of watching a roomful of strangers autopsy True's unrecognizable corpse. Now there was nothing left to do. The deserted streets were vaguely unsettling at 2:00 A.M. We had no way of getting to the Hotel Fiesta Americana, where we had reserved rooms.

One of the medical technicians pulled up in his small sedan to pick up a colleague. Sensing our plight, he offered us a ride in his overcrowded car. Just as we began to squeeze in, two burly men in leather jackets approached the vehicle and ordered us to stop. I turned around, surprised. The men looked hostile and both wore sidearms. They didn't identify themselves. "Can you tell us where you have been for the past ten days?" one of them asked.

Exhaustion and disbelief made me laugh derisively as I looked at the two men, who resembled character actors in a B movie. The investigation had begun. No stone would be left unturned. Everyone was suspect.

"Who are you?" I asked.

"Investigators," they replied.

"I'll tell you where we've been," I said. "We've been in the sierra searching for our reporter. Where have you been for the past few days? Why don't you go up there and find the men who killed him?"

The two investigators stared for a moment, then turned and left.

Back at the hotel, we found Hayward, but we were too beaten up to talk much. None of us had eaten anything since the previous day, and we needed to shower and change clothes. First we had to call Martha and tell her Philip was murdered. We didn't want her to hear the news watching television or from a reporter's call.

Chase said he wanted to make the call to Martha, reminding me he was Philip's best friend. I looked at him. Chase, a tightly wound guy, intuitively suspected murder earlier than I, and his pent-up anger had threatened to boil over all day, complicating things from the time he came on to the helicopter, making it harder to maintain peace with the general, himself a tense bantam of a man. But Chase also was a man with a big heart, the kind of loyal friend few of us ever find. He had come a long way to help find True and bring him home. It was selfless of him to offer to call Martha. How do you break the news to someone that her husband was murdered, possibly tortured and sexually assaulted? It would be hard to offer much consolation in such a moment.

Martha had been prepared for the worst, and Chase said she took the news as well as could be expected. Afterward, I spoke briefly with Martha and Juanita, though I had little to offer. Martha was like a rock, amazingly composed and clearheaded. Anyone else would have been a basket case. She thanked me for coming to Mexico and helping find Philip. She and Juanita were coming to Guadalajara the next day to claim Philip's body. She wanted to have him cremated as soon as possible. After a few more minutes, we said good night.

I shed my clothes and placed the foul-smelling laundry bag in the hallway outside my room, feeling guilty that an attendant would have to handle the clothes in the morning. For a long time I stood in the shower, trying to wash the stench from my body. The simple act of donning clean clothes, of buttoning a shirt, of zipping shut a pair of denims, somehow made me feel safe, reminded me I was alive. I felt awash in gratitude. It was nearly dawn now, and sleep seemed out of the question. I opened the windows to let in fresh air and survey the view seven floors below, an empty soccer field in the distance.

I retrieved my notebook. I had not made any notes since midway though the autopsy and I wanted to record the events of the last hours before memory played its tricks. I had written my name and home address on the reporter's notebook I grabbed before leaving San Antonio. Now that struck me as absurdly funny. Who did I think was going to mail the notebook to me had I lost it while hiking through the Chapalagana or even here in Guadalajara?

Hours later I woke up, sitting in my hotel room chair, notebook still in hand.

*

After breakfast, Chase and Hayward left to meet Martha and Juanita at the airport, while I grabbed a cab to the U.S. consulate. We were counting on consular officials to take on True's case and pressure Mexican authorities to pursue his killer or killers. No matter what they told me that morning, though, I knew Washington's interests would come first. It always works that way. American diplomats would not squeeze their trading partners to the south for the sake of one murder case. It sounds colder than it really is. The reality is that no government anywhere allows a single criminal case to define or over-shadow bilateral relations. What if our interests conflicted down the road, I wondered? We could retain our own lawyers, but what good would that do? An American newspaper makes an inviting target for anyone interested in an easy payday. How could we be sure our money was not being pocketed without any real work performed? Experience told me a thorough investigation would not happen by itself. Mexico was a country where the powerful were protected from the law and where the powerless feared those in power, especially those charged with keeping the law—the police, prosecutors, and judges. Consequently most murders went unsolved. There were at least a dozen pending cases that involved the murder of Mexican journalists. None were being pursued, even where there was evidence leading to the killers.

We didn't have to wait long for things to get complicated. Back in Mexico City, Zedillo administration officials were alarmed by Rivas Souza's findings. A murdered American journalist was a more serious matter than one killed in a hiking accident. If the killers were Huichols, administration officials faced yet another confrontation with members of an indigenous group who wanted to be left alone. Things were bad enough in Chiapas with the Zapatista rebels and the restless Mayans of the region, tired of endless land grabs, broken government promises, and countless other injustices that kept them in a permanent state of poverty.

The situation was further complicated by Mexico's lack of experience with political plurality. Zedillo had led the way in forcing his own party, the PRI, to respect the outcome of state and municipal elections, which had led to a steady increase in opposition governors and mayors taking office. The Jalisco governor came from the National Action Party (PAN), which was conservative, pro-business, and Catholic. Its candidates had won more and more gubernatorial and mayoral seats in recent years.

Before the PAN's rise, someone from the president's office would have picked up the telephone, issued orders to the local party bosses, and then sat back. Now officials from the two parties in the federal and state administrations found themselves without any real working connections or relationships, each having to contend with the other in a case suffused with political ramifications. Working together sounds simple, but you just don't flip a switch and turn on democracy after seven decades of one-party rule.

To make matters worse, Zedillo's team had been taken by surprise and learned of the unofficial homicide ruling on the morning television news. No one from the governor's office had bothered to call and brief the president's advisers. A story broadcast on the country's leading network, Televisa, included an on-camera interview with Rivas Souza, who did not mince words. "It is a homicide," he said. "It is not an accident."

It was a nightmare for Los Pinos. True was the first accredited American newspaper journalist ever to be murdered in Mexico. Unhappy officials braced for the worst as they were besieged with calls from the international press as well as the Mexican media.

At the consulate, officials introduced me to Dr. Phil Weigand, a noted U.S. anthropologist who had married a Mexican anthropologist and lived and worked in Mexico for three decades. They had lived among the Huichols for several years in the 1960s, had stayed in touch with their contacts in various Huichol communities, and were recognized experts in the field.

Weigand proved to be a valuable tutor. I summarized True's story proposal and the background leading up to his solo trek into the Huichol sierra. Weigand was the first to express surprise that True, who had previously visited the Huichols, would venture into the sierra without a Huichol guide and official approval from Huichol authorities. Such permission, he said, was nonnegotiable, even for outsiders who were known from past visits. Yet he could not recall a single instance where a trespasser had met with violence, much less death. Most unwelcome visitors were simply expelled.

He offered me a view of Huichol society that differed from what True had written. Weigand agreed with many of True's observations about the more appealing aspects of the culture, but he also talked about the historic tensions between the Huichols and outsiders. Any larger appreciation of the Huichols, he said, had to include the land wars with mestizo ranchers earlier in the century and the invasion of peyote-seeking American hippies in the 1960s. Huichols, Weigand said, had spent decades staving off unscrupulous mestizos who coveted their land to graze cattle or cultivate poppies and marijuana.

The Huichols, as well as all other indigenous groups, were mindful of the treatment they received when they left their own communities. Huichols forced by economic necessity to hawk folk art in the cities or work as pickers on lowland tobacco farms were treated like second-class citizens, or worse.

Mexico celebrates its indigenous roots, but reality is something else. Throughout its history, Mexico has mistreated its Indians. Many Mexicans consider indigenous people little more than savages. Mexico's mosaic of Indian groups—and there are hundreds, each with its own history, language, and culture—occupy the lowest rungs of the social ladder. Most upper-class Mexicans consider it a point of pride to describe themselves as Spanish in origin, thereby differentiating themselves from Mexicans of mixed ancestry.

"The report of sexual assault with a stick, however, suggests the killing was the work of mestizos," Weigand said, adding that such brutality was more in keeping with drug traffickers sending a message to outsiders rather than anything characteristic of Huichols. "The Huichols are capable of violence, of course, just like anyone else. But if that were the case, the probability is that alcohol was involved and that it was not premeditated."

Martha, Hayward, and Chase joined us at the consulate, and for a few minutes everyone exchanged sympathies. Shortly after their arrival, however, we were informed that the Zedillo administration was intervening in the state criminal case. True's remains would be transferred to federal custody and flown to Mexico City so a second autopsy could be performed. It was a precaution, we were told, and the federal attorney general's office had agreed to allow a forensics expert hired by the FBI to observe the procedure. Dr. Emma Lew, the assistant coroner in Dade County, was flying down the next day from Miami. The news caught me by surprise, sinking in slowly beneath the fatigue and shock. Higher powers, I realized, were intervening for political reasons. It was becoming more than just a murder case.

"What's wrong with the first autopsy?" I asked.

Consular officials told us about the strained relationship between Rivas Souza and the ruling party. In short, Zedillo administration officials wanted their own independent examination separate from a state government they did not control or trust. Later, officials close to the president would deny the federal government conducted its own parallel investigation, but a cable from consular offices to the State Department released years later told a different story. The morning after the Rivas Souza autopsy, Lieutenant Colonel Roberto Aguilera, chief of police of the Mexican army at the defense ministry, appeared in Guadalajara to ensure a timely transfer of True's remains from state custody to federal control.

"He informed post that he had come at the request of President Zedillo," a U.S. official in Guadalajara informed Washington. "He explained that although the state of Jalisco still had jurisdiction in the case, President Zedillo had recommended that federal authorities assist by performing a second autopsy and conducting a parallel investigation. Lieutenant Colonel Aguilera said that his investigation results would be provided to the state of Jalisco as well as to the consulate general."

Aguilera told consular officials that he already had investigators in the sierra at the crime scene. The official who wrote the cable concluded by noting, "Comment: State authorities have devoted

considerable time and energy to this case, but the federal involvement has added considerable resources. The office of President
Zedillo has clearly taken the leading role in the investigation."

Rivas Souza was the old man of forensics in Guadalajara and a
widely known teacher, consular officials told Martha and me. But
some considered him a loose cannon who looked a bit too comfortable in front of a television camera.

International press groups had begun a public campaign on behalf
of True while he was still missing and presumed alive, and now they
were calling on the Zedillo administration to solve the crime. Officials
in Mexico City wanted to issue their own ruling.

Back at the hotel, I called Larry Walker, the *Express-News* publisher, and recounted events since we had last spoken. We discussed
the government's decision to conduct a second autopsy, and I mentioned Martha's plan to hold a memorial service at her home. I raised
the possibility of returning with her to Mexico City to await the eventual release of the remains and to represent the newspaper at the service. We didn't know how long that would take, but I felt guilty about
leaving her alone in Mexico. Walker said I had accomplished what I
had set out to do in Mexico, and my place was back in the San Antonio
newsroom. I reluctantly agreed to fly home, a decision I came to regret
when the remains were released one day later and Martha held her
memorial on Saturday, the day after I arrived home in San Antonio.

I booked a flight to Mexico City to return to my hotel there and
collect my baggage. That night in Guadalajara we had a quiet dinner in
the hotel, more of a family gathering than a meal. In such moments,
the details and logistics are a blessing, giving everyone something to
talk about and fill the space otherwise occupied by grief and emotion.
We checked out Friday morning, and consular officials arrived at the
hotel to escort us to the private side of the airport. Two executive jets
belonging to the federal attorney general's office were parked on the
tarmac, one to carry True's remains back to Mexico City, the other
reserved for Martha and Juanita. David Nájera, the president's liaison
with the foreign press, was there with other federal officials.

We watched as workers from the coroner's office loaded True's remains, now encased in a rubber body bag, onto a wheeled gurney that was rolled up to the rear baggage hold. Two crew members leaned out and hoisted the bag aboard. Seeing True's remains loaded like cargo hit home for everyone. It was a depressing moment, and we hugged and said good-bye. Chase and Manuel Obaya, Martha's brother-in-law who had returned from Monterrey, boarded the jet with True's remains. Martha and Juanita ascended the stairs of the second airplane.

I watched the two jets taxi and take off, and then accepted a ride to the bustling commercial terminal where life was proceeding as if nothing had happened. Families awaited arriving relatives, passengers hurried to their gates, and departing tourists browsed the tequila displays in the duty-free stores. As I checked in, however, airline employees and security guards glanced my way, remarking among themselves. The local television news was playing the story over and over, showing our late-night arrival with the body, the woman reporter asking me if I thought the Huichols killed True, and Rivas Souza's declaration that True had been murdered.

"I'm sorry about your reporter," the counter agent said, looking at me with sympathy.

There wasn't much to say. I had developed an abiding love for Mexico since arriving at the border twenty-five years earlier and finding my first newspaper job. Guadalajara had been the scene of some memorable family times. Now I wanted to leave and never come back.

My driver was waiting at the Mexico City airport. As I walked back into the hotel I felt the stares of other guests as I stepped out with my dusty backpack, rumpled clothes, and hiking boots. I didn't look like a Four Seasons client. Yet the hotel staff had thoughtfully packed up my belongings in my absence and now declined to charge me for my room. There had been no time to pack and check out when the call came from Los Pinos to meet General Fonseca. Now the sympathetic gestures of hotel employees made me feel badly about the anti-Mexican sentiment I felt welling up inside myself.

A pile of faxes was waiting, copies of stories about the case, more calls from reporters. George W. Bush, the two-term governor of Texas, had offered his condolences on Thursday through a senior adviser, Karen Hughes.

Monika met me at the San Antonio airport and brought me home. We enjoyed a simple supper with our boys. I had been gone five days, but it seemed much longer. It was impossible not to compare my circumstances, surrounded by family, with Martha's devastating loss.

The second autopsy was performed Saturday in Mexico City shortly after Dr. Lew arrived from Miami. Sensitivities in the case were multiplying, and Los Pinos issued a press release claiming that Zedillo had not ordered the second autopsy, as had been widely reported. Rather, the decision had been made by the attorney general's office which, after all, was part of his administration and headed by Jorge Madrazo Cuellar, a member of Zedillo's cabinet. About the same time, Madrazo's office issued its own contradictory statement affirming that it had conducted the second autopsy, while declaring that it was not intervening in the state investigation. The same Alice in Wonderland press release also stated that it was Madrazo's office, not the U.S. embassy, that had invited Dr. Lew to observe. The FBI, the statement added, was not investigating a death on Mexican soil as reported in the local press. A second release followed the very next day, stating that Madrazo's office was now working alongside state authorities. It also clarified Dr. Lew's presence, saying that Mexican officials had consented to a request by the U.S. embassy to have an FBI consultant present during the second autopsy even though the FBI would not be permitted to play any role in the case. There was an Orwellian quality to the flurry of statements and counterstatements, all stemming from historic Mexican sensitivities to any perception that U.S. authorities, onetime invaders and occupiers, were exerting any influence south of the border.

Before the second autopsy was performed, Clinton administration officials issued comments through an unnamed State Department spokesman. Clinton himself said nothing, a disappointment. Any presidential comment would be front-page news in Mexico and would serve to pressure Mexican investigators.

Ambassador Davidow was in Washington when the search and recovery efforts took place, but he called me in San Antonio after he returned to Mexico City. The ambassador said he was determined to push for prosecution of True's killers and that he had urged officials in Washington to speak out and send a strong signal of concern and interest to Los Pinos. But he was candid. "If you don't stay on the Mexicans, nothing will happen," he said. "They'll drop the case."

A State Department spokesman in Washington that Friday had told reporters the administration was following the case very closely. "We have seen the news accounts indicating that Mr. True was murdered and have been informed by the coroner in Guadalajara that the cause of death was strangulation," the spokesman said. "While we reserve making a judgment until the final report of the Mexican authorities is made, we are very disturbed by what appears to be the violent demise of a journalist who had undertaken an effort to report on a little-covered region of Mexico. Mr. True's death has saddened all his friends in Mexico City, including those in the embassy who knew him well."

The *Express-News* had placed announcements in several Mexican newspapers expressing appreciation for the government's assistance in the search. Before leaving Mexico, we announced that Díaz, the Huichol hunter, would be paid the 10,000 pesos as a reward for finding True. We also offered a second payment to anyone who provided authorities with information leading to the arrest of True's killers. I couldn't help thinking of the Huichols who had led us to the canyon bottom on Wednesday, wondering if one might come forward.

Rivas Souza, meanwhile, told reporters from Mexico City and Guadalajara newspapers that he could no longer discuss his homicide ruling because an unnamed official with the Zedillo administration had ordered him to shut up. "The order just arrived from Mexico City for me to not give out information of any kind," Rivas Souza told reporters, who had asked him to expand on his earlier comments about the autopsy. "Those are the kinds of details that they ordered me not to give out. Forgive me, but those are the orders."

From afar, it was becoming hard to tell if the Zedillo administration was worried more about investigating the crime or limiting negative publicity. Years later, Nájera, working at the Mexican embassy in Belgium, admitted to me that he was the official who called Rivas Souza.

"There was a tendency on the part of this doctor to make controversial public statements. I think he saw himself as the protagonist in this drama," Nájera said. "My impression is that he enjoyed being the center of attention. I was listening to the radio or watching the television over the weekend, and he was being interviewed, and he suggested True's killing could have been an attack by homosexuals. He started to change his story, and the Mexican press now was speculating that True might have been a CIA agent or a DEA agent, and suddenly the whole world was speculating wildly."

Nájera said he had called Rivas Souza, intending only to reason with him and did not mean to intimidate the pathologist into silence. "I did call him, introduced myself and said, 'Please, I'm asking you, please don't make any more statements to the Mexican or foreign press.' He said, 'Okay, that's fine.' There was no fight or disagreement.

"The next day he told the press, 'I can't talk to you because the presidency has told me to shut my mouth.' I think my telephone call, in the end, contributed to the confusion that ensued," Nájera said, reflecting on how the case quickly became enshrouded in rumor and speculation. "But I tell you that the decision to bring the remains to Mexico City, to conduct a second autopsy, to bring in an FBI observer—that all happened without the president's involvement. We didn't know anything about that."

Did Nájera regret the Zedillo administration taking an active role in the case? He said that Mexican and U.S. embassy officials believed True's killing was a simple robbery and homicide, not something that would create tension between the two governments. But, he added, "the newspaper, Martha, and the Foreign Correspondents Association made it evident that it could become a bilateral scandal, depending on the outcome and our reaction."

As we talked more than five years after True's death, I posed the same question to myself that I had asked Nájera. Had our actions, however well intentioned, caused good people under intense pressure to make bad decisions with lasting consequences?

"Someone, I don't know who, in the federal attorney general's office or maybe in the presidency, decided, 'Let's do a second autopsy and clear up all this confusion,'" Nájera said. "I think, in retrospect, that the state pathologist in Guadalajara is deeply responsible for creating a situation that led to confusion instead of clarity. Everyone was worried that we'd never resolve what really happened."

For once at least, the Zedillo administration acted like the ruling party of old, taking matters into its own hands. Politics trumped the law.

The memorial service for True was held Sunday "in a backyard garden filled with the hibiscus and irises he nurtured and loved," John Mac-Cormack, True's friend and fellow reporter, wrote from Mexico City. Both he and Fred Bonavita, True's editor, were on hand to represent the newspaper amid the larger gathering of Martha's family, friends, and fellow journalists who came together to remember True's passion for hiking and telling the stories of people who had no one else to tell them.

A small makeshift altar stood near the entrance of the garden, covered with a brightly striped Mexican blanket. A handworked Oaxacan crucifix that Philip and Martha had found on a visit there was surrounded by cut flowers: purple irises, white carnations, yellow sunflowers, delicately blooming lilies, and pale roses. A reporter who knew of True's love for irises had placed dozens of them throughout the house and garden. The altar held photographs of True taken on assignment by *Express-News* photographers and a small snapshot of Philip and Martha on one of their many road trips. One photo showed True in a coat and tie, his official newspaper photograph. Another showed True, more typically clad in a T-shirt, with Fidel, his cranky parrot, perched on his shoulder.

Ochre-colored archways and floor tiles washed in a fading pink hue separated the small home from the large garden. Various correspondents in attendance came forward to remember and praise True.

Tim Padgett, a veteran Mexico City reporter first for *Newsweek* and then *Time* who compared True to Jack Kerouac, said True reminded him of a man he knew who traded secular life for the priesthood when his wife died after years of marriage. The priest, who found his calling late just as True did, converted Padgett to Catholicism. Padgett said both men brought other life experiences to their work, experiences that set the priest apart from other clerics and True from other reporters.

Tracey Eaton, the correspondent for the *Dallas Morning News,* spoke emotionally of his lost friend. Members of True's adopted family came forward to remember the American journalist whom they had welcomed into their fold.

"Philip came to our family through Martha, and it has always been a celebration whenever we were with them," said Ana María de la Garza, one of Martha's cousins from Matamoros. "He showed us that our country was his favorite. It was fascinating to hear him talk of Mexico with such admiration, him being a foreigner, and it was our luck and our country's good fortune that he was a voice for the foreign press. His journalistic work always filled us with satisfaction because we knew that the truth and love of Mexico always compelled him to write."

Obaya had spent a restless night in the True home, perusing Philip's bookshelf. He, too, was an outdoorsman. While many would question the wisdom of True's solo outing into the sierra, Obaya refused to second-guess his slain brother-in-law.

"Philip took many more risks in Mexico City as a journalist than he took on that trip," Obaya said. "I believe the whole thing was very bad luck. Unfortunately, he came across bad people, but he faced greater dangers from bad cops and criminals in Mexico City. Did he take a risk going alone? I don't deny that, but it wasn't the first time he made such a trip."

Obaya had come across True's worn copy of *The Complete Walker,* the trekker's bible. Now, as he stood before the gathering in True's garden, he read from its inscription:

Now shall I walk or shall I ride?
   "Ride," Pleasure said.
   "Walk," Joy replied.

Obaya recited the verse again, this time in Spanish.

¿Ahora, caminaré o pasearé?
   "Pasea," dijo El Placer:
   "Camina," replicó El Gozo.

True lived fifty years, and his life unfolded in distinct chapters: a boy trapped in a troubled family, a 1960s hippie who found his intellectual freedom on a Southern California campus, a blue-collar working man on Long Island, and finally a newspaperman, husband, and expatriate living on the border and in Mexico City. In the end, True accomplished more, personally and professionally, than he ever imagined he would. Throughout his life, True walked. Riding was for others. So too he had walked into his death and, in so doing, finally received the recognition and appreciation denied him most of his life.

Part 2

11

Who Killed Philip True?

> There are plenty of opportunities
> to lead a lonely life. Somebody's
> husband may never come home, may
> come home changed. A man might lose
> every friend and come home without
> much of himself inside his own skin.
>
> —Marlys West, "Details from the Southeast Quadrant,"
> *Borderlands: Texas Poetry Review*

While True was being commemorated in the garden memorial, I spent the morning in my office, reading coverage of the story in the Texas and national newspapers. Someone had dropped off a front page torn from the Sunday, December 6, edition of the *Express-News* with a story that True had filed on the eve of his trek. It proved to be his last byline. Later we would learn that it was published the very day True was murdered in the Sierra Madre.

AHUACUATLAN, Mexico – High in a valley here in the Sierra Gorda mountains of Queretaro and San Luis Potosi, a woman in a denim jumper and straw hat squeezes an ancient accordion and leads 150 schoolchildren in a laughing, clapping song.

No Sesame Street dropout, Martha Ruiz Corzo is a frontline

soldier in the fight to preserve the remnants of Mexico's fast-dis-appearing wildlife habitat.

"Unidos en la lucha por la Tierra, no nos moverán (United in the fight to save the Earth, we shall not be moved)," rang the verse that Ruiz, director of the Sierra Gorda Biosphere Reserve, sang with the children of the Jóse María Morelos Primary School.

Deforestation, overpopulation, streams and rivers awash in human waste and garbage now threaten Mexico's vast and diverse collection of plants, animals and resident and migratory birds.

If they are to be saved, it will be children like these, schooled in Earth-friendly principles of conservation, recycling and respon-sible reproduction, who ultimately will carry the battle, Ruiz said.

And here at the Jóse María Morelos Primary School, Ruiz's message seems to be taking root.

It was True's kind of story, one that celebrated the disappearing wilderness and the power of people, even children, to make a differ-ence. Looking back over True's life, it is easy to see his progression from student protestor to young strike organizer to mature reporter writing about a Mexican teacher and her clapping students. True would have chosen just such a story to be his last.

Express-News columnist Rick Casey caught True's spirit better than anyone else:

He had the two traits necessary to take a journalism career into middle age. One is intense curiosity, the fierce need to know. For most good reporters, writing is slow death. Research—the portfo-lio to go out and explore—is what revives you, repairs your spirit. Curiosity may have killed True, but it also gave his life intensity and joy. The other trait that sustains a veteran reporter is anger. If the world were the way it should be, there'd be no story. Anger provides the edge. Journalistic training just polishes that edge, provides techniques of fairness and analysis that raise writing from a primitive cry of the heart to reportage that can be relied on even by those who don't share the anger. . . Philip True had that anger.

Later I reread True's body of work from his six years at the *Express-News*. He wrote hundreds of stories about Mexico, but none of them were about the Huichols or the two previous trips he had made to their stretch of the sierra. It was one more mystery to ponder.

Monday was my first full day back at work. Editors sat quietly around an oval table in the second-floor conference room, awaiting the start of the afternoon page one meeting. The usual premeeting chatter and the clamor of late arrivals had been replaced with silence. People were waiting for me to say something. We couldn't just go to the day's news. Terry Scott Bertling, the senior editor for arts and lifestyle, softly remarked on everyone's appreciation of the newspaper's efforts to find True. "Can you tell us more about what really happened down there?" she asked.

No one in the room of editors, I realized, knew anything more than what they had read. Even in grief, newspaper people do not lose their curiosity, their need to know. Susana Hayward and I had been so involved in the search that we had paid too little attention to the story. No one had written a detailed account of the efforts by Manuel Obaya and Fred Chase, later joined by Hayward, as they crisscrossed the sierra in a small plane, landing here and there as they retraced True's intended route. The story about True's autopsy was written by a reporter in San Antonio and included only a few lines about our search party finding True's hidden grave after picking up the trail of feathers.

I found myself telling the story of how Chase and I dug with our hands to unearth True. It was the first time I had talked about it at any length, and it unleashed emotions. Heads bent down around the long rectangular table. Editors convene every day in newsrooms across the country to sketch out the next day's edition. At their best, the meetings are a free-spirited exchange of views punctuated with one-liners, a ritual that favors the quick of mind. It is not where editors come to tell stories and weep. But this day it was. The *Express-News* family had lost one of its own for the first time in its 133-year history, a record extending back to the end of the Civil War. True's death had affected each member of the newsroom, including people who had never met him but knew his work. Editors left the meeting as quietly as they had come.

Someone in the newsroom started *un altar de muerto*, a Mexican death altar. Such altars are adorned with objects that help mourners appreciate and honor a lost friend or family member. It began simply with a lighted votive candle and a framed photo of True. Day by day, hour by hour, it grew. Rick Hunter, the photographer who accompanied True to the mountain reserve on his final story, added the last photograph taken of True, standing on the edge of Sierra Gordo in central Mexico. Martha sent her husband's leather huaraches, which were placed alongside a reporter's notebook, True's story proposal, and a copy of his map of the Huichol sierra. I added my own *recuerdos*, or remembrances: the small vial of sand from True's grave and a few smooth river stones from the Chapalagana.

More votive candles appeared each day until the *altar de muerto* took on the appearance of an indoor grotto, a sort of spiritual retreat inside the newsroom. Fresh candles burned until the night editors shut down and left for home. Employees from all corners of the company came to pay their respects. It was not uncommon to see a pressman in uniform standing next to an editor in a shirt and tie, each lost in thought.

True's death transformed the newsroom in unspoken ways. For nearly six years we had been divided by our own bitter history, some from the Murdoch-era *Express-News,* some from the defunct *San Antonio Light,* and still others who arrived after the end of the newspaper war. Now we found ourselves bound by a shared loss. Fewer than fifty members of the newsroom had known True, yet in death he united us.

True's last trek might have been a personal quest, but for journalists, he died as a reporter because he was a reporter. That meant something. Journalists who have worked in danger zones know that you are always a reporter, always on duty, always identified by locals as a journalist. And they know that such work often is dangerous.

That same week I received a call from George Irish, my former publisher at the *Light* who had moved up to head Hearst Newspapers in New York. Irish had brought me from New York to San Antonio nearly ten years earlier, and now he was calling "as a friend" to check on me and inquire about Martha. Then he called Martha. It brightened a gloomy week to know that True's death and the well-being of his widow mattered to the executives in New York.

The next day Frank Bennack called, "just to talk," he said. There are 20,000 people who work for Hearst around the world, and Bennack, the longtime CEO and now the vice chairman of the board, is the modern architect of it all: newspapers, magazines, broadcast stations, cable networks, entertainment programming, Internet businesses, the list goes on. Bennack is a legendary deal maker, and for twenty-three years he was known as a tough and demanding CEO. But he was equally comfortable working the *Express-News* newsroom on occasional visits, trading quips with columnists, even greeting pressmen by their first name decades after he left his hometown. I called him "reader number one," knowing he received the *Express-News* at his Eighth Avenue office in New York and on frequent visits to his picturesque Hill Country ranch. Bennack had built a global media empire, yet he still had ink in his veins, and it first flowed in San Antonio.

"Tell me, how is Martha?" he asked, after we had talked a while.

I paused at his question, marshalling my arguments for why the company should go beyond its legal obligations to provide for True's widow and her unborn baby. True's colleagues and readers were contributing to a fund we had established, but the sum would be small in the scheme of things and such generosity would dwindle once the story faded. Before I could speak, Bennack read my mind: "You always want to do the right thing in these sorts of terrible situations," he told me. "No need to discuss it now. I'm calling to check on you today, but we will wait to hear from you and Larry [Walker] with your recommendations."

We said good-bye and I hung up, pleasantly stunned by Bennack's intuitive style.

Thursday, Christmas Eve morning: *Who killed Philip True?* I stared at the four words on my computer screen, the first sentence in my narrative of recent events, an unanswered question. Before I could finish my story, which was scheduled to appear on Sunday, editors approached my office with the look of people bearing news.

"They've caught True's killers," Fred Bonavita said.

Details were sketchy, but sources in both governments told Hayward that two Huichol Indians had been detained at a small ranching outpost not far from where True had been killed. They had been found with his camera and had led investigators to the missing backpack. The two men had confessed to killing True and were now being held in custody awaiting formal charges.

Martha heard the same news from reporters at her Mexico City home. I remained wary, remembering the Truempler episode when Mexican authorities had plucked the wrong man from the sierra. We were cautious for another reason: Mexican cops and federal agents are notoriously corrupt and inept. Beatings and torture are standard investigative methods. There is an adversarial relationship between reporters and the Mexican army and the various federal and state law enforcement bodies. True's murder had forced us into an uneasy arranged marriage; forces we did not trust or respect were our only hope of catching the killers.

Mexican reporters wasted no time asking if we believed the two men were really True's killers or hapless victims framed by authorities. I wrote out my response, knowing whatever I said would appear in every major Mexican newspaper the next morning.

"We are obviously heartened at the news they have detained two individuals who are said to have confessed their role in the homicide, and who were found with Philip's personal property, including his backpack and camera," I wrote. "We need to be very careful about getting our hopes up prematurely. Independent access to the suspects will be essential in convincing us of their culpability. Nevertheless, we commend the Mexican authorities for their vigorous efforts in both the search and recovery operations, and now the criminal investigation."

I returned to my computer screen and the draft of my Sunday story. *Who killed Philip True?* Possibly we had our answer. It was a start.

Martha and I spoke briefly that Christmas Eve, and then it was time to go home. She had friends and family to comfort her at her Mexico City home, but this first holiday without Philip and each passing day must have been exceedingly hard even as their baby grew in her womb. I had neglected my own family since my departure two weeks earlier, and it was time to count our blessings together. Proximity to death heightens one's appreciation for being alive. I found my wife and sons waiting for me, as always that night of the year, gathered around the Christmas tree.

Editors staged a mid-January newsroom memorial to True with readings, songs, and remembrances. Fred Chase, True's best friend and my companion in the search party, drove up from Laredo to attend. Carlos Sada, the Mexican consul general in San Antonio, praised True's journalism and his emotional connection with the country he had covered and made his second home. Larry Walker, the publisher, spoke about the newsroom culture and the way people pulled together and kept vigil for the missing True and later mourned his death. He remarked obliquely about the company's measures to provide for the financial security of Martha and the unborn baby. Nothing else was said on the subject, but it was reassuring news to concerned journalists.

I had been editor for a year and a half now. Our new team, a mix of *Express-News* and *Light* veterans and newcomers from other cities, was still defining itself, working to make the *Express-News* a newspaper of regional distinction. The loss of True bound us more closely.

The memorial service also helped us get on with life. Yet with each passing day, True's death stayed with me. I would wake at night, sweating from nightmares that moved between the Chapalagana and the autopsy room. Lurking vultures and True's decomposing remains filled my dreams. I pictured him suffering at the hands of his killers, and I felt somehow responsible for his death, even as I told myself there was nothing I could have done to prevent it. I still felt guilty about missing Martha's garden service. As True's top editor, I should have been there. It had been wrong to leave Martha and return home so quickly. I stopped working out, too busy or preoccupied to make it to the gym or go for a run.

Something else was nagging at my conscience: someone had to go back down there and push for the prosecution of his killers. Reporters around the country had sent letters thanking me for going down to Mexico to search for True. Some wondered if their editors would have done the same. The notes were gratifying, but the next minute I would catch myself dwelling on the days I let slip by before I headed south.

Nothing could have changed the outcome, I reminded myself. Had I not gone at all, we might not have persuaded the president to order a reluctant military to mount a full-scale search. We might never have found True's grave. Manuel Obaya, True's brother-in-law, left the rim of the Chapalagana convinced that True was down there somewhere and that the villagers in Amoltita were involved. But he also left believing that the truth was beyond his reach. I knew I had helped prevent True's disappearance from becoming a mystery we would never solve.

Mexican authorities, left alone, would do as little as possible. Few significant crimes are solved in Mexico, and few crime victims win justice. Sooner or later, U.S. officials in Mexico would move beyond True's death to the next issue, the next crisis. I decided I would make it my job to pursue justice in the True case. I was determined to show Martha, and one day her child, how important True had been to the *Express-News*. This was something worth fighting for, something that would give meaning to my time as editor.

If I had gone missing in the Chapalagana, True would have come for me. The column that Rick Casey had written about True's qualities as a journalist helped connect me with True in a way I never connected with him when he was alive or fathomed in the canyon bottom as we unearthed his grave.

True and I shared early lives that were unhappy, buried in our memories with the passage of time, perhaps, but always present in terms of who we were and how we saw the world. Each of us struggled as young men to harness those experiences and remake our lives. After idle, rootless years, we both managed to untangle ourselves with the help of good therapists and strong life partners. I should have reached out and made an effort to get to know True better in the preceding years, and perhaps he could have moved past his distrust of authority and done the same with me. I still didn't know much about True's earlier life, but I knew that both of us escaped bad circumstances and eventually found something good.

True had never said much about his family. Monika, my wife, and our two boys, Nick and Alex, were my road forward in life, leading me far away from my own upbringing when I felt unwanted and dreamed mostly of escape. Many abused children grow up to be abusers, perpetuating the cycle. I knew I had broken the cycle, and I knew that my children would not grow up the way I did. The farther in life I moved along, the less I needed to dwell on my own early circumstances. True, until his death, had been on the same path of building his own strong family on the ruins of his past.

Each of us broke free of our families after high school, and each of us stayed cut off from our parents for many years. Unlike True, after many years of estrangement, I had reconciled with my parents. True's parents died before he developed such an interest or need—if he ever did. Theodore and Christeen True never told Philip, their only son, they were sorry and they never asked his forgiveness. Ken and Betty did tell their middle son, the one they knew as Bobby, they were sorry. Yet before that happened, a decade passed as we lived disconnected lives, never speaking or writing even once to each other. They didn't even know that I lived in Texas, far from my memories and their own world in suburban Philadelphia.

I was an ambitious young reporter working in Corpus Christi when a postcard arrived from my mother, written as if we had spoken the previous Sunday. A letter from my father followed, expressing hope that I would come home for a sibling's wedding. It was a beginning, and I reached out to them in response.

The road back to some sort of normal relationship has been a rough one over the decades. Sometimes, when I think about things that happened to me as a child or teenager, the memories surface like events from another lifetime. With each year of reconciliation putting distance between the present and those experiences, I have become more aware of the gifts my parents gave me: my mother's ambition, intelligence, and razor-sharp wit, my father's empathy and disciplined work ethic, their faith-based belief as Catholics in nonviolence.

My own upbringing was nothing like the one True endured. The scars I carried out of adolescence and into adulthood all came from an early subconscious belief that I was an unwanted child. Two sisters came along years later, but in the beginning, we were three boys who came into the world in the space of twenty-four months: Ken Rivard on December 8, 1951, Peter on November 7, 1953, and me in the middle, on November 17, 1952.

Elizabeth Gallagher Rivard, my mother, was the daughter of an Irish-Scotch, alcoholic mother and an Irish-American cop in the New York City borough of the Bronx. Strong on the street and at the precinct, which included Yankee Stadium where he frequently rubbed shoulders with his pin-striped heroes, Lieutenant Al Gallagher, who also sang as an Irish tenor in a barbershop quartet, was gentle at home, happily surrounded by his four little girls. Beneath the surface, my mother told me, he feared that Florence O'Neil, his often raging wife, would grab his service revolver and kill him. With Florence living in a gin-induced stupor, my mother, the second oldest of the girls, spent her childhood raising two younger sisters. She was robbed of a normal life as an adolescent and teenager. Even as Florence lived into her nineties, by then a lonely nursing home charge, my mother remained bitter and unable to forgive her. My mother rejected Florence's one effort to reconcile when Florence refused to face up to her own abusive parenting.

As a newlywed in the early 1950s, my mother found herself far from her New York roots, halfway across the country in Michigan, an unfamiliar state without friends or relatives to lend support. Kenneth Rivard, my father, came from a family of French-Canadian immigrants who lived in Ticonderoga, a small mill town on Lake Champlain in the Adirondack Mountains in upstate New York. His mother gently but firmly ruled the roost. His diminutive, selfless father said his prayers in French, tended the coal stove at home, and toiled double shifts at the International Paper Mill. Like most shift workers, he walked to the mill with lunch bucket in hand, guided by the billowing smoke and foul stench pouring from the smokestacks that settled over the small town like a medieval plague.

For years my father struggled professionally, despite his World War II service in the U.S. Navy that allowed him to attend Columbia University in New York on the GI Bill. He met my mother on a blind date while she was earning her nursing degree at St. Vincent's in Greenwich Village. He was going to be "somebody, someday," he promised her, probably a surgeon, at least a doctor. But the Ivy League remained a foreign, uninviting world to the small-town navy veteran, and he bounced from pre-med to pre-law and finally to liberal arts studies as he tempered his ambition.

We lived at the "top of the mitten" in the small town of Petoskey on the shores of Lake Michigan, where my father had found work in a lethargic, postwar economy as a shoe salesman for JC Penney. Even then, before he began to earn his living on the road, my father was emotionally absent, content to bring home his wages while my mother bore the burden of keeping house and tending three baby boys all clamoring at her breast. Good jobs were scarce, but my mother prodded my unconfident father to reach higher. The husband of a young couple they befriended in the neighborhood was "somebody," at least by his own measure, a cocky traveling salesman who worked for Armour Star, a meat company. His employer provided him with a car to ply his canned meats through the small towns and back roads of northern Michigan. My parents envied such status. They lived week to week, and after paying the rent and grocery bill, found themselves too short to buy a used vehicle or even a television. When the couple told my parents of a new territory opening in western Michigan, a job that came with an automobile, my mother pushed my father to apply.

Soon afterward we moved to Kalamazoo, where my father sold meats, fresh and canned, out of the trunk of his new company car. It was a step up from measuring feet and selling shoes. Family photographs from that period include one that shows my mother, a smiling, beautiful young woman, lying in the park grass next to my father, the two of them a picture of youthful bliss and infinite possibility that, sadly, did not endure. Ken left Betty at home to mind the three toddlers while he serviced customers in an era when grocery stores were still mostly mom-and-pop affairs and traveling salesmen were still part of the retail landscape. My father liked the work because he was paid to gab with strangers, who welcomed him as a friend, even as he resisted the intimacy of real communication with those closest to him. He is still every stranger's best friend, still more comfortable at home when the talk is small.

As my parents made new friends on Mapleview Avenue, where they bought their first home for $12,700, my father tried and failed to get on with Upjohn, the pharmaceutical giant then based in Kalamazoo. I was still a little boy, perhaps six or seven, when the living room filled one weekend with other young men bragging to my father and mother about the generous salary and benefits packages they were bringing home, their young wives looking on, nodding with undisguised admiration. It was a measure of my father's attempts to fit in that I remember him reluctantly accepting a cigarette from one of the men after much razzing. They urged my father to inhale like a man, but he could only puff and cough, clearly out of his element. He looked weak. I retreated to my baseball cards, finding promise in my imagined future as a starter for the Yankees, scoring from third as my grandfather, Lieutenant Al Gallagher, in full dress uniform, with polished shield and holstered sidearm, looked on with undisguised pride.

My mother's burden took its toll. Whether it was my nature as a rebellious boy or my place as the middle child, I drew the brunt of her building frustration and anger and violence.

My first memory, fittingly, is of being in the doghouse. I must have been three or four years old. My mother's favorite place to strap me with one of my absent father's leather belts was in the bedroom we three boys shared, bent over my own bed, the lower of two bunks. "Pull down your pants and bend over" were the first words I learned to fear. I can't remember what I did that particular morning to anger her. As my mother confined me to bed for the afternoon, she taunted me by saying she was going to bake homemade brownies for my brothers. I would not be allowed to have any because I was bad. As I lay crying in my bed, my mother came back to say it would get worse if I continued. "Do you want me to get out the belt?" The words made me cower like a kicked dog.

A year or so later, I found myself in the same hospital where she worked as a nurse, emerging from a cloud of ether after having my tonsils removed. My mother loomed over my hospital bed while my father, as always, stood back in her shadow, clutching the brim of his felt hat in his hands, silent and remote while she did the talking. "I have something for you," my mother said, thrusting a present into my hands. It was a stuffed animal, a black sheep.

"I thought black sheep were bad," I told her, even as I hugged it close, a new friend.

Years later, my mother would recall the same scene, but she also remembered sitting up with me all night in the hospital as I struggled with the pain of the surgery, while my father remained at home. The black sheep, she said, enchanted both of us with its tinkling wind-up nursery rhyme music. I don't doubt her. Memory often erases the full picture, leaving only the one-dimensional recollection of pain and rejection.

One day my mother spotted an ad in the *Kalamazoo Gazette*

placed by Smith, Kline, and French, a pharmaceutical company based in Philadelphia, seeking a "detail man" to pitch the company's line of prescription drugs to doctors in western Michigan. My father balked after being rejected by Upjohn, but my mother insisted, and soon he was headed to Philadelphia for training before returning home to take over his new territory.

His career with SK&F, as we came to know "the Company," uprooted us twice in the next three years, first to suburban New York, then to suburban Philadelphia. We found ourselves saying good-bye to one set of friends, only to be unsure what to say when new, less friendly boys asked where we were from. The new job also kept my dad on the road. My mother, who now had two young girls to go with three boys, continued to work occasional nights and odd hours as a hospital nurse whenever he was home. Even when my father was present he seemed absent, always retreating after supper to his home office, content to toil away at his paperwork and sales reports until long after my mother went to sleep. Much of it probably was make-work, but for him it was the most important thing in life.

The repetitive belt whippings continued until puberty, later replaced by weeks, sometimes months, of mandatory confinement to the house and extra chores. I also experienced continuous verbal abuse and alienation—fueled by my mother's anger and my father's weakness and denial. I was happy when I eventually escaped my family, and they were happy to be done with me. I was written out of their will and forgotten. I left as a confused teenager, hating life with them but beaten down and thoroughly convinced of my own lack of worth.

There was, however, enough of the rebel spirit in me to carry me forward and, lucky for me, to stay out of serious trouble long enough to meet my savior, a high school teacher named Mike Walker. A bit of the rebel himself, Walker convinced wary high school administrators to give him the worst-performing smart students in the system, kids with high IQs who were headed nowhere, or worse. One Monday morning, I found myself sizing up eight other well-known troublemakers and underachievers as Walker explained we had been pulled from regular classes and were now known as SNAP students. What did that stand for? we asked. Superior nonachieving pupils, Walker replied. Ostensibly the class would cover literature, writing, English, and history. In fact, Walker taught us one subject: building self-esteem and believing in the unlimited possibility of the future, irrespective of the past.

For me, it was a new lease on life, the beginning of a decade-long trek away from delinquency and failure, toward a new understanding of myself and my potential. It would be years before I felt fixed, or at least no longer broken, but by age twenty-five I had won my first job as a newspaper reporter. I never looked back.

This is not a book about my life, and such a book would have to give my parents more credit that I've given them here for struggling to atone for the past. Limited therapy helped my parents, and more serious therapy led me to understand that even the most strained family bonds retain remarkable resiliency. People can endure a great deal and still find love within themselves toward those who mistreat them if it stops. My biggest unanswered prayer is that my mother let go of her anger and pain and that my father find a way to reach her. Neither possibility seems realistic to them as they enter old age together, and so we go on imperfectly: my parents, my brothers and sisters, and our children.

My background helps explain the bond I felt with True after his death. True found his own release in life by seeking out the stories of people whose stories otherwise might not be told. Believing no one would ever come to my rescue as a young boy, I also came to understand newspaper reporting at some unconscious level as an avenue to help myself by helping others. Eventually I learned that being the editor of a newspaper is about more than the journalism. It's also about service—to your employer, your staff, your community. Editors are judged by the journalistic quality of the newspaper they edit, but also by how they stand up for their people and their work, fight for resources, and stand by people in their time of need.

Searching for justice in the case of Philip True would allow me to do something for Martha and the unborn baby. Monika had surprised me when I had approached her about going south to search for True. "Of course you have to go," she had said. Now, weeks later, I was lying in bed and backing my way into telling her I needed to go down to Mexico again, to pick up where I had left off and make sure True's killers didn't go free. True was my reporter. I was his editor. We had not been close friends, not even friends really, but that didn't matter. Monika told me she knew I would have to go back even before I told her.

12

The Case of Mexico

Prosecutors, judges, and police all contributed to the system's ineffectiveness. The unprofessional work of prosecutors, known as "ministerios públicos," was one of the country's most serious but least understood problems. Crucial gatekeepers to the justice system, the "ministerios públicos" were often young men and women just out of law school, with monthly salaries of only a few hundred dollars. Since they enjoyed considerable discretion over which arrest warrants would be served and which cases sent to a judge, they were easy targets for bribes. They were not infrequently accused of writing mistakes into criminal complaints, for a price, thus forcing judges to dismiss charges.

—Julia Preston and Samuel Dillon,
Opening Mexico: The Making of a Democracy

We do not have any interest in not arriving at the truth.

—Jorge Luis Ramos, deputy attorney general
in the Zedillo administration

Two men were accused of killing Philip True and, not surprisingly in the closed world of Huichol villages, the suspects were related. Juan Chivarra de la Cruz, 28, and Miguel Hernandez de la Cruz, 24, were brothers-in-law. Miguel was married to Juan's sister, Amalia Chivarra de la Cruz. Beyond that, the family tree was complicated by the marriage of blood relatives, an inevitability in isolated settlements where there often are few other choices.

The suspects' identities and alleged motive were disclosed to the press on Sunday, December 27, three days after their alleged arrest in the sierra not far from the place where Margarito Díaz Martinez, the Huichol hunter, first spotted True's corpse. One day later they were paraded in front of the press, a time-honored tradition in Mexico designed to convince the public that the guilty-looking prisoners on display were in fact guilty.

Horacio Vega Pánames, a criminal investigator with the state attorney general's office, did most of the talking at the press conference, obviously enjoying his unusually large audience of reporters, including some who had traveled to Guadalajara from Mexico City. "We have clarified the facts surrounding the death of Philip True," Vega declared. "They were not interested in his belongings. They did not even know how to use his camera. He offended them because he had been taking photographs."

The two Huichols decided to kill True one day after he arrived in the San Sebastián area without a guide or written permission from community authorities, Vega said. It is customary for outsiders visiting Huichol lands to first call on town elders and request permission to visit Huichol villages or lands. Once they give their approval, the elders typically issue a written letter authorizing the visit and assign a Spanish-speaking Huichol to serve as escort and guide. Vega, however, said that True had been under no legal obligation to seek such permission in advance of his trek.

True was attacked on Sunday, December 6, about 8:00 A.M., Vega told reporters, after the two Huichol men and Chivarra's wife, Yolanda Chivarra López, encountered him in the Chapalagana on the path to San Miguel, True's next destination. The Huichols had left Amoltita that morning on a pilgramage to Jesús María, a day's walk north of San Miguel, where they intended to leave a religious offering.

Amoltita, of course, was the same village where Chase and Obaya encountered the hostile, machete-wielding villagers who claimed that an injured True passed through the area after he had been attacked by wild dogs. In retrospect, the villagers appeared to be complicit, if not in the actual killing, then at least in misleading searchers and protecting True's killers.

Mario Hernandez, one of Vega's fellow investigators, said Chivarra grew angry over True's solitary presence in the sierra when he first encountered him on the trail one day earlier, taking photographs of the Chapalagana landscape and asking for directions to San Miguel. It wasn't until the next morning, when Chivarra in the company of his wife and Hernandez encountered True again, that his anger turned to violence.

"They [the suspects] were crossing the river when they saw Philip," Hernandez said. "They were carrying herbs and other offerings to Jesús María. Philip asked if they could all go together." True fell in with the Huichols as they began to make their way up and out of the canyon, unaware of Chivarra's brooding resentment.

As they made their way up the steep path, Chivarra whispered to Hernandez that they should "kill the gringo." He then grabbed True's leg from behind, causing True to fall backward and strike the back of his head on a rock before tumbling face down under the weight of his own backpack. Chivarra threw his weight onto True's legs and ordered the younger Hernandez to strangle True, trapped face down in the dirt and helpless to fend off his attackers. Hernandez told investigators that he pressed his forearm into True's throat and cut off his breathing. Once True lost consciousness, Chivarra directed Hernandez to remove a red bandana tied to True's backpack to finish the job. Hernandez tied the bandana tightly around True's neck. Then Chivarra cinched the bandana even tighter and doubled the knot to be sure. The Huichols then pushed True off the narrow footpath and down a steep ravine.

Chivarra's pregnant wife, Yolanda, witnessed the attack and "ran off scared," investigators said. When the three Huichols returned more than one week later from their pilgrimage to Jesús María, they learned that search parties were closing in on the area where they had left True's body. Chivarra told investigators that he instructed his wife to continue walking home while he and Hernandez stayed behind to dispose of the corpse. Her statement was never entered into evidence.

If the Huichols were telling the truth about the time and date of the attack, True had fallen far behind schedule. He was only halfway along his hundred-mile route nine days after leaving Mexico City. Yet he might have died only one day short of finishing his trek. While much of his planned trip lay ahead, True could not have continued past San Miguel without extending his time away from home. Martha, awaiting the results of her amniocentesis, surely would have suggested that True end his trek short of his intended goal. True only had to radio a message to the bush pilot, Chuy López, in Tepic with a change of pickup point. Instead, True's fateful second encounter with Chivarra along the canyon trail led to his death.

The confession conformed in large part with Rivas Souza's autopsy report, but not completely. There was nothing in the confession to support the coroner's finding of sexual assault. Chivarra's claim that he sat on the back of True's legs while Hernandez used his forearm to cut his windpipe is contradictory, since True was allegedly face down. The coroner had noted what appeared to be defensive wounds on True's arms, suggesting a longer and different kind of struggle. But the investigators seemed disinterested in clarifying any unresolved discrepancies. With statements in hand from the two suspects, Vega told reporters, the case was solved. He acted as if a conviction was a mere formality.

"It was easy, very easy for them to do it," Vega said, adding that Hernandez was "under the influence of" his older, domineering brother-in-law, which enabled him to overcome his own misgivings when ordered by Chivarra to kill True. "The only hard part was getting there," he claimed, referring to the remote corner of the sierra where investigators located the suspects.

Susana Hayward, along with Gloria Ferniz, an *Express-News* photographer, awaited the formal arraignment before a civilian judge in Guadalajara the next day. Editors asked them to look closely for any signs of abuse or torture. We wanted justice, not scapegoats.

The next morning, the two Huichols were escorted to a patio outside the prosecutor's office as photographers jockeyed for position and reporters fired questions. The Huichols stood silently, True's red backpack and camera placed beside them.

"I was on my knees in the courtyard, waiting for them to come out, and suddenly Chivarra was standing right next to me, inches way,"

Ferniz said. "All I could think of was, 'You son of a bitch, how could you have killed Philip?' It was hard for me to do my work."

The two men were "silent and disheveled," Hayward wrote, and dressed in Western clothes, like many Huichols who come and go from their traditional communities, taking seasonal jobs in the tobacco fields and agave farms or peddling handicrafts in the cities. Chivarra wore a burgundy shirt and jeans. Hernandez sported a green Coca-Cola shirt. "Both looked bleary-eyed, but showed no signs of physical abuse," Hayward reported. No reporter there that day, American or Mexican, reported that the suspects showed signs of abuse.

Incriminating statements, called *declaraciones,* carry significant weight in the Mexican criminal justice system, even though they often are coerced and, when necessary, even manufactured. Americans can hardly appreciate the contrast to our own system where a suspect has a constitutional right to remain silent and to seek legal counsel.

Mexico clings to its archaic system. A "trial" includes nothing more than an individual judge's review of written evidence presented by the state and the defense. In theory, the judge reads the case file and renders a fair verdict. Reality is something else. There are no grand juries to assess the fairness of the charges or the weight of evidence to support the charges and a trial. There are no citizen juries, no open courtrooms, no oral presentations or witness examination and cross-examination. Judges accept written evidence from both sides, review it without prejudice, and then issue their verdict. Often enough, it is their clerks who file and read the legal pleadings and then prepare the written verdicts for the judges to sign and issue. A signed confession under such circumstances carries a great deal of weight, especially when the defense has no opportunity to challenge police methods or present evidence of torture. Too many in the system are prone to influence and corruption.

"I have an autopsy and the confessions of two people," a cocky Vega told reporters during the Monday arraignment. "It's proof enough for me."

Editors in San Antonio read the investigator's glib remarks and grew worried. President Ernesto Zedillo and state officials alike had promised a thorough investigation and timely prosecution. Now it appeared that investigators had no interest in pursuing additional evidence or witnesses.

Investigators permitted Hayward to listen from an adjacent room as they took formal statements from the two suspects. "They spoke in normal voices, in Spanish, and didn't seem scared or sound forced," she reported, suggesting they were voluntarily confessing their crime without coercion. Perhaps they were sufficiently intimidated by their arrest and transport to Guadalajara to cause them to cooperate.

We were disappointed to learn that investigators had not located True's journal or the rolls of film he had shot. The film found in the camera did not include photographs of the suspects. When asked if they knew more about the motive, one of the investigators said Chivarra "got the devil in him and he killed him."

The confessed killers' motive struck many at our newspaper and in the foreign press corps as contrived. True was sensitive to indigenous customs and sensibilities, and he intended to spend less than one day crossing through San Sebastián, an impoverished expanse of the Huichol sierra that includes Amoltita and Yoata, the Chivarra family ranch several hours away from the village. Had True successfully crossed the Chapalagana and reached San Miguel, chances are none of the Huichols he encountered in that neighboring indigenous community would have been offended by his presence. Chase and Obaya had felt unthreatened everywhere except Amoltita.

A small campfire containing a cigarette butt was found next to the spot where Díaz said he had found True's corpse, apparently built by Chivarra and Hernandez to ward off the cold as they prepared to move True's corpse Sunday night, December 13, exactly one week after they killed him. For the next four hours they labored to drag their heavy load down the seldom traversed game trail to the canyon bottom, a serious challenge, even for two Huichols accustomed to strenuous travel on foot through the sierra. Once they reached the bottom, Chivarra and Hernandez dug a hole in a sandbank not far from the river and buried the corpse. Then they cut river reeds to erase their footsteps and obscure the disturbed sand mound.

Chivarra and Hernandez made three mistakes after killing True. First, they left their victim exposed in the wilds long enough for Díaz, the hunter from Popotito, to happen by the morning of December 13, a half day before the suspects returned from their pilgrimage and decided to hide the corpse. Realizing he had found the missing journalist who was the object of so much attention in the normally quiet sierra, Díaz immediately set out for San Miguel to report his find. Díaz probably passed the killers somewhere along that trail, each traveling in the opposite direction. True's killers, of course, had no way of knowing their decision to move the body would only heighten suspicion about the circumstances surrounding his death.

Their second mistake was to move the decomposing corpse under darkness. Shortly after they set out, the sleeping bag fabric snagged on the rough terrain and ripped. Goose down feathers spilled out, leaving a trail of feathers that followed them down into the Chapalagana and led us to the hidden grave only two days later.

Their third mistake was behaving in a way that must have led other Huichols in San Sebastián to conclude that they were responsible for the journalist's disappearance. Vega said the two men decided not to return to their ranch in Yoata after disposing of their victim and stayed out in the wilderness until their arrest on December 26. A more accurate assessment is that the brothers-in-law panicked when they realized that soldiers and police were searching for the missing foreigner and fled their ranch. Staying away from home for such a prolonged period must have heightened suspicion among others in the community. A relative who had been involved in a long-running land dispute with Chivarra apparently helped identify the killers to authorities after the two flashed True's money, traveler's checks, and binoculars around the community.

Vega, in his hurry to take credit for breaking open the case and seeing the two Huichols imprisoned, paid scant attention to unresolved details. He discounted robbery or the involvement of other Huichols. Yet he admitted that some of True's personal effects, including his wallet containing $400 in pesos, were missing.

Vega was vague about the actual time the suspects were taken into custody, reportedly by a dozen soldiers and state investigators, including himself. Hayward and other reporters received unofficial confirmation on Christmas Eve that the two suspects had been apprehended and were being flown to the military base outside Guadalajara. Did authorities disclose their arrest immediately, or were they detained days earlier in the sierra and held for days before their first public appearance? One can only speculate what might have transpired in the time between the apprehension of Chivarra and Hernandez and their appearance in Guadalajara, "silent and disheveled."

After a night in jail and a conversation with their court-appointed lawyer, Chivarra and Hernandez changed their story. They returned to court the next day and told the presiding judge, Jesús Salvador Rivera Claro, that they had killed True in self-defense. The headline in *La Jornada,* a Mexico City daily, laid out the new version of events: "I killed True because he wanted to rape my wife."

Hernandez offered the judge and others in attendance a narrative of events the same newspaper summarized under the secondary headline, "Multiple Contradictions."

"On December 4, at 10:00 A.M., I was at my ranch, sitting inside my house when the gringo arrived," Hernandez said. "He spoke to me, but I didn't understand him very well, and the gringo gave me a kick and he came inside my house without my permission. My family was inside the house, my three sons, who are little, and my wife, Amalia Chivarra de la Cruz. The gringo came inside and, likely as not, he wanted to rape my wife...I became angry and after forcing the gringo out through the door of my house, I grabbed a bandana that the gringo carried on the back of his backpack and with the bandana I grabbed him around the neck and I strangled him."

Judge Rivera then asked Chivarra for his account of the killing.

Chivarra said he was vaccinating cattle nearby when True barged into Hernandez's house, causing Miguel's wife and the children to come running out of the house, crying. Chivarra said Hernandez spoke Spanish poorly and could not understand True, spurring him to act in self-defense. "I just heard shouts and wailing, and when I finished vaccinating I went over to Miguel's house," he told the judge. "When I saw him [True] it frightened me and Miguel told me he had killed the gringo because he had come into his house without permission and he had wanted to rape his wife."

U.S. and Mexican newspapers, meanwhile, were reporting that toxicology tests from the Rivas Souza autopsy showed that True had an extremely elevated blood alcohol level at the time of his death. The tests also revealed traces of *aminovalérico*, an over-the-counter derivative of a local plant used as a stimulant in the sierra, that True might have used to counter the effects of high altitude and cold temperatures. Some Mexican press accounts speculated that True was intoxicated and, under the influence of alcohol and the drug, had fallen to his own death.

The suspects offered no explanation of how they moved the body a distance of several miles from their ranch to the canyon bottom. They also denied robbing him. "We didn't take anything from the gringo," Chivarra added.

Vega remained confident. "It happens in 85 percent of the cases," he told Hayward. "Nearly all of them change their declarations. It's something unique to our judicial system . . . unless there is something extraordinary, we expect formal charges."

Judge Rivera wasn't persuaded and ordered the men held. Something else the defendants said in a jailhouse interview with Mexican reporters worried us far more than their self-serving revisionism.

Chivarra told reporters that soldiers arrived in Amoltita while he and Miguel were hunting in a distant canyon after burying True. The soldiers demanded to know Juan's whereabouts and allegedly hit his ailing mother, Angelina de la Cruz de la Cruz (sic), and then beat his father,

Francisco Chivarra López, a Huichol shaman, so severely he vomited blood. For three days, Chivarra claimed, his father was unable to eat. Later he claimed his parents suffered recurring psychological problems.

Chivarra said he and Miguel were flushed out of hiding by the mistreatment of their family and other Huichols, including the traditional governor, Isidro López Díaz, who claimed he was hung upside down on a tree and beaten. The suspects were detained by "green judicials," or army troops, when they returned to the area on Christmas Eve. Soldiers put the suspects aboard a helicopter and threatened to throw them out if they didn't reveal where they hid True's backpack and show them the burial site. Miguel claimed they were taken to a military warehouse and beaten throughout the night.

In a country where official abuse is common, the Mexican press treated the accusations as fact, as if such stories were standard second-day fare in any Mexican criminal case. Vega denied the two men were mistreated and said the army's role was limited to transporting state investigators into the remote sierra and providing security as state police made the arrest.

Meanwhile, a week had gone by and the Zedillo administration continued to delay release of the second autopsy report. Dr. Emma Lew returned to Miami without meeting the press but spoke briefly by telephone with Dane Schiller, who had been sent to Mexico City from his border post to buttress our reporting efforts.

Lew said she could not file a conclusive report with the FBI until her Mexican counterparts provided toxicology test results. Scheduling conflicts, she said, had prevented her from following her customary practice of visiting the scene of the crime.

Much later, Dr. Sergio Ramirez, the young resident working in San Miguel who was present when we found True's grave, told me that officials with the federal attorney general's office, including members of the second autopsy team, arrived by helicopter in San Miguel and ordered him and Díaz, the Huichol hunter, to accompany them back to the Chapalagana and the site where Díaz first spotted True's corpse and then on to the gravesite.

"They searched the area carefully and collected cigarette butts in the ashes of the small campfire near where the body had been," Dr. Ramirez said. "They took pictures of everything and asked a lot of questions. I had to walk all the way down and back up the canyon again. I'll never forget it."

Dr. Ramirez, now working as a physician who oversees ten public hospitals in central Mexico, said he was asked twice to return to the scene as federal authorities sought to collect more evidence. Those federal investigative efforts were never publicly disclosed; if U.S. officials were aware of such efforts, they never released the information.

Jorge Madrazo, Zedillo's attorney general, was named Mexico's consul general in Seattle after Vicente Fox took office in 2000, to protect him against drug traffickers angered by his aggressive investigations. After ignoring interview requests, he finally agreed through another Mexican diplomat, a mutual friend, to answer questions about his role in the case. After I reached him by telephone he insisted on receiving questions via e-mail. In the end, he never responded to those questions.

Don Finley, the *Express-News* medical writer, had contacted several U.S. forensics experts to ask about reports of high alcohol levels in True's body, which the Mexican press was reporting as evidence of his intoxication at the time of death. Finley was told that microorganisms in decomposing bodies frequently produce alcohol at levels exceeding legal intoxication.

"Postmortem alcohol production is a very odd thing," said Gary W. Kunsman, the chief toxicologist with the Bexar County medical examiner's office in San Antonio. "It doesn't occur in all bodies, and it doesn't occur at the same rate in bodies, even under the same conditions."

Kunsman, a former medical examiner in the U.S. military, said he had examined pilots who died in crashes and were not located for two weeks, who registered alcohol levels of 0.2–0.3 percent, double and triple the legal blood alcohol level in Texas at the time.

"So you know the pilot's not drinking," he said. "He crashes, it takes a week or two to locate the body, get him back, autopsy him," and measure the alcohol levels.

Three days after the second hearing, on the last day of 1998, Judge

Rivera ordered Chivarra and Hernandez held for trial on charges of homicide and robbery. We had scored an important first-round victory in the legal battle, but we had lost momentum in the court of public opinion. The state human rights commission announced it was opening an investigation into the claims of torture and mistreatment leveled by Huichol authorities:

> Initially the only ones who were there were Mexican army personnel and five people dressed in civilian clothes, who appeared to be in charge of the investigation. They arrived in the indigenous community of San Sebastián Teponahuaxtlán on December 20 and the next day they tortured the traditional governor, Isidro López Díaz, to force him to tell them the whereabouts of [the suspects]. The same day, they detained and tortured with the same end in mind Francisco Chivarra, the father of Juan Chivarra. They searched people's homes in Yoata, they treated everyone with arrogance, and, finally, without an arrest warrant issued by the appropriate authorities, they detained the two Huichols against their will, they transported them by helicopter on December 24 to a military security facility, and only on December 26 did they turn them over to civilian law enforcement authorities.

The Mexican press quoted unnamed Huichol authorities who said two thousand army troops had invaded the sierra, including two who died in a car accident near Tuxpan de Bolanos, where True was last seen as he began his trek. The Huichols claimed army troops used a rope to hang the local governor, López Díaz, upside down from a tree, and then beat him while demanding to know where they could find Chivarra and Hernandez.

The troops surely numbered in the dozens, but the sequence of events described by the Huichols, which begins December 21 and includes the detention of Chivarra and Hernandez on December 24, suggested an official cover-up.

More challenges lay just ahead. On Tuesday, January 5, a source

By the time he was 11 years old, his father had been banished from the house for molesting Bonnie.

Philip and his sister, Bonnie True, at the chicken farm in Pacoima.

True, sporting long hair and his trademark floppy felt hat, in his late-60s hippie phase with Bonnie and his mother, Christeen, on a visit home from the University of California-Irvine.

Now a teenager, Philip posed for a family portrait alongside his stepfather, Steve Vadovich, the neighborhood mailman who married True's mother, then exiled his stepson to a bedroom in the garage.

Checking notes in his pensión room while covering the Zapatista uprising in Chiapas in 1994 for the *San Antonio Express-News*.

Standing atop Sierra Gordo, the central Mexican gorge that was the scene of True's last story, published the day he was murdered in December, 1998.

Philip and Martha walking arm-in-arm in Mexico City.

An overview of the Chapalagana where True was killed and his hidden grave was later located alongside the river in the canyon bottom.

Margarito Díaz, the Huichol hunter who first spotted True's corpse in the wilds, and Dr. Sergio Ramirez, the young physician serving his residency in the Huichol sierra, who led the small search party down into the Chapalagana.

Next to a Huichol dog that helped locate True's shallow grave, Díaz and Julian Carrillo, Dr. Ramirez's assistant at the health clinic in San Miguel, take a turn digging out True's corpse.

The author, wearing a face mask, pauses while digging out True's corpse.

Mexican army soldiers watch as a state forensics team carries True's enshrouded corpse to a waiting helicopter.

Huichol brothers-in-law Juan Chivarra and Miguel Hernandez at their arraignment in Guadalajara, two weeks after True's grave was located in the Chapalagana Canyon in the Sierra Madre. Their defenders claimed they were tortured before confessing.

True's backpack and .35 mm camera were recovered from the Yoata ranch where the Chivarra clan lived and put on display for the press. Investigators would go months without finding True's journal inside the backpack.

Investigators, declaring the case solved, also put on display True's passport and other personal effects recovered from the suspects' ranch huts.

Martha True and the author meet with President Vicente Fox at Los Pinos in Mexico City to press for action in the case.

The defense: U.S. expatriate Miguel Gatins, high profile defense lawyer Arturo Zamora, and defense investigator Patricia Morales address the Guadalajara press after the suspects' sudden release from jail.

Colatlán Judge Reyes Contreras, who was befriended by Morales and declared the Huichols innocent before suddenly ordering their release. Afterwards, he immediately left town without notifying the government or True's family and friends of his controversial legal ruling.

A newly freed and made-over Juan Chivarra tells *Express-News* reporter Susana Hayward, who interviewed him several times at the Colatlán jail, that he had never met her or True. Miguel Hernandez and Patricia Morales look on.

Martha holds "Teo," Philip Theodore True Jr., after a press conference in Guadalajara.

Huichols in the village of San Miguel study reward posters circulated in the sierra in January, 2005 that offered a 50,000 peso reward for information leading to the detention of fugitives Chivarra and Hernandez.

Juan Carillo, a Huichol elder in Tuxpan de Bolanos, examines photos of two fugitives after the state Supreme Court issued a final verdict of guilt and sentenced the pair to 20-year prison terms. The Huichols failed to help authorities locate the two convicted killers, thought to be hiding out in the remote sierra.

told Schiller in Mexico City that pathologists who participated in the second autopsy did not agree with Rivas Souza's ruling of strangulation. Federal and state forensics experts were convening in Guadalajara the next day, according to the source, to try and resolve their differences. Dr. Lew was returning from Miami for the meeting. Incredibly, Rivas Souza was not invited to attend.

As the Wednesday meeting got under way without him, an unhappy Rivas Souza broke the silence imposed by Los Pinos two weeks earlier. "They don't believe us that it was a homicide," he told Schiller, referring to federal officials. "I am not telling lies." He wondered aloud how federal and state authorities hoped to reconcile the differing conclusions while excluding him from the meeting. "Medicine is not mathematics, two and two does not equal four," he said. "If someone else has another conclusion, they should have to defend it."

Thursday morning, Martha received a call at her Mexico City home from Dr. Lew, the FBI consultant, now back in Miami. It was the first time they had talked, and Lew expressed her sympathies before turning to the reason for her call. The Dade County assistant coroner wanted to share her conclusions with Martha before she learned anything from television or print news sources. "It's complicated," Lew said. She sounded hesitant to speak as frankly as she wanted to, even in private. "I believe your husband was murdered."

Others in the federal attorney general's office were not prepared to go that far in their public statements because it was a politically sensitive situation, explained Lew, who would be far less forthcoming in her own public statements.

Lew explained to Martha that her husband probably died from a combination of factors, including a blow to the head and another one behind the left lung that probably caused him to lose consciousness and stop breathing as fluids filled his lungs. That injury went undetected in the first autopsy, she said. The Huichols might have strangled True with his own bandana, Lew said, but she did not believe strangulation was the actual cause of death. The small hyoid bone in the throat was not broken, a telltale indicator of death by strangulation. To Martha's relief, Lew also disagreed with another important finding in the Rivas Souza autopsy.

"Your husband was not sexually assaulted," Lew told Martha.

The damage to his anus was the result of the body being dragged such a great distance down the steep canyon, Lew said. She could not say if the high alcohol levels were the byproduct of decomposition, or if True might have been forced to swallow a massive quantity of grain alcohol, a torture tactic associated with drug traffickers.

Law enforcement and forensics sources in San Antonio told the newspaper that True's blood alcohol measurement of 0.26 percent—far in excess of the 0.1 percent legal drunk driving level in Texas (later lowered to 0.08)—was the equivalent of fifty mixed drinks. If the alcohol wasn't the result of decomposition, they said, it must have been forced on True. Most U.S. experts, however, questioned Mexican forensic methods as outmoded and unreliable. Still, some PGR officials believed—and were eagerly telling Mexican reporters—that True probably was drunk and fell to his own death. Lew told Martha that federal pathologists were unwilling to rule her husband's death a homicide.

Martha called me to share the details of her conversation with Lew. It was evident that the second autopsy, while not admissible in the state case according to the Jalisco attorney general's office, would raise doubts with the public and possibly influence the trial judge.

A press conference given by PGR officials in Mexico City on Friday confirmed our worst fears. A senior PGR official told reporters that True died from a "severe concussion" that probably rendered him unconscious and a second blow to his back that damaged his lungs and cut off his breathing. He wasn't strangled to death or sexually violated, he said. True's death, said Jorge Luis Ramos, deputy federal attorney general, could not be ruled a homicide. "We are not dismissing the possibility of homicide," Ramos said. "There could have been one, but it is not our role to decide. Who or how the blows were produced, we do not know. We do not have any interest in not arriving at the truth."

Ramos's contorted double negative was a perfect expression of the tortured path the case had taken after only one month. The pathologists who performed the second procedure would not speak to the press. Zedillo administration officials at Los Pinos were no longer commenting publicly on the case as they readied for a February state visit by President Bill Clinton. The assistance that officials had rendered during our search for True now was overshadowed by the doubt they had sown.

It had taken three weeks for the federal attorney general's office to finally make public its findings, which it had promised to disclose in a matter of days. Outside of Texas, few newspapers were following the case closely. The situation was different in Mexico. True was back on the front page and nightly news. The entire country, led by the administration and the national press, seemed ready to grasp at any evidence, however flimsy, that True's death was his own fault.

Back in Miami, Dr. Lew spoke briefly by telephone with Schiller. She had not spoken publicly in Mexico or otherwise made known her views. "There's more than one of us scratching our heads on this case," Lew said. "I'm not sure it will ever be resolved to my satisfaction. I don't know if we will ever find out what led to his death. Accept that this is a very complex case pathologically."

Very different words than those she spoke to Martha.

Administration officials refused to release the second autopsy report to Martha or the *Express-News*. For the first time, we found ourselves on the outside of the case, cut off.

Dr. Vincent J. DiMaio, the Bexar County chief medical examiner in San Antonio and a nationally regarded forensics expert who played no role in the case, told Schiller that the advanced state of decomposition appeared to make a definitive ruling all but impossible in the second procedure. "When you have a decomposing body you get one shot," DiMaio said. "The body was bad off to begin with."

I thought back to the autopsy and visualized the scene where

Rivas Souza and his team studied True's swollen neck and the bandana tightly affixed around it. It had been tied in a Huichol knot, Rivas Souza had pointed out at the time. Now, if Mexican officials could persuade its own nationalistic press that True might have died in an accidental fall, it would be able to put the unfortunate incident behind them.

A memorable column was published that January, written by Arnoldo Kraus in the Mexico City newspaper *La Jornada,* titled "The True case, the Mexico case."

"The history of the True case is a sad imitation of the Case of Mexico," Kraus wrote, lamenting that True's actual death was now the only certainty remaining in the *telenovela,* or Mexican soap opera. Mexicans so disbelieved what their government told them, he wrote, that everything else—the cause of True's death, the two unreconciled autopsies, the manner in which the suspects were hunted down, and even their possible guilt—was beyond popular grasp. "While nothing is surprising anymore in Mexico, two causes of death in one person...is cause for disbelief."

Kraus left little doubt that he believed True was murdered, but he, like many Mexicans, would conclude that the muddled trail leading back to the foreign reporter's death made it impossible to believe justice would be served. "It's very probable that the cause of True's death will never be known," Kraus wrote. "Any claim will be unbelievable: the wake of contradictions and abuses is gigantic. The journalist's death, whether it was accidental, murder, or whatever other cause, is the amen to a terrible outcome and the premature widowhood of a pregnant mother, it is a journey and look at the incredible state of disbelief, hopelessness and the chokehold on justice and reason in Mexico."

If Chase was right, if there really were no secrets in the Huichol communities, there still seemed to be no one in the Mexican government or press interested in finding out what others in the small villages of San Sebastián knew about True's death.

Several U.S. reporters showed more enterprise than Mexican investigators. Tracey Eaton, True's friend and the Mexico City bureau chief for the *Dallas Morning News,* was the first reporter to visit the sierra and make his way to Yoata, the small ranch that was home to the suspects and their families. The *Express-News,* among other newspapers, published his lengthy account on March 1.

"He had no business being here," Martin Chivarra, Juan's younger brother, told Eaton, who was accompanied by one of the newspaper's photographers. "It's like me going to the United States without a passport. *La migra* catch you, they abuse you, they mistreat you. Here, it is the same."

Carlos Chavez, the director of the Jalisco Association for the Support of Indigenous Groups, told Eaton that True's failure to obtain written permission from Huichol elders was a serious mistake. Without it, Chavez speculated, True's killers might have concluded that his presence in the sierra was unknown and they could kill him with impunity. "If a Mexican had been killed, the government wouldn't have lifted a finger," Chavez explained.

"People are getting the wrong idea, they think we are all violent," said Jésus Lara, president of the Union of Huichol Indian Communities of Jalisco. "But it's not true. We have welcomed many strangers into our villages, and nothing has happened. We feel deep shame over the murder. Now we only want justice. So if these two Huichol suspects are guilty, they should be punished."

Eaton found other Huichol experts who had followed the case and read True's original story proposal. They expressed misgivings about True's picture of Huichol society and whether he really comprehended indigenous sentiments toward outsiders.

"Huichols, especially when they drink, often show a real hostile attitude toward foreigners," said Stacy Shaeffer, an American anthropologist and expert on Huichol culture and peyote use, then teaching at the University of Texas–Pan American. "They sometimes kick foreigners out of their communities or throw them in jail. Inequality is at the heart of a lot of it. The foreigners have money, they have all these fancy gadgets, cameras, and sleeping bags. But many don't have a clue about Huichol culture. And they don't give anything to the community. It's just take, take, take."

Shaeffer, who had known True as a reporter on the Texas border, said she did not mean that True fit that stereotype, but she wasn't the first person to publicly question True's view of Huichol life, the "constant sound of children laughing." Other journalists were writing critically of True's story proposal and his decision to undertake a solo trek through Huichol lands without permission.

"He loved the Huichols so much," Martha told Eaton. "He had studied them and visited them on and off for fifteen years."

It was a defense she would repeat again and again to reporters on both sides of the border with each twist or turn of the case. Publically I espoused the same position, but as time passed, I too wondered what True was thinking when he left behind his wife and unborn child to pursue one last wilderness quest.

Amid the legal wrangling in Mexico City in the months after True's death, the suspects were transferred from the maximum-security prison in Guadalajara to the small jail in Colotlán, a mestizo town of 16,000 people located four hours to the north, closer to the Huichol sierra. Eaton was the first U.S. reporter to speak with them.

Chivarra disavowed his two previous confessions and offered yet another version of events. He told Eaton that he glimpsed True hiking on a trail and never encountered him again. True stopped only long enough to ask Chivarra for directions to the next town. Chivarra pointed True in the right direction and then returned to his work, vaccinating cattle.

"I was coming down a trail when I saw him. He was on a mule trail, not an Indian trail," Chivarra said. "He said he liked walking there. I got scared. He was carrying a big backpack. I thought he was probably going to kill me."

Chivarra denied ever confessing his guilt.

"I didn't kill him," he said. "I want to leave this jail."

Hernandez was less assertive in proclaiming his innocence. He stayed back, Eaton wrote, "glancing around nervously, wringing his sweat-drenched palms. Asked about his purported confession, he stared at the ground, finally mumbling, 'I don't remember anything.'"

The same scene played out again and again as other reporters traveled the mountain roads to Colotlán to interview the suspects. Chivarra swaggered and spoke with menacing bravado one moment, then shifted roles and became the bewildered Indian fearful of foreigners the next. Oblivious or indifferent to the glaring inconsistencies in his constantly changing story, Chivarra relished sparring with journalists. Hernandez, clearly dominated by his older brother-in-law, said little, but he never denied his role in killing True. He simply did not have an alternative story.

A more detailed picture of the Yoata clan, particularly Chivarra himself, emerged during the course of my own reporting.

General Fonseca had denied the presence of drug cultivation in that part of the sierra as we headed into the Chapalagana looking for True, but he was badly outnumbered by credible sources that said otherwise. One had to look no further than the Mexican newspapers for the periodic account of a Huichol "mule" being busted while delivering a marijuana load from the sierra to traffickers.

My first inkling of Chivarra's involvement in illicit activities came in a letter mailed to me only weeks after True's death from an American man living in Arizona, who once was a regular visitor and occasional resident in San Miguel, where his mother taught at the village school.

One day while walking on a common path linking San Miguel to the San Sebastián side of the canyon, the young man came across Chivarra standing by a barricade that he had built to block the path, forcing locals to detour away from a nearby marijuana plot he was cultivating. "He was bad news even back then, and that was the last time I walked down that path," the man said.

Others with a personal connection to the region said Chivarra had been involved in various incidents since his youth, including petty theft, cattle rustling, and assault. Chivarra's father was a Huichol shaman, but Juan had not followed in his footsteps. He and his family had been expelled from their former community, thus explaining their life in Yoata on a remote ranch peopled only by immediate family members.

The Huichols do not keep written records, but the Chivarra family name is widely known in the sierra, and no one I encountered holds the clan in high regard. For some generations, one anthropologist told me, the Chivarra family had controlled the "moonshine business" in that part of the sierra, distilling spirits from the sotol cactus.

There is another disturbing aspect to the suspects' families. For at least two generations, the two families have repeatedly intermarried. Juan's mother is a de la Cruz de la Cruz, meaning she married into the same extended family from which she came. Juan Chivarra is married to Yolanda, who happens to be his aunt, the sister of his father. Miguel is married to Amalia Chivarra de la Cruz, Juan's sister.

"In any human group you are going to find bad apples and these guys are bad apples," said Dr. Phil Weigand, an anthropologist whose published writings on the Huichol communities, where he has worked on and off for decades, are widely respected. "Marijuana cultivation has penetrated that area, along with cattle rustling and moonshine alcohol . . . these kinds of people alienate their neighbors. The people in this region have had a history of in-breeding, and it's not a good thing in terms of physical or mental health, and violence among these elements is not uncommon."

Relations were never good between residents in San Sebastián, especially around Amoltita, and San Miguel, larger and more productive, across the canyon in San Andrés, but they deteriorated in 1997 after a few youths from Amoltita showed up in San Miguel, smoking marijuana and offering to share it with others in the village. While cultivation was an undeniable reality in the region, the specter of Huichols consuming drugs was a new phenomenon.

The teacher's son who sent me the letter said he had used the radiotelephone at San Miguel to alert his contacts in the governor's office in Guadalajara. Soon an army unit arrived in Amoltita and burned the crop only weeks before the harvest. The incident escalated tensions between the two communities and added to Amoltita's unsavory reputation. It was into this milieu that True walked, oblivious to the heightened hostility toward outsiders. It doesn't take much imagination to wonder if Chivarra and Hernandez attacked True fearing that he had come across and might photograph marijuana fields they were protecting.

In his unpublished dissertation, anthropologist Paul Liffman writes that San Sebastián was one of the hardest hit counties during the violent battles with Cristero ranchers in the 1920s. Much of San Sebastián was seized and held by mestizos until the Huichols rose up two decades later and regained their lands, eventually winning legal recognition and title in the 1950s.

"Basically, the *comunidad* has been closed since the revolutionary period," Liffman wrote. "At the very least, visitors . . . are subject to serious scrutiny and must have official permission or significant local sponsorship before they can travel freely within its boundaries. Even unknown Huichols are viewed with suspicion."

True's Huichol experiences were limited to Tuxpan de Bolanos, a town that is home to both Huichols and mestizos and where the rules that govern the more remote, outlying communities do not apply. It was a fatal mistake for True to assume the welcome he received there would be the same deeper in the sierra. If only he had asked; if only someone had explained.

13

The Depth of the Holes
You Climb Out of

> Men speak of blind destiny, a thing without scheme or purpose. But
> what sort of destiny is that? Each act in this world from which there can
> be no turning back has before it another, and it another yet. In a vast
> and endless net. Men imagine that the choices before them are theirs to
> make. But we are free to act only upon what is given. Choice is lost in a
> maze of generations.
>
> —Cormac McCarthy, *Cities of the Plain*

Alan Zarembo, a reporter for *Newsweek* magazine, never met Philip
True. His assignment as Mexico City bureau chief didn't begin until
January 1999, one month after True's death. But Zarembo's intrepid
reporting uncovered a compelling and incriminating link connecting
Chivarra to the killing of True. Zarembo arrived in Mexico intrigued
by the True case and determined to retrace the slain journalist's footsteps through the Sierra Madre. No journalist had reached the Chapalagana since our search party found True's hidden grave. Tracey
Eaton would get there and publish first, but Zarembo was unaware of
his planned trip.

"One of the reasons I was driven to this story was that I identified
with Philip," Zarembo later told me. "There's something about foreign
correspondents; something in life is pushing them and pulling them.

You have a sense that we're all running away from something in our home countries to something else in another country. Most foreign correspondents believe there is more to life than America, in my case, more to life than the Pittsburgh suburbs. It appears to me Philip was in Mexico reinventing himself, something I sense in a lot of foreign correspondents. The fact that I had never met him, I think, was a real advantage. All the other journalists liked him, and not having that emotional connection with him gave me a distance that was helpful."

In the first week of March, Zarembo paired up in Mexico City with Sergio Dorantes, a local freelance photographer who frequently worked for the news magazine. Dane Schiller petitioned his bosses in San Antonio to allow him to go along, but skittish editors vetoed the idea. A frustrated Schiller was forced to remain behind in Mexico City. The *Newsweek* team flew to Guadalajara, rented a car, and drove to Colotlán, where the two suspects were jailed. Zarembo hoped to meet the judge assigned to the case and interview the two suspects, even though other journalists had failed in their attempts to press the small-town magistrate, Felix Enrique Aguiar, for information.

"The judge didn't seem to know very much, but there was an album of photos of evidence that had been collected: Philip's plane ticket, one of his boots, and a picture of the notebook," Zarembo said.

The photograph of the notebook stopped Zarembo in his tracks. "Can I see this notebook?" Zarembo asked Aguiar.

"No, it's evidence," the judge told him.

We knew True had carried a notebook with him, in addition to his new camera and numerous rolls of film. We also knew from True's last telephone call to Martha from Tlaltenango that he had whiled away his unscheduled day there shooting photos and getting the feel of his new camera. We urged investigators to redouble their efforts to locate the journal and the missing film, but were told nothing had been found. We often wondered how hard they looked. Certainly, U.S. officials in Guadalajara made no effort to review the seized backpack, or the journal would have come to light immediately. Horacio Vega Pánames and others in the state prosecutor's office were complacent, satisfied with the sworn confessions, reluctant to travel to the sierra and pursue other witnesses and evidence, too indifferent or disorganized even to search a backpack.

"Now my interest was high," Zarembo said. "Every story I had read said his notebook was gone, and there I am looking at a photograph of his notebook. We asked to see the file, but Aguiar said it was confidential and still under review. It was clear he hadn't done anything on the case, and we went away empty-handed. There was another guy in his office, telling him the whole time not to talk to us."

Zarembo and Dorantes turned their attention to the suspects in the nearby municipal jail. "We talked to them in jail, and Juan denied everything. He claimed he only saw True once and that was it. Miguel actually told me True was drunk. Their stories didn't match up."

Zarembo knew a great story might be found inside True's notebook, but he also knew that *Newsweek*, with a circulation of more than 4 million, would not be interested in another jailhouse interview. Plenty of other reporters already had cast doubt on the suspects' changing accounts of True's death.

Zarembo and Dorantes headed into the sierra to look firsthand for their story. No one in the Mexican press had made such a trip. As Zarembo entered the mountains, Eaton was coming out, but their paths never crossed.

Looking back, I fault myself for not sending Schiller and a photographer into the sierra on the same journey, but True's death weighed heavily on me and other editors at the newspaper. I allowed my trepidation to overcome my journalistic instincts.

"The first thing we did was fly to San Miguel and get permission from the local Huichol governor," Zarembo said. "We had to wait in a little shack for him, and he had to dictate the letter. There was another Huichol there who knew how to write, and I remember he used one finger to type it all out. They also gave us a guide. The idea is we were going to trace Philip's route."

Their charter pilot retraced the route taken by Manuel Obaya and Fred Chase in December, banking out of San Miguel and heading east toward Amoltita. They made a hairy landing on Amoltita's overgrown runway. But this time there were no menacing men with machetes in the welcoming party. They unloaded their gear, and the pilot agreed to meet them three days later at noon. Zarembo and Dorantes and their guide walked into Amoltita late in the afternoon and headed toward a few Huichols milling about a small pavilion in the center of the village—a few dozen scattered, low-slung cinder block dwellings.

"There was a little tension, but I was so new to Mexico I didn't know enough to feel threatened," Zarembo said. "There was a lot of gossip about what happened to True. People pointed out to us the hillside where they first saw True. There was a sense of shame, as if people knew these guys in jail were the ones, at least somehow involved."

The villagers allowed the visitors to spend the night in the small village school. The next morning the guide led them out of Amoltita toward Yoata, the small settlement where the Chivarra and Hernandez families lived. "It was far and really steep. And I say that having done a lot of hiking and some mountaineering, glacier climbing," Zarembo said. "This was a the hardest thing I've ever done. It was extreme terrain. The guide kept telling us we were almost there, and we kept clearing one hill and seeing another."

They finally reached Yoata as night fell. What they found was a settlement of five dwellings built on stilts and dramatically seated atop a sheer cliff. The view into the canyon, Zarembo said, was staggering. Yoata did not exist on any maps.

The family was not happy to see the visitors, but after speaking with the guide, offered to let them men sleep on woven bamboo floor mats in a vacant house. "As we lay down that night on these woven mats they use, we realized we probably were sleeping in the houses of True's murderers," Zarembo said.

The new day began on a testy note when Zarembo awoke to observe angry family members glaring at Dorantes as he bathed in a nearby spring above the dwellings. "They were really pissed because he was using their water source, a natural spring, as a bathtub," he said. "They had turned it into a little pool and fenced it off so the cows couldn't get in there. And there's Sergio soaping up."

The guide convinced the family to speak to Zarembo. Everyone, he said, had a different story to offer. Juan's brother, Martin, was more forthcoming than he had been with Tracey Eaton, essentially confirming that Juan and Miguel killed True.

"Martin said Juan and Miguel had walked to the village of Jésus María to make this religious offering and that they caught up to True and he was drunk," said Zarembo. "He wanted to take their picture and they pushed him off a cliff, and when they came back they saw the body and took it down to the river."

Yolanda, Juan's pregnant wife, also was there. She had accompanied the two men on their walk to Jésus María, and according to what she told authorities at the time of their arrest, she had fled after witnessing the attack on True.

"When I asked her about it she started crying. She said, 'They told me to walk ahead. I didn't see what happened.' When they got to the same spot on the way back, they told her to keep going while they stayed to dispose of the body," Zarembo said.

Zarembo and Dorantes stayed a few more hours and then headed back to Amoltita. The return hike was more than Dorantes, in his forties, could handle. After two hours, he stopped, too fatigued and dehydrated to walk under the weight of his own gear. Zarembo and the guide divided up the load, rested, and resumed their hike. They soon met a Huichol man leading a mule along the path in the other direction. After some negotiation, they persuaded him to rent out the mule and accompany them to Amoltita. With the mule bearing their backpacks and gear, the group made it to the village just after nightfall and slept once more in the village school.

Zarembo and Dorantes had exhausted their food supply and were famished after two days of vigorous hiking. The next morning, they paid several hundred pesos, an extravagant sum, to a village woman to kill one of the skinny hens they saw pecking at the dirt. "This woman cooked up the smallest chicken I'd ever seen," Zarembo said. "What came out of the pot was practically all bones."

They met their pilot at noon and were soon airborne, headed toward Guadalajara. "I couldn't stop thinking about this notebook," Zarembo said. "We heard some pretty damning stuff up in the sierra."

Over the noise of the engine, he convinced the pilot to alter course and turn toward Colotlán. "We were filthy, dusty, and this time we found the judge alone, and I think he felt sorry for me," Zarembo said. "I told him there might be clues to the case inside the journal and I would help translate any English notes for him. He made a call and then told me I could see the notebook the next day."

The judge told Zarembo that the notebook was locked up in an evidence room at Puente Grande, the state prison in Guadalajara where Chivarra and Hernandez were first held. The next morning Zarembo arrived at the prison where a guard accompanied him into the evidence room. He saw True's size 9 1/2 hiking boots on a shelf. The guard and Zarembo rifled through True's backpack, still packed with dehydrated food, camping gear, and clothing. Zarembo was tempted to study True's trip map and look for possible markings and notes on his progress, but time was short and the guard was nervous. Zarembo ignored the map and soon laid his hands on the notebook. He opened it and saw True's handwritten journal entries in English and Spanish. Now, Zarembo knew, he had his story, right there in his two hands. First he had to get it out. "The guard agreed to let me use the photocopy machine there in the office and then he took the notebook back and told me, 'Get out of here.'"

Zarembo left before anyone could challenge him, eager to get back to his Guadalajara hotel and read True's notes. For the first time, someone would be able to walk behind True and recreate his journey and the events leading up to his death in the Chapalagana.

As Zarembo leafed through the pages, he was startled by an entry toward the end in which True recorded a tense confrontation with a Huichol named "Juan" outside Amoltita. As True came down the trail, Juan ignored his greeting and demanded to know if True had permission from local authorities. When True said he had permission from Huichol authorities in Tuxpan de Bolaños, Juan said he needed permission from San Sebastián authorities. He was hostile and told True to follow him to his village, where he might be jailed. While the entry itself is not definitive proof that "Juan" was Juan Chivarra, how many other men named Juan could be found vaccinating cattle in such a sparsely settled area? Didn't Chivarra tell authorities in his first confession that he had encountered True on the trail one day before deciding to kill him? Surely the man True encountered was Juan Chivarra.

Zarembo's story took up three pages of *Newsweek's* U.S. edition, an unusually generous allotment of space for a foreign-news story with no major policy implications. An even longer, more detailed story with more photographs made the cover of *Newsweek's* Latin America edition. The cover image was Rick Hunter's last photo of True standing placidly over a gorge in central Mexico.

I will never forget receiving a message from my assistant that Monday in early March asking me to call Zarembo at *Newsweek's* Mexico City bureau. We did not know each other, but the message line, "found True's journal," said everything I needed to know.

True's journal begins in Tlaltenango, where he last telephoned Martha, a typical small Mexican city located along a secondary highway, a onetime Indian village that grew over the centuries to become a bustling town. It's a visual mix of colonial and late-nineteenth-century preserved churches, homes, and government buildings, surrounded by uninspiring contemporary construction. The meeting of the indigenous and Hispanic is most felt in the main plaza, where people look more Indian than Mexican as they gather in the shadow of the handsome church.

The plaza is the town's public gathering spot. Locals of all ages flock there at night and on weekends to share a park bench or stroll around the square in quiet conversation. The plaza's margins are home to a friendly mix of newspaper vendors, rag-snapping shoeshine boys, and an old man tinkling his handlebar bell announcing the arrival of the *paleta* or Popsicle cart.

True spent an unplanned day exploring the town and chatting up locals when his Sunday bus to Tuxpan de Bolanos failed to show. The town shops feature handmade straw cowboy hats, leather huaraches, and hand-tooled leather belts with *ixtle*-embroidered cowhide, handiwork known as *cinturón piteado*. Artisans work with thin strands of thread from the maguey plant, the same succulent used to make tequila, and deftly weave the white filaments into images of fighting cocks or bucking horses. The belts are an essential piece of *vaquero* or cowboy fashion for men throughout Mexico.

Amid traditional pursuits, True saw signs that locals were leaving Tlaltenango for a new life north of the border. Stucco and concrete building walls advertised cheap airfares and package deals to Los Angeles and San Francisco. Boys wearing Dallas Cowboys T-shirts pedaled U.S.-made mountain bikes. Stateside license plates hung on battered old vehicles that somehow had made the long journey south for the December *fiesta* and Christmas holidays with returning migrants behind the wheel. A large street banner advertised a peso-for-dollar exchange house with the latest buy and sell rates.

Miguel Sanchez was a seventy-year-old huarache maker and Tlaltenango native. He told True he lamented the effect of migration on the city and his family. He especially missed his children, who had left Mexico. Sanchez's shop and home occupied a quarter of a block off the plaza, thanks to the U.S. dollars that family members regularly sent back from the states. The family patriarch would readily trade it all for the return of his far-flung sons. "My wife made a tragic journey to Alaska to visit our younger son, seriously hurt in a car accident, but I have never left," Sanchez said. "I told him, 'Why not stay here? I will lend you money to start a business. You won't be rich, but you can make a life. Look at what I've done for you all.'

"He moped around for a month," Sanchez continued, and then he said, 'I will go one more time. I will come back, and here I will plant myself.' And it came true. He went, and after his accident he came back home to plant himself. He is buried there in the village cemetery."

Monday morning, November 30, three days after he left Martha in

Mexico City, True finally boarded the "Huichol Express" for Tuxpan de Bolanos. His journal reveals little about the trip on the "ancient Mexican road on the left from the Sierra." The inside of the bus, he noted, was "saturated with the smell of human sweat and wooden smoke."

True jotted down some reflections, noting the Huichols' mixed success over the centuries in resisting Western pressure to assimilate. He also made some interesting observations about Mexico that reveal his sometimes critical, sometimes romantic take on his adopted home.

Mexico has given the world many negative standards of measure. Mexican jails, dogs, buses. In Sierra Madre, John Huston gave another: The Mexican outback, one of the greatest uprisings of peaks and canyons in the world, where Geronimo and Pancho Villa both hid out from civilization, was used by Huston to spawn his federales, a brand of lawless lawmen that Humphrey Bogart found out the hard way didn't need no "stinking badges."

Dry and High, the southern sierra are ridges, mesas and plunging canyons with clear rivers at their bottoms. The remote past belongs to the Huichol Indians. Proud, positive and tenacious, the Huichol man resisted Spanish, Mexican and Catholic efforts to blot out their nation's culture with clothes, peyote, etc.—beads, masks [sic].

Although their numbers are diminishing, those who hang on here seem happy, taking the best of what is offered as roads and electricity and government influence gradually push into their frontier . . . although many have to work or sell beaded masks or dream pictures in Guadalajara or Mexico City, it is here that they are at home, and here they will stay for as long as they can.

Huichol resistance to the Spanish conquest and proselytizing Franciscans who accompanied the Spanish conquistadores is well documented. Nonetheless, the Huichols continue to succumb to the temptations of Western culture. True only had to look out his bus window to observe a "burro train packing shelled corn, construction materials, and a brand new TV set back to Mesa el Venado, a community with no electricity."

Such telling observations, unfortunately, are few in number.

Journalists who have reviewed True's journal are stumped by the absence of daily diary postings. Notations recording activities and experiences on the road are largely absent. True seldom records the date or time of day he wrote, or his location. He omits any mention of meals, *pensiónes* where he slept on his way to the trailhead, or his peso expenditures, however modest.

How True expected to recall the details of his journey without reference notes is hard to imagine. Perhaps he had stopped thinking as a newspaper man, given the disinterest among editors in San Antonio, and had come to see the trip only as a personal quest, a last solitary experience in the outdoors before the birth of his son or daughter and his passage into fatherhood.

I came to see his trek as a way of breaking with his sad past and embracing the future, one in which he would leave behind the burdens of the family of his youth for the promise of his new family. If that was the case, True might have abandoned journalistic inquiry for a more personal memoir. Yet he wrote nothing about his past on this trip, just as he had hardly ever written about the past.

Perhaps his lack of formal training as a journalist made him less attentive to the basics, but that is improbable. True's undergraduate degree from the University of California–Irvine was in comparative cultures, a course of study that surely honed his observational skills, an essential talent for a good newspaperman. True knew it was often the little things that yielded the best descriptive material. His newspaper work had always been built on solid reporting. But this time, at least, there was little of either.

Near the end of his journal he pays some attention to time as he falls farther behind on his ambitious ten-day, hundred-mile route. His journey in words was a puzzle that slowly took shape as I matched his notes against the map and the suspects' statements.

One mystery not cleared up by the journal is where True spent

Monday night, November 30, when he boarded the bus from Tlaltenango to Tuxpan de Bolanos. Only when another U.S. magazine journalist arrived in the sierra did some of the missing puzzle pieces fall
into place.

Paul Kvinta, an intrepid reporter for *Outside* magazine, retraced
True's footsteps in an impressive ten-page spread published in the
magazine's June 1999 issue, perhaps the most exhaustive story on
True's walk through Huichol country. Kvinta also struggled to make
sense of the journal as he tried to match diary entries against True's
intended route and actual rate of progress. "That is some of the
roughest country I've ever encountered," Kvinta told me. "I was
amazed to learn that True went in there alone and without a guide."

Kvinta knew that Philip carried with him a gift of green parrot
feathers for Jesús Gonzalez, a *mara'akame* (Huichol shaman) who
lived in Tuxpan de Bolanos. Philip and Martha had befriended Gonzalez on a previous journey during Holy Week of 1998, when they
were invited to witness a peyote ceremony. But True failed to meet up
with Gonzalez to give him the colorful feathers. He was seen walking
out of Tuxpan de Bolanos, according to Kvinta's reporting, on Tuesday
afternoon, December 1. Somehow True lost another day between his
presumed Monday departure from Tlaltenango. What did he do with
himself from Monday night through Tuesday afternoon?

"We were good friends. I don't know why he didn't stop by to see
me," Gonzalez told Kvinta.

While reading Paul Liffman's unpublished dissertation, I came
across the name of someone else True failed to call on: Maclovio
Curiel Mayorga, the unnamed PRI mayor True alluded to in his original story proposal as "that rarest of things, a decent PRI politician."
How could True pass through town without calling on the man at the
center of his proposed story exploring the clash of tradition and
modernity in the Sierra Madre?

Did True have a full appreciation of Huichol sensitivities to outsiders, even those who, like himself, had visited previously? We will
never know.

The journal tells us little about True's days and nights on the trail: making and breaking camp, weather changes, meal preparation, the sounds of animals at night, or the pleasure of espresso at sunrise.

The lack of writing, together with True's late start—he did not begin his walk until his fourth afternoon away from home—suggests that he focused on making up lost ground rather than taking notes. True seemed to abandon the walker's mantra that the journey is more important than the destination. Or he concluded that the epic trek he had plotted was overly ambitious. In order for him to reach his destination by the appointed day, he would have to sacrifice much of the reason he came. In that sense, True lost control of his trip at the very outset.

He might have realized, early on the trail, that his romanticized view of "life in a Huichol village" was terribly wrong. The Huichols he encountered along his path were not the Huichols described in his story proposal. His first village experience introduced him to Huichol aloofness and what awaited him all along his path.

Ironically, a single word, "friendly," is written across the top of page 11 of his journal in what appears to be his first notation once he left the trailhead and began his hike. Under this optimistic heading he added, "People met on the trail are albeit [sic] invariably friendly. ¿'Pa' donde (va)? Que milagro,' a vernacular greeting that translates to, 'Where are you going, what a miracle,' but typically means, 'Long time no see' or 'Fancy meeting you here.'

These first Huichols seemed mystified at the sight of the tall gringo with the even taller backpack. "Friendly," he would soon learn, was a hasty conclusion.

Before his first night on the trail, True reached Mesa el Venado, described by Kvinta as a small cluster of simple dirt brick dwellings surrounded by forest. "Come into Venado and it's different, a group of people sitting around, drinking at the tienda supplied by burro [which True had seen from his bus window], scatters as backpacker shows up. Taciturnity. 'Buenas tardes—Tardes. ¿Como le va?' Stoic, silent faces. 'It sure is hot.' Long silence. 'Si.'"

True's encounter with the sullen villagers was brief. Given the silent treatment, he wasted little time exiting the village. He was an unexpected and unwelcome stranger, and clearly he would not be invited to stay for a drink, share a meal, or make camp. He turned back to the trail in search of a place to pitch his tent.

Gonzalez's son, Tomás, served as Kvinta's guide. He told the *Outside* magazine correspondent that he was near Venado the night of December 1, when he noticed a figure in a sleeping bag in a "grove of large leafed oak trees." Unaware that it was True, whom he knew, Tomás continued on his way.

Kvinta and Tomás received a somewhat more welcoming reception in Venado, but only after Tómas presented paperwork affirming Kvinta's right to be there, papers that were carefully scrutinized by the village men, Kvinta noted in his story. While the two were eventually invited to spend the night on the dirt floor in one of the humble dwellings, they were told by the village men that True "walked right through the village . . . he didn't talk to anyone, and no one talked to him."

Such a self-serving version of events can be traced to Huichol sensitivity to the attention that True's murder had brought to the region. The Mesa el Venado villagers, in the wake of the killing, did not want to appear inhospitable or in any way responsible for True's death. But they were guilty of something. There is no reason to doubt True's journal entries, while there was ample reason for the Huichols to recount events in a manner that masked their unwelcoming behavior. It can be argued that True should have sought permission to make his trip. But it is equally true that the men of Mesa el Venado shunned the visitor who interrupted their daytime drinking jag.

Kvinta recalled later how valuable his Huichol guide was as they entered other villages. "When we came into a village, everyone would just stare at me, and not in a hospitable way," he said. "Then the guide would formally address everyone and tell them who I was and why I was there and you could just see everyone relax and change their attitude."

If True misjudged his reception by isolated Huichol villagers, he also romanticized the rugged backcountry of the Sierra Madre in his story pitch. *The Treasure of the Sierra Madre* is vintage Hollywood, a backdrop landscape painting of an untamed frontier where a good man with a trusty six-shooter and a sturdy horse could conquer all. Up close, the Sierra Madre is all together something else, a place that renders the individual trekker insignificant. Any visitor, no matter how skilled, contemplating a solo crossing would take pause at the endless ranges of peaks, high mesas, and narrow canyons, a world stretching endlessly into the cloudbanks.

That seemed to be the case as True set out the next morning for Popotita (to be distinguished from Popotito, farther along his route), the next village on his map. Along the way, a passing Huichol remarked to True, "I never saw one of you people here before."

If the people did not live up to True's expectations, the landscape did. The wilderness vistas True evoked in his proposal revealed themselves as he skirted the rims of several sheer precipices leading down to the distant river. It was True's first look at the enormity of the landscape.

"Leaving Venado, the sierra opens up, with the land plummeting down to [the] bottom of Rio Camatlán, hills and ridges in the distance. Maybe not Copper Canyon," he wrote, referring to Mexico's grandest canyon in Chihuahua state to the north. "But [it] seems scary to someone who will traverse it alone on foot."

"Scary" was a word True did not use lightly. Even when others marveled at his adventures and misadventures or expressed reservations about his planned solo treks into the wilderness, True tended to smile knowingly. Such trips were not for most people but were fine for someone with his experience.

Now days behind, True might have wished to be at home with Martha rather than alone in the vastness of a place he had underestimated, amid a people he did not really know. "Gorges so deep, and the cost of access so high, that you just might call them evil and forget about going down there," True wrote. "It can take you two days of hard walking to reach a place you can see and almost reach out and touch."

True must have made a striking figure on the horizon as he walked alone high above the deep, slithering cut in the earth, slowly and steadily moving forward, the silhouette of his tall backpack signaling Huichols near and far that an outsider was afoot on their lands.

True arrived that afternoon in Popotita, in time to witness the corn harvest in progress. The few frames of film retrieved from his camera document the workers in the field. One photograph shows a young boy with stalks in hand, another a woman turning away shyly. True's photos are unexceptional, taken at a distance and, it appears, in fading light. The frames suggest he was not at liberty to work openly amid the harvesters.

Huichols, like many indigenous people, feel violated when their image is reproduced against their will or without their consent. Some believe the camera and its user rob people of their spirit. Others worry about foreigners profiting from their captured images, and some are concerned that photographs copy what is sacred and should remain singular. Huichols typically give or deny permission to take photographs based on their assessment of the visitor's comportment and motives. Paul Liffman, the anthropologist and Huichol expert, once photographed a Huichol with his permission, only to be startled by the man's question afterward.

"How many Huichols have you got inside that machine?" the man asked, as if the camera somehow was the repository for something physical or metaphysical.

Huichols understandably resent being objectified by Western outsiders. Huichol village elders expect visitors to look on with respect and to resist the temptation to photograph religious ceremonies. When photography is allowed, it's not unusual for Huichols to request token payments in return. In all cases, maintaining control of their situation rather than surrendering it to strangers is understandably paramount to the Huichols.

There is no record of where True made camp his second night on the trail. The Huichols he encountered in Popotita proved to be as reclusive, if less surly, as those he had met in Mesa el Venado. He must have staked his tent outside of the village, bringing to a close one more day without an invitation into Huichol life.

True retired for the night knowing the biggest challenge of his journey lay just ahead, a descent into the *gran barranca*, the great gorge. Strangely, he closed his journal with a note to himself identical to one he wrote on the bus from Tlaltenango to Tuxpan de Bolanos: "Mexico has given the world some of its great negative imagery." The reappearance of the line suggests he turned in feeling rather negative. If his journal is a reliable guide, True was five days out of Mexico City without a single sustained conversation with a Huichol.

On the next morning, Thursday, December 3, True's spirits seemed reinvigorated. It was nearly a week since he had left Mexico City and he was now three days into his hundred-mile journey. Surely he realized that he could not cover the entire distance in the few remaining days, but he was only two hard days' hike from San Miguel and a lifeline to Martha.

"Goats baahing, children screaming from the distant rancho, the blinding face of the morning sun bathes the russet grasslands in golden light, and casts every blade of grass, every pebble, a shadow," True wrote. "I nosed over the final summit toward the barranca. It was a good morning to be alive."

Later he wrote an appreciation of the Huichols' legendary endurance in the sierra: "Huichols are the original trekkers, going to Real de Catorce on foot."

Real de Catorce is a small silver mining city in north central Mexico founded by the Spaniards in the early 1700s high in the desert-rimmed mountains of San Luis Potosí state. It lies a few hundred miles south of the Texas border and just as far due northeast from the heart of the Huichol sierra. The meaning of the name remains a mystery, though the most quoted version refers to fourteen Spanish royalists killed there defending the Crown's silver mines and mint. Built entirely of native stone and rising up a steep slope, Real is a resurrected ghost town nestled into the backside of a mountain at an altitude of 2,750 meters (10,826 feet).

The Huichols are less interested in the colonial-era town than in Catorce, the desert expanse that stretches for miles below, a place they know as Wirikuta, where the sacred peyote cactus is hunted and gathered during annual dry season pilgrimages. The Huichols have a word, *yeiyari*, that represents the ceremonial cycle and can be translated as "path" or the "way." One creation story tells of a caterpillar laying out the original pathways from the sierra to the peyote region.

For the Huichols, territory is central to identity, and historically they trace their existence over a space "90,000 square kilometers (56,250 square miles) in five states of western and north-central Mexico," according to Liffman. Today, the 20,000 or so Huichols dwell in a much smaller world, an area that encompasses 5,000 square kilometers (3,125 square miles) and the three indigenous communities recognized by the Spanish Crown in the early eighteenth century. Even within that reduced expanse, Huichols find their land holdings constantly under challenge.

While the peyote-producing desert is now far from the Huichol communities, they remain connected to the land. Aspiring *mara'akames,* Huichol healers, must make the pilgrimage five times to achieve their desired rank and status. But the days are long gone when Huichol pilgrims braved mountains and desert and made the 500-mile round-trip journey on foot or burro with only as much food as they could carry. Since the 1950s and 1960s, what was once a three-week journey now is accomplished in a matter of days in trucks and buses on roads that bypass fenced-off ranches and other modern-day impediments as well as the many sites the Huichols hold sacred that now lie beyond their reach. Yet the romantic myth persists, even in True's journal. Even now, however, as Liffman notes, it can still be an "exhausting, costly and even dangerous trek," and for the Huichols an important rite of passage.

The town's legend and continuing attraction begins with a long, narrow tunnel, nearly a mile and half in distance, that cuts through the mountain and is the only roadway to the outside world. Travelers on Mexico's Highway 57, which connects Laredo, Texas, to Mexico

City, turn off the highway and, after a half hour's drive, arrive at an old cobblestone road that climbs and twists for sixteen miles up to the mouth of the tunnel. Traffic in each direction takes turns moving through the single lane subterranean passage.

Most Huichols avoid the town and tourists, instead finding their way to the place of the emerging sun at Cerro Quemada, a mesa 11,000 feet above the desert reached on foot or by horseback from Real. Numerous campfire rings attest to the number of peyote worshipers who have spent a night there as part of the pilgrimage, under the influence, gazing into the seemingly infinite distance.

After encountering Huichols in and around Real during frequent visits over a twenty-five-year stretch dating back to the mid-1970s, I came to regard them as a private people, not interested in interacting with gringos. Maybe I lacked the anthropological curiosity of True, maybe I was less taken with Carlos Castañeda's New Age fictional writings, but I never wanted to intrude on Huichols during a peyote ritual. Westerners tend to ingest drugs to get high, to alter their state of mind or escape reality. Huichols use the cactus in religious ceremonies to commune with ancestors present at the creation of the Wixárika, the Huichol people and their world. Whatever insights one experiences in a hallucinatory state, to the sober observer the peyote eater appears wasted, sometimes catatonic, other times alternately laughing, crying, and incoherent. Like True and others who came of age in the 1960s and early 1970s, I had my own experiences with LSD, peyote, and other drugs. Most of those so-called trips long ago had settled deep into the subconscious, beyond memory or articulation.

True had his own long challenge looming. While he would be halfway through his journey once he overcame the Chapalagana and reached San Miguel, the 3,000-foot-deep canyon he faced would pose the severest challenge of the trip for the fifty-year-old hiker. Beyond San Miguel lay the last three villages on his map. San Miguel was approximately fifty miles along the trail from where True started, by my calculations. Liffman's dissertation, which includes his own thoughtful views on True's death in the sierra, places the distance at sixty miles.

After San Miguel, True's map would have taken him northwest to San Juan Peyotán and Santa María de Octotlán, a journey equal in distance to what he already had covered, but a much more forgiving trek signaling his approach to the end of the trail. One or two days' walk west of San Miguel, True would have crested one last ridge and then gained a view that on a clear day extends to the Pacific Ocean. From there the ground beneath him would have sloped downhill and away from the isolated canyon country. Any thought of reaching his final destination, however, would require extending his trip. Because of the various delays that began in Tlaltenango, True was averaging closer to six miles a day, well short of the ten-mile days he planned.

From the depths of the Chapalagana, he likely entertained the thought of calling it quits in San Miguel. Why press on when there was zero chance of achieving the full distance in the allotted time? Even if True wanted to make it all the way, out of pride or simple enjoyment of the trek, he knew he was not going to find the Huichol world he envisioned that March day in his home office.

His feelings of homesickness for Martha and their unborn baby were intensifying and he must have been burdened by his promise to return in ten days. The Huichol universe remained almost hermetically sealed to him, even as he walked through its rugged heart. The only reason for continuing, really, was True's long ingrained habit of never quitting in the face of inevitable adversity.

One of the government-built dirt landing strips was in San Miguel, otherwise unreachable by any roads. Any distracting thoughts that True had of quitting his journey as he neared San Miguel, however, must have been dispelled by the panoramic views that grew more dramatic with each step. He made camp that night on the eastern edge of the canyon. "I love you, Martha and bebito," he wrote in his final journal entry for the day.

The next morning, Friday, December 4, he set out early, in time to pause later and observe, "The great barranca—maybe there are bigger ones around here, but nobody talks of them. It is a great thing to have accomplished the relatively easy task of getting in here. Now to get out.

> Down here it looks like watered desert with organ pipe cactus (and) scrub trees . . . Huichol country. This may not be the heart of it, but it seems like the main ventricle. No Catholic or Protestant churches at all. The one priest mentioned in five days lives up on the way to Huastita. Most place names still seem Huichol: Popotito, Chalmotito, Salmontito . . . lots of abandoned homes in Salmontito. Maybe has to do with the late rains, poor harvest. People have to buy corn and beans and spend money to do it, and maybe just a lot of people abandoned the Huichol country . . . When a Huichol official goes out, he wears his full typical garb.

True's random entries provide few clues to his exact whereabouts Friday morning. At first glance he appears to have descended into the canyon bottom, but he also places himself in the abandoned seasonal village of Salmontito. His references to Western religions and a priest and then to Huichol privations suggest he had a conversation of some length and substance with one or more Huichols that gave him some sense of life and conditions around the canyon. Yet no one is directly quoted or otherwise described.

On this fourth day of his trek, at 7:30 A.M., True encounters the first and only Huichol he names in his journal. The man's name is Juan. "Juan sitting on a hillside about 7:30, hunting and whistling to somebody barely visible in rancho below. THIS IS THE PICTURE OF THE TRIP."

For the first time since he left Tuxpan de Bolanos, True witnessed a scene that fired his reportorial instincts. The always friendly True reached out. "Saludos, but declines," True wrote, suggesting he reached out to shake Juan's hand, but the Huichol did not reciprocate.

True then reconstructs the following exchange:

"I'm periodista."

"Did you get authority from San Sebastián?"

"No, from Tuxpan [de Bolanos]."

"We are in San Sebastián, and you must get permission. I am going to rancho and I will send some guys to get your pack. Will take you to San Sebastián and maybe put you in jail. You can't come into Huichol land without permission."

True then writes: "Tells me of some prospectors who were jailed, refused permission to look for minerals and forced out. It looks bad for a bit."

By now True probably realized he would have to talk his way out of his predicament. If he were expelled from the community, he would suffer a serious setback and face two choices: attempt a roundabout circumvention of San Sebastián, exceedingly difficult because of the canyon's reach, or turn back and go home.

It isn't clear if True recorded his notes almost immediately, while awaiting Juan to lead him down to San Sebastián, or if he recorded them later. "Then," True adds, Juan "says something about how even Huichol people from San Miguel Huaixtita need permission to do things here."

"Even passing through?" True asked.

"Nothing more," Juan answered.

"Well then, if I take no pictures, can I pass on?"

"Yes, follow me to my rancho," Juan responds obliquely.

True apparently felt he had no choice but to follow Juan's order. Perhaps True sensed from the start the disturbing nature of Juan's demands and obediently followed while calculating how best to extricate himself from the situation later. Perhaps he didn't. The two men reached Juan's ranch before nightfall.

True writes that Juan "left San Sebastián at 3:30 A.M. with vaccine-tick spray, walked six hours to his rancho, calling out down canyon to other rancho. Along [the] way vaccinated and dipped about 30 head of cattle and burros at ranch. Intended to do some up hill, then walk back five hours back to San Sebastián to be back at his rancho tomorrow."

He seems to be recounting Juan's day that led to their meeting that morning. Perhaps True accompanied Juan on his rounds caring for the livestock. Either way, when the two reach Yoata, heads turn. "Rancho is protected by a pack of mangy, howling dogs that look like eating visitors is their one job in life. Everybody down at the corral watching. Women wash ropa, cows, which Juan vaccinates and sprays. Women are bold, scolding creatures. . . Cattle in open side of corral. Juan is a different man, Shed typical garb for work boots, jeans and shirt—T shirt. Rancho has staggering vista up canyon."

True's handwriting here is partly incomprehensible, but it appears he comes into the village, once again unexpected and unwelcome. Howling dogs snap at him. Surprised villagers, pausing from their chores, turn to stare. No one greets him.

There is nothing in the journal about his escape. The next entry is almost bizarre in its serene observations of True's natural surroundings. It's as if the encounter with Juan and the threat of being jailed were nothing more than a bad dream. His next journal entries begin with his description of a heron, or two different herons, which some would see as harbingers:

"A great white heron glides over running water down canyon in the pre-dawn light. A great blue heron glides over running water, down canyon in pale dawn light.

"There comes a moment in the rising light of day when these leafless, gnarled, spikey, ghost-like trees come alive. Silver branch tops in not yet light strengthen here, looking like snow dusting the limbs."

Then he changes the subject. His attention turns to the challenge ahead. "Trail."

Once again, a single thought compels True to set aside everything else. "A trail is the way—it is a companion. It tells you that you are getting somewhere, even if it's not where you were going, or wanted to, you are not alone, you are accompanied by the legacy of the spirits who went before you, the trail.

"Trail," True wrote, "is security."

He seems relieved to be back on track and more cognizant than ever that a trek through the Sierra Madre was not a trek through Big Bend, Death Valley, or Joshua Tree. At the same time, he may have

been lulled into a false sense of security, having somehow left behind
Yoata and Juan. Knowing True, one has to assume he struck a bargain
and left of his own free will. Perhaps Juan grew tired of playing sheriff
and decided not to pursue the matter because True was willing to
leave San Sebastián that day.

> If you're bushwhacking, you're never sure. You're glad to get back
> on the trail, no matter how adventurous, because you can stop the
> thousand calculations per minute unknown terrain requires—you
> can rest, and glory in just how rugged it is out there. Trail acquires
> personality. It has bones, lines, logic, purpose and spirit. They are
> custom built by the people who want them. Park service trails are
> fat, wide and graded, designed to make plodding feasts of week-
> end backpackers and day hikers. Indian trails are working tools
> designed to get local experts where they want to go quickly. They
> don't need to be much for a superbly conditioned, nimble Indian
> to get on down the road. The savior for an in-between gringo
> backpacker is that here in the Sierra Madre, Indians drive animals
> sometimes, and a loaded burro and a loaded gringo back packer
> can strike a happy balance.
>   Following a trail is like a greyhound following the rabbit—it
> goes ever on, just out of reach. It twists, it curves. Sometimes fat,
> sometimes a gossamer strand, sometimes fiendishly obvious,
> sometimes known only as a particular tilt to a piece of ground.
> The pursuit of it becomes everything. It is the journey upon which
> you are embarked. Lose it, you have lost your way, your purpose,
> your goal. Oh black moment. Find it again, the sun rises on a val-
> ley of waving flowers, the world is all right again—such is the
> drama of trail walking.

I read that passage over and over, coming to see it as a great subconscious burst of insight, foreboding, and relief by our reporter, anxious and under threat one moment, suddenly released back into
freedom and his trail the next. He seems aware of his dire circum-

stances yet is consciously oblivious to the darker possibilities. The same words can be read different ways. Only True knew at that time and place what he really felt or meant.

That night Philip began to compose the last love letter of his six-and-a-half-year marriage to Martha, one that he would continue writing into the next day. He wrote it in Spanish, his adopted language, in his adopted country, while wandering in a strange land where his presence was neither understood nor welcome. By now, even True, lover of Mexico, its people, its history and its culture, knew that the feelings were not mutual in Huichol territory. True was a trespasser in the eyes of the Huichols he had encountered. It began badly in Mesa el Venado and never got better. If anything, the deeper in he walked, the farther from friends he found himself.

> Dear Martha,
> Here I am in Salmontito. How I arrived here I will tell you later because the light is fading. It is the end of a late day of walking. Minor problems, but surmountable. Tomorrow the biggest canyon of all, according to the Huichols. We will see. I miss you every day. I think about you and the little baby. I hope that you are well and secure in my love for both of you. I wanted to write you because I miss you and it's the thought of talking to you in Huastita, to send you a message. I love you, Felipe.

It would be impossible later to read Philip's last love letter to Martha as simply a journal entry; impossible not to view it as a final, unconditional affirmation of all that was good about their life together: a strong marriage, the coming baby, commitment. Philip True no longer harbored doubts.

He closes his journal Friday night with one final thought:

> Some people test their mettle by climbing high peaks. In the Sierra Madre it's the depths of the holes that you climb up out of that is the mark of your mettle.

True arose Saturday morning, deep inside the Chapalagana, and added another note in Spanish to his wife.

> The next day, my dear one. I am accompanied in the bottom of the canyon, possibly the biggest one here. The people told me it would take me three hours to descend, but I needed five! I am coming to a wall of rock, clear brown with a bit of red... The water was rose colored under the rising sun. Above the rock, is a waiting cactus, above that, huisache or something. Above that is the sky, still blue. To the left, a rock tower that reaches toward the sky, and not very far from it.
>
> I hope that you can enjoy this with me. I know that you will never be able to come here, but you will know something of me. Maybe the baby. This place is very wild. It is hard, difficult, beautiful, and terrible. It is good to know it.

These passages reveal more of True's feelings than anything else he had ever written. Over the preceding twenty-four hours, True's journal had turned into a letter home, one that would not arrive until months after his death, on the cusp of his son's birth.

True wrote one more passage in Spanish, the language he reserved to express his innermost personal feelings to Martha:

> I am going to pass tomorrow, Saturday, here. I've been thinking about a day of rest, and I believe this is the moment. I have to go up, more or less, 1200 meters (3,700 feet) to reach San Miguel to call you via the radio there, so because of that, I've been pushing. But the last four days have cost me, and I am taking into account that I am going to need all of my strength for this ascent. So, please understand me if I don't arrive in time to call you before Monday. For the time being, that's it for now. It's time to cook the beans and dried beef. I love you and the baby.

The next morning, Sunday, December 6, True awakes and begins his day's journal, pages 43–44, with another single word: "Bird."

Size of large jay, dark (black?) tail with two feathers middle about 12" long, yellow belly and crest. Squawks and talks like a parrot. Tail feathers tipped white with crest, dark head to yellow of lower throat and belly, flies lightly and gracefully, landing in slender branches.

True again described the bird as if it were an arriving messenger harboring news. Those were his last written words. How he spent his last morning on the trail will never be known.

He broke camp and began his climb out of the Chapalagana and onward to San Miguel. Sometime that morning, Chivarra and Hernandez set upon True. While we may never know the truth surrounding his murder, we know that on this day, in the Chapalagana, True met his death. His long journey had come to an end.

14

Mexican Justice

O! what came so close
that we were never able to know.
O! what was never able to be
That maybe could have been.

— Pablo Neruda, "Time That Wasn't Lost"

While the suspects sat in the Colotlán jail and the case faded from public view, Martha made plans to leave Mexico City. The house on Sierra Amatepec, which once seemed so cozy, now felt empty, a tomb of memories. An embracing fold of family and friends awaited the expectant mother at home in the sister cities of Brownsville, Texas, and Matamoros, Mexico. Martha was back on the border by February.

For True's friends and colleagues in the *Express-News* newsroom, the prosecutorial lethargy was disheartening. How could authorities inventory the contents of the backpack, photograph True's journal, and then return it unread to his backpack? It was hard to say if incompetence or indifference explained the oversight. U.S. officials in Guadalajara, meanwhile, failed to undertake their own independent inquiry. Certainly the FBI's local office had the necessary contacts to gain access to the backpack. But it didn't happen.

The majority of U.S. reporters in Mexico believed the suspects were guilty, but many Mexican reporters, accustomed to Jalisco-style justice, assumed that the two Huichols were coerced into confessing and might be random victims of investigators looking to close the case. Over and over again, we heard people in Mexico complain that the government would have ignored the case if the victim had been a Mexican. They resented what they saw as special attention paid to one dead U.S. journalist.

Martha remained outwardly stoic, but she was grief-stricken and depressed by the horrible nature of her husband's death, which was not conducive to a happy pregnancy. Three months before her due date in June, she went into what her doctors called stress-induced labor.

Philip Theodore True, 3 pounds, 4 ounces, was born March 9, 1999, at Valley Central Hospital in Brownsville. Martha had lost one Philip True. Now she and her family prayed she would not lose another. Little Philip True, who would be called Teo, short for Teodoro, spent his first six weeks in the hospital's neonatal unit on a respirator, struggling to breathe and eat on his own.

Newsweek's story disclosing the existence of the journal the same week of little Philip's birth ignited a new wave of media coverage. True's journal reference to his hostile encounter with "Juan" near Amoltita gave reporters new reason to suspect the two Huichols charged with the murder. Susana Hayward, who had moved permanently to Mexico City to take True's place, made her first trip to the Colotlán jail in early April in the company of Bob Owen, the newspaper's chief photographer.

"Go away! Leave!" Chivarra shouted at Hayward after learning she worked for the same newspaper as True.

He stomped off but returned shortly, preening before Owen's cameras, donning a pair of sunglasses belonging to a jail guard. While

Chivarra held the stage, Hernandez accommodated his antics with laughter.

"Give me money," Chivarra told Hayward, peering through the bars of his cell, refusing to grant her an interview even as a prison guard urged him to meet with the visiting journalists.

Chivarra offered the same story he gave the *Newsweek* reporter. "I'm telling you the truth," he said. "I saw him walking by when I was vaccinating cows, that's all. I never saw the gringo before in my life. I didn't touch him. I didn't kill him."

The two men told Hayward they confessed only after enduring beatings and torture. "They hit us a lot, so I decided to say, 'Yes, yes, we did it!'" Chivarra said.

"They hung me by the neck from a tree," Hernandez chimed in, speaking for the first time. "If you are hanging from a tree, you will agree to anything."

Later Hayward asked the local prosecutor, David Magdaleno Rodriguez, about the journal. He hadn't even read it.

A new defense lawyer, Juan Pedro Salas Castillo, had replaced the Huichols' public defenders, but he refused to tell Hayward who was paying his fee. Salas was taking his job seriously, though, by seeking the suspects' release on the grounds that they spoke poor Spanish and were denied access to a Huichol interpreter during their interrogation. He also convinced the trial judge to let him amend the defendants' previous confessions months after the fact. It was a move the prosecution missed or ignored, despite the state's reliance on those statements to pursue a swift conviction.

"Legally, they have a right to do that," Judge Aguiar told Hayward. "One of them said he had an encounter with Mr. True, but obviously he is saying he did not kill him."

The differing autopsy results were also complicating matters. Aguiar seemed to accept the second autopsy performed by federal officials to be evidence worth consideration, and he appointed an independent expert to reconcile the contradictions in the two reports.

More than once I imagined True, alive and on the job, assigned to cover the story of an American journalist's death and the arrest of two Huichols charged with his killing. Would the suspects' admission of guilt and other circumstantial evidence persuade True of their guilt, or would he have sided with the defendants and their claims they were tortured and denied due process? There was no easy answer to that one.

As Martha spent her days traveling to the hospital to be with baby Philip, the case against True's confessed killers seemed less certain than ever. Only one month earlier, the near miraculous appearance of True's journal and the circumstantial link it established between True and "Juan" had persuaded doubters and strengthened the case against the jailed Huichols. Now a speedy verdict seemed unlikely.

In April, I traveled to Washington to attend the annual convention of the American Society of Newspaper Editors and to ask the organization's board to approve a resolution calling on Mexico to deepen the investigation and prosecute True's killers. Speaking with individual board members, I was struck by how few of them knew much about the case. True's murder had been front-page news in Mexico, but many U.S. editors seemed only vaguely aware of the fact. Yet that May, six months after True's death, his name was added to the roll call of 1,200 other journalists etched on the Freedom Forum Journalists Memorial in Arlington, Virginia, a monument honoring the work of reporters, photographers, and editors killed in the line of action. True was one of twenty-nine journalists killed worldwide in 1998.

We were weighing our scant options when a call came from Julio Muñoz, the executive director of the Miami-based Inter American Press Association. The IAPA has a long tradition of fighting for press freedom in the Americas, especially in countries ruled by undemocratic military regimes.

"Bob, what do you think about an official mission to Mexico to meet with President Zedillo and everyone involved in the case?" Muñoz asked me. He said the delegation would meet with Zedillo on behalf of several journalists killed in recent years in Mexico and then travel to

Guadalajara for face-to-face meetings with the prosecutors and governor in the True case. "Would you be willing to join that mission?"

There was no need to answer yes.

Our seven-member delegation gathered outside the Hotel Marquis
Reforma on the first day of June, a clear, cool morning, the kind of
day that tricks the visitor into momentarily forgetting the chronic pol-
lution that plagues Mexico City most of the year. This was my first
stay at the new Marquis, an opulent art deco palace of polished gran-
ite, marble archways, and upscale shops. It was not a place True in
his blue jeans and flannel shirt would have been found. Many rooms
overlook Chapultepec Castle and Park, and after checking in, I found
myself gazing down at the tiny human forms walking, jogging, enjoying the open spaces. A guest with a good pair of binoculars could have
spotted True trudging under the weight of his rock-filled backpack in
the weeks before his departure.

A handsome, silver-haired, and always impeccably tailored Argen-
tine named Jorge Fascetto, the publisher of *El Día* in La Plata, a city
outside Buenos Aires, headed the delegation. Most U.S. newspapers
belong to large corporations, while most Latin American newspapers
are still family businesses. Publishers and editors are often family
members and many of them, like the Fascetto family, had endured
years of dictators, censorship, and human rights violations in their
countries.

Fascetto's elegance was matched by a broad intellect and a razor-
sharp sense of humor that he plied with equal skill in Spanish and
accented English. He always travels in the company of his warm-
hearted wife, Bunty.

Fascetto had been to San Antonio years earlier, and he liked to
tease me about the "ditch running through San Antonio," his irrever-
ent description of the River Walk, a major downtown amenity and
tourist draw. He joked with me again as we boarded several hotel
sedans for the ride across the city to the offices of Zedillo's attorney

general, Jorge Madrazo Cuellar. Fascetto could keep any group loose, even on the way to an adversarial meeting with a high-ranking political appointee.

Madrazo was a cipher to the delegation. He was a nationally respected expert on the Mexican constitution and a former professor and researcher at UNAM, the National Autonomous University of Mexico, the hemisphere's largest university. He had served as president of the national human rights commission before joining the Zedillo administration. We later wondered if that experience had led him to conclude reflexively that the two Huichol suspects were victims of torture and probably not responsible for True's murder. It was Madrazo's ministry, known by its Spanish initials, the PGR, that had carried out the second autopsy.

The attorney general had been unavailable to Martha and me, even in the immediate days after the recovery of True's remains. Los Pinos seemed to have distanced Zedillo from Madrazo and the PGR with its press bulletin issued weeks after True's death in December stating that Zedillo did not order the second autopsy. The attorney general had responded by going to ground.

After our arrival, an aide ushered us into a small, windowless conference room. A secretary served coffee and then retired. Madrazo entered, clad in an ill-fitting black suit, tense and disinterested in small talk or introductions. Even Fascetto had no luck putting Madrazo at ease.

We wanted to discuss the confusion brought about by the second autopsy, which everyone in the Zedillo administration denied ordering, and we wanted to know if the federal government could and would intervene in the state's legal process.

Why did the federal government order a second autopsy and who ordered it, we asked? Madrazo rambled, not offering a direct response. Why had his office refused to release the full report after initially promising to do so in three to five days? The mood grew tense, the conversation combative. Madrazo chain-smoked.

Fascetto turned the conversation from True to the slain Mexican journalists whose cases remained unsolved. He proposed that the attorney general create a federal task force charged with investigating crimes. Madrazo said it was a novel idea but added, with no sense of irony, that his office was constitutionally prohibited from interfering with state authorities charged with such investigations.

I noted the language contained in a statement issued by Los Pinos on December 17: "The President of the Republic has sent instructions to the appropriate federal judicial authorities to fully assist local authorities in the investigation of [True's death]."

The issue was muddled and Madrazo was not offering any clarity. After forty-five minutes, an aide appeared and whispered in the attorney general's ear. Pleading a busy schedule, Madrazo restated his commitment to democracy and press freedoms, then stood up and wished us well on our stay in Mexico.

The next day we climbed back into the hotel sedans for the short ride through Chapultepec Park to Los Pinos. Zedillo had agreed to receive our group for a thirty-minute private meeting, a promising sign that he wanted the IAPA to recognize his commitment to a free press and a working judicial system. Most of the unsolved killings of Mexican journalists had occurred before Zedillo took office and some dated back almost a decade, so the president did not seem overly sensitive to the delegation's presence. Zedillo knew the the visit would center on the True case.

Zedillo was the first Mexican president to embrace democratic rule. He quietly declined to exercise the autocratic power wielded by his predecessors, even when it would have advanced his own agenda, such as dismissing corrupt governors tainted by drug money. He wanted, above all else, to be remembered as a democratic reformer. Zedillo refused to hand-pick his party's candidate to succeed him as president, a time-honored tradition in the ruling party, thus leaving the decision to primary voters, a historic first in Mexico.

David Nájera, Zedillo's liaison with the foreign press, greeted me warmly and led us up the stairs, past the familiar Dr. Atl volcanoes and into a conference room with a long oval table. A small Diego

Rivera painting of *campesinos* graced the wall behind the president's chair. Zedillo came in moments later, walking around the table, exchanging introductions with each of the editors.

Several years had passed since I had seen Zedillo in person, yet he greeted me by my first name. Personal encounters, I knew from experience, say nothing about how a president wields power. It is easy to charm reporters, to tell them yes when you mean no, and I certainly was not immune to the president's personal attention. But Zedillo always struck me as sincere.

Zedillo was an Ivy League–educated technocrat who had never run for elective office until an assassin's bullet felled the party candidate and he was cast into the presidential race in 1994 as the "accidental candidate." He had cordially agreed to receive our delegation. From time to time he met with select reporters from foreign publications, but he loathed the Mexican press, with its traditions of accepting payoffs from party officials in return for subservient coverage.

He had a low-key political style, and he cared little about drawing attention to his administration's accomplishments. He was indifferent to photo ops and other media exercises, and he tended to measure democratic reform step by small step. He preferred slow, steady momentum to the sudden, spectacular gesture that played well on television and the front page. Most of his progressive moves lacked drama, and to Mexicans, he sometimes looked weak or indecisive when he was merely restrained in style. Zedillo did not like confrontation, and while privately he might have abhorred the lawlessness and lack of justice in so many parts of the country, he was unwilling to act unilaterally.

Fascetto, seated to Zedillo's left, opened the meeting with an overview of press issues in Mexico, in particular the unresolved cases of interest to the IAPA. As he spoke, Fascetto lectured the president on Mexico's dysfunctional judicial system. Leaning back in his chair, speaking with flourishes of his hands and a slightly ironic smile creasing his face, Fascetto seemed oblivious to the Mexican president's darkening countenance. Zedillo stiffened perceptibly in his chair as

Fascetto continued. When the president finally spoke, his face was flushed and there was ice in his voice. He offered a stern defense of his administration and its accomplishments fighting organized crime, defending press freedoms, and working for democratic reforms. Then he looked away.

There is no love lost between Argentines and Mexicans, each at its own end of the hemisphere. Mexico is built on the history and myths of its indigenous culture and the clash of the Spanish conquest. Argentines are New World Europeans.

Fascetto was factually correct in his wide-ranging assessment of the Mexican political landscape. But no Mexican president cares to be dressed down by a newspaper publisher from a country reeling from its own official corruption and a half-century of coups and military juntas responsible for the disappearance and death of thousands of students and leftists in the 1970s.

Alberto Ibarguen, then the *Miami Herald* publisher, jumped in, outlining IAPA's new impunity project, which he would be leading. The strategy was to focus attention on countries and governments where the killing of journalists occurred regularly and where their killers went unhunted and unpunished. Zedillo commented positively on the project but said it would be undemocratic for his administration to intervene in criminal cases, which were the purview of the states, just as they are in the United States, he pointedly said.

When I was given the opportunity to speak, I thanked Zedillo once more for helping us find True. The president nodded as I expressed our fears that a sloppy investigation, coupled with allegations of torture and the controversial second autopsy, might result in True's killers going unpunished. Couldn't he task an aide to prod authorities in Guadalajara into action? The mood grew more relaxed and Zedillo stayed nearly an hour, even trading quips with Fascetto toward the end. We stood up as the president prepared to make his exit. Once again he circled the table to shake hands.

"How are Martha and the baby?" he asked, coming to a stop and holding my hand in his own. "Please tell her I send my personal sympathies and my admiration for her, and please tell her we will do everything we can to get this case finished before the year ends."

Zedillo mentioned that he hoped to travel to San Antonio a few weeks later for the U.S.-Mexico Economic Conference. He left the room, Nájera trailing behind him.

Our meeting the next day with state officials in Guadalajara seemed choreographed. They knew we had been to Los Pinos to see President Vincente Fox, and their renewed commitment to the case seemed rehearsed. Jalisco Governor Alberto Cardenas Jimenez was one of several opposition governors to win state office during Zedillo's administration. In the past, members of the opposition PAN had scored probable victories at the state level, but organized voter fraud by the ruling PRI had kept them out of office. Even Fox had been cheated out of victory in the governor's race in his home state of Guanajuato several years earlier, a PRI-engineered fraud that would propel him into the national arena and eventually lead to his election as president.

Attractive young women in matching miniskirts escorted us to our seats around an enormous conference table with Cardenas at the head. The state attorney general, Felix Ledesma Martinez, also was there with his team of prosecutors and investigators, who sat stiffly with thick case files stacked before them. A supporting cast of subordinates and other local officials rendered the meeting little more than a photo op. Local television cameramen, print reporters, and photographers crowded around us, recording all of us in the act of doing nothing.

Cardenas, like the president, seemed equally sincere in his expressions of sympathy for True's death, but Fascetto pressed him for a timetable. Ledesma answered for him, saying the judge was obligated to rule within a year of the day the two Huichols were formally charged. Prosecutors, however, expected a verdict even sooner, no later than August. One of Ledesma's prosecutors informed us that an "independent doctor" had examined Chivarra and Hernandez after their arrest and had determined that the two men had not been tortured while in army custody.

"If that is true, then why don't you release that report to us and the Mexican press?" I asked. "We'd like to speak with the doctor."

Ledesma consulted with an assistant. They did not have the report with them but promised to retrieve it and make it available to the delegation.

We also questioned the prosecutors' failure to return to the sierra to track down more witnesses, and their failure to treat True's journal as an important piece of evidence. *Outside* magazine had just hit newsstands, and once again an American journalist had proven more enterprising than Mexican authorities.

The prosecution team, unable to hide its nervousness in front of the governor and attorney general, sidestepped our many concerns. They insisted the evidence in hand would lead to a conviction. It was the same posture struck by Horacio Vega Pánames in the first weeks of the case. Clearly nothing more had been done since the initial arrests.

A far larger press corps than we had seen in Mexico City had assembled outside, suggesting significant coverage of our visit on the nightly news and in the morning newspapers. But the reporters finished with us abruptly and then stampeded like a herd toward Ledesma as he exited the building and made a fast break for a waiting car. A young reporter from *Reforma* whom I had met on my previous stay came over to talk.

"A lot of reporters and cameras," I said, somewhat self-importantly.

"Yes, everyone is waiting to see if it is true the governor is going to fire Ledesma today," she said.

I was taken aback. "But we just met with the governor and attorney general, and Cardenas told us he has full confidence in Ledesma winning a conviction in our case," I said.

"That's because he is going to tell you whatever you want to hear," she said.

"Why is there pressure to get rid of Ledesma?" I asked.

"Accusations of repeated abuse and torture of prisoners by investigators during his administration," she said.

My spirits sank.

Indeed, Ledesma soon resigned under a cloud and declined through his U.S.-born wife to be interviewed for this book. The delegation moved on to Guatemala, while I flew home to await a verdict later that summer.

Back home, a U.S. Justice Department official monitoring the case told Gary Martin, the newspaper's Washington bureau chief, that the FBI now considered the case solved. The two Huichol suspects in custody, the agency had concluded, were guilty of killing True just as they originally confessed. A newly elected Democratic congressman from San Antonio, Charlie Gonzalez, had been pressing authorities for some sign of progress in the investigation. His request led the Justice Department official, Jon Jennings, to send him a letter stating the FBI's conclusion. "The FBI is confident the investigation shows the two individuals in custody are the persons responsible for the death of Mr. True," Jennings wrote. "Moreover, while the Mexican prosecutors work to conclude the investigation, the suspects remain in custody without bail."

Gonzalez told Martin the letter still did not give him any certainty the case would be resolved by a set date. "What we're looking for is a timely resolution," Gonzalez told Martin.

Ambassador Jeffrey Davidow, in San Antonio for the U.S.-Mexico Economic Outlook Conference, echoed the letter's findings: "From what I've seen, the case against them is very strong." Later he told me that if we ever let up, the case would go away.

Martha and I met again in October at the IAPA convention in Houston. The organization bestowed a posthumous award on True for his work in Mexico, and Martha, with seven-month-old Teo in arms, accepted the honor. The ceremony was moving, held in a small room after a luncheon speech by Colombian President Andres Pastrana Arango, a former journalist and onetime victim of a political kidnapping. Hundreds of newspaper publishers and editors and their spouses from the Americas were on hand, many of whom had been victims of political violence. All knew the True case, but this was their first contact with Martha.

"I receive it in his name, the name of his son, and in the name of all those who have lost their lives as working journalists," Martha said as she accepted the plaque. Later, she added, "It was very emotional. For me, it was a beautiful, peaceful presentation. It made me feel Philip was very close. And I know wherever he is, he is very proud."

Late in November, Susana Hayward made one more year-end journey from Mexico City to Guadalajara, where she met Gloria Ferniz, the *Express-News* photographer who had accompanied her to the December 1998 arraignment of the two Huichols. They struck a bargain with a driver who owned an aging decommissioned taxi to drive them up the winding mountain road to Colotlán. Ferniz found the narrow switchbacks and plunging gorges almost more than she could bear.

Once there, they met with Judge Aguiar, who admitted to Hayward that he would not render a verdict within the mandated year. Various defense motions were delaying resolution of the case.

The two journalists made their way downstairs to the jail entrance, where the head guard prepared to let them in to meet Chivarra and Hernandez. The two Huichols, perhaps lonely for the attention, spent two hours with Hayward and Ferniz.

Chivarra displayed his trademark bravado, while Hernandez stayed in the background. "People come take notes, always taking notes in their little notebooks, and then they leave," Chivarra said. "They are making money off me, and then I never see them again."

Then Hayward wrote:

He ran his index finger across his neck. He is a dead man.

"You might as well bring in the casket," Chivarra told her, indicating he and his brother were resigned to their fate.

Hayward told Chivarra for the first time about True's journal and the entry recording his confrontation with Juan on the trail.

"I didn't do anything to him. I didn't hit him. I didn't kick him," Chivarra said. "Maybe I can die without thinking about it so much. Already I want to die. Only my God and I know the truth."

Her story appeared in the *Express-News* on Sunday, December 5, one year to the day that True began his ascent from the canyon bottom. We marked the first anniversary of True's death with a relatively brief newsroom ceremony. A muted version of the Mexican altar reappeared, candles were lit, and a few editors made brief remarks. It was short and somber. The year had ended without a verdict.

Newspapers went to press with the January 1, 2000, edition amid sighs of relief and the clinking of champagne flutes. The feared Y2K meltdown never happened. Clocks moved past midnight and all the world's numbers moved from "99" to "00."

Something was happening in Mexico, however, and growing numbers of editors in cities that did not usually pay close attention to events south of the border now wanted to go see for themselves. Editors wanted to meet Vicente Fox, just as editors had wanted to meet Mikhail Gorbachev, Nelson Mandela, and Lech Walesa—individuals who changed the course of history in their countries. Fox held the potential to change Mexico if he could finish first in the three-man presidential race in July. The polls indicated the Mexican people were ready for change. A Fox victory and the fall of the ruling party loomed like a historical inevitability.

There was another growing reason for U.S. editors to show newfound interest in Mexico. Almost anywhere you looked, communities of Mexican migrants were sprouting up, especially in the Southeast and Midwest, which had not been traditional destination points for Mexican laborers. Newspapers in those communities needed to make sense of the situation for their readers even as they struggled to find ways to reach the newcomers.

When I approached the ASNE leadership in April 1999, many editors were unfamiliar with the True case. Now, at the 2000 convention, editors approached me. A group was being assembled to travel to Mexico in June to meet the three presidential candidates, and board officers asked if a smaller delegation should press officials about the True case while there. Nothing had come of the IAPA delegation's visit, but every chance to meet with the president and his possible successors had to be taken.

The group's new president happened to be Rich Oppel, the editor of the nearby Austin *American-Statesman,* a friend and mentor of mine during my first two years as editor in San Antonio. Tony Pederson, then the executive editor of the *Houston Chronicle* and Fascetto's successor as IAPA president, also agreed to join us, along with several other editors from around the country.

"Clearly we are frustrated with the lack of progress in the Philip True matter," Pederson told reporters upon our arrival in Mexico. "It is unfortunately similar to the murders of numerous other journalists in Mexico, in which investigations for whatever reasons seem to stall and those responsible are not brought to justice."

The delegation began its work in Guadalajara this time, where we found ourselves looking across the table at unfamiliar faces. In the one year since I had visited Guadalajara with the IAPA delegation, Ledesma had resigned and his replacement had come and gone just as quickly. Gerardo Octavio Solís Gomez, the third attorney general in as many years, had been named to the post five days before our arrival. An owlish man wearing round, wire rim glasses, he said all the right things and promised a swift resolution. "It is our view, supported by the evidence, that Mr. True was victimized by the two Huichol suspects," Solís told Hayward. "In three to four weeks the evidence part of the trial should be concluded. They should be sentenced for the crimes of homicide and robbery."

In the actual meeting, Solís made it sound like a guilty verdict by decree was forthcoming. "The word has come down from the governor, so the case will go to trial in three to five weeks. You should be reasonably assured, based on the evidence, that the Huichols will be sentenced for homicide and aggravated robbery."

He predicted a prison term of fifteen to thirty years.

Writing later about the trip, Oppel noted, "It is unsettling to have one's objective—justice—quickly converge with a legal official's promise that a conviction will occur, but Solís would not be the first prosecutor to promise a guilty conviction. A judge will have his say."

Those would prove to be the most prescient words written about the case to date.

Solís also informed us that the forensics expert assigned by the judge to reconcile the two autopsies had concluded that the cause of death was edema, the accumulation of fluid in True's lungs. The edema resulted from strangulation, a blow to True's head, or the impact of the blow to his back behind his left lung, perhaps after being shoved down the ravine, or all of the above. Once again we were promised a copy of the report; I reminded the attorney general that we were still awaiting the promised report by the unnamed "independent doctor" attesting to the condition of the two defendants after their arrest. He just looked at me blankly.

Solís and his deputy, Jorge David Delgadillo, introduced us to León Beltrán, the latest prosecutor assigned to the case in Colotlán. He had traveled several hours to Guadalajara to meet with us, the officials emphasized, as if that signified some special commitment to the case. Once again, an August verdict was predicted with confidence. I could only stare at them in frustration.

Afterward, Oppel and Pederson spoke with reporters and expressed optimism about a verdict in the near term. I did my best not to sound a sour note about unkept promises in front of my colleagues. My fellow editors had traveled a long way on behalf of the Express-News and our cause. Several Mexican reporters, now familiar faces, asked for my opinion of the meetings. "The only measure that matters is where we stand in August," I said.

Back at the hotel bar, I had a frank conversation with a Mexican newspaper editor who had joined the delegation. He was an IAPA board member who ran a respected string of independent dailies in northwestern Mexico. I told him I was growing cynical after repeated visits to his country. Every Mexican we had met in the revolving door of Guadalajara justice was either incompetent or a liar.

"Todos son cabrones," he agreed, shaking his head. "They're all fuckers."

The next morning we flew to Mexico City.

We met on June 1 with Zedillo at Los Pinos, almost one year to the day since my last visit. Part of me felt like the unwanted relative who visits too often, and I wondered if there was anything to be gained from a second meeting with a president who had no intention of intervening with state authorities on our behalf. If the case did not get resolved soon, we would be dealing with a new administration.

This time a well-briefed Zedillo wasted no time in outlining his administration's position. Shortly after Oppel made some opening remarks, the president jumped in. "Yes, I know the case very well," he said. "It is a very sad situation."

Recalling his approval of military resources for the search effort, Zedillo added, "It was federal authorities who found his body and caught the criminals. It will be up to the judge to say whether they are guilty."

I smiled as I took notes, thinking there was little doubt how Zedillo himself viewed the suspects if he was labeling them criminals. For the first time, however, Zedillo questioned True's judgment in entering the Huichol sierra without permission and a guide. "This case should not be interpreted that journalists are not safe in this country; this case is not a typical crime situation," Zedillo said. "Mr. True went to this place, these primitive communities, and he was not informed, he was not aware of this, and the tragedy evolved."

Zedillo remained as warm as ever toward me, and as we shook hands, I realized this would be my last meeting with the man who used his son's head to mark his ballot. Mexicans were about to return to the polls, and this time they would carry out a revolution at the ballot box.

15

A Second Anniversary

Most opposition leaders and many independent analysts believe that Mexico's road to democracy will not be completed until the PRI is ousted. Their reasoning: There is such an entrenched system of mutual protection among PRI members that the country will never be able to fight back corruption and restore confidence in its institutions until it is run by a new cast of characters.

—Andres Oppenheimer, *Bordering on Chaos*

On July 2, 2000, voters across the country went to the polls to select a new Mexican president for the *sexenio*, the single six-year term allowed under the national constitution. Many watched with trepidation. In the past, the period between the July vote and the December changing of the guard at Los Pinos had been marked by economic instability and peso devaluations that had devastated both middle-class and working-class Mexicans. Ernesto Zedillo had promised to hand his successor a stable economy and government.

For the past seventy years, "successor" had been synonymous with the handpicked PRI candidate. But the relatively new science of polling in Mexico showed Fox surging. For the first time the PAN sensed the possibility of winning the presidency. Three years of non-stop campaigning by the six-foot-six charismatic rancher, outfitted in cowboy boots and shirtsleeves, was paying dividends. Mexicans wanted change.

Fox projected a more independent image, a plainspoken populist to working-class Mexicans and an experienced, no-nonsense business executive to the country's urban elites. Both voting blocs were fed up with the PRI, its pervasive corruption and cronyism, and its resistance to reform. No one had forgotten that the economic upheaval six years earlier after the last presidential vote had led to near collapse averted only by a massive financial bailout engineered by the Clinton administration.

Francisco Labastida, the ruling party's choice, was proving to be a complacent candidate, overly dependent on the party's machinery and uninspiring on the campaign trail. Labastida represented more of the same, and in many ways was a step back from Zedillo. Whereas Fox was running against the system, there was little Labastida could do or say to excite voters about the future under the PRI.

The third candidate was the dour, dark-haired Cuauhtémoc Cárdenas, the popular mayor of Mexico City and the son of Lázaro Cárdenas, a former president still revered for his bold nationalization of the oil companies and massive agrarian reform earlier in the twentieth century. Cárdenas once again represented the left-of-center Democratic Revolution Party (PRD). Many Mexicans believed the PRI stole the presidency from the younger Cárdenas and his party in 1988. Salinas, the ruling party candidate, was installed as president after an extraordinary postelection week when the PRI-controlled election commission refused to disclose vote counts after early returns foreshadowed his doom. With the opposition parties literally locked out of the counting rooms and without access to the electronic tallies, ruling party leaders spent an entire week carrying out backroom ballot fraud under the guise of resolving computer glitches. Twelve years later, though, polls showed that voters had lost faith in Cárdenas as the heir to his father's office at Los Pinos, perhaps because of his decision not to rally party militants in 1988 to take to the streets and challenge the questionable Salinas victory.

The final vote tally, this time counted the night of the election by a truly independent commission, gave Fox 43 percent of the popular vote versus 36 percent for Labastida and 16 percent for Cárdenas.

A shocked Labastida went into seclusion and refused to deliver a concession speech or speak by telephone with Fox to offer his congratulations. His only hope was massive fraud, no longer possible in a changing Mexico. It was left to a stone-faced Zedillo, in the ultimate test of his democratic principles, to announce the official results to the Mexican public that night on national television. Fox's victory, he assured the nation, would be honored.

"Just now the Federal Elections Institute has informed us and all Mexicans that it now calculates with information that is certainly preliminary, but sufficient and reliable, that the next president of the Republic will be Vicente Fox Quesada," Zedillo said. "A moment ago I telephoned Mr. Fox to express my sincere congratulations for his electoral triumph, as well as to express the absolute disposition of the sitting administration to cooperate from now until December 1, in every aspect that could be important for the successful start of the next administration."

Zedillo had words of praise for Labastida, his party's humiliated candidate, the only PRI presidential candidate to lose in the party's history. But for millions of viewers, the outgoing president's words mattered far less than what they were witnessing for the first time in their lives: the transfer of power from the PRI to another party.

Fox, suddenly standing on a world stage, promised nothing less than the transformation of Mexico. Every problem had a waiting solution: a settlement of the simmering Zapatista uprising in southern Chiapas, a frontal assault on the country's drug cartels, a crackdown on corruption and a reorganization of the country's feared security forces and police, continued record economic growth.

The president-elect had promised everything to everyone in the course of his long campaign, commitments that spoke to the desires and ideals of the nation but proved impossible to fulfill. Standing in his way was the PRI, now an opposition party with enough votes and allies in the Congress to thwart Fox's every move over the next six years.

For at least one night, however, as television cameras recorded a euphoric Fox swigging from a champagne bottle on the balcony of his Mexico City apartment, change electrified 100 million Mexicans. The longest-ruling party in Latin America had lost an election it could not steal.

We knew that Fox's victory meant little or nothing in the short term for our case. The Mexican justice system would not miraculously transform itself because of one election. August, the month of a promised verdict, came and went. Nothing changed except the players in the case.

Susana Hayward spoke with the third prosecutor assigned to the case in Colotlán, Jaime Ruiz Sandoval, who predicted a verdict within a month after numerous delays and attempts to "buy time" by Pedro Salas Castillo, the Huichols' defense lawyer.

The journalist in me questioned the fairness of what was becoming an indefinite incarceration of Chivarra and Hernandez while both sides awaited a verdict. We certainly wanted them to have a capable defense attorney and did not want them to be summarily convicted. Some in our newsroom questioned their guilt and believed their claims of torture. Then I would think of Martha, baby Teo, and True's violent death in the Chapalagana, and I would find myself reacting more viscerally, determined to see True's killers punished. At any rate, Salas was doing his best to defend Chivarra and Hernandez and head off their conviction. If they were found guilty, it would not be for his lack of effort.

"This is a very clear case of homicide. They are guilty," Ruiz told Hayward in a telephone interview. "There is sufficient evidence, they are detained, and they will be sentenced."

Even Salas seemed resigned to a conviction. "It probably will be resolved soon and my two clients will likely be denied liberty," Salas told Hayward. "But if they are freed, will the American media lynch us?"

To make matters worse, Felix Enrique Aguiar, the trial judge, had been transferred. State officials assured us such disruptive rotations were routine, and a U.S. consular official said such moves were designed to thwart corruption. We saw the changes as a comedy of errors. We had seen three state attorney generals, three prosecutors, and three judges in less than two years. We were never informed of the changes; we always learned about them after the fact.

There was little to do now but look ahead to Fox's inauguration at the beginning of December, just days before we would mark the second anniversary of True's killing. Democracy was coming to Mexico, but it wasn't coming fast enough for us in San Antonio or for Martha in Brownsville. Mexico was a government and society built on corruption, including the corruption of its legal system. One honest national election could not cure a disease that occupies every part of the body politic like a cancer.

Fox was sworn into office on the first day of December 2000. Zedillo and his PRI cohorts sat like carved statues as the former Coca-Cola executive spoke to the Congress and the nation in his inaugural address, promising a complete break with past regimes. While Mexicans celebrated, we prepared for a second anniversary memorial in the newsroom. After so much time had passed, we had little to show for our efforts.

The ceremony took place December 8 in the newsroom. A San Antonio folkloric group of three sisters and a brother, Los Inocentes, stirred the emotions of those gathered with traditional Mexican ballads and a moving song they composed in memory of True, which they sang in Spanish and English. Bonavita, recently retired, and I both spoke. The altar was resurrected and there were words of consolation from many of the journalists for Martha, who was there with Teo, Juanita, and a few relatives.

That Sunday I wrote an open letter to Fox. For the past three years, Fox had accepted petitions from everyday citizens while traveling to every corner of the republic, a Mexican tradition linking the humblest constituent to the most powerful political figures.

"Use this case to show those who voted for you, and those who did not, that you truly are committed to seeing justice done," I wrote. "Show those watching on this side of the border who support a free and democratic Mexico that there is no impunity in the Mexico of

Vicente Fox. Send a signal that you cannot murder a journalist from the United States or anywhere else without paying the price. Give us the justice every Mexican seeks."

I sent a translation of the column to *Reforma* in Mexico City and *Mural* in Guadalajara, both of which published it. The open letter to Fox was a calculated move. We risked irritating the president in his first month in office, but what did we have to lose? In a second, private letter, I asked Fox for an audience for Martha and myself. I wanted him to meet True's widow, a Mexican citizen, to create a personal connection. Martha was an empathetic, intelligent figure. I wanted to appeal to the new president's heart, not just his intellect.

I called Martha to discuss the case and a change in strategy. It was time, I suggested, for her to return to Mexico and meet the president and then the press. Perhaps her presence as a Mexican citizen, a mother, and a widow demanding justice would be more impressive than delegations of editors. A meeting with Fox, together with the attendant press coverage, seemed like the best way to bring the case back into the spotlight.

Martha was settling into her new life in Brownsville and was understandably busy as a single parent, mothering a baby not yet two years old, whose premature birth had resulted in developmental problems. She was less than eager to return to Mexico and all the memories it held, but she agreed to go if Fox would see us. She too had grown tired of false promises.

While we waited to hear from Los Pinos, Hayward made her third trip to Colotlán, accompanied by Jerry Lara, the photographer who worked closely with True in Chiapas. This time she met with Jóse Luis Reyes Contreras, who became the third judge to handle the case on October 1. "I have to start from the beginning, but the case is moving forward," he told Hayward. "I can't give you a date . . . but it shouldn't be long now."

Lara loathed the assignment to photograph the suspects. "That was one of the hardest days of my life, taking their photograph," he said. "There they were, smirking, changing their story, saying they never met the gringo. It was hard for me to hold back. I wanted to tell them what kind of guy they killed, but if I had said one word I would have lost it."

Chivarra told Hayward he was tired of talking with outsiders. He walked back to his cell, hollering in Huichol. With his older brother-in-law out of the picture, the reticent Hernandez finally decided to speak. Drawing near and speaking in a whisper, he said, "Sometimes I feel remorse, but if I think about it too much I get sick. I don't expect to get out of here. This is like home now."

Hernandez then gave Hayward a Huichol bracelet he had braided in jail.

The call from Los Pinos to my office came late in January. Only two months into his presidency, aides said Vicente Fox was ready to welcome Martha and me to Los Pinos. We arrived one week later. This time there were different paintings on the walls. The traditional works that had endured as one PRI administration gave way to the next had been removed and replaced with the work of contemporary Mexican artists.

Fox, sporting an open white dress shirt with the sleeves rolled up, rose from behind his desk and welcomed us, in his deep, booming voice, into his private second-floor office. He seemed even taller in person, standing there in cowboy boots. We shook hands and introduced ourselves: Martha, myself, Hayward, and Lara, there to photograph the meeting. Fox invited us to seat ourselves at a small, round table, where we were joined by Juan de Dios Castro, the president's legal counselor and a trusted family friend from Durango.

There were no other aides in the room and no security detail at the door. I had shaken hands with five Mexican presidents and once ate breakfast with Salinas in the working office at his living quarters elsewhere on the grounds, but I had never been inside the inner sanctum. This was informal working space. Paperwork and framed family photographs covered the top of his desk. Streaming sunlight showcased a hand-tooled leather saddle with elaborate silver detail displayed beside his desk.

"Okay, what do you want?" Fox asked as he turned toward me once we were seated.

I was caught off guard by his bluntness and heard myself stammering out congratulations on his recent election, noting how closely Texans had watched the race. He seemed impatient or perhaps irritated by my column.

"We want justice," I said, finally collecting myself. "More than two years have passed without a resolution in the case of our reporter Philip True. He was murdered by two Huichols. The evidence is strong, including their confessions. We want you to use the moral force of your office to help us win a verdict."

Fox turned to his legal adviser. "We do not have the legal right to intervene, but the federal government can establish communication with Jalisco authorities to sensitize them about this case taking so long," the lawyer said. "The delay is also hurting the two suspects because they remain in jail."

We listened intently as he summarized the case history for Fox. It was the first time we met a Mexican official who knew the case in detail. De Dios Castro, older than Fox, spoke casually and with confidence. Clearly he and the president went back a ways. He told the president he had spoken days earlier with the state attorney general. The delayed resolution of the case, he told the president, was inexcusable.

Fox nodded. "You know I can't intervene in a state case," he said, "but we can arrange for you to meet with officials there at the top if that would be helpful. Of course, we can't do more than that, because that would be interfering with the decision of the judge . . . there is no inconvenience in [arranging the meeting] and hopefully it will speed things up."

Martha told Fox she had brought photographs of her husband and her baby to show the president. Fox's dealings with me had been formal, but his expression softened as he admired the baby photos. He chatted with Martha like an uncle talking to a favorite niece, as if the rest of us were no longer there.

"This is the last photograph taken of my husband alive in Mexico," she said, handing him the Rick Hunter photograph of True posing over a steep gorge.

"Sierra Gorda!" Fox exclaimed, as Martha nodded in agreement.

Fox had instantly recognized the familiar vista, located not far from his ranch in Guanajuato in Mexico's Bahia, or central plateau.

"My husband knew you, Señor Presidente, since the time you were governor," Martha said. "He traveled with you on some of your trips through the country."

Fox nodded his head in affirmation. He told Martha he remembered her husband well. "It is a shame what happened to him. I am very sorry and you have my sympathy. We will do what we can."

The interview came to an end and we walked out, unsure of what had been accomplished. Fox made no promises; offering to facilitate a new round of meetings with state officials was not exactly what we had hoped for, but we took a positive view with reporters.

"I told the president how much Philip adored Mexico and the Huichol culture, which he had written about and photographed before," Martha said. "I feel very grateful as a Mexican that the president of my country took the time to hear our appeal for justice. I felt President Fox was concerned for the well-being of myself and my son, and he told me to look to the future."

We left Los Pinos with hope tempered by experience. Later that day, we glimpsed the tops of Popocatépetl and Iztaccihuatl, the twin volcanoes standing sentinel outside Mexico City, normally obscured by the capital's polluted air. An earthquake had shaken the city three hours after Fox was sworn in on December 1, and "El Popo" had sent a storm of smoke and ash into the sky. Now it stood serenely in the distance. It seemed like a good omen.

That night Martha and I hosted a dinner for the Trues' Mexico City friends and fellow journalists. This was their first chance to visit with Martha since she left Mexico City, more than two years earlier, and their first chance to meet Teo, who would turn two on March 9.

One of the guests was David Nájera, who had returned to the foreign affairs ministry after Zedillo left office and was awaiting an assignment abroad with the diplomatic corps. *Newsweek's* Zarembo, who had found the journal, also was there. It was the first time Martha and I had met him and we thanked him for his doggedness. It was a low-key evening, a matter of friends breaking bread. The unresolved case hung in the air like an uninvited guest. People shook their heads in disbelief as they reflected on the fact it was entering its third year in the courts.

I enjoyed a long conversation with Dudley Althaus, the veteran correspondent for the *Houston Chronicle* who had been a good friend of True. Dudley and I first met in Managua when the Sandinistas were still in power in the early 1980s, before he landed his first newspaper job. He too had found his first job at the *Brownsville Herald*, at my suggestion, and I had watched his career progress with interest and pride. Now he was the dean of U.S. newspaper correspondents in Mexico.

Fox, meanwhile, already was experiencing problems in office, unable to win cooperation from the other parties to help him deliver the reforms he had promised on the campaign trail. How was he going to deliver on the True case, Althaus wondered. More than one person expressed the same pessimism, and none thought there was much chance True's killers would ever be convicted. It was a gloomy finish to yet another trip to Mexico.

Part 3

16

Friends of the Defense

Mexico's geographic diversity and complex political and judicial structures make it impossible to assert that a single government agency is responsible for committing or tolerating the vast array of human rights violations that take place—the evidence points at time to state or federal authorities, police or army officials, prosecutors, medical personnel or judges. Some abuses are committed in a local context, while others are carried out in the name of the national interest. These complexities, however, should not detract from one fundamental reality: Mexico's federal government is obligated under international law to ensure that all people under its jurisdiction are able to fully exercise their human rights, to be free from torture and other abuses, and to have effective access to judicial remedies when violations take place. When such violations occur, the federal government is responsible.

—Human Rights Watch, *Systematic Injustice: Torture, "Disappearance," and Extrajudicial Execution in Mexico* (1999)

The second reform would be the substitution of written trials for oral trials. Paradoxically, in a country like Mexico where illiteracy prevailed for decades and decades, all of the legal proceedings are written.

—Jorge Castañeda, *We Are Many*

December 2000, Guadalajara

Miguel Gatins was enjoying a Marlboro cigarette and his first double espresso of the morning. It was a good day to be an American expatriate living in Mexico, and not just because winter in Guadalajara meant warm temperatures and blue skies. Ruby, his Mexican wife of sixteen years and a former local television and radio personality, already was at work in her home office as the Mexico manager for a Boston-based travel service that catered to seniors. The only item on Miguel's agenda that morning was dropping off Francis, 14, and Remy, 12, at school. Both children attended the prestigious American School, where 1,500 of the city's most privileged children went from kindergarten through high school before moving on to universities in Mexico or abroad in the United States or Europe.

The family would celebrate Miguel's forty-ninth birthday in two days on December 17, and Christmas would come one week later. He and Ruby had much to be thankful for as they marked the passage of another year in his adopted country. Miguel did not work, at least not in the conventional sense. He had gladly walked away from his career as an international banker a few years after marrying Ruby, and now he was a full-time house husband, father, and active school board member. He had hated working, and a surprise inheritance from an aunt in Atlanta allowed him to quit for good. He discovered that he was much happier unemployed and made no apologies for it. The important things in life, his marriage, the kids, were all that mattered.

He called for Francis and Remy, telling them it was time to leave for school. They kissed their mother good-bye and piled into the 1998 Volkswagen Jetta with their father waiting behind the wheel. It was a short drive from the Gatins' two-story home on Paseo San Arturo in Colonia Valle Real, an upscale gated community in the wealthy enclave of Zapopan on Guadalajara's outskirts, to the nearby American School.

Miguel and Ruby lived modestly by local standards. They drove small economy imports, in contrast to the latest model SUVs and expensive luxury sedans that crowded the driveways of their neighbors. The Gatins' home was somewhat smaller than most of the others in the richly landscaped *colonia,* yet a glance inside suggested a privileged pedigree. Many of the furnishings were period French antiques inherited from Gatins' parents. A large painting of Pantaleon Germán-Ribón hung over the fireplace, a national hero executed in 1816 by the Spanish in Cartagena on the eve of their defeat in the Colombian war of independence. The rebel leader was an ancestor on his mother's side of the family.

After dropping off Francis and Remy in front of the busy school, Gatins turned the corner onto the Avenida López Mateos, one of the principal thoroughfares in the city, and parked his car outside Jacinto's, a favorite breakfast café. He settled into a table and asked for his second double espresso of the morning and ordered a hearty breakfast of *huevos rancheros,* fried eggs nestled on a tortilla and smothered in spicy *ranchera* sauce, and *bolillos,* fresh-baked bread rolls.

Gatins lit another Marlboro and turned his attention to the front page of *Publico,* the morning newspaper. His two-pack-a-day habit and espresso addiction hinted at a certain intensity beneath his outwardly placid personality. On the outside Gatins came off as a relaxed man with a good sense of humor, always ready to volunteer at the school, help with a community project, or make a financial contribution to a worthy cause.

He wasn't the only American living the good life in Guadalajara or its wealthier sister city, Zapopan. For decades, the city and outlying area had been home to tens of thousands of American retirees. It wasn't the same now, of course, as it had been for the first wave of newcomers after World War II. But a dollar still went a lot farther south of the border, where anyone with a decent pension and enough savings to purchase a home could easily afford stateside luxuries such as a housekeeper and gardener. The year-round mild climate was another attraction. Even the better homes did not have heating or air conditioning because there was no need for it.

Gatins was not the typical American retiree. He and True were of the same generation, and both had married strong Mexican women and left behind their lives in the United States. But unlike True, who spent his childhood on a working chicken farm, Gatins hailed from a privileged background.

He was born in Paris and raised in Atlanta, one of six children born to Joseph Gatins, who held dual citizenship in France and the United States, and Sylvia Germán-Ribón y Valenzuela, who came from a distinguished Colombian family that dated to the eighteenth century. Joseph was a French resistance fighter in World War II, captured by the Nazis early in the war and sent to prisoner of war camps, first in Germany and then in the Soviet Union. Joseph made several failed escape attempts and was finally sent to the Rawa-Ruska death camp in the Ukraine, reserved for French escape artists and other troublemakers. Unlike many there, he survived.

After spending the postwar years in Paris, Joseph moved his wife and six children to Atlanta, where his father's roots predated the Civil War. Joseph managed the family-owned Georgian Terrace Hotel, the historic Peachtree Street landmark built by his grandfather and frequented by celebrities and notables. Clark Gable and Vivien Leigh stayed there during the 1939 world premiere of *Gone with the Wind*.

Miguel, the youngest child, lived an extraordinary life by any measure. At home, the Gatins, considered a pioneer Atlanta family, enjoyed membership in the exclusive Piedmont Driving Club and they socialized with other old-line families. Miguel spent carefree summers with relatives in Paris and with his grandmother in her thirteenth-century castle in the French countryside, or with an uncle who owned an island off the coast of Cartagena.

Miguel grew up speaking French and English and graduated from the University of Georgia with a degree in Spanish, his mother's native language. Gatins, like True, set out to explore the world as a young man, although his view was a far more comfortable one, whether he was backpacking through Europe, Mexico, and Central America, or traveling abroad as a young international banker.

Despite such advantages, Miguel was not a happy man. He hated his work, his first marriage floundered, and he detested the conventional social scene. He was an alcoholic.

When his marriage ended in 1981, he moved on to a new city and a new job, finding work as an international banker in Miami. There he met Ruby, whose Guadalajara roots reached back several generations. She had her own career, and she was smart, fun, and unencumbered by family history or expectations. They lived in different cities, but their relationship quickly grew serious. There was something about Ruby that compelled Miguel to try marriage again, and in October 1984 they were wed at the historic St. Anthony Hotel in San Antonio, a place they chose for its geographic convenience and Mexican ambiance, ideal for family and friends from both sides of the border.

Meeting Ruby was the first of several good turns in Miguel's life. A little more than a year after they were married, as they welcomed in the New Year 1986, Ruby and one of Miguel's older brothers convinced him to check into the Betty Ford Center in Rancho Mirage, California. One year after he achieved sobriety, his Atlanta aunt died and left Miguel and his siblings a significant portion of her multimillion dollar estate, enough money for Miguel to quit his job in Miami and move with Ruby to Guadalajara. Work had been a central source of his unhappiness, and Gatins resolved to never hold another job. Now, fourteen years later, he was still sober and content, his addictions limited to high-cholesterol foods, strong espresso, and cigarettes. Gatins took life one day at a time and lived for his wife and children. He made no apologies for not having a career or holding a conventional full-time job. He had discovered a balance in his life, and he no longer felt an obligation to justify his existence to others.

As he waited for his breakfast to arrive, a story in that day's edition of *Publico* caught his eye. Two Huichol Indians, Juan Chivarra de la Cruz and his younger brother-in-law, Miguel Hernandez de la Cruz, were still awaiting trial after spending two years in jail on charges they robbed and killed an American reporter named Philip True while he was hiking solo through the Sierra Madre. The faces of the two forlorn Huichols, seen sweeping out their jail cell in the photograph accompanying the article, peered back at Gatins from the page as he read about their unresolved status and lengthy confinement in Colotlán, a town way off the beaten path. Even worse, the story reported that Juan Pedro Salas Castillo, the defense lawyer who had successfully delayed a verdict with his various motions, had abandoned his clients and fled, presumably to the United States, to avoid criminal charges.

The whole sorry incident struck Gatins as inhumane. He was familiar with the general outline of the True story, which had made page one headlines two years earlier and certainly had been the topic of conversation around the American School and the expatriate community. Violence and crime were popular topics of social conversation. Everyone had been a victim at one time or another, or at least had a family member or close friend who had been victimized. Outside the gated communities and well-guarded upscale commercial districts, Guadalajara could be unsafe. Kidnappings and extortion were common, drug-related shootings broke out periodically as competing cartels vied for turf, and street crime was a constant. But the case of the reporter had been unique, occurring in remote Indian country, where few Guadalajarans had ever ventured. For the average person, it had been hard to tell from the local coverage if True had been murdered or simply fell to his death in a hiking accident after a night of drinking the local moonshine.

Gatins had forgotten about the case until now, assuming it had gone away, just as most murder cases go away in Mexico. The article caused him to recall True's newspaper editor, who had come to Guadalajara at the time and several times later to push local authorities for action in the case. He admired the guy for coming down and searching for his missing reporter, making sure the journalist was not left unfound. It reminded him of the old U.S. Marine adage about never leaving a man behind. But otherwise, Gatins didn't like him or what he stood for, even if they had never met.

The man seemed far more interested in winning a conviction than in finding out whether the two jailed suspects were actually guilty. Such grandstanding by a powerful newspaper editor north of the border struck Gatins as the kind of typical arrogance that Americans show their southern neighbor. He was, Gatins thought to himself, the picture of the gringo bully. The San Antonio newspaperman seemed bent on avenging the Mexican victory at the Battle of the Alamo.

As the days went by, Gatins found his thoughts returning to the two jailed Huichols and the injustice of their indefinite incarceration. He wished there was something he could do, someone he could call, to counter the bullying and the pressure. But Gatins was not an activist; in fact, he had an aversion to pressure and conflict. Yet an internal voice was urging him on, spurring him to do something about it. For reasons even he did not fully comprehend, he decided to look further into the matter, to see if there was some way he might help win justice for the defendants. What began as a casual reading of the morning newspaper after dropping off the kids at school slowly grew into an obsession.

After more than a week of such deliberations, Miguel showed Ruby the article he had clipped out and asked her what she thought about his getting involved in the case. She readily agreed, even after her husband underscored the possibility that they might have to spend some of their savings in order to help.

"You could have knocked me over with a feather," said Sims Bray, a magazine publisher and a lifetime friend of Gatins from Atlanta whom Miguel called to discuss his intentions. "Miguel has never taken a stand like that before in his life."

"It seemed incredibly unfair that these two Huichols had spent two years in jail when they hadn't been convicted of anything," Gatins said. "It also seemed apparent that the army had illegally detained them and almost certainly abused them. On the other side, you had the U.S. government, a powerful Texas newspaper and its editor pushing hard, and other U.S. reporters supporting that effort. It just seemed like two poor, defenseless Indians up against a lot of power."

Few Mexican murder cases receive the attention given the True case, which led many in Mexico to believe True's widow and the newspaper were receiving preferential treatment reserved for influential Americans. Mexicans, accustomed to injustice, official corruption, and rampant crime waves ignored by authorities, did not see the case from the same perspective as Americans. Instead of demanding a fair and thorough inquiry into the reporter's death, Mexicans reflexively disbelieved official claims and assumed the worst about their own judicial system. Better that the case go away like so many others than let the gringos push Mexico around.

Gatins was not the first individual to come along, on either side of the border, who viewed the *Express-News* as the powerful bully north of the Rio Bravo. We, too, worried about the indefinite jailing of the Huichols, even if their two-year stay behind bars resulted from tactics by the defense. We also were concerned about the abuse claims, although there was no direct evidence to support them. Mexican human rights groups and some in the Mexican press simply accepted the claims as fact.

One person came to Gatins's mind as he decided to take action. He and Ruby periodically made small donations to Patricia Morales, a thirty-five-year-old former police investigator and self-described human rights lawyer. Morales operated the Reconocimiento Posthumo a los Policias Caidos en el Cumplimiento de su Deber (REPOS), a charity that aided the widows of policemen killed in the line of duty. It was a big name for a solo practitioner, but Morales, with the drive and passion of a do-gooder, was well-connected in Guadalajara law enforcement circles. She seemed to know everyone who mattered.

In a meeting at the Gatins home, Miguel laid out for Morales his desire to help the two jailed Huichols and his willingness to finance an investigation if Morales thought there was any chance of winning their freedom. She was eager to take up the challenge and agreed to look into the matter. She reminded him that criminal cases in Mexico are processed in secrecy and records are not generally available to the public.

What Morales and her organization lacked in size she more than made up in what would become a fanatical commitment to Chivarra and Hernandez. While Gatins was struck, as an outsider, by the inequities of the Mexican justice system, Morales was driven by more nationalistic feelings; she was offended by the way Mexican authorities seemed to be under the thumb of the Americans. It came as no surprise that the accused were Indians, who occupy the lowest rung of the country's social ladder. Morales also had a natural affinity for the two Huichols, growing out of her own humble and indigenous roots. Her paternal grandparents were Huichol and Cora Indians from the bordering state of Nayarit. Her widowed grandmother, like many impoverished Indians unable to survive alone, made her way to Guadalajara. Two generations later, those roots were not forgotten.

"There was a scarcity of material goods in my childhood, but we were rich in principles and love," Morales later said.

Once she and her younger brother were left alone in their modest house with only a little bread, a tortilla, and some beans to hold them over for the day while their mother went out to work. "We were sitting down, looking out the window, when a poor little girl came by and told us she was hungry," Morales said. "We decided to share our little bit of food, knowing we would then go hungry. Ever since that day I've known that you don't live by bread alone."

Morales operated out of a large house in Santa Anita, a cobble-stoned, colonial era town slowly being surrounded by gated communities, imported auto dealerships, and worsening highway traffic. Federal police confiscated the home from one of Mexico's most notorious drug traffickers, Joaquín "El Chapo" Guzmán, and then gave it to Morales *en comodato,* or deeded to her in trust. Americans would find such an arrangement a bit too cozy to pass the smell test, but it is common in Mexico for law enforcement authorities to entrust such properties to sympathetic social organizations.

After Morales took on the True case, she renamed REPOS more grandiosely as the Institute for Latin American Philanthropy, expanding its mission to include prisoners' rights. It was still basically Morales operating out of the seized drug lord's house, where she also lived with her husband and three children on donations from individuals like Gatins.

El Chapo, Spanish for "Shorty," was linked to the 1993 Guadalajara airport shootout that killed Cardinal Posadas. He was serving a twenty-year prison term for bribery when he engineered his first escape. El Chapo fled to Guatemala but was caught and returned to Guadalajara's maximum-security prison, Puente Grande. He escaped a second time several years later, concealed under a truckload of dirty laundry after bribing the prison warden and jail guards. Embarrassed officials in Mexico City fired and then jailed the warden and dozens of prison guards after the escape. El Chapo, more than a decade later, remains on the loose, one of Mexico's untouchable drug lords, wanted on both sides of the border, with a $5 million U.S. government bounty on his head.

The home, while somewhat rundown, befits a drug lord rather than a small nonprofit endeavor. Guests enter the two-acre compound on the edge of town through high metal gates. A fountain feeds into a tiled swimming pool, while an adjacent cabana is used by the feds to store furniture and other property seized from other drug traffickers. A dilapidated tennis court conceals a large underground chamber accessible only by activating a secret switch that caused the concrete steps leading up to the court to swing open like the belly of an airplane. Underground, El Chapo had ample room to store drug shipments, weapons, and operate a clandestine jail and torture chamber. Morales found chains, ropes, tape, and blood spatters on the walls when she first took custody of the property.

For all its grim history, the Santa Anita compound provides Morales with a rent-free home and workplace. Charitable donations afford her a comfortable lifestyle. She dresses smartly, drives a late-model SUV, often employs a driver, and is familiar with the city's best restaurants. She is the breadwinner for her children, while her husband Oscar, a gentle man with a goatee, supervises activities around the compound and serves as her general fixer.

Morales's claim to be a lawyer said something else about the country's judicial system. She did not attend law school or earn a conventional four-year university degree, but Mexicans can represent incarcerated individuals without possessing such credentials. The more unscrupulous types are known as *coyotes* because they prey on their victims, but there are people who work selflessly and honestly inside the system, and indigent prisoners rely on sympathetic individuals like Morales who charge modest fees or nothing at all.

Morales traveled to Colotlán, met with José Luis Reyes Contreras, the third judge appointed to the case, and spoke with the defendants, who told her that their defense lawyer had disappeared after collecting money they raised by selling the family livestock. Nothing in the Huichol sierra is a better measure of family status than cattle. Huichols who own cattle are relatively secure. Huichols without cattle often live in misery. If Chivarra and Hernandez somehow won their freedom, they would have nothing to support themselves and their families.

At first, neither the court nor the defendants welcomed Morales's involvement. Her first interview with Chivarra and Hernandez went nowhere. Chivarra refused to speak with her and Hernandez just smiled at her as she sat there for three hours, trying to win their confidence. Juan finally told her to leave.

"Get out, and don't come back," he stormed. "A woman has no business in these affairs. Go home and take care of your kids."

Morales, not easily intimidated, exploded. "You have no idea how much trouble you are in and how few friends you have," she said. "Look, you thankless Indian, you don't see the damn truth that you're in the hands of the devil now, and your ignorance and stupidity is going to kill you."

She stood up and left, but she had no intention of following Chivarra's dictate to go home. She checked into a local hotel, filled that evening with carousing *federales*. Morales spent the night wide awake fearing that the armed men would burst into the room and assault her or fire an errant round through the thin walls.

The next morning Morales and her driver went to a local grocery and stocked up on canned goods and delicacies for the prisoners. Having sensed the previous day that Chivarra had established himself as the local jail boss, Morales entered the communal cell area a second time and asked Chivarra to help her distribute the surprise feast of ham, sausages, cheese, and fresh bread she had brought for the inmates. Morales ate alongside the prisoners and then poured herself a soft drink and lit a cigarette. As she smoked, she casually asked Chivarra, who had been watching sullenly but with unconcealed interest, if he was hungry. "That's okay, perhaps you prefer the jail food," Morales suggested.

She looked at the underweight Chivarra, and while he was unsure and distrustful of mestizos, he also was starving. After hesitating, he reached hungrily for the food. "I swear he took that food into his hands with the same pleasure as a father holding his newborn child," she told Gatins.

Within minutes Chivarra was telling Morales all about his family, his children, and life in the sierra. She had just won a new client. As she slowly gained their confidence, Morales coaxed the two Huichols into sharing their account of how they and their relatives were beaten and threatened by army troops. As the judge and his clerk, who actually tended the case file and would recommend a verdict for the judge to sign, watched Morales tend to the two despondent Huichols like a watchful mother in the ensuing days and weeks, they too began to treat her with special consideration.

Then Morales did something no member of the prosecution team had done. She traveled to the sierra to meet with family members and local Huichol authorities in the San Sebastián community to ask for their accounts of being beaten and tortured by the army during the search for the defendants. In one month, the one-woman head of the Institute for Latin American Philanthropy had shown more enterprise and investigative vigor than the entire prosecution team had over the preceding two years. Her arduous trip into the sierra convinced her the two defendants were telling the truth.

Prosecutors, U.S. diplomats, and the Guadalajara press remained oblivious to the new defense effort. Miguel and Ruby moved in the same social circle as senior U.S. consular officials, who reacted with indifference when Miguel casually mentioned his newfound cause. Consular officials had stayed in close touch with Martha, and they periodically spoke with me in San Antonio and with Susana Hayward in Mexico City. They regarded the case as closed, the verdict inevitable. No one seemed to understand the significance of Gatins's involvement. Miguel and Ruby, not wanting to call attention to themselves, decided to say nothing more.

Morales returned to Guadalajara in late January, convinced of the two Huichols' innocence and eager to take the case. She brought home more than her convictions. Somehow Morales had managed to obtain case documents, usually not available to outside parties. She paid the judge $250 for a copy of the voluminous file. The same judge had declined to make the file available to Martha or the *Express-News*. Miguel and Ruby listened as Morales sat in their living room and laid out a comprehensive plan to win the Huichols' freedom, an undertaking she estimated would cost $25,000.

Mexico's judiciary is notoriously corrupt, and judges and prosecutors are easily bribed or intimidated, according to a 1998 Human Rights Watch report. But Gatins did not believe Morales intended to bribe Reyes Contreras. The money, she explained, would cover her time and travel costs, better meals and clothing for the jailed Huichols, and such expenses as charter flights to ferry Huichols from the sierra to Colotlán so they could provide the court with sworn statements attesting to their mistreatment and to Juan and Miguel's good character. She also intended to hire medical experts to examine the defendants and their family members to assess the aftereffects of torture, the prolonged incarceration of Juan and Miguel, and their separation from traditional Huichol society.

Miguel's considerable inheritance had enabled the Gatins to pay cash for two houses, one to live in and one as an investment. They lived on Ruby's salary and spent frugally, except for the tuition costs at the American School. While many would envy such comfortable circumstances, what Morales was proposing actually was a lot of money to the Gatins, nearly 20 percent of their life savings. Miguel and Ruby, already committed to the suspects' innocence, agreed to finance a new defense. Over the next eight months, the couple paid out nearly $28,000 to Morales. There were no receipts or records of her expenditures, nor did Miguel and Ruby ask for any. They had faith in Morales and faith in their shared cause.

Such support was unheard of in Mexico; the Gatins had never even spoken with the two Huichols and, beyond what little they knew from press accounts and Morales's anecdotes from her jail visits, they knew practically nothing about the defendants. Neither Miguel nor Ruby had ever ventured into Huichol territory.

Morales became a familiar figure in Colotlán, where her work was hardly a secret. As she continued to visit the judge's office and argue anomalies in the prosecution's case, the court staff began treating Morales as the de facto case expert. Although she had no legal standing, they listened to her arguments that the first autopsy was in error and that the second autopsy, which drew no firm conclusions about whether True's death was a homicide or an accident, was more credible. Local prosecutors, meanwhile, paid her no mind. They had their confessions, normally insurmountable in Mexican criminal cases.

She also became a welcome presence at the jail, bringing Chivarra and Hernandez new shoes and clothes, good food and medicine, even toothbrushes and nail clippers, all financed by the Gatins. She and Chivarra became so close that he sank into a depression when weeks passed and he did not see her. One time the head jailer called her in Guadalajara. "Your little Huichol, Juan, doesn't want to eat," the guard told her. "He's been sick, and he doesn't want to talk to anyone else but you."

He handed the telephone to Juan.

"When are you coming?" Juan beseeched Paty. By now they called each other by their first names, each dependent on the other. Chivarra wanted his freedom; Morales wanted a major victory for herself and the Instituto. Listening to Chivarra lament her absence, Morales promised to drive to Colotlán that night to see what was ailing Juan. As soon as she arrived, Juan miraculously regained his appetite for both food and conversation.

"Your Huichol dies when you're not here," the jailer teased her.

The emotional dependence became mutual. "I felt that he was so defenseless and dependent on me, that he needed my protection, my affection, and my protection against the danger he faced," Morales later said.

If Morales and Chivarra developed far more than a lawyer–client relationship, it would not be the first time a man jailed for murder won the heart of a woman on the outside. A Huichol elder who knew Juan's troubled history commented to Morales on the positive effect she was having. "Juan has become a completely different person, a real gentleman, respectful, well dressed, well fed, and so well cared for," he told Morales.

"Our defense grows stronger each day, and my relationship with the defendants, and they with me," Morales responded.

As he came to know Morales, even joining her for dinner at a Colotlán restaurant where she pleaded her case and picked up the tab, the judge felt no obligation to alert the other parties with an interest in the case.

Morales gathered momentum in February and March. She confidently told Gatins that the prosecution had stopped working on the case after the arrest of Chivarra and Hernandez, despite official pronouncements in Guadalajara and at high-level meetings between state officials and True's editor and Martha. There was more, according to Morales. The two Huichols had been arrested without an official detention order and illegally detained by army soldiers rather than civilian law enforcement. The two conflicting autopsies, she said, offered ample opportunity to argue that True had been drunk along the trail and had died in an accidental fall. In her view, Reyes Contreras could not find the Huichols guilty if he relied on the evidence rather than outside pressure.

Gatins, more convinced than ever of the Huichols' innocence, decided to call Hayward in Mexico City to introduce himself and disclose his intervention in the case. "I reached her at her home one night in late February or early March and I told her who I was and explained my interest in the case, but I don't think she connected with what I was saying. I told her I was an American and that I thought the evidence indicated that True had died in a hiking accident and I intended to get involved. She didn't seem to care. In any event, she was in the middle of cooking something and obviously enjoying a glass of wine or two, something I commented to my wife after we hung up."

Hayward disputes that account, saying Gatins awakened her late at night and claimed that the two jailed Huichols were innocent while the evidence indicated True had been drunk when he plunged to his death. Hayward, a friend of True's as well as his successor in Mexico, had a considerable emotional stake in the outcome of the case and was personally affronted by Gatins's interference. She later said she didn't take him seriously and assumed he was a naive interloper.

Whatever Hayward thought about Gatins and his call, alarms did not go off in Mexico City or San Antonio. Gatins would be ignored, his motivation misunderstood, his influence underestimated.

Late that spring, Gatins decided to call Martha. He dialed information in Brownsville, jotted down Martha's home number, and placed the call. Martha answered, and Gatins earnestly launched into an introduction and explanation of his efforts to free the two men charged with the murder of her husband. Philip was the victim of a hiking accident, Gatins told the widow, not a murder.

Martha finally broke in. "Why are you doing this?" she asked coldly.

"From all I know and have read about your husband, Philip would be the first one to stand up and fight for the rights of these two Huichols," Gatins said.

There was only silence on the other end of the line.

"I just want you to know that I think the verdict is coming down in a few weeks and we might meet down here and I wanted you to know who I was," Gatins added.

It was an uncomfortable conversation for both sides, ending as quickly as it had begun.

Afterwards, Martha called me in San Antonio and described the strange call from an American living in Guadalajara who insisted that the Huichols were innocent and claimed to be financing a new defense effort. She gave me Gatins's telephone number. He sounded to me like another meddler, one of many who came along in the course of the case, operating with the idealistic belief that indigenous people were incapable of such a crime. I paid him no mind and told my assistant, Marie Martinez, to ignore him if he called.

Over the previous two and half years, I had received numerous calls, letters, and e-mails from strangers offering information about

True's murder. Most were conspiracy theorists or mentally unbalanced. One persistent ham radio operator, who still checks in periodically, claimed to have taped radio conversations with a man who witnessed the murder, recordings that he never produced. In the beginning, I returned every call, answered every letter, and chased every lead, no matter how unbelievable. In time I learned to ignore such implausible offers. Ignoring Miguel Gatins was a terrible miscalculation on my part.

As Morales finished her work on the case in June, she realized she needed an experienced trial lawyer to draft the final written defense argument. The self-described lawyer had accomplished a great deal in Colotlán and in the sierra, convincing hesitant Huichols to travel to the court and give sworn statements on behalf of the defendants and attesting to the army's brutality. While her investigative work and all-around energy had impressed everyone but the prosecution, Morales knew she lacked the legal education or trial experience to draft final arguments that would be key to influencing the judge's decision. She turned to Samuel Salvador, the only Huichol law professor at the University of Guadalajara. He recommended Arturo Zamora, a former prosecutor, respected defense lawyer, and rising political star in the out-of-power PRI. Zamora was the leading candidate to challenge the PAN for the mayor's office in Zapopan in the elections scheduled for 2003. Gatins liked Salvador's suggestion. He didn't know Zamora well, but they lived on the same street and he knew his reputation and political ambitions.

Zamora agreed to draft the final argument for a modest fee of 10,000 pesos, about $1,000. His name alone was worth the expense. His involvement surely impressed Reyes Contreras, a small-town judge who seldom if ever encountered politically connected lawyers. Zamora further promised Gatins and Morales that he would file an appeal pro bono if the Huichols were found guilty and sentenced to prison terms. Such a high-profile case was certain to keep the candidate's name in the newspapers and on the local television news. Once word spread he was defending two indigent Huichols for free against powerful American interests, the boost to his political stature would be enormous.

Reyes Contreras told Hayward in a mid-June telephone interview that he intended to rule within forty days. His remarks suggested a decision in early August, the third year we had been promised a verdict in August. "There is no more time for presenting evidence," he told her. "The case is in my hands. Soon there will be a sentencing. It's been a controversial case because there have been many disparities with the parties involved."

Hayward also learned in the course of her interviews that one month earlier, yet another prosecutor, Monica del Rosio Estrada Gomez, had been assigned the case. The state had changed prosecutors three times now. A newcomer could not master the case file this close to a verdict even if she tried, much less establish a relationship with the judge. Estrada Gomez didn't seem overly concerned or focused on the case; she never even called Martha or the editors at the *Express-News* to introduce herself.

Martha, however, had been calling the judge on a regular basis, and Reyes Contreras had assured her that he would provide advance notice of the verdict to give her time to travel to Colotlán for the ruling. U.S. consular officials received similar assurances from the president of the state supreme court in Guadalajara, who privately predicted a guilty verdict and stiff sentence.

In late July, the well-connected Zamora arranged for Morales to meet with the newly elected governor, Francisco Ramirez Acuña, and Solís, the attorney general, to lay out her findings and argue for a dismissal of the charges. The officials listened politely out of deference to Zamora but did nothing.

Yet rumors began circulating in the Guadalajara press corps shortly afterward that the judge intended to rule in favor of the jailed Huichols. One Guadalajara reporter I knew shrugged his shoulders when asked on what basis he thought the defendants would regain their freedom. "I am only telling you what I hear around," he said. "They say the judge is inclined toward the defense. That's the *chisme*." That's the gossip.

Morales, meanwhile, had practically become a resident of Colotlán as the judge and his clerk labored over the written verdict. On Thursday, August 2, she telephoned Miguel and Ruby and for the first time summoned them to Colotlán. "Friday might be the day," she announced.

The next morning, the Guadalajara newspaper *Mural* reported that the pathologist assigned by the court to reconcile the two autopsies had rejected Rivas Souza's conclusions and affirmed the cause of death as edema, or fluid in the lung, leaving open the drunken hiking accident scenario.

By now, the Mexican press had repeatedly distorted the sequence of forensics examinations, widely referring to three separate autopsies in the case. Rivas Souza and his team were the only pathologists to fully examine an intact, if badly decomposed, corpse. Federal authorities examined the remains transferred from Guadalajara to Mexico City, but they had less to work with. Clothing had been cut away, the tightly knotted bandana had been removed from the neck, the throat had been partially dissected to examine bloody striations visible inside the throat wall, and organs had been removed for testing. The third pathologist only reviewed the paperwork from the state and federal autopsies and did not even interview the principals. The Mexican press also failed to understand or even explore the nature of True's blood alcohol level—measurements dismissed as unreliable by U.S. forensics experts. Instead of reporting that decomposition produces alcohol in some corpses and not in others, the Guadalajara media simply reported that True was drunk when he died.

The *Mural* story closed with one other development favoring the defense. The judge had accepted as evidence a report written by Dr. Jorge Armando Hidalgo Moreno, a physician hired by Morales, which asserted that Hernandez had been tortured for four days after his capture in the sierra. It seemed irrelevant to the judge that a physician with no training or expertise on the subject could make such an assertion so long after the fact.

Nervous with anticipation after spending so much money over the past eight months and becoming wed to the welfare of the two Huichols, Miguel and Ruby left for Colotlán early the next morning, packing enough clothes to stay several days. They arrived at noon and made their way to the Hotel Colotlán, next to the bus station on the town's outskirts. Paty was there with Oscar and her chauffeur.

The group whiled away the hours in small talk. As the afternoon wore on and they grew stir crazy in the hotel room, everyone walked outside and headed for a nearby restaurant for coffee. As they sat in the café, the newly appointed prosecutor and her assistants passed by on their way to the bus station. It was Friday afternoon and the state's team was clearing out early, going home to Guadalajara for the weekend. No one enjoyed being assigned to an outlying judicial district like Colotlán, and state workers customarily spent only the required time on the job, always eager to return home to the bustle of the capital. As Gatins and the others watched in astonishment, the other side, with so much riding on the verdict, left town.

Shortly afterward, around 4:00 P.M., Reyes Contreras's clerk called Morales on her cell phone and summoned the group to the judge's office. After the short ride from the hotel to the rundown building that housed the jail and court offices, Morales led the group up the stairs to Reyes Contreras's second floor office over the small jail. Gatins watched as Juan and Miguel followed behind them, accompanied by the head jailer. It was the first time he and Ruby had seen the defendants, and the two Huichols seemed unaware that the Gatins were their benefactors.

As the group crowded together in front of the judge seated at his small desk, Reyes Contreras asked his clerk to read a brief statement: Chivarra and Hernandez were not guilty and were ordered released from custody. The judge then asked them to sign the official verdict, but the two defendants just stood there, not comprehending the significance of the moment. The two Huichols turned to Morales, who assured them they were free and were not going back to jail. She told them to sign the verdict. Chivarra signed and Hernandez made his mark. Gatins watched, struck by the obvious emotional connection that had developed between Morales and Chivarra, who relied on her yet also seemed to hold sway over her.

There were no grand pronouncements, no sense of high drama. The judge declared the case closed and the group walked back down the stairs and into the afternoon sun, the first time in more than two and half years the Huichols had stood outside as free men. Tension gave way to relief as reality slowly sank in.

"I think the judge let them go on purpose late Friday so he wouldn't have to take a lot of calls," Gatins said. "I think by law he didn't have to advise the other side for seventy-two hours."

Reyes Contreras prepared to leave immediately after issuing his ruling. With his wife and clerk, he left for his home in Autlán, located on the old road to the Pacific beach resort of Manzanillo.

Chivarra and Hernandez readily accepted Morales's invitation to come to Guadalajara rather than return to their families and ranch in the sierra. She wanted to present them as wrongfully prosecuted victims to the press and avoid any impression that the judge had sprung them so they could disappear into the vast sierra.

On the way out of town, the two-vehicle caravan stopped at a gas station. As Gatins stepped out of his car, he glanced toward the Huichols seated in the back of Morales's vehicle. He and Juan made eye contact for the first time, and Gatins suddenly felt uneasy as he met Chivarra's penetrating stare. "I felt he was thinking, 'Who the hell are you?'" Gatins said.

Farther down the highway, with Guadalajara still hours away, the group decided to stop at a popular highway restaurant for a meal. When they walked inside, they found Reyes Contreras and other court and family members already seated. The judge invited the new arrivals to pull up chairs and join his party. Suddenly the judge, the freed Huichols, and their defenders were one big family gathered around the same table, enjoying a communal and celebratory meal.

"This was sort of a surreal scene, very Mexican, in a way, where now all the participants were equal citizens, and bygones were bygones," Gatins said. "Juan and Miguel were rather quiet, as could be expected, and I was pleasantly surprised by their polite behavior and manners, which contrasted with the image one has of inmates, much less with that of crazed murderers."

Not all the participants were on hand. Somewhere south of Colotlán, the afternoon bus sped on toward Guadalajara, carrying the prosecution team home, unaware that a verdict had been reached. The accused killers, still in custody when the bus departed, were now free men, enjoying a cozy supper with the judge and his clan.

One telling moment unfolded toward the end of the meal when Miguel Fonseca Murillo, the court secretary, took advantage of a lapse in the conversation to pose a mischievous question to Chivarra. "Now that you are free, tell us if you had anything to do with the death of Philip True," he said, only half jokingly.

Gatins just sat there, privately wincing at the question. He turned toward Chivarra to listen to his response. Chivarra just stared at Fonseca and did not answer. Morales also remained silent.

"At the time, I thought his comment was in bad taste, but at the same time I realized that while there was no doubt as to the legal verdict, based on the evidence, I also realized that many questions remained unanswered," Gatins said.

The two groups parted ways after the meal, and the two vehicles carrying the defense team and the Huichols rolled into Guadalajara late that night. "We all went our own way, quite exhausted from the day's events and still not quite believing what had happened," Gatins said. "We knew the following day the news would come out and, frankly, we were scared."

Morales brought Chivarra and Hernandez home to stay with her and Oscar. There were two new house guests to enjoy the comforts of El Chapo Guzmán's former lair now known as the Institute for Latin American Philanthropy, victorious in its first and only undertaking.

*

The news broke Saturday morning. Ruby called an old college friend, Roberto Ruvalcaba, the station director at Radio Metropoli, the all-news station in Guadalajara, and gave him the scoop. He trusted Ruby from her on-air days as an anchorwoman and decided to go with the story without seeking confirmation. The news flash caught officials with the attorney general's office completely by surprise, and they telephoned Ruvalcaba to dispute the broadcast. Solís's staff in Colotlán had checked in with the judge just two days earlier, on Thursday, and had been told a verdict was not imminent. Finally convinced by the station manager that the story of the Huichols' release was true, a flabbergasted Solís dispatched a staff member to make the four-hour drive to Colotlán to check the jail and hunt down Reyes Contreras. U.S. consular officials also were caught flat-footed and unable to reach anyone over the weekend.

"It was obvious the judge had favored us with a jump start on this developing story," Gatins said. "Further it was evident that we had caught the authorities, including the governor and the attorney general, by surprise and that they had no way of responding since it was the weekend and the court was closed and the judge was nowhere to be found."

Gatins placed a telephone call to Alan Zarembo, the *Newsweek* correspondent who had first discovered True's journal. It was too late for Zarembo to file his own story since the magazine had closed its next edition that morning. But word spread quickly through the Mexico City press corps. Hayward notified editors in San Antonio and began placing calls to Guadalajara and Colotlán. She managed to reach the duty officer at the small jail, who told her the judge had left town after releasing the defendants. Hayward now realized Gatins was someone to reckon with, and she quickly reached him by telephone. He recounted his original interest in the case and his hiring of Morales, and offered to give her copies of the case file. "I paid [Morales] a few hundred thousands of pesos, which by Mexican standards is a lot of money," Gatins told her, for the first time disclosing the cost of winning the Huichols' freedom.

Mexican reporters, soon followed by their U.S. counterparts, besieged Martha at her home in Brownsville, everyone wanting her reaction to the news and what she thought of Gatins and Morales. "I don't understand how they could be set free when they confessed to killing him, when Philip's things were in their possession; they didn't even get sentenced for robbery," Martha said. "I'm hurt, somewhat indignant, because Mexican officials told us this case would be handled professionally."

Gatins told Hayward and other reporters that True would not have wanted to see innocent Huichols victimized. "Martha is the one who suffered most in the final analysis," he said. "In our version, her husband didn't die in horrible circumstances."

Gatins's words galled Martha, who had no interest in expressions of sympathy from a stranger whose money had upended the case against her husband's accused killers. "How can it be that a third party who wasn't even involved with the case from the beginning could have this influence?" she asked. "It's like nobody considered Philip was hit, robbed, or even had alcohol poured into him. The autopsies weren't even taken into account."

Convinced that yet another August would pass without a verdict, I had traveled with my family to the Texas coast for a few days of vacation before the start of the new school year. We were watching a soccer match on television when the phone rang. I don't remember who in the newsroom delivered the bad news to me, but I began to scribble notes. As I listened incredulously to the news that the judge had ruled with only the defense team present and had not even informed the prosecution of his act, I made a note I still have: "They bought the judge."

I started responding to reporters calling my cell phone. "The judge has confirmed everyone's worst beliefs about Mexico and its weak and corrupt judicial system," I said. "It's now up to the Mexican prosecutor and the administration of President Fox to demonstrate to the world that judges can no longer act with such impunity or make a mockery of the law."

I dictated the same statement to our own reporter. The story editor paused after reading it and asked if I intended to speak so harshly. I thought about it for a moment and said, "This is exactly what I want to say. I don't care anymore if the truth offends someone in Mexico."

Monika had come into the room after the first phone call. When I hung up, she asked what had happened. I could hardly get out the words. From the moment True was reported missing nearly three years earlier, I had never doubted our purpose. Now I found myself sitting in a rented hotel room, a thousand miles away from events in Mexico. We had lost.

I gathered my feelings and called Martha. All I could think to tell her was how sorry I was. We knew the two Huichols had killed Philip, but now hope gave way to despair. The words wouldn't leave me: We had lost. The men who killed Philip True had gotten away with murder.

Out in the free world, Chivarra and Hernandez underwent hasty makeovers under the protective eye of Morales and the benevolent patronage of Gatins. Stylish haircuts, new clothes, a succession of good meals, and hours spent splashing in the Instituto's swimming pool washed away two and half years of incarceration in Colotlán.

A smiling, triumphant Gatins with one arm around each of the freed Huichols appeared in newspapers, as he readily acclimated to sudden notoriety.

The selling of Juan and Miguel to the Mexican and U.S. press began in earnest from their newly adopted home. Comfortable beds, clean clothes, plenty of food, television, and other entertainment—it was a new world to Chivarra and Hernandez after life in the sierra and thirty-one months in a shabby, rundown jail. The next ten days were a whirlwind as Morales and the Gatins fielded interview requests and manned their overworked copy machine, providing reporters with copies of documents from the case file, autopsy reports, and the judge's final order.

The two Huichols became celebrities of sorts, condemned men liberated against all odds, now graciously meeting with one journalist after another, shyly smiling for the cameras, appearing on national television, offering their story of torture, incarceration, and finally salvation and redemption. They were simple Indians who had fallen into the malevolent grip of the army and state investigators, innocent victims who lost two years of their lives after being forced to confess to a killing they did not commit. All they wanted now was their simple life back in the sierra, reunited with their families and their land.

The brothers-in-law from Yoata had suffered greatly these past two and half years, and there was no one better to describe the painful experience than Juan. As always, Chivarra did the talking while Hernandez played a supporting role. Chivarra covered his talking points with the skill of a practiced hand, even remembering to express sympathy for Martha and her travails since her husband's lamentable death. There is no one quite so convincing as a pathological liar, I thought, watching their performance on Spanish-language television.

Hayward flew to Guadalajara to interview Chivarra and Hernandez. Most of what they told her in a Tuesday interview, four days after their release, conformed to what they said to other reporters, with one significant exception. Sitting with Hernandez and Morales listening, Chivarra looked at Hayward and calmly denied ever meeting her before now. "I never met you," Chivarra told Hayward. "I never met the gringo [True]. I never told you any of that."

When Hayward reminded Hernandez of the bracelet he had given her in the Colotlán jail and his apology outside Chivarra's earshot, Hernandez just looked down at the ground, not speaking.

Chivarra's bald lie even unsettled Morales. Hayward had come into contact with the defendants twice in Guadalajara at the time of their arraignment and three more times at the Colotlán jail. Three different *Express-News* photographers had accompanied her and taken photos of Chivarra and Hernandez that were published with her articles, all of which Morales and Gatins had seen in their regular visits to the newspaper's website.

Chivarra, it seemed, could no longer keep track of his own comings and goings, or his own story. Or he felt no need, having embroidered his story so many times he now felt beyond challenge. Once again, Juan Chivarra was in control.

He told Hayward he had only glimpsed True as he passed by on the trail. "I never said a word to him, I didn't think anything of it," Chivarra said. "I know myself. I'm not bad. If people go to my village, I won't bother them. People say I'm mean, but I'm not. I haven't hurt or robbed anyone. I'm happy now, at peace. Being on the outside is not the same as being in jail. I didn't kill him. We didn't harm him. But we feel for all the pain his wife went through."

In denying he killed or even met True, Chivarra also seemed to be denying long-standing accusations that preceded True's visit to the Huichol sierra. "My heart was aching," Chivarra said of his time behind bars. "I was sad and worried about my family. I was jailed without having committed any crime. I cried and cried."

Morales added her assurances. "What I want last in the world is to send criminals back on the street," she said. "We went in to find out the truth, because Mexico is tired of lies."

Like Gatins, she invoked the spirit of True. "We felt his presence," Morales told reporters in her breathless, almost mystical speaking style. "He is the first one who would not have wanted the Huichols convicted. If this has served for anything, Philip True was an example that we can do something about corruption."

Gatins displayed the same absolute conviction about the miscarriage of justice. "The moment the Jalisco [autopsy] report was discounted, the Huichols should have been released," he told Hayward. "We only set out to find the truth. And the truth is this was an accident."

Hayward said Gatins told her that he believed True was drunk that Sunday morning in the canyon bottom, perhaps after overindulging while trying to stay warm the previous night, causing him to set out inebriated. He then fell to his death along the steep, narrow trail. Gatins later denied making that statement, but at the time I wondered if a recovering alcoholic might see excess drinking at the root of all evil and a convenient explanation whenever events spun out of control in someone else's life. Hadn't that been his personal experience?

Rivas Souza's original autopsy negated any possibility of accidental death in a fall. There were no broken bones and no internal bleeding or organ damage suffered in the fall. True was a dead man when he tumbled down the steep ravine. The federal autopsy mentioned the presence of vomit near the spot where the Huichol hunter, Margarito Díaz, said he first spotted True's corpse before it was moved. This led Gatins and Morales to believe that True survived his fall and later died from his injuries.

The science of forensics went unexplored as an essential element of the story. The small amount of vomit could have escaped True's mouth as a result of the impact, but such nuances were no longer subject to debate. In a country long accustomed to the abuse of its lowliest citizens, nothing could compete with the story of the two humble Huichols, the Mexican woman who fought the aggression of powerful American detractors, and the shy expatriate and his Mexican wife whose selfless generosity had made it all possible.

Rivas Souza was among the few in Guadalajara who did not celebrate the sudden turn of events. The tall, white-haired pathologist, now 75, fumed over the damage to his reputation built over a half century. The respect he was paid by the U.S. press was not matched in the Mexican press. He was all but ignored now by the Guadalajara media. "I am sick of being harassed," he told Hayward. "I have given my report, and I stand behind it 100 percent. Philip was strangled, he was killed."

Gatins and Morales packed their bags for a road show. It was time to take Chivarra and Hernandez to Mexico City. The two Huichols from Yoata were about to meet the capital press.

In retrospect, our single greatest mistake was underestimating the defense. We had worked hard in Mexico City and Guadalajara to pursue what we believed was a fair verdict. We failed to make the same effort in Colotlán, a small city of 16,000 people, a distant world from

Mexico's capital cities. U.S. consular officials, like their counterparts in the U.S. press, traveled to Colotlán to stay abreast of the case, but they too relied on assurances from senior judicial officials in Guadalajara, who told them that a conviction was inevitable.

Martha and I decided to return to Mexico City to consult with President Fox's legal adviser, Juan de Dios Castro, and to hold press conferences there and in Guadalajara to urge the state appeals court to overturn the lower court's verdict. One other difference between the two countries' legal systems, we had learned, was the state's right to appeal the judge's decision, a right that offered some protection against arbitrary rulings by local judges.

Press groups protested the decision to absolve the men of the killing, and even the U.S. government set aside quiet diplomacy. A State Department spokesman in Washington and Ambassador Davidow in Mexico City said the U.S. government was convinced that True's death was a homicide and expected Mexican authorities to apprehend and punish the killers. Two South Texas congressmen, Ciro Rodriguez and Charlie Gonzalez, also decried the verdict and the nature of the judge's action.

If Morales and Gatins enjoyed a burst of publicity favoring the Huichols, we made our own case in Mexico one week later. Reporters there seemed surprised that we were not quitting the case now, and our demands for an appeal were widely reported. "This case is not a situation of Mexico against the United States," I said at our press conference. "It is not a soccer match, and the fact that these suspects were released does not represent a victory for Mexico. We have a journalist who was killed. It doesn't matter whether he was Mexican or American. It is important the killers be punished."

John MacCormack profiled Gatins for the Sunday, August 12, edition. It was a testament to MacCormack's professionalism that he produced a balanced story about Gatins, given his impact on the case. He was, MacCormack wrote, the "unforeseen wild card in a complex criminal case that involves delicate international sensibilities as well as troubling issues of fact and law."

Gatins displayed no misgivings in the interview. "I'll scream this to the day I die," he said. "I was a witness on this case, and from my point of view, justice, to my great amazement, was served. These were Indians from the other side of hell. No one knew them. It was a formula for the classic scapegoat scenario. True died of tragic accidental means, or possibly someone else killed him, but the Huichols were made into scapegoats to get the Americans off our backs."

Gatins was surprised at the balance and objectivity in MacCormack's story, given his employer and his own personal relationship with True. He telephoned MacCormack to compliment his professionalism. To his surprise, MacCormack was "standoffish." "As far as I'm concerned, you helped set free the two men who murdered Philip True," MacCormack told Gatins.

As she prepared to leave Guadalajara after interviewing Chivarra and Hernandez, Hayward turned to Gatins and made a prediction: "You spent your money on the wrong side; you'll see one day."

Gatins thought otherwise, of course. He made an ideal defender of Chivarra and Hernandez, and not only because he had the necessary resources to help them. All his life he had been an outsider, someone who did not quite fit. His father's prisoner-of-war stories he heard as a boy were not lost on Miguel as he contemplated the long incarceration of Juan and Miguel.

"I particularly remember, as we grew up in the Deep South of the 1950s and 1960s, when my father would stop the car and he would offer a pack of cigarettes to prisoners on the chain gangs working on the highways," Gatins said. "After a time, I came to realize that this gesture was one that only a person who had also experienced the loneliness of prison, and the agony of torture, could feel in seeing another prisoner in chains."

One of Miguel's older brothers, Martin, told MacCormack, "We grew up where there was discrimination, and not only racial. It wasn't so long ago that being Catholic was not very high on the list in the South. We were raised on the beliefs of equality and so forth, and that it's a worthwhile thing to do, if you believe people are being treated unjustly or not being treated properly."

Life as a recovering alcoholic also influenced Gatins's outlook. "I think it is important to note that my alcoholic recovery has played a role in who I am today and indirectly was a factor in my involvement in this case," Gatins said.

"He always told me he wanted to marry a woman from another country, and he always told me when he was in banking that he didn't like what he was doing and didn't want to work," said Sims Bray, his Atlanta friend. "He's always been his own man."

The surprise inheritance had made such a life possible. "It was during that time that I discovered being away from the stress of the workplace and not being obsessed with making another dollar was not only okay, but in my case, healthy for my well-being," Gatins said. "I came to realize that a person's self-worth did not have to be associated with their social standing, professional employment, bank account or automobile, contrary to what the system leads everyone to believe."

Gatins said he developed an appreciation for True as he read more about his life and realized they shared similar outlooks on life and priorities not built around material gains.

Despite his outward support of Chivarra and Hernandez, Gatins nursed some private reservations. The more he came to know Chivarra, the more he thought the Huichol knew more than he was saying. He was so controlling, and there were unresolved details in Chivarra's story, as well as vague hints dropped here and there by Morales during the course of her investigation.

Gatins had read the Hayward interview with Chivarra in which he claimed they had never met, an obvious lie. He shared his misgivings with Morales, who acknowledged that Chivarra had met Hayward on several occasions. She attributed the lie to Chivarra's excited state after his release from jail.

Martha's suffering also nagged at Gatins. First she lost Philip and now she lost again, this time a protracted and very public fight for a conviction of her husband's accused killers and the hearts and minds of the Mexican people. "I know she must think there is a monster down here," Gatins said. "I hope she will think differently later on."

Gatins was right. Martha did not regard him or Morales as do-gooders. "The truth has to come out," she said. "I can accept a verdict, but I cannot accept the truth not being known."

At the press conferences Martha and I held, we focused on the revolving door of judges and prosecutors and Reyes Contreras's indefensible conduct in handling the verdict. Afterward, several prominent Mexican journalists began to question the verdict.

"It is inexplicable they are free," said Homero Aridjis, a Mexican writer, journalist, and human rights activist who served as the president of PEN, an organization of 15,000 writers in 90 countries. "There seems to have been a machine of corruption to free these people. All the judges involved should be investigated. There is something very rotten in this process."

Whatever misgivings Gatins privately harbored, he believed that he and Ruby had done the right thing. Speaking weeks later to Hayward, he continued to defend his belief that True died in a hiking accident. "I know we probably will never know everything about this case, nor was I there when Philip died, but I know it was no murder," Gatins said.

We failed to reach Reyes Contreras in the weeks after the verdict. Officials in Guadalajara said that he had been suspended from the bench and was unavailable even as they refused to explain the disciplinary action. Gatins told reporters that the suspension was a political gesture meant to appease our side.

Yet the judge seemed to go out of his way at the time of the verdict to manipulate events. Prosecutors told us they had visited with the judge the day before he released the two Huichols, the same day that Morales was tipped, and received assurances that a verdict would not be issued before the following week, prompting them to start their weekend prematurely. The president of the state supreme court told U.S. consular officials that he was "confounded" by the verdict.

"He [the president] said he had not seen the text of the decision yet, but that it is likely the decision will be appealed and the case be re-tried—this time in Guadalajara where it will be handled 'according to the law,'" consular officials cabled Washington. "We were quite disappointed by the release of the defendants and the secretive way the decision was handled. The fact that senior local judicial officials seem upset about the decision bodes well for an appeal, however."

What was the exact nature of Morales's relationship with Reyes Contreras? At the very least she befriended the judge, winning access not accorded anyone else. The fact that they shared meals alone should have been sufficient reason to remove him from the case. The specter of the judge and defendants and their respective retinues coming together for a meal one hour after the verdict was even more questionable. Certainly the two groups might have coincidentally selected the same roadhouse eatery, but neither side expressed awkwardness or felt the need to keep their distance. It didn't seem implausible that the communal dinner was arranged in advance.

We were not alone in our suspicion that Morales used Gatins's money to influence the judge. It's impossible to prove such claims, but neither Gatins nor Morales provided any detailed accounting for the $28,000 in expenditures.

I asked Morales for an exact accounting of the money. "If you believe that we took the money you are making a grave mistake," Morales said, angered by my inquiry. "And yes, I spent my own money on this case, and never earned one cent of [Gatins's] money myself."

My line of inquiry also offended Gatins. He cited several legal cases in Guadalajara where lawyers earned even larger fees. "She didn't give me anything," Gatins said, adding that he trusted Morales and never asked for receipts or an accounting.

"I would ask you to consider, if this win was based on a bribe, why would Paty have spent so much time in Colotlán, etc., working the case until the very end?" Gatins asked. "Had she reached such an agreement with the judge, the logical thing would have been for her to keep a low profile away from the court... She did not know until the very last minute which way the judge would rule."

Gatins suggested my original reaction on hearing the verdict, when I scribbled a note to myself that the judge was bribed, prejudiced my later thinking. "This is where Paty deserves credit. She felt our only chance was to convince the judge to make an independent decision based strictly on the evidence," Gatins said. "There was no way we could compete with you and your network of influence at high levels, but I think she felt the country had begun to change and that maybe the time was ripe for such a decision."

I in turn wondered if Gatins truly believed the Huichols went free based on the evidence. Just as many in Mexico accept as fact the abuse and torture of jailed suspects, we knew that bribery of judges and other officials also was routine.

"Do you think she bribed the judge?" I asked Gatins outright in early 2004.

"I have thought about that subsequently, I admit," Gatins answered. "I knew she got very friendly with the judge, took him out to lunch, that's common around here."

Gatins also acknowledged that Morales's obtaining a copy of the case file from the judge was unusual. "In the end, I don't think she did bribe him," Gatins said. "I think one of her qualities is her ability to make contacts and make friends of all these officials in and around the courts."

Gatins, I concluded, might be right. He impressed me as one of the more trusting and generous men I had ever met—and perhaps one of the most misguided.

Prosecutors fashioned an appeal arguing that Reyes Contreras ignored key evidence, including the state autopsy, while accepting the extraofficial autopsy performed by federal coroners with no standing in the case. Forensic pathologists are taught that a primary indicator of homicide is the movement or concealment of a corpse. The nature of True's death, followed by his burial days later and his missing valuables, pointed to the commission of a crime, yet Reyes Contreras somehow neglected to rule either way on the robbery charge in his verdict.

Reyes Contreras ignored the Huichols' first and second statements, in which they admitted killing True.

Yolanda Chivarra, Juan's wife, told investigators she witnessed

Juan and Miguel attacking True and later returned with the two men along the same trail when they decided to conceal the corpse. The judge made no mention of her in his ruling.

"It is obviously discouraging to think that this whole civic action we sponsored would boil down or be cheapened to a simple bribe; I cannot buy it," Gatins said. "Not to be arrogant, but, in my view, we simply did a far better job than the prosecution."

Gatins was right. The defense did work harder and more effectively than lazy, incompetent prosecutors, and it is discouraging to think the entire effort might have come down to a bribe.

17

Injustice North of the Border

It is unacceptable to the Mexican government that a judicial system can allow a person who has shot someone from behind to walk away without the jail sentence such a crime deserves.

—Marco Antonio Fraire,
Mexican consulate spokesman in San Antonio

In Washington, George W. Bush prepared to host the first-ever White House state dinner in honor of Vicente Fox. Bush's first foreign trip as president had been a visit to Fox at his ranch in Mexico, and now his first state dinner would honor the Mexican president in September. The Texas governor-turned-president had an aversion to nation building and global activism, and a lack of affinity with our European allies. But he felt differently about our neighbor to the south. A new era of openness and respect between the two countries seemed to be in the offing. Bush and Fox talked as if the first significant immigration reform in two decades was within grasp.

While friendship and diplomacy were about to take center stage in Washington, a less trusting relationship between the United States and Mexico that reflected our real history continued to play out. We knew the Mexicans harbored many unspoken reasons justifying their reluctance to rule on the side of justice in the True case. Some were historic, some were xenophobic. And another reason was the widespread view in Mexico that the U.S. legal system did not extend rights and protections to Mexicans, especially the millions of undocumented workers here illegally.

Mexicans believe our system is as arbitrary and corrupt as their own. That will strike American readers as absurd. Two cases in Texas, however, that became big news south of the border around the same time as the True case illustrate how Mexicans are victimized north of the border.

On New Year's Day 1997, Eli Montesinos, a forty-four-year-old businessman from Monterrey, was shopping with his wife, Susana, and three of the couple's four daughters at the Dillard's department store in Rivercenter Mall, a popular tourist destination on San Antonio's downtown River Walk.

San Antonio police officer James A. Smith, in full uniform and armed with his loaded service weapon, was moonlighting as a private security guard. As the holiday closing hour approached, Smith started steering customers toward a single exit door as store managers began to lock up.

According to the officer, Montesinos, who weighed more than 300 pounds, grew belligerent when he was not allowed to exit the store with his family through a more convenient door. A shouting match escalated into an altercation and Smith said the two men traded blows with the policeman's metal baton. Smith and Montesinos fell to the ground, wrestling. Montesinos's wife said Smith applied a chokehold that caused her husband to stop breathing and pass out. He died five days later in a San Antonio hospital without recovering consciousness.

The story was front-page news in Texas and throughout Mexico. A Mexican visitor to San Antonio during the festive holiday season—when tens of thousands of Mexicans pour into the city to shop and visit—was killed by a moonlighting policeman because he would not leave through the designated exit door. It seemed a terribly unjust end to a minor dispute that might have been better handled if Smith had followed standard department policy and called for backup. Most police departments have banned the chokehold Smith employed to subdue Montesinos.

From the outset, police and city officials seemed more interested in defending an off-duty cop than investigating the incident. No one in the city leadership called to comfort the widow or her four children, even though the family kept a second home in the city, and the victim's mother lived there.

Montesinos's death was ruled a homicide by Vincent J. DiMaio, the Bexar County medical examiner. DiMaio said death was hastened under the stress of a violent struggle by Montesinos's obesity and undiagnosed heart disease.

The Bexar County district attorney's office took ten months to review the politically charged case before declining to file charges. An internal police investigation exonerated Smith of any wrongdoing. Dillard's and local authorities refused to release the store videos of the incident.

Mexican diplomats protested the outcome, and the U.S. attorney general's office in San Antonio announced it was opening an investigation into the possible violation of Montesinos's civil rights.

Dillard's eventually paid the Montesinos family $1 million to settle a negligence lawsuit, and in return the family waived all claims against the city and police.

"I never heard from anyone in the Justice Department or U.S. Attorney's office about the supposed civil rights investigation," Mexican Consul General Carlos Sada said three years later. "I couldn't even get them to return my telephone calls or answer my letters on the subject. Most Mexicans do not believe there was an honest, complete investigation because the policeman was an American and the victim was a Mexican."

A second case also was page-one news in Texas and south of the border, the kind of story that causes people elsewhere to shake their heads and talk about frontier justice in Texas.

In May 2000, Sam Blackwood, a seventy-six-year-old South Texas rancher, shot and killed an unarmed young Mexican laborer named

Eusebio de Haro, who hailed from the state of Guanajuato, home to Fox and to many Mexican workers living in South Texas.

Blackwood claimed self-defense, but there were two witnesses to the shooting, Blackwood's wife and a second Mexican worker who was accompanying de Haro on their return trip to Kerrville, where they lived and worked one hour northwest of San Antonio. The two laborers were returning on foot from an Easter week visit to their village.

The surviving Mexican testified that they were walking across Blackwood's ranch, parched and searching for water, when they spotted the approaching rancher and his wife and asked them for a drink of water. Blackwood refused and ordered the men off his ranch. As they turned to leave, he aimed his pistol at de Haro and fired.

Blackwood claimed the Mexicans were rushing him with a weapon, which was never found, and the coroner refuted the rancher's claim of self-defense by establishing that the Mexican was shot from behind. Even Blackwood's wife, testifying under oath, contradicted her husband's assertion that the Mexicans had threatened the couple and were armed.

Murder? A thirsty, defenseless Mexican migrant bled to death in the South Texas brush country while a seventy-six-year-old rancher holding a pistol looked on. Blackwood was convicted of one count of misdemeanor deadly conduct, fined $4,000, given a 180-day suspended sentence, and allowed to walk away a free man.

"Can anyone imagine a Mexican worker shooting to death a Texas rancher and being let off with such a light charge and his freedom?" I wrote in a column published three weeks after the release of Chivarra and Hernandez.

My inbox was filled Monday with vitriolic e-mail from Mexican haters. The column was translated and published in *Reforma*, prompting a second wave of e-mail from Mexicans who believed the killings of True and de Haro were one and the same; in each case the system denied justice to outsiders. Mexico had its Philip True case, and San Antonio had a case of its own.

18

Murders, But No Murderers

The time has come for Mexico and the United States to trust each
other. Simple trust, that is what has been sorely absent in our relationship in the past.

—President Vicente Fox, September 6, 2001

Mexico is a magical country where there are murders but no murderers.

—Homero Aridjis, Mexican writer and human rights activist

After the press conferences, Martha and I remained in Guadalajara to
hire our own lawyers—a move we should have made two years earlier.
We settled on Ochoa & Associates, led by Jorge Ochoa, a young, polished lawyer with good connections. Ochoa's legal aide brought us to
Ochoa's offices on a shaded residential street in Zapopan. We sat down
with Ochoa and his partners and outlined our interest in retaining
counsel for the duration of the case.

They seemed eager to represent us and, to our surprise, suggested a
modest fee of $3,500 to handle the appeal, with an equal sum due if they
prevailed. Gatins had spent so much more. Our lawyers, of course,
would not conduct an independent investigation into True's death.
They were hired to be our eyes and ears around the appeals court,
watch Arturo Zamora, and represent Martha before the magistrates.

"What do you want to have happen to these two men who killed Mr. True?" Ochoa asked us.

Martha and I turned to each other with the same look on our faces: what exactly did he mean? "We want justice, not revenge," I said.

It had been a mistake not to hire Ochoa earlier. He would have learned about Miguel Gatins and Patricia Morales, and worked to prevent the judge from rendering such a one-sided decision. We reviewed the case for an hour. Our new partners agreed to work with state prosecutors to see that a timely appeal was filed and vigorously pursued. They seemed confident that Reyes Contreras had committed key errors that would result in a reversal. It was a strange experience, pursuing onetime defendants found not guilty by a trial judge. They would have been home free, untouchable in the United States.

"The right to appeal is necessary because of the total discretion and power the judges have in our country to rule however they want," Ochoa told us.

Shortly after our visit to Guadalajara, Vicente Fox traveled to Washington as the guest of honor at George W. Bush's first state dinner. On the surface, they shared much in common, two cowboy presidents more comfortable on their ranches than in the presidency. Both came to politics as wealthy businessmen. Bush welcomed Fox to Washington with hyperbole, declaring Mexico to be "our most important ally." The next day, Fox addressed a joint session of the U.S. Congress and received several standing ovations during his spirited thirty-minute speech delivered in excellent English. "The time has come for Mexico and the United States to trust each other," Fox declared. "Simple trust, that is what has been sorely absent in our relationship in the past."

He used the word "trust" over and over again, and called on Congress to legalize the status of millions of Mexicans already living and working in the United States without papers. "Migration has always rendered more economic benefits to the United States than the cost it entails," Fox told the senators and congressmen. After the speech Fox told reporters, "It's not an amnesty. They haven't committed any crime."

Fox challenged lawmakers to overhaul U.S. immigration policy by year's end, a deadline even Bush knew was impossible in Washington, where there was more support for immigration reform among Democratics than Republicans. The two presidents then traveled to Toledo, Ohio, to visit the city's growing Mexican and Mexican American community.

Fox left for Mexico in an optimistic mood. No Mexican president had ever come to Washington and challenged U.S. lawmakers to enact such ambitious change. The move was risky, but Fox came to office on the winds of change, and Mexicans filled with nationalistic pride as they watched their new president project strength and engage American political leaders on equal terms. Days later, the September 11 terrorist attacks on America changed everything. All discussion of immigration reform was forgotten. Border security became the new watchword. The Bush administration, meanwhile, was caught off guard by the level of anti-American sentiment unleashed in Mexico after he declared that other countries were either "with us or against us" in his newly declared "war on terror". Suddenly our "most valuable ally" no longer wanted to play the part. Relations between the White House and Los Pinos chilled as Bush weighed his military options.

Meanwhile, we still had a case to appeal. The first appeals court hearing was held Monday, September 24, in Guadalajara's colonial supreme justice tribunal. This was the first open hearing in a courtroom since the arraignment of the defendants nearly three years earlier. Three magistrates were on hand to receive arguments from both sides before retiring to study the voluminous case file and eventually render a verdict. It would take two judges to agree on a verdict.

The prosecution caused a sensation when it presented graphic photographs from the Rivas Souza autopsy. A new prosecutor in the case, Liliana Iris Moran Ferrer, argued that the autopsy photographs clearly demonstrated that True was beaten, strangled with his own bandana, and then thrown down a steep ravine. Cuts and abrasions on his arms and legs suggest he fought back while still alive. The state presented nineteen photographs and a video of the first autopsy, evidence it said was ignored by Reyes Contreras.

"The judge had an obligation to see evidence we presented, not to omit it," Moran told the magistrates. "This was totally illegal and violates the basic principles of law. The judge only considered evidence relevant to his sentence. It showed a lack of knowledge of the law."

Zamora's presence in the courthouse drew widespread attention because of his rising profile as a likely mayoral candidate. "I'm sure of the innocence of the Huichols, but not of what happened to Philip True; or if anyone killed him, who?" Zamora said.

Attorney General Solís was there to underscore the importance of the case to top officials, who had been embarrassed by the surprise verdict in Colotlán. "The results are clear. There was the autopsy proving strangulation, there was a confession, and the accused returned the property they stole from Mr. True," Solís argued.

Rivas Souza was on hand to defend his findings. "This was a homicide," he said. "All the black marks are bruises and they were made while Philip was alive—bleeding doesn't occur after death. There are signs Philip fought with his aggressors, who probably killed him while conscious, strangling him with a bandana that had two knots made in the back of the neck."

He questioned the political motivation of the Zedillo administration in ordering a second procedure. "A second autopsy is difficult to do," he said. "There was a putrid body, and it was lacking basic organs undergoing blood tests. Why would I lie? All I care about is the dignity of a person."

Back in San Antonio, John MacCormack seized the opportunity to take the autopsy photos, along with Rivas Souza's report and the summary findings of the second autopsy, and submit them to five leading forensic pathologists around the United States. None were paid or had an interest in the case.

Four of the pathologists told MacCormack they believed True had been murdered. "In my opinion, he died of strangulation. Everything

points to homicide," said Dr. Robert Kirschner of Chicago, a former
deputy chief medical examiner for Cook County, Illinois.

Kirschner, who has conducted autopsies in the developing world
for human rights organizations, said True definitely did not die in an
accidental fall. "There's nothing to suggest evidence of a fall," he said.
"There are no serious head injuries, no other fractures or ruptures of
internal organs. We can disregard that theory immediately."

Only one of the pathologists, Dr. Sparks Veasey, the former head
of the autopsy section for the University of Texas Medical School at
Galveston, did not reach a conclusion. "I'm unable to state, in reason-
able medical probability, the cause and manner of death," he wrote
back to MacCormack.

Veasay was the only one of the five experts who thought True
might have been drunk, while the others dismissed the significance of
the blood-alcohol levels and attributed the reading to postmortem
decomposition.

"I seriously doubt this death is from a fall from a height," said Dr.
Nizam Peerwani, the Tarrant County medical examiner in Fort Worth.
"I truly believe that, based on this material and these pictures, he was
strangled to death." Peerwani also cited other findings by Rivas Souza
that support strangulation, including hemorrhaging of neck muscles
and a groove around the neck caused by the bandana. "There are at
least two pictures that very clearly show a very tight ligature around
the neck," Peerwani said. "One shows the ligature being removed, and
it shows a deep furrow in the lateral aspect of the neck."

Peerwani also said the blood-alcohol test conducted in the
Guadalajara laboratory, known as an oxidation test, was meaningless.
"The method they used is totally unacceptable in our legal system,"
he said.

Dr. Jerry Spencer, the medical examiner in Lubbock, Texas, who
helped conduct the 1985 autopsy in Mexico on slain DEA agent
Enrique Camarena, said he concluded True probably was beaten to
death. "There is sufficient evidence of blunt-force injuries of the head
to result in the death of Philip True," he wrote. "He may also have

been strangled, but I cannot concur with that opinion based on the available evidence." He added, "The blood alcohol concentration is not unexpected from the fact that the body was moderately decomposed. Finally, based on the injuries and circumstances of death, the manner of death of Philip True should be classified as a homicide."

Dr. DiMaio in San Antonio agreed. "If we found this body in a shallow grave in Bexar County, it's going to be a homicide until proven otherwise," he told MacCormack. "If there's no evidence of serious head injury, and the bandana was around the neck, and it wasn't a heroin or cocaine overdose, and we didn't find anything else, we'd most likely say the cause of death was asphyxia.

"I'd make this case a homicide by virtue of the way the body was concealed and the absence of significant trauma or natural disease," he concluded.

None of the pathologists agreed with Rivas Souza's original finding that True had been sexually brutalized, saying the changes in the anus occurred during the decomposition process.

After rereading MacCormack's story, I began planning a return trip to Guadalajara. It was time that Martha and I held another press conference. We would invite Rivas Souza to give the local press a lesson in forensics. The third anniversary of True's murder was less than a month away, and there was no sense sitting still in San Antonio, waiting for an appeals court to rule in the case. Perhaps we could send a message to the three magistrates via the Guadalajara press.

We arrived in Guadalajara ready to spoon-feed the local media. We knew most of them would not bother to do any independent reporting, so we translated the findings of the five U.S. pathologists and packaged them with copies of the graphic autopsy photos. We also photocopied the pages of True's journal describing his confrontation with Juan on the trail near Amoltita.

Rivas Souza willingly appeared alongside us in his trademark white laboratory coat. Our best witness, as always, was Martha, who brought Teo with her. Their presence was a powerful reminder to all present that a husband and father had been lost.

We urged the press and the magistrates to recognize that True's death was a homicide and that the verdict handed down by Reyes Contreras was a miscarriage of justice that perpetuated a negative image of Mexico beyond its borders.

Some of the reporters were openly hostile and demanded to know why an American newspaper editor kept returning to challenge the Mexican legal system. What about your own problems back home? We fired back, asserting that Mexican journalists should be outraged that reporters are murdered in Mexico and their killers routinely act with impunity.

Rivas Souza reiterated his determination not to alter his findings in the face of political pressure or controversy. He was gratified to receive the indirect support of so many U.S. forensic experts who reviewed his work. "I never said who killed him, only how he died," he stated. "There is no reason why I should change my opinion."

The next morning we reviewed the newspapers and discussed the television coverage. Given the confrontational atmosphere at the press conference, we had done very well. Back at home, the third anniversary of True's death came and went. And with each passing month, it became more obvious that our case was mired in politics that transcended True's murder.

Court officials told Susana Hayward in early February that a decision was imminent, but months went by without news. Finally, in April, the presiding magistrate, Tómas Aguilar Robles, told our reporter the court had reached an unanimous decision that would be announced in three or four days as soon as the paperwork was completed. Aguilar spoke extensively with Hayward and made it clear that the lower court judge had erred by giving legal weight to the second autopsy and ignoring the findings of Rivas Souza.

April came and went without any new word.

By law, the magistrates had fifteen days to review the lower court verdict and issue a decision. More than six months had passed now since the state's appeal was filed, nine months since Chivarra and Hernandez had been set free. Once again politics, not the law, appeared to be guiding events. We were told the magistrates feared ruling against Zamora, who might retaliate somehow if elected.

Martha's Guadalajara lawyers filed a petition in federal court seeking to compel the state magistrates to rule. Federal courts wield absolute power over the state courts; any decision or ruling is subject to federal appeal. To demonstrate his authority, the federal judge, Gerardo Eduardo Garcia Anzures, requested the entire four-volume case file from the state appeals court. His request promised to delay resolution of the case even longer, but it also prodded the state high court.

The magistrates, perhaps fearing the embarrassment of federal scrutiny, finally ruled on Thursday, May 30. They found Chivarra and Hernandez guilty of *homocidio sencillo*, or simple homicide, the equivalent of manslaughter. They sentenced the two Huichols to thirteen-year prison terms.

Martha reacted with relief. "The first thing is, I want to thank God because my husband and I received justice," she told Mexican reporters from her home in Brownsville. "I am in a state of shock, joy, now I have a story to tell my son, that in Mexico you can find justice, that his father was a brave man who loved Mexico and the Huichol culture. This case was never against an indigenous people, but against people who took my husband's life."

Gatins, meanwhile, thought politics swayed the judges in our favor. "As a matter of first impression, the magistrates are trying to make everyone happy," Gatins told Hayward. "They convicted them, but they lowered the sentence from thirty to forty years to just thirteen years, and they did away with the allegations of robbery, which was the alleged motive. They were completely railroaded. An acquittal would have been the proper verdict."

Rivas Souza felt vindicated. "I never wavered from my findings, that he was strangled to death," he said. "When I heard the news last night, I was so pleased the truth came out, not just for me but for

Philip's wife, Martha. In this world there are so many shameless people, it's good to know there are also admirable people."

The three magistrates issued a 582-page ruling that charged Reyes Contreras with lying about some of the details he cited to justify his verdict. It was a rare public rebuke of a judge. For Martha, the verdict brought the first good news in three and half years. "I heard about the verdict while I was driving home in my car, and I shouted and shouted and shouted," she said.

It was satisfying to see her smile again. Yet, after three and half years of false starts, setbacks, broken promises, and disregard of the law, it was impossible to let down our guard completely.

Zamora quickly negated the detention order by filing an *amparo,* a motion that prevented authorities from arresting the two defendants while the appeal was considered.

Our next best chance to advance the case would come in late August, when Fox was scheduled to visit Bush at Prairie Chapel Ranch in Crawford, Texas, a small town a few hours north of San Antonio. Fox also intended to visit San Antonio for the first time since being elected president. I sent him a private invitation to meet with newspaper editors and asked him to publicly call for a resolution in the True case. Such a statement by Fox on foreign soil was unlikely. But if we succeeded in winning an audience, his traveling press entourage would propel the story back onto page one of Mexican newspapers and raise the pressure on authorities to act.

Relations between the two countries were fraying at the edges. Weeks before his August trip, Fox personally telephoned Texas governor Rick Perry and asked him to cancel the planned execution of Javier Suarez Medina, a Mexican national convicted and sentenced to die for the 1988 murder of an undercover Dallas police officer.

Mexico, like most Western nations, does not have the death penalty. The refusal of U.S. authorities to stay executions of Mexican citizens or transfer them to Mexican jails was a growing issue between the countries. Most cases are in Texas and Florida, states with the biggest death row populations and the highest number of executions. Convicted murderers are unsympathetic figures, but there is an important legal issue that goes beyond the death penalty debate. International law requires law enforcement agencies in any country to notify arrested foreigners of their right to meet with officials from their own country before submitting to questioning. The law, of course, is routinely ignored.

"Human rights is a key issue to this government. We will always ask for clemency [for Mexicans facing execution]. In cases where legal rights were violated, we will demand it. The legal rights of Javier Suarez Medina were not complied with, particularly with regard to the Geneva Convention," Fox told Dane Schiller in an interview at Los Pinos.

Governor Perry rejected Fox's request, knowing the implications for the Mexican president's scheduled visit with Bush at his Texas ranch. "He received the justice that in the sovereign state of Texas is meted out for the penalty of killing a police officer, and that is death. One way not to have that problem is don't come to Texas and kill a police officer," Perry told reporters after the execution had been carried out, only two days after Fox's public appeal.

Fox immediately canceled his U.S. visit, ending our hopes for a meeting in San Antonio. Both governments put their best spin on the situation, but clearly relations between Washington and "our most important ally" had deteriorated. The spirit of the state dinner in Washington was long gone.

The fourth anniversary of True's killing slipped quietly by the first week of December 2002, and we found ourselves in a standoff. We wanted a final verdict, while the Mexicans wanted us, and the True case, to go away.

The federal court finally acted in February 2003, four years and three months after True's death. Neither side liked the decision. The court returned the case to the state appeals court, declaring that one of the three magistrates had a relationship with Zamora, the defense lawyer and mayoral candidate, which should have precluded his involvement in the case. It was a catch-22: a pro-defense judge was caught in a conflict of interest, so the verdict of guilt and the prison terms against the Huichols he represented were vacated. We found ourselves where we were at the outset of the appeals process in late 2001.

"There is nothing I can do but keep fighting until they get what they deserve," Martha told reporters. "It's hard to live day to day, but I still have faith in the Mexican justice system."

Jalisco's newly elected governor, Francisco Ramírez Acuña, was scheduled to deliver an address the very next day at St. Mary's University Law School in San Antonio. We sent a reporter to ask him about the True case. It seemed curious that an elected official from Guadalajara would come to San Antonio, of all places, to extol the virtues of the Mexican legal system. Ramirez, a member of the PAN, told his audience that under PRI rule, "there was a climate of impunity in which citizens did not follow the law and authorities did not enforce it."

All true, but we didn't see much change under the PAN. Afterward, Lucy Hood, one of our reporters, pressed Ramirez about the True case. The governor was not happy to be confronted unexpectedly by a reporter in public. He had come to give a speech. A defensive Ramirez told his audience that the state supreme court had convicted the two Huichols, who were now wanted men. He was wrong on both counts. Our story the next morning sent a message to the embarrassed governor: we were not going away.

19

Revelations in Guadalajara

I don't want to die with a secret. I don't want to pay for someone else's mistakes before God, nor do I want to live with my conscience burdened.

—Patricia Morales, defense investigator and director of the Institute for Latin American Philanthropy

Nights around here are filled with ghosts. You should see all the spirits walking through the streets. As soon as it is dark they begin to come out. No one likes to see them. There's so many of them and so few of us that we don't even make the effort to pray for them anymore, to help them out of their purgatory. We don't have enough prayers to go around. Maybe a few words of the Lord's Prayer for each one. But that's not going to do them any good. Then there are our sins on top of theirs. None of us is still living in God's grace. We can't lift up our eyes, because they are filled with shame.

—Juan Rulfo, *Pedro Paramo*

A one-paragraph e-mail written in garbled English arrived Thursday afternoon, March 27, 2003, as I sat at my office computer. It came from Guadalajara and it changed everything.

Mr. Robert Rivard, editor in boss of the San Antonio Express-News:
Respectable Mr. I am the Directress of the Latin American Institute of Philanthropy that I investigate about Philip's death True me if the whole absolute truth of their death, in fact I am writing a book, I believe that it would really surprise him, I am not against the alone North Americans that I never gave myself had conquered in finding the truth, and I have given myself bill that you have looked for the truth but this confused one, I would like

to speak with you, with al respect he will be surprised a lot the true truth.

The note was from Patricia Morales.

Since the surprise release of the two defendants, our focus had been on Miguel Gatins, the financier, and Arturo Zamora, the formidable lawyer. Susana Hayward, who had met Morales at her home when she interviewed the released Huichols, considered her flighty.

Morales asked me to reply in Spanish, which I did with a curt dismissal. Her answer, written in Spanish, brought me to my senses. Having dismissed her as just another peculiar character in our long-running soap opera, I reversed course when I realized she was reaching out to me.

"I have found the truth and I know that it will surprise you once you know everything," she wrote in Spanish. "At this time I do not want to speak publicly about this matter, and later you will know why, if only you will allow me to know you and let me confide in you."

This time I wrote back immediately and asked her to tell me more. In the deepest reaches of my brain, I allowed myself to fantasize actually meeting Morales in Guadalajara. At our meeting, she unburdens herself, admitting that she knows the defendants killed True. I ask her to join Martha and me at a press conference in Guadalajara, and when the truth is revealed, the press, the public, and the judges all concede that the two Huichols killed True and must be punished. I chided myself for indulging in such cinematic fantasy.

We continued to exchange e-mails, each one giving me a bit more reason to believe she had information that was weighing on her conscience. Still, she kept her distance, resisting my efforts to pry out the truth. Neither Gatins nor Zamora was aware that she had contacted me, Morales wrote. Then she fell silent for days.

When she returned to her keyboard, Morales wrote with a torrent of emotion and spirituality. "The problem is big, understand me. I am alone in this, and I do not know where I am finding the strength to communicate with you; remember at this very moment that Mr. Zamora is in the middle of his campaign and everything is in his favor to become the president of the Zapopan county. After that he wants to be the governor of Jalisco and I can assure you that is very possible. Arturo is a close friend and I respect him a lot. This case made him very popular and if I do something that turns things the other way I will have very serious problems.

"A few months ago I fell sick. A doctor told me I would die, and to appreciate life. What would become of my children without me? Today my health is much better and I believe I am free of the illness, but I don't want to die with a secret. I don't want to pay for someone else's mistakes before God, nor do I want to live with my conscience burdened. This thought is why I decided to contact you. Thank you for your consideration. All I ask of you is much prudence and a little calm."

Four days later, Morales wrote again to tell me she would no longer confide in me by e-mail. She refused to discuss her "secret" with me over the telephone. For reasons only she knew, Morales swung from a confidant offering to share an intimacy to an arm's-length adversary. I told myself to be patient, to avoid making the wrong move that might drive her away. I did not know which side of Morales's troubled conscience or volatile personality would surface on any given day. One moment she verged on confession; the next she stood firmly in Zamora's court, distrustful of an American newspaper editor.

Morales feared that the *Express-News* would publish a story disclosing her e-mail communications and thus endanger her life. She wanted to meet face to face. Struggling to control my excitement, I casually agreed to call her on my next visit to Guadalajara; what I didn't tell her is that I had plans to travel there in a matter of days.

Martha and I planned to attend a scheduled court hearing on April 9, a little more than a week later. I didn't tell Martha about my planned meeting with Morales, knowing it would upset her, but I did share the information with Dane Schiller, who had replaced Hayward in Mexico City and planned to cover the hearing.

Schiller and I met for dinner Tuesday evening, April 8. We didn't feel like leaving the hotel, so we walked into the Angus steakhouse located inside the Hilton, where we were staying. The room was packed with traveling businessmen, served by a tribe of young, attractive women dressed in revealing red leather Indian costumes. The notion of middle-class Mexican women pretending to be sexed-up Indians struck us as absurd. We were the only ones who seemed to think so; everyone else was eating, drinking, and gawking.

Schiller was a former navy intelligence clerk, fifteen years younger than I, another gringo journalist from somewhere else who found his start in newspapers on the border at the *Brownsville Herald*. We shared similar views about Mexico and what made the country simultaneously alluring and repelling. His somewhat unconventional sense of humor made him the ideal dinner companion in such surroundings.

After breakfast Wednesday morning, Ochoa drove us to the hearing. It would be my first chance to observe Zamora and, four-and-a-half years into the case, the first time Martha and I would actually attend an open legal proceeding in the case. We arrived at the colonial-era courthouse, entering through the massive doorway into an open, landscaped courtyard. Onlookers gazed down from the second-floor balcony. A broad staircase led to the courts and magistrate offices. We had hardly made our way up the stairs when the prosecutor gave us the bad news. The hearing had been abruptly canceled.

Zamora, she told us, had petitioned the president of the Supreme Court to disqualify the two magistrates who remained assigned to the case, both of whom had ruled against Chivarra and Hernandez in the first appeals court ruling. The last-minute maneuver was legal, we were told, but it struck us as a telling demonstration of Zamora's political influence. Court officials knew Martha and I had traveled from Texas. The court clerk neglected to place a courtesy call to either the prosecutors or Ochoa, our lawyer. All of us were caught flat-footed.

"As a candidate, he has a strong public image, but that does not impact justice," Tómas Aguilar Robles, the chief magistrate on the first appeals court panel, told Schiller in a brief interview defending his action. Zamora, he said, was only exercising his right as defense counsel to ask that the original magistrates be replaced. The Supreme Court president refused to meet with Martha or me. I had never seen Martha so angry. We just stood there, steaming, until a group of Mexican reporters approached.

"We are looking for justice in a country where it's very easy to lose faith in the judicial system," I said. "The fact that the defense lawyer casts such a long political shadow is influencing everything and everyone."

"It is hard to live with this feeling of injustice," Martha told them. "He [Philip] is not coming back, no matter what happens."

We retreated with Ochoa to the balcony.

"I don't think I can take any more of this," Martha said. "What's the use? I'm not coming down here anymore. I feel like quitting."

She had every right to feel demoralized. We looked like fools in a drama in which all the actors except us knew the outcome. It would have been easy to quit, but I didn't want to give the locals the satisfaction of seeing us limp off, defeated. "Let's just go home and see how we feel in a couple of days," I said. "We don't want to make any big decisions while we're so angry."

I turned to Ochoa. "Whatever we decide, we're not coming down here anymore," I said. "We're not going to let them make *pendejos*, fools, out of us."

Back at a lunch table in the hotel restaurant, I broke the news to Martha about the e-mail exchanges between Morales and myself, and my plans to meet with her that afternoon. A look of bewilderment crossed Martha's face. It was the second jolt of bad news for her in one day. I could tell she disapproved of my decision. Whose side was I on?

Morales answered her cell phone on the first ring. She must have learned that we were in Guadalajara, and she agreed to meet me at the Hilton, saying she would recognize me from newspaper photographs. I posted myself in the hotel lobby to discreetly observe arriving traffic to make sure she came alone. Perhaps I was being paranoid, but Guadalajara could turn from a quiet colonial capital into a lawless place in matter of seconds for the unwary.

Then I saw her walking toward me. Morales was a striking woman in her late thirties or early forties, sporting large, dark sunglasses and dressed in a stylish black suit and a revealing blouse, not the kind of outfit one would see in an American office setting but not uncommon in Mexico.

We shook hands and relaxed with our first eye contact. She was warm and personable, given to emotional highs and lows, but sincere. She seemed relieved to finally meet me and discover I was not Davy Crockett incarnate. We rode the elevator to the executive floor and a private lounge. Schiller, by prior agreement, discreetly observed us from an internal balcony.

First we negotiated the ground rules. Morales wanted assurances that we were speaking off the record. I resisted. What good would it do for me to learn about something that might turn the case in our favor if I had to keep it secret? "Don't worry, I'm going to tell the whole truth in a book I am going to write," she said.

"What good is a book if True's killers are set free for good first?" I asked.

We sparred for a few more minutes and finally agreed that I would hold the information in confidence until she shared the truth with Gatins and Zamora, which might take weeks or more because of his campaign schedule. I insisted on taking notes.

"I could always deny meeting you," she said.

"I could publish our e-mail exchanges," I countered.

She couldn't resist spilling the truth. Morales spoke without punctuation. Words came as fast as her brain could push them out. She gestured continuously with her hands, her facial expression changing from joy to sorrow, her tremulous voice rising and falling. One moment her body leaned intimately into mine as she prepared to share some hidden truth, then she pulled back, veering in another verbal direction, expressing distrust of me as a gringo. It was almost impossible to get down any coherent notes. I tried to break in, encouraging her to finish a thought or anecdote before racing ahead, with little luck.

For two hours I listened intently as Morales poured out an emotional, often confusing narrative, interspersing revelations about True's killers with references to a nameless, life-threatening illness she had contracted in the sierra. The defense of Chivarra and Hernandez had become her whole life, she explained.

"You have to know that I am a deeply spiritual woman, a very sensitive person, someone who could only think of Juan and Miguel for all this time, and never myself," she said. "Only my relationship with God gave me the strength to recover and be here with you today, giving me the strength to meet with you and admit my own errors. There is so much to tell you, so much you cannot understand about the Huichols, so much that only I know, that it will take many, many weeks for me to try to explain you so you will understand."

How about, I suggested, the simple truth. Did Juan and Miguel kill True?

"It's what you have been saying all along; I feel so sorry for the widow," Morales answered. "She has to know that my only interest, Miguel's only interest has always been nothing but the truth."

"What is the truth?" I demanded, exasperated. "Did those two Huichols kill Philip?"

"Yes, Juan and Miguel killed your reporter, Mr. True, just like they confessed the first time."

The words left her mouth and moved toward me in slow motion, as if it had taken years for this simple sentence to take root in her conscience and be spoken aloud.

I struggled to extract corroborating details, but names, dates, and places were of little interest to Morales. Our meeting, I realized, was this self-described devout Catholic's visit to the confessional, her attempt to unburden herself of sin and guilt. Reconstructing a years-old homicide was incidental.

After Chivarra and Hernandez were released in August 2001, she said, Huichol elders invited her into the sierra to observe a "spiritual ceremony" customarily closed to outsiders. Their invitation was an expression of gratitude for the institute's efforts on behalf of the communities.

Shortly after the defendants were let out of jail in 2001, Morales had welcomed a large delegation of Huichols into her home after they traveled to Guadalajara from the sierra. Her offer of lodging had bound her even more closely to the Huichols, who couldn't help but notice the comfortable Western lifestyle that Chivarra and Hernandez were enjoying.

After digressing, Morales shared a few more details. Several elders had drawn her aside after the ceremony and told her, "You are defending the wrong people. Juan and Miguel are responsible for killing the foreigner."

Then Chivarra's father, Francisco, who had been in the delegation that visited Guadalajara and was present at the ceremony, spoke to her. "My son Juan killed Philip True and I will never forgive him," he told Morales.

About the time of the ceremony, which she said took place early in 2002, her health began to fail. More than a year of toiling on the case, traveling back and forth into the sierra, had taken its toll. On one occasion, a truckload of Huichols traveling from Mezquitic and San Sebastián rounded a curve in the one-lane dirt road just as Morales, along with her driver and two young women working as interns at the institute, appeared from the opposite direction. Several Huichols climbed down from the back of the open truck, lurching and brandishing machetes. The women, improbably dressed for the office in Guadalajara right down to their high heels, makeup, and pedicures, locked the car doors in panic as several of the men peered through the windows. After a minute, Morales rolled down her window and, in her inimitable, rapid-fire chatter, somehow talked them into accepting a gift of clothing in return for the women's unmolested departure.

Beyond such physical dangers, Morales said, her time in the sierra took a physical toll. Huichols truly live off the land, and as a visitor goes deeper into their territory, modern conveniences disappear. Even latrines are rare in the outlying villages and settlements. Huichols spend much of each day in the elements, working, walking great distances, and subsisting on far fewer calories than even a lean Westerner consumes. When traveling on foot through the sierra, they eat, sleep, and defecate in the wild. At home, families sleep communally in a single room on woven mats placed on earthen floors. There is no electricity or running water.

Morales took to her bed, ravaged by an unidentified viral or bacterial infection that destroyed her appetite and spawned high fevers, vomiting, and dysentery. A devout Catholic, she soon concluded that her symptoms were brought on by an underlying spiritual crisis. Morales began to fear death and the prospect of eternal punishment if she went to her grave without disclosing the truth about True's murder. Her soul held a secret that had to be released, but just as she prepared to contact me, the case took a new turn.

"That's when the magistrates ruled they were guilty and sentenced them to thirteen years," she said. "I felt a burden lifted from my conscience. I told myself, 'Now I will not have to say anything since they are going to pay for what they did,' so I decided not to write to you."

She had kept her secret for more than a year, assuring herself that the new verdict would save her from eternal damnation.

Thirteen years for such a vicious murder and robbery would have been a small price to pay, I suggested. When Chivarra and Hernandez killed True, they left his wife a widow, pregnant with a son who would never know his father. My reporter and his family lost far more than thirteen years, I reminded her. "All that time you let pass. Didn't you at least owe Martha a telephone call to tell her the truth and to ask for her forgiveness?"

Morales dabbed at her tears and sat in silence before resuming her narrative. Sometime later that year, she confronted Chivarra and Hernandez after they arrived at the institute's compound for a visit. "I demanded they tell me, once and for all, exactly what happened to True in the sierra," Morales said.

When the Huichols answered vaguely, Morales said she lost her temper and demanded that Juan tell her the truth. Until now, he had enjoyed an unspoken dominance over his benefactress, growing in part out of her need for him to be found not guilty, thus justifying her efforts in the sierra and Colotlán and the expenditure of so much of Gatins's money. Now her blind loyalty finally gave way, at least for a moment, to accusation.

Chivarra shouted back, infuriated by her challenging tone. Yes, he angrily admitted, he and Miguel had killed True. The gringo was trespassing and taking photographs, and he claimed that True asked him for help obtaining semiprecious stones that Huichols consider sacred and off limits. This was yet another rationalization offered up by Chivarra, something he never once mentioned in the preceding four years.

The morning after he first encountered True, Juan, along with Yolanda and Miguel, set out on a religious pilgrimage, only to encounter True searching for gemstones along the river. It was after that, Chivarra said, that he decided to kill True. Chivarra gave his brother-in-law the order to assist him in the attack as the small traveling party ascended the steep canyon trail. I thought back to the afternoon I spent at the bottom of the Chapalagana, awaiting the return of the helicopters, and how I whiled away part of the time casually examining river stones, looking for fossils. Perhaps True had been doing the same.

"Juan showed no remorse at all as he told me everything. He was angry that I challenged him," Morales said. "Miguel told me they turned Philip face up after they killed him and put some flowers in his hands. He said the gringo looked like a sleeping angel."

Morales also helped clear up the confusion about the killers' whereabouts in the days after they returned from their pilgrimage. Before they changed their stories, Miguel told investigators that he and Juan grew fearful of the search parties after Chase and Obaya arrived in Amoltita in Chuey López's small airplane. Miguel was there when the angry, machete-wielding villagers ordered the visitors to leave. Afterward, they concluded that Chase and Obaya were police investigators. As soon as the searchers left, Juan and Miguel returned to the killing ground to conceal True's corpse deep in the canyon, apparently getting there right after Margarito Díaz, the hunter, had passed by and spotted the decomposing corpse and True's backpack. Her account meant the entire village knew of True's fate when Chase and Obaya arrived. Chase had been right that afternoon when we stood at True's open grave. There are no secrets in the sierra.

Juan's story about semiprecious stones was ridiculous, I argued. It was too coincidental that True's journal entry about his confrontation with Juan quoted him complaining of other trespassers hunting for the minerals. Morales and Chivarra seemed to be turning True into the embodiment of every gringo who had ever troubled the Huichols.

Morales countered that the official inventory of True's backpack entered into evidence mentioned a small bag containing a handful of stones. How, she asked, did I explain the presence of stones in his backpack if he had no interest in collecting valuable minerals? I told her I had done the same thing the day I spent at the bottom of the Chapalagana, collecting a few stones and a vial of sand to give to Martha without giving the matter much thought. That didn't make me a thief.

Weigand, the noted Huichol anthropologist, later impressed on me the extraordinary sensitivity the Huichols exhibit toward outsiders who show an interest in the region's semiprecious stones. They are even more suspicious, he said, of anyone who tries to gain access to any of the abandoned mines that harken back to an era when the Huichols performed forced labor in silver mines under the watch of the Spaniards. The sensitivity, frankly, is disproportionate to any material value the stones or minerals might hold, but the Huichols accord a spiritual value to the living and inanimate alike that together form their universe. True might have shown a passing interest in bringing back a few stones collected for souvenirs, especially after Juan's warning along the trail about others expelled for such activity, but there was no way he was in the sierra to exploit the locals and their mineral deposits.

I continued to suggest other possible motives for True's killing. How could she be sure that True at some point hadn't stumbled onto Chivarra tending his marijuana crop, I asked. Whatever she thought of the two Huichols, everyone who knew the region described the Chivarra clan as inbred ne'er-do-wells.

Morales, who only months earlier had extolled True's qualities when the Huichols were released from jail, now demonized him. He was up to no good, she insisted. The Huichols had issued an all points bulletin in their communities announcing that True was persona non grata because of previous forays into Huichol territory made without permission in search of agates and opals to enrich himself. He had been caught trading in gemstones before, she assured me, and on one such trip had been detained and held in a crude Huichol stockades.

"Believe me, there are secrets they will only tell me, things they are afraid to tell outsiders, but every word is the truth," she insisted. "Philip True was very well known to the Huichols. They liked him, but they had warned him he had to stop his illegal activities."

I shook my head in disbelief. Morales reminded me she was a trained investigator. "Let me ask you a question if you are so sure I am wrong," she said. "You have read his journal, and so have I. How come there isn't one single interview with any Huichols, not a single one?"

Her question was one I had asked myself. I had no answer, other than my assumption that the Huichols had shunned their uninvited visitor.

"Let me ask you another question," she said. "I have gone to the archives on your newspaper's website and I have read everything Philip True ever wrote in Mexico. He never wrote a single story about the Huichols in your newspaper. So tell me, how is it possible that people now say this reporter loved the Huichols and knew them well, and yet he never wrote about one of those visits? What was he hiding?

"I will tell you," she said before I could respond. "He had a business buying and selling stones."

I could not believe her; True was not a schemer. It wasn't in his nature to operate an illicit business, and it would have been hard to do so while working as a reporter. He could have made more money cheating on his expense account than he could traveling to the remote sierra to acquire hard-to-find uncut semiprecious stones.

Morales said that that even True's illegal activities in the sierra did not justify his murder. "I have been forced to admit that my work has been carried out on behalf of two guilty men," she said. "Now you have to allow yourself to understand True was not necessarily the person you thought you knew."

I tried to steer the conversation back to the business at hand, getting her to agree to publicly disclose the truth that Chivarra and Hernandez had murdered True. "We can talk all day about these theories, but your moral obligation will not be satisfied until you disclose the truth," I said. "Telling me does not save your soul."

A lapsed Catholic myself, I felt only a slight twinge of guilt for playing to her fear of burning in hell. "We want you and the Huichol elders to appear with Martha and me at a press conference in Guadalajara," I said.

"A press conference now before the July elections is impossible," she said, fearing she would be made a scapegoat if Zamora lost his race. "You have to give me time to meet privately with Miguel, who treats Juan and Miguel liked adopted sons, and with Arturo [Zamora], who is a very powerful man."

"How about if we agree that I will call Miguel Gatins in two weeks to discuss his willingness to go public?" I asked. "That should give you all the time you need."

Morales promised she would speak to Gatins and ask the Huichol elders if they would meet with me. What about her? I wanted all of Guadalajara to hear the killers' most ardent Mexican defender condemn them.

Morales said a decision by a federal judge to remand the case to the state high court had brought back her worst fears. The Huichols might never pay for their crime if she didn't speak up, she admitted.

Zamora had brought the case to a standstill, she said, because the magistrates were intimidated and no one wanted to be selected for the next appeal. The president of the state supreme court knew, she said, that Reyes Contreras had ignored convincing evidence gathered in the first autopsy, so none of the magistrates wanted to affirm the judge's indefensible ruling, either.

Why, I asked her, did she choose to contact me now?

"I read the story your newspaper published on the fourth anniversary of True's death, and I realized his son would turn four the following March," she said. "That is when I decided to send you an e-mail."

"Forgive me," she had written just before my departure to Guadalajara, "and understand me when I tell you I have always felt your sorrow over the loss of your friend and the sorrow of Mrs. True, the widow."

Gatins, she said, would be devastated to learn Chivarra and Hernandez killed True. "But Miguel is a very good man, an honest man, a true benefactor," she added. "I know he will want to do the right thing after he knows."

She agreed to call me as soon as she had spoken with Gatins. I escorted her to the lobby and then made my way toward the coffee shop to meet with Schiller and Martha. Both anxiously awaited news.

"The good news is she admitted she knows the Huichols killed Philip and her conscience bothers her," I said. "The bad news is she said Philip was up there trying to trade in illegal gemstones, and that he had been caught before and told not to do it."

I paused to let the information sink in.

"Martha, is there anything we don't know?"

Martha looked at me as if I had lost my mind. She shook her head vehemently, hurt that I would even ask. I instantly regretted my question, but I had to pose it. Later I gave Schiller a more detailed accounting of my conversation with Morales. He, too, doubted her claims. Both Schiller and Hayward had told me that their own experiences interviewing Morales convinced them she was unreliable and emotionally unstable. Anything she said had to be taken with a dose of skepticism. I wondered otherwise, without saying so at the time, believing for the first time that we had erred in not understanding her as a seminal character, perhaps our most formidable adversary. Gatins, a university-educated, English-speaking American, had received most of our attention. He was easier to categorize, to understand. He was more linear; Morales was a maze.

The important thing, we agreed, was convincing her and Gatins to go public with what they knew. Martha, I told myself, was not allowing herself to even consider such an unlikely turn of events. She loathed Morales and Gatins. Sit beside them before the press and cameras? I didn't blame her.

20

Wooing the Defenders

You, the sought for; I, the seeker; this, the search:
And each is the mission for all.

—Kenneth Patchen,
"The Character of Love Seen as a Search for the Lost"

There is no I, we are always us,
life is other, always there,
further off, beyond you and
beyond me, always on the horizon,
life which unlives us and makes us strangers,
that invents our face and wears it away,
hunger for being, oh death, our bread.

—Octavio Paz, "Piedra del Sol (Sunstone)"

I left Guadalajara knowing Martha was uncomfortable with my efforts to convert adversaries into allies. Until now we always had acted together. Still, back home I soon wrote to Morales. "I have thought of very little since our meeting in Guadalajara last week and afterward my return to San Antonio. First of all, I want to thank you. I really appreciate your invitation to get together there. I know you could have decided not to contact me, and I see your efforts to share the truth with me and your change in view on the True case as a significant moral act."

Urging her once again to speak with Miguel Gatins and Arturo Zamora as soon as possible, I suggested that Zamora might be able to negotiate a plea bargain of some sort if Chivarra and Hernandez would agree to publicly admit their guilt. "I think I can speak for the widow, Martha True, when I say vengeance was never our objective," I wrote. "We've never wanted anything more or less than justice. The sentence, while important, is less important than the truth."

Fiesta, the annual ten-day spring celebration of the Battle of San Jacinto and Texas Independence, was under way when I finally spoke with Patricia Morales by telephone, three weeks after our meeting in Guadalajara. Any hope that she would go public was dashed when she began to ramble about her close relationship with Zamora and the need to protect his candidacy through the Sunday, July 6, vote.

A week later, she sent me an e-mail message that once again undid earlier progress. She was ending the discussion of a near-term agreement and withholding any assurances that she would go public even after the election. She rejected my latest proposal that she contact the supreme court president to brief him on the turn of events. "I can assure you that they [the Huichols], while free today, carry with them the blame and the penance for what they did, and they are prisoners of that and of the daily misery of their lives," Morales wrote. "The last time I saw them they told me they missed their lives in jail because they ate and lived better there. I know you are a good person, and you cannot know how much I lament my error."

Morales renewed her promise to write a book.

I decided to wait one more week for her to budge and then I would contact Gatins. Before I could act, Morales wrote again to tell me she had spoken with Gatins, who had been stunned to learn the truth. He proved to be every bit as good as she had described him. The next morning Gatins took the initiative and sent me a warm note by e-mail, which included the text of a letter he had written to Kevin Richardson, the U.S. deputy consul general in Guadalajara, advising him of the defendants' admission of their guilt to Morales and his subsequent decision to withdraw his support.

"The information Morales has, in my opinion, goes a long way in explaining the many missing links in the case, including the real motive, which was territorial in nature, and even goes as far as possibly explaining how both autopsies could be partially correct," Gatins wrote in his letter. "This obviously does not justify the actions of these individuals who at the moment of truth, notwithstanding a possible motive in their eyes, went through with their diabolical plan to commit a murder.

"Here we are in what I guess is an unusual twist of roles in a long and complicated case," Gatins wrote. "My purpose, at this point, in coming forward to you with this information . . . is simply to try to bring this matter to a satisfactory closure, particularly for the True family. Our purpose was always to get at the truth, and as it turns out, the truth was not on our side, and thus it is our duty to say so."

I was moved by Gatins's willingness to admit he had placed his faith and his money in the wrong cause. Two years of his life and a good bit of his savings were wrapped up in defense of Chivarra and Hernandez and his support for Morales's casework. Rather than tiptoe away from the mess, he was stepping forward to correct the record. Many people would not have had the guts to acknowledge the truth. Now, thanks to Gatins, the U.S. government also knew. Richardson would send a cable to the U.S. embassy in Mexico City, and the ambassador or a senior political officer would then send his own cable to the State Department and the secretary of state in Washington. How long would it be before embassy contacts quietly shared the information with officials in the Fox administration? The more people who knew, the better chance we had of prevailing.

It was my turn to reach out to Gatins. "You and Patricia have taken some very brave and moral steps, and I admire you for that and for your long devotion to seeing justice done, even if there have been turns in this case over the last four and half years where I might not have spoken so generously of your efforts," I wrote. "I made my own share of mistakes along the way in this case, at times driven by frustration and emotion rather than common sense, so please believe me when I say there are things I would do over in this case, too, were I given the chance."

I laid out my proposed plan for a press conference in Guadalajara, and we agreed to speak by telephone for the first time.

"Whatever pain and embarrassment we might incur by admitting that we were wrong does not compete with the freedom we feel of sharing this latest information," Gatins wrote back.

Gatins was a special man, I now realized, misguided in his decision to spend tens of thousands of dollars defending two jailed Huichols, murderers he had never even met. But there was no mistaking his moral convictions. If anyone could talk Morales into going public, it would be her benefactor.

Our e-mail exchanges continued through the summer. Gatins confided in me that Morales, a close adviser of Zamora's, had once again withdrawn and decided she was unwilling to confess her secrets to a larger audience. So much for eternal damnation. She was hoping instead for an appointment to a city council seat or other important advisory position if Zamora won the mayor's race in July. She had worked hard to help Zamora in his political career, even serving as the divorced candidate's social companion at political dinners and public events, helping dampen rumors and speculation about his sexual preferences. I knew Morales and her husband had a strained relationship, and I knew she was close to both Zamora and Chivarra, two men from the opposite end of the social-cultural spectrum in Mexico. Only three generations removed from indigenous roots on her father's side, Morales straddled the two worlds. She had become increasingly emotional, even paranoid, in her messages to me, obsessed with the possibility that she and her children would suffer if we went public.

Zamora won his race to become mayor of affluent Zapopan. As he began to organize his administration team prior to taking office, it became clear to Morales that she was no longer in the inner circle. Her unpredictable personality made her ill-suited to hold public office. Her usefulness had passed, and Zamora now was too busy to return her calls. She felt betrayed by the mayor-elect, a betrayal I wanted to exploit.

Gatins, far more adept at handling Morales, found himself in a new role as mediator: I pressed aggressively for public disclosure while Morales stalled for time. The low-key Gatins refereed.

Morales raised a new complication, citing her possible attorney–client relationship with Chivarra and Hernandez, even though she was not the attorney of record. A frustrated Gatins finally decided to travel to San Antonio so we could meet. I assured him he would be welcomed as a friend.

On Friday, October 17, Gatins walked into the newsroom of the *Express-News*. As we shook hands, I found myself looking at a man my own age and stature. We established an instant rapport. How had we been cast in opposite roles in this case?

Schiller happened to be visiting from Mexico City. He, MacCormack, and Gatins settled into my office to discuss a timetable for going public in Guadalajara without Morales. Gatins had never met MacCormack in person, and now he complimented his work once more. MacCormack gruffly deflected the praise, saying he did the same professional job on his earlier profile of Gatins as he would any other assignment.

The four of us walked downtown to Schilo's Delicatessen, the city's oldest German restaurant. We continued to feel one another out, each side trying not to get too argumentative about aspects of the case on which we still disagreed. The lunch was about building trust, and we knew we were asking a lot of Gatins. He still believed in the validity of the second autopsy and the third pathologist's review of both procedures. We argued there was no proof the suspects were tortured by the army or police after their arrest. Who needs proof in Mexico that the police torture suspects? Gatins asked incredulously.

After lunch, we walked back to the newspaper. I escorted Gatins through the second-floor newsroom, introducing him to wide-eyed reporters who wondered what he was doing at the *Express-News* with the editor serving as his tour guide. Wasn't Gatins the enemy? Only a few editors and reporters knew what was unfolding behind the scenes.

Back in my office, Gatins and I found ourselves talking about our families and high school children. He and Ruby were thinking about leaving Mexico, perhaps moving to San Antonio, the city where they were married, so they could enroll their children in U.S. schools to prepare them for college.

The news that Chivarra and Hernandez were guilty of murdering True had hit hard in the Gatins household, where the two Huichols had been welcomed like adopted sons. Miguel and Ruby did not regret their decision to take up their defense, but they were soured by their experience with the legal system as much as they felt betrayed by True's killers.

In addition to this disappointment, the Gatins had recently suffered a serious scare in Guadalajara. Months before his visit to San Antonio, Miguel was robbed at gunpoint. It all began when he purchased several $100 raffle tickets in a charity auction of a new vehicle to benefit the American School, where his children were enrolled and he served on the board. Gatins had bought the tickets to goose slow sales, but then he actually won the new Nissan sedan. One week later, he was carjacked. He hadn't even had time to register his windfall with his insurance company.

"Having a revolver pressed into your ribs until you feel cold steel is something else," Gatins said. He could have been one more victim in a city with too many victims. It was a deeply unsettling experience for the man who had made Mexico his adopted home.

Before Gatins left, we agreed to hold the press conference in the last week of November or the first week of December, in advance of the fifth anniversary of True's death. The symbolism seemed potent. The magistrates still had not ruled. What would they do once members of the defense team publicly capitulated?

Gatins promised he would participate, regardless of how Morales reacted to news of the agreement reached in San Antonio. In an ideal world, we wanted her as a Mexican citizen in front of the microphones. Some in Mexico might argue that we had pressured our fellow American to change sides, but they wouldn't be able to say that about Morales. If she balked, we would give reporters copies of my e-mail correspondence with her.

Martha embraced our plan. "It still seems incredible to me that Gatins is willing to speak publicly about the matter, if it really is about to happen," she wrote. "It will be very interesting to see how the press reacts after learning the news. Do we have a date yet?"

We did: Tuesday, November 25. With luck, it would be a memorable Thanksgiving, the first in many years to find reason to give thanks in Mexico.

21

Final Verdict

The lesson is that people endure, and enduring, may yet hope to prevail.

—T. R. Fehrenbach, *Fire and Blood: A History of Mexico*

This is the moment to prove that together we can end the corruption, impunity, discrimination, and injustice. We can show that we want our nation's destiny to be ruled by law.

—President Vicente Fox,
speech calling for an overhaul of Mexico's judicial system

Dane Schiller, Martha, Teo, and I met in Guadalajara for dinner the night before the press conference. Our upbeat mood masked nervousness. Miguel Gatins had called shortly after our arrival to say that Patricia Morales had changed her mind yet again and now intended to appear alongside us. He warned us we would not like much of what she intended to say. The specter of her claiming that True was a dealer in illicit semiprecious stones could turn the event into a circus and provoke Martha to storm out. But hearing her admit Chivarra and Hernandez killed True would hit the Mexican press corps like a bomb. We had to take our chances.

The next morning was a tense one. We had arranged for all parties to meet in the private dining room on the hotel's nineteenth floor, where we could break the ice out of the view of the press and the public. It was the same place where Morales and I had met earlier in the year.

I awaited our guests in the hotel lobby. Miguel and Ruby came in first. As we chatted they confirmed that Morales intended to tell reporters that the Huichols killed True after they caught him hunting semiprecious stones, and not for the first time. Her statement had been even more accusatory in tone before Ruby edited it, as she struggled to somehow justify the homicide and, in turn, her involvement with the defendants.

I found myself wondering how intimately involved she and Chivarra had become. Perhaps she was unable to admit that this man she felt close to had actually killed True without any real motive, unable to contain his own rage. She seemed unwilling to confront the truth except by degrees. Chivarra still seemed to have a hold on her, as if she needed him and not the other way around.

Morales arrived minutes later and we made our way upstairs, where I introduced everyone as we sat down to breakfast. The presence of Teo, now a cute little boy intent on raiding the buffet table, was a welcome distraction. Ruby, experienced at hosting groups of strangers, stepped in and helped ease the tension. Her natural warmth made it impossible for anyone to regard her as an adversary. Martha and Morales, however, sat at opposite ends of the table and avoided eye contact.

We discussed the press conference and agreed in principle to limit our prepared statements to a few minutes each. I told Morales that the longer she talked, the less the press would grasp and the more likely they were to misquote her. In truth, I wanted to prevent her filibustering.

Downstairs we entered a packed room, television cameras arrayed on tripods behind rows of filled seats. I made some brief introductions and turned the microphone over to Gatins, who spoke excellent Spanish and stuck to his script. He came right to the point. "Good morning... Almost two years after the initial verdict that set the defendants free, I received information from Patricia Morales, the lead investigator for the defense, who advised that Juan Chivarra and

Miguel Hernandez had finally voluntarily offered a detailed account of their participation in the murder of Philip True. With this latest information, I have no doubt that [they], for reasons that perhaps will never be fully understood, murdered Philip True in the Sierra Huichol in December 1998."

Gatins then gave the Mexican press some more news. "I have been authorized by Arturo Zamora, the lead counsel for the defendants in the appeals process, to inform you that he and his cocounsels have officially removed themselves from the case in the interest of justice."

Gatins told the assembled reporters that he had no qualms about publicly disclosing his reversing his position in the case. I listened with admiration. How many others might have taken their secret to the grave? Without this public admission, I knew, there was little chance of ever winning a final verdict against True's killers.

"Our participation in the case was always based on a search for truth and justice," he said. "With this declaration, my involvement in this case and support, moral or otherwise, for the defendants, comes to an end. In closing, I would like to express my deepest sympathy to the family of Philip True, especially to Mrs. True, here with us today, for the anguish and pain she has had to endure in this personal tragedy and for a process which has been too long in closing."

It would be Morales, however, who offered a spellbinding confession that yielded significant new details.

The defendants, Morales said, confided in her much earlier than she had ever admitted. During one of her visits to the Colotlán jail they told her they guarded a secret they would share with her if they won their freedom. Gatins and I exchanged surprised glances as we listened to her ramble in Spanish. Morales was saying she learned of their probable guilt at least one, perhaps even two years earlier than she had previously acknowledged.

Some weeks after Reyes Contreras released the two Huichols in August 2001, Morales was invited to the sierra to attend a ceremony in a Huichol temple to give thanks for the two men's release. "There they told me they had had sworn an oath to break their silence that they had kept to protect their ethnicity and their mother earth," Morales said.

I looked over the packed room of U.S. and Mexican journalists. Everyone was busy scribbling down her words. Nothing in our advance press release had given any hint of this kind of disclosure.

"We left [the temple] and we sat down in one of some small rooms that they indicated were utilized as a confessional," Morales said. "Juan confessed to me the following and Miguel confirmed all that Juan said. He told me there, before his gods, that he would tell me the truth about the death of Philip."

Morales said the Huichols claimed to know about True, that he had been arrested three times on previous forays into the region for stealing semiprecious stones. I looked over at Martha, who was seated on my right, at the opposite end of the table from Morales. She was poised to walk out. I placed my hand on hers and whispered. "Take it easy, and wait until I get the microphone and I will deal with her," I said.

Morales continued: "The authorities had alerted the community that if someone saw Philip return to the San Sebastián region, they should capture him and take him to jail. It was known that he was a journalist. The veracity of those three arrests I was able to confirm with Isidro López, the traditional governor at that time and who confirmed that he had personally arrested Philip True on those charges."

López was the same Huichol elder who claimed he was tortured by army elements during the original search for Chivarra and Hernandez.

In Morales's version, Chivarra recognized True on the trail and demanded to see written permission authorizing his presence, which True could not produce. Chivarra said he believed True was getting rich selling gemstones while Huichols like himself went hungry. When Juan and Miguel, along with Yolanda, encountered True on the trail the next morning, they decided to kill him, Morales said.

"Juan told me he came up behind Philip and grabbed him around the legs, causing Philip to fall face down, and Miguel with his bandana, tying the knots, tried to strangle him." She said. "Once they saw he wasn't moving, they turned him face up, and they crossed his hands across his chest and placed some herbs in them. Juan commented to me that he looked at peace, 'pretty like an angel.' Afterward they continued walking, but they went back, thinking someone might find him. They threw him down a slope, thinking he wouldn't be found there."

Morales did not realize, as she continued with her stream-of-consciousness account, that everyone in the room was thinking the same thing: She had known for a long time that the defendants were guilty and had said nothing.

"I want to point out that Juan and Miguel's confession was confirmed to me on three occasions when they visited me in Guadalajara," she added, as if we needed any further evidence of their guilt.

Why, I wondered, had she finally come forward after so long?

"I made my decision to disclose what I know because even though it gives me great sadness because of the deep affection I have for these two Huichols, I am not in agreement with what they did," she said.

I was indebted to Morales for coming forward, but I had no reason to sit by while she voiced Chivarra's constantly evolving deceits.

"There is absolutely no evidence to support that claim," I said, reaching for the microphone after she finished. "This is just another story, their latest justification. Philip was murdered by Juan and Miguel and nothing can justify what they did."

I reminded the assembled reporters that it was easy to lose track of the various confessions and excuses that Chivarra and Hernandez had offered over the years for killing True.

When Martha finally spoke, she recognized Gatins but withheld comment on Morales other than to note that the only one who knew what her husband was doing in the sierra was dead and was not present to speak for himself. Her words hit home.

"I recognize Gatins's effort in looking for justice and his courage to recognize it publicly," she said. "Now we can only wait and hope that the Mexican legal system will conclude its verdict in our favor and that true justice will be done for Philip True, a man who had tremendous respect and admiration for Mexican culture."

With the statements concluded, reporters, many of whom had been de facto supporters of the Huichol killers, turned on Morales. How could she have concealed such evidence for so long? Morales was stunned. She saw her disclosure of the truth as a noble act. The Mexican reporters asked if her timing was related to a change for the worse in her relationship with Zamora.

"I am doing this as a moral act," she snapped. "I do not have to carry a cross that is not mine. I want to live in peace."

Her baseless assertions about True the gem scavenger seemed of no interest to the reporters. We had accomplished all we hoped to accomplish. Zamora's resignation was even more telling. A powerful political force no longer stood between the magistrates and a fair verdict, or obsequious elements of the local press and stories disclosing the truth about True's murder.

Later that evening Schiller and I joined the Gatins, Morales, and a few members of their extended family at Santo Coyote, a popular restaurant in Zapopan housed in a huge thatched *palapa*, with narrow streams musically coursing through dense tropical foliage. Martha understandably declined to attend. As our team's ambassador, I had no trouble engaging Morales, even after the press conference. I knew what kind of beating she would take in the morning newspapers for withholding her secret for so long. Gatins was convinced of her good intentions, however obscured they were by her procrastination, emotional swings, vague mysticism, and continued efforts to somehow exculpate Chivarra.

We sat around a circular wood table as waiters brought large platters of sizzling meat for all to share. The symbolism of both sides breaking bread after years as adversaries was not lost on anyone. During the course of the meal, Morales leaned over to me and whispered, "Everything I've told you about Philip is true. None of you knew what he was doing there. Do you know that he has a secret Huichol wife and a child, or two children?"

I stared at her for long moment.

"*¡Estás loca!* You are crazy!" I told her. I meant it, too.

"There is so much you do not know, that you cannot understand about the Huichols as a foreigner, so many things I could tell you that are beyond imagination," Morales said, casting a knowing eye my way.

Morales was unlike anyone I had ever met. She was warm, well-meaning, and likeable even as she struggled to justify an unprovoked murder. Even Gatins acknowledged that her emotional attachment to Chivarra robbed her of objectivity. I wondered if it had robbed her of her sanity. None of that mattered. Morales had admitted publicly that the two Huichols she held so dear were killers. That was the only reason we were there.

I had one piece of unfinished business before heading home to San Antonio. More than five years earlier, consular officials suggested we get the reward money to Margarito Díaz Martinez by sending it to Susana Eger Valadez, a Berkeley graduate who first visited the Huichols as a graduate student and later founded the Huichol Center for Cultural Survival in Nayarit. The money, wired to her bank, somehow disappeared, and we eventually gave up hope of tracing it; Díaz went unrewarded. Gatins knew we wanted to fulfill our obligation to Díaz and had contacted Samuel Salvador, the Huichol professor at the University of Guadalajara who told Gatins he was related to Díaz. He agreed to hand deliver the money on his next trip into the sierra. The next morning I withdrew the money in pesos, moving from one ATM to another until I had enough cash. Gatins and I met in the hotel lobby and signed a note confirming the money exchange. I handed him an added gift of tail and wing feathers from a turkey I had shot that spring in the Hill Country. I hoped Díaz, also a Huichol shaman, would find good use for them. A month later, Gatins called to say that Salvador had returned from the sierra and the reward money had been delivered. It probably made Díaz the richest man in his village.

"I hope he actually gave him the money," a doubtful Gatins said a year later, after telling me that Salvador had borrowed money from

him afterward and never repaid the loan. Gatins no longer seemed
certain of anything in Mexico.

On March 29, 2004, President Fox delivered one of the most important
speeches of his administration. Fox was now in the second half of his
six-year term and, long stymied by a divided Congress, faced the
inevitability of lame duck status. So the speech he delivered calling for
historic reforms in the country's justice system had to be considered in
moral terms rather than short-term political or legislative gains.

Fox called for sweeping changes. He dismissed the current system
of closed trials by judges, the absence of witness testimony and citizen juries. The system, he said, was archaic, inherently unjust, and
easily corrupted. Nothing Fox said that night was news per se, but no
Mexican president had ever said as much out loud. In some ways, Fox
was summarizing the True case.

The first democratically elected Mexican president in modern
times was now declaring that Mexico could not call itself a democracy
until the rule of law became a way of life. Impunity stood in the way
of Mexico achieving its civic potential at the start of a new century.

The next day brought more good news. Our Guadalajara lawyer,
Jorge Ochoa, had won another federal order mandating the intransi-
gent state magistrates to issue a ruling. The state's high court had
been silent since February 2003, more than a year earlier, when a federal judge had set aside the conviction and thirteen-year prison term
and ordered a new review. Now another federal judge had handed
down an "act now" order.

The ruling came on the eve of Semana Santa, Holy Week, a traditional vacation period in Mexico when offices close and official business comes to a halt. Still, we told ourselves that the political impact
of our Thanksgiving week press conference followed by the public
rebuke from the federal judge would finally force the state court to act.

Gatins also connected the same dots from his vantage point in
Guadalajara. "If there has ever been a case which illustrates the many

reasons for a meaningful judicial reform in Mexico, as proposed just this week by the president, you need to look no further than the torturous case of the Philip True affair," he said.

Late in April, a group of Hearst editors and executives were gathered outside New York for a management seminar. Skipping the buffet lunch, I returned to my room to check e-mail. A message from Luis Carlos Sainz, a Guadalajara newspaperman I knew, stopped me in my tracks. "Do all of you know the new verdict in the Philip True case?"

Part of me had believed there never would be a verdict. Now, Thursday, April 27, five years and four months after True's murder, there was news.

As I began to type a response, the telephone rang. It was managing editor Brett Thacker calling from San Antonio with the answer: Chivarra and Hernandez had been found guilty and sentenced to twenty-year prison terms.

The sentence would soon be followed by an arrest warrant for the two Huichol men, who were somewhere in the sierra. Morales had spoken to them two months earlier. Chivarra had told her he didn't blame her for publicly disclosing their guilt, and he said that if they were convicted they intended to turn themselves in rather then flee. I didn't believe him.

I felt a slight shaking as I sat there speaking with Thacker, and realized it was my legs and arms. This moment was a long time coming. He patched me through to Martha in Brownsville so the three of us could talk. She, too, had just heard the news.

"We won, Bob," Martha exalted, more relief than joy in her voice, a sentiment I shared. "I know we won once before, but this time we won for real."

"Martha, thanks for not quitting," I said.

"Thank you for not quitting," she said.

In a moment it was over. I felt strange, dislocated, so far from the San Antonio newsroom with such momentous news in the air. I wished I were there, absorbing the late afternoon energy generated by journalists on deadline with a big story to tell. I walked back to the meeting room, where the afternoon session had already started, and took my seat. But I was somewhere else, my mind wandering, somewhere back in the Chapalagana.

Three days later, back in the San Antonio newsroom, I received a call from Agustín Gutiérrez Canet, Vicente Fox's spokesman for the international press. He told me that Fox sent his best wishes in the wake of the verdict. "The Philip True case is precisely one of the reasons why President Fox has introduced this comprehensive judicial reform initiative," Gutiérrez said. "It is a pity what happened to Philip, but we hope justice finally has been served. We are confident the president's project will be approved once the internal political issues are resolved."

Then another e-mail appeared, this one from Susana Hayward, now working for the Knight-Ridder newspaper chain in Mexico City. It included a statement released by the U.S. embassy there.

U.S. ambassador Tony Garza, who took over from Jeffrey Davidow one year after Bush took office, was an old friend from, where else, Brownsville. Garza and I got to know each other when he served as Texas secretary of state under then-Governor Bush.

"Philip's family and his colleagues at the San Antonio *Express-News* tirelessly pushed for a full accounting of the circumstances of his death," Garza said. "While Philip's death is still deeply felt, there can be some satisfaction that those who took his life are finally being brought to justice by the Mexican judicial system."

It was a fitting benediction from a Brownsville native to two of the town's adopted sons, the place a mother and child had returned to call home. Martha could now find closure and look ahead to the future.

22

The Silence of the Huichols

Perhaps the only thing not stolen from the Indians has been their soul,
their inaccessible world of strange languages and dialects, of hidden
pride and strong hierarchy, of deep religious sensitivity and powerful ritual, of mystery and magic. It is the continuity of communion with this
past—not the past of museums and statues but the past of spirits and
beliefs—that has protected Indian culture from destruction.

—Alan Riding, *Distant Neighbors*

Finding Juan Chivarra and Miguel Hernandez in the Huichol sierra
would not be easy if they did not want to be found. True's killers
would have to turn themselves in, an unlikely scenario despite Chivarra's earlier promise to Patricia Morales, or the Huichol elders
would have to support their detention and arrest. The sierra was too
wild and inaccessible to find two locals on the run. The remote ranch
that hugged the precipice of the Chapalagana was hours away by foot
or mule from the nearest settlement; even an experienced helicopter
pilot would be hard-pressed to find a landing spot within easy reach
of Yoata, and the roar of the rotors would echo off the canyon walls
and alert the Huichols long before the craft came into view. By then
they could be safely hidden in one of the area's many unmapped

caves or moving down a steep path on their way to seek refuge with relatives who were unlikely to cooperate with outside authorities.

The attorney general first asked Miguel Gatins and Morales to broker the peaceful surrender of the killers, but news of their public admission that they had helped guilty men win their freedom had made its way even to San Sebastián, and attempts by Morales to contact Chivarra and Hernandez went unanswered. Once a benefactor, she was now their betrayer.

Solís's investigators then asked the army to send in troops aboard helicopters to effect the capture, but the military was not interested. Under prodding from Los Pinos, they had made the original arrests in 1998, but the army was widely condemned afterward for reportedly resorting to beatings and threats to flush out the killers.

"That's the only way they ever found these guys the first time," Gatins said. "Juan and Miguel only came in because of what was happening to their families and the others."

Morales and Gatins agreed to accompany investigators in a caravan headed for a meeting in the village of Mezquitic to meet with Huichol elders. It was not a promising start. Several of the Huichols were drunk, including Juventino Carrillo de la Cruz, Juan Chivarra's uncle. Carrillo accused Morales of betraying the Huichols with her public disclosure of the two killers' guilt. The search party would never capture its prey, he predicted, without help from Huichols. Would they help? The elders were evasive one minute, cooperative the next.

As the discussions between investigators and the Huichols dragged on, Gatins listened to Morales tell a Guadalajara newspaper reporter yet another version of how and when Chivarra confessed his guilt to her. Morales was never able to abandon the killers, especially Chivarra. She also hinted mysteriously to the reporter, as Gatins remembered her once saying to him, that some of the clan's children might have participated in True's murder.

The talkative Morales also repeated a story that Gatins had heard from her shortly after the Huichols were released from jail in 2001.

After Chivarra and Hernandez stayed two months at her home in Guadalajara, Morales drove the reluctant Huichols, now accustomed to their comfortable lifestyle, as far back into the sierra as possible until the road gave out in San Sebastián. Along the way, they were stopped at an army drug and weapons checkpoint, a familiar sight in the region. The officer in charge hailed Chivarra as "Cesar," a nickname Morales had never heard. Clearly the officer and Chivarra knew each other and had some sort of relationship.

Gatins, Morales's onetime financier, found himself wondering more and more about her role in the case, and whether she had allowed Gatins to continue funding the Huichols' defense after she learned they were guilty. "It was kind of a circus in Mezquitic," Gatins said. "The Huichol governor was drunk; they said they would help us but it didn't really seem they were sincere. There was resentment, particularly toward Morales. Meanwhile, she had this doctor along who was supposed to tend to her emotional state. The whole thing was crazy. After two days I went home."

Hearing this account later, as search parties supposedly pursued Chivarra and Hernandez, I wondered whether we would ever know what Morales knew, and whether she could distinguish between reality and imaginative supposition. As the search efforts slowly took shape, Morales sent me several long e-mails offering additional details about Chivarra and his family, her effort to explain Chivarra's downward spiral in life. As always with Morales, any gleanings had to be extracted from her breathless and verbose delivery.

"I will try to transport you to the Huichol essence of Miguel, and principally of Juan, so that you will personally come to know the encounter that caused Philip's murder, and at the same time transport you to the habitat and the mysticism of the killing ground, even more mysterious."

Morales said Chivarra's father, Francisco Chivarra López, like his father before him, is a *mara'akame,* or shaman, one who "practices witchcraft, casts spells, practices natural medicine, and is an adviser, priest, and cantor."

Mara'akames are held in high esteem in Huichol communities, and the most accomplished are regarded as humans with almost godlike powers. They embody Huichol traditions and spiritualism.

"Francisco is a very esteemed and serious man, who always has one facial expression, not smiling, not sad or hurt, nothing ever but a serious, profound look," she wrote. "He speaks little, but when he does talk he utters very important things and he knows, acts and speaks, and conducts himself like someone who knows everything.

"He practices levitation and transporting men from one place to another, and not always walking on two feet. On some occasions they walk like coyotes on all fours, and move with great speed, climbing in and out of the canyons."

As the eldest of six children, Juan should have followed in his father's footsteps, learning from an early age to sing the oral histories, make the ritual journeys to Catorce to hunt and consume peyote, commune with the ancient spirits and gods in nature, and cure other Huichols. It is an exalted role in Huichol society.

Chivarra was ill suited to the job, the result of his confused childhood. When Chivarra was six, Morales wrote, he overheard his grandparents questioning whether he was Francisco's legitimate son. Stung by such talk, the young boy left on foot, taking advantage of the freedom Huichol children enjoy from an early age, when they are taught to survive unattended in the wilds. He wandered westward for weeks, fed by Huichols along the way, sleeping wherever he found himself as the sun set, making a trek familiar to Huichols who descend into the western lowlands in search of seasonal employment in the tobacco, chile, and maguey fields. Huichols would not be alarmed to encounter a child walking alone, but a mestizo shopkeeper who lived in the lowlands and was out hunting reacted like any adult would in such circumstances: he took Juan home to feed and care for him.

Chivarra lived with the man until he turned ten, when Francisco located him after years of searching, apparently learning of his whereabouts from other Huichols who had returned to San Sebastián after working in the fields. The mestizo had come to see Juan as his adopted son, and had even registered him as his godchild. He did not want to return the boy to Francisco and agreed to do so only after Francisco promised that Juan could come back when he turned eighteen to marry the man's only daughter.

Years later, when Juan's godfather reaffirmed his desire to see Juan and his daughter wed, Francisco balked, knowing that his son's marriage to a mestizo woman would end the Chivarra line of *mara'akames*. He exercised his authority as family patriarch and offered Juan his own sister, Yolanda Chivarra López, as a wife. Torn between his boyhood love, his taste for mestizo life, and his obligations as the eldest son of a Huichol shaman, Juan agreed to marry Yolanda. Once again in this remote fold of the sierra, husband and wife came from the same bloodline.

"Juan had loved the mestizo woman since she was a girl, but he was conscious of his commitment to his ethnicity and tradition as the next *mara'akame,* so he married Yolanda, who, of course, is very ugly and much older than him," Morales wrote.

Later, investigators tracked down Chivarra's benefactor, suspecting Juan might turn to him while on the run.

Morales cited evidence of Francisco's powers of persuasion and his ability to work magic, describing how the *mara'akame* settled scores with the men who mistreated the family when Chivarra and Hernandez were first arrested. She said Juan's mother, Angelina, admitted that True's backpack was hidden in her house after the soldiers beat her, and that Juan himself admitted he killed True after watching his father cough up blood as he was beaten. Francisco, she now wrote, used his powers while recuperating to condemn his tormentors.

"He had faith the gods would act justly, and there were many other Huichols who were present when he was tortured and they knew who his torturers were," Morales said. "I personally investigated and another group confirmed that the four persons who tortured Francisco all died, two in automobile accidents, one of illness, and the other committed suicide. All Francisco would say is that he knows his song reached the gods and they delivered him justice."

Amid such mystery, Morales now hoped Chivarra and Hernandez would leave their mystical world in the sierra and surrender once again to outside forces. With Morales and her attending physician along the next day, the search party made its way over the rough dirt road, where traveling a few miles in the dry season can take hours, until even that gave way to foot paths. Yoata, the ranch where Chivarra and Hernandez lived, was only an hour's jog away for a Huichol runner the elders had arranged for the investigators to hire, according to guides.

While the investigators, Morales and her doctor, and others cooled their heels alongside the now-useless vehicles, one of the guides set out on a trot down the path supposedly leading to Yoata. He returned a few hours later to report that the ranch was deserted. Even the women and children had cleared out. It was an odd, even unbelievable claim. Carrillo, the inebriated governor in Mezquitic and Yolanda's brother, had told the search party one day earlier that Chivarra and Hernandez were there. Even more suspect was the speed with which the guide returned. On a map, the road ends as the terrain becomes a seemingly endless series of gorges, with the isolated village of Amoltita still several punishing kilometers away. The reporters who made it to Yoata after True's murder described a grueling daylong hike to reach the remote ranch from Amoltita, itself reachable only on foot or by small airplane.

The investigators had been duped, but none showed any particular desire to challenge the guide or plunge ahead on their own. Dane Schiller had been told that his presence in Colotlán and his constant inquiries were unnerving local authorities.

"If we weren't here, I don't think there would be a search," Schiller told me. "We're a big pain in their ass." When investigators called on Gatins earlier in the week at his Guadalajara home—so uninformed of current events that they actually hoped to find the killers hiding there—they complained about the pressure they were under because the *Express-News* Mexico City office manager, Minea Nieto, kept calling their offices in Guadalajara asking for a status report.

"She might only be an office assistant, but to them it's like the governor of Texas is calling," Gatins said.

Nearly a month passed before state investigators made another attempt to enter the Huichol sierra to apprehend Chivarra and Hernandez. But their efforts, however well intentioned, were sadly comical and a failure. Schiller had gone to the end of the road with a couple of the investigators, but two flat tires on their rented SUV sent them back to Colotlán. Once again, investigators arrived poorly prepared for their mission, lacking any outdoor gear or money for food and lodging. Investigators told Schiller they were drafted for the assignment without warning at the end of a day's work in Guadalajara and told to head out immediately and enforce the detention order in twenty-four to forty-eight hours, hardly enough time in the sierra to move from one community to the next. Some forty investigators in the state were working more than 1,200 active cases, and none of those assigned to the job were familiar with the True case. Bob Owen, the newspaper's chief photographer, joined Schiller for a second outing to search for the killers. Investigators, however, didn't even have photos of the two killers and had never seen them. Editors in San Antonio hurriedly e-mailed a selection of photographs to Owen in Colotlán to share with the search team. The only camping gear, food, and water on hand was in the big red Suburban rented by Schiller and Owen.

"These Huichols all look alike," said Juan Manuel Vargas López, the frustrated Colotlán delegate for the attorney general. Dressed in street clothes and equipped only with sidearms, the investigators were far out of their element. Once again investigators told Schiller their only real hope was to persuade Huichol elders to surrender the two men. Searching for the two men in the sierra could turn into an endless game of hide and seek if the communities decided to protect Chivarra and Hernandez. In Tuxpan de Bolanos and San Sebastián, Huichol governors promised to cooperate, but investigators felt they were being run in aimless circles by the elders and local guides. Yet investigators were unwilling to enter the sierra unaccompanied by Huichols. Cultivators overseeing marijuana plots in the area were heavily armed and could easily overwhelm the outgunned searchers if they stumbled down the wrong path.

A Huichol woman selling soft drinks in a village along the road looked at the photographs and told the searchers they had missed Hernandez by minutes. He had boarded a bus that the team had just passed on a narrow one-lane mountain road but had not bothered to stop and search. True gave himself ten days to traverse the roadless expanse of Huichol sierra, and he made it less than halfway. After a night and two days the investigators returned home empty-handed without covering a single kilometer on foot, never venturing beyond the margins.

The state attempted to find and imprison the two killers employing the same haphazard approach that characterized the rest of the case. In defense of the actual searchers, they were victims of the country's law enforcement culture. Police are underpaid, ill equipped, and poorly trained, and, given their own history of violence, understandably unwelcome in indigenous communities.

Huichol leaders, especially in the county of San Sebastián where True's killers live, are caught between colliding forces. The traditional elders face an almost impossible task in trying to preserve and protect their space and culture amid the relentless outside pressures that lay siege to their communities and lure Huichols away from traditional life.

Drug trafficking and alcohol have irreparably changed life in the sierra for the worse. Anywhere rural poverty and hopelessness rule, illicit drug cultivation and the money it brings are not far behind. Huichols who tend marijuana or poppy patches for mestizo traffickers have money for food, medicine, and clothing, as well as cattle, seed, and tools, the essentials that stand between security and starvation in the sierra. Alcoholism in traditional cultures is a plague. There is little social drinking, and home-distilled tequila—*tuchi*—and a home-brewed corn drink—*tejuino*—are too often consumed in excess, an escape from the harsh daily life in the sierra. Under the influence, Indians expect outsiders to drink with them, and they are offended when a visitor declines their invitation. Drunkenness fuels violence, provoking normally peaceful Indians into unplanned acts of rage they later cannot explain.

"Almost every single Huichol serving time in prison or a jail is in there because he committed an assault or murder while drunk, or he was caught running a drug load," said Phil Weigand, the American anthropologist and Huichol expert.

Poverty and the prospect of work in nearby towns and cities pulls many Huichols away from their traditional life as highland farmers living in the natural world. Huichols migrate in and out of Mexican society the same way Mexicans migrate back and forth across U.S. borders. It's an act of necessity, yet with each venture out of the traditional communities the Huichols come back changed. While they return with money, they also come home less committed to traditional life and the old ways.

Slash-and-burn subsistence farming is hard work under ideal conditions, more so with primitive tools at high elevations where the soil is thin and water can be scarce. The eldest son inherits the land and authority from his father, leaving other offspring to fare for themselves. Some feel they have nothing to lose by leaving. Others are simply run off and forced to find abandoned land, however uninviting, to start from scratch.

The Huichol elders and priests, then, have ample reason to resent outsiders. While they struggle to preserve their ancient culture and hold together their communities, they see little reason to cooperate with outside authorities that want to put two more Huichols in their prisons.

For decades, the Huichols have looked without success to the Mexican legal system to protect them against mestizo ranchers who have stolen Huichol lands to graze their cattle and cultivate their drugs. Many cases linger for years and even decades in the courts; few are resolved in the Huichols' favor. If Mexican law does not serve their interests, why should the Huichols cooperate in the detention of Chivarra and Hernandez?

"Juventino Carrillo definitely knows where Juan and Miguel are, I swear to you," Morales told me, adding that the entire episode of defending guilty men, being fooled by them, and then seeing the case implode had left her emotionally devastated. Yet Juan and Miguel surely nursed similar feelings about Morales, the one Mexican they thought they could trust. Instead, she too turned on her former charges. As the two men stayed beyond reach, Morales grew morose over their deception.

"It wasn't ugly, it was monstrous, cruel, merciless, to think that they were never mine, that I was theirs, that I never protected them, that they used me, they never confided in me, they made a fool of me, they never wanted me, they played with me, and their best weapon was my pride and vanity. How can I accept his?"

The Huichol elders issued a public statement in late 1998 declaring their opposition to violence and their desire to see True's killers caught and punished. But the truth is more complicated.

Many Huichols have long known that Chivarra and Hernandez were guilty of murdering True, and there have been intimations from some of them that his killing was more complicated than previously disclosed. As early as 2001, the Huichol elders allowed Morales to witness the confessional ceremony in which Chivarra and Hernandez admitted their guilt and sought to cleanse their spirits—a fact she finally disclosed to me in our first conversation and in greater detail at our joint press conference. Perhaps that confession was enough for the Huichols. Perhaps it takes a village to conceal a murder and hide a corpse. Perhaps the Huichols cannot condemn the two confessed killers without also condemning the larger Huichol community. Or the Huichol leaders might believe that as long as Chivarra and Hernandez remain free in the sierra, the Huichols have shown outsiders, at least in this case, that they remain an independent people.

December 2004, six years after Philip True disappeared and died, came and went and his two confessed killers remained free.

23

A Return to the Chapalagana

For me it had something to do with the colossal sameness of the Canyon; but that was sameness not of monotony but of endlessly repeated yet endlessly varied pattern. A prodigal repetition of terrace, mountain on terrace, mountain on terrace, of canyon after canyon after canyon after canyon. All of them, one succeeding the other, almost unknown to man, just existing, existing, existing, existing. There seemed at first no hope of a beginning, no hint of an end.

—Colin Fletcher, *The Man Who Walked Through Time*

Chuy López banked the aging Cessna 182 hard as he sighted San Miguel Huaixtita and then circled over the gaping abyss of the Chapalagana, preparing to land on the short dirt runway that began at the open jaw of the canyon and ended at the village's footsteps. The view from above was startling: a line of tall metal towers led from the nearest hill to the village, awaiting wires that would bring electricity to the village. A curving single-lane dirt road led into and out of the once roadless San Miguel, and a few pickup trucks were visible on the ground. Everywhere, piles of bricks marked sites where villagers were replacing traditional thatched huts on stilts with sturdier multiroom dwellings. The meeting of the ancient and the modern anticipated in True's story proposal was unfolding before our eyes.

January 7, 2005. More than six years had passed since our army helicopter had set down on the village soccer field. Sitting in the copilot's seat, I watched our approach with a mix of awe and dread. I had written about this very descent after interviewing Fred Chase and Manuel Obaya at the end of their search, but any vicarious appreciation paled in comparison to the actual experience.

"I've never flown this plane before," López had casually told me a half hour earlier as he fussed with dials and gauges and we tried to make small talk over the noise of the engine as we ascended into the sierra.

We had returned in pursuit of True's killers. Along with López, there were three of us aboard: myself, Dane Schiller, our Mexico City correspondent, and Dr. Sergio Ramirez. I had called Ramirez months earlier to enlist him in our campaign. Now serving as chief administrator for ten hospitals in central Mexico, he listened to our plan and readily agreed to return to San Miguel as our guide.

Schiller and I had met with the current governor, Francisco Ramirez, and Solís, the attorney general, days earlier in Guadalajara to complain that eight months after the final conviction of Chivarra and Hernandez, little was being done to capture them. We described Schiller's personal experiences accompanying the hapless investigators sent into the sierra so ill prepared they stood no chance of succeeding. Our criticism was not well taken; both officials insisted that the killers were being aggressively pursued. We thanked them for the meetings but left convinced that we had to bring the search back to life.

Miguel Gatins, once our adversary, now volunteered to drive us to Tepic, where we would meet López. We had become friends since our October 2003 press conference, and on this visit he and Ruby welcomed me to his home to meet their children. Later we also visited Patricia Morales in the nearby town of Santa Anita where she and her husband, Oscar, hosted Gatins and me for lunch. Our only adversaries now were the two men who killed True.

Six years ago, Ramirez was a young medical school graduate serving his year of public service in the Huichol sierra when True disappeared. He selflessly helped organize local Huichols to join the search, and along with his assistant at the village health clinic, Julian Carrillo, personally accompanied us down into the Chapalagana and helped unearth True's corpse. It was obvious then that the otherwise reticent Huichols held Ramirez in high esteem, a trust he earned by his willingness to walk two days over mountain trails in driving rains to distant settlements to treat a sick child, deliver a breech baby, or attend someone too frail to journey to the clinic. Before his year ended, Ramirez was anointed by the elders as a *mara'akame*—an unprecedented honor for an outsider. Since then we had stayed in touch.

We didn't expect to encounter True's killers on our journey, but we had a plan to hunt them down, and we intended to buzz their rancho. Our small airplane was stuffed with duffel bags, most of them filled with glossy reward posters picturing Chivarra and Hernandez and offering 50,000 pesos for information leading to their capture. Other duffels held soccer balls and basketballs to distribute to children in San Miguel and nearby Popotito. The basketballs, purchased at a Wal-Mart in Guadalajara, were emblazoned with the San Antonio Spurs logo.

Schiller had bought dozens of hard plastic tubes and stuffed them with reward posters so that we could drop them over small settlements in the neighboring county of San Sebastián, an area that included Amoltita and the Yoata ranch, where the killers lived, places we deemed to dangerous to visit on foot.

Ramirez cautioned us to leave the posters stowed in the hold until we assessed the mood in San Miguel. He too had not been back for six years and was not sure how he would be greeted. "Maybe they won't even recognize me," he joked, alluding to the weight he'd put on since his year in the sierra.

We trudged uphill into the village toward the small clinic. An advertisement on the side of a hut stopped us in our tracks: Cell phone cards sold here. Cell phones?

San Miguel was one of several primitive villages where the only access other than by foot was the airstrip built by the government for supplying the rudimentary health clinic. Now the Huichols had cell phones and could buy cards programmed with minutes that could be inserted for use. Villagers later told us that the first vehicle to lumber up the newly constructed road was a red Coca-Cola truck, soon followed by a Corona beer truck, whose driver left behind a small sign tacked to a tree, the village's first advertisement.

We walked into the clinic.

"I've been bitten by a scorpion," Ramirez said in Huichol as we entered. Marina, the Huichol nurse he had trained six years earlier, was turned away from Ramirez, attending a seventy-year-old woman with a crude bandage wrapped around her leg. Her husband shyly explained that she fell out of a *copal* tree she had climbed to harvest resin used to make adhesive and incense, leaving an ugly gash that ran from below her knee to her ankle. "Take a seat; I'll be with you soon," the nurse replied without looking.

"Are you going to make your old boss wait?" Ramirez teased her.

Marina turned, gave a joyous cry, and then fell into Ramirez's long embrace, laughing and crying at once as she switched to Spanish and told him that she had feared he would never return.

A knot of mournful Huichols related to the old woman looked on blankly during the emotional reunion.

"Okay, what do we have here?" Ramirez said, picking up where he had left off six years ago, examining the old woman's lean, still muscled leg. I marveled at her ability to climb a tree at her age, but she only drew her veil more tightly and turned toward the wall, stifling soft whimpers of pain.

Ramirez wasted no time snapping a pair of surgical gloves over his hands while Marina affixed a face mask to his head. Schiller and I stood by quietly as he cleansed and then began to close the wound. He introduced us only as *amigos,* not wanting to associate us with Philip True. I studied the ancient, World War II–era radio, a squat box that sat on the floor. Ramirez told me that it only worked as a two-way radio that connected the village to health officials in Guadalajara; in other words, True could not have called Martha, as they both intended, although he probably could have relayed a message to her.

"What's the gossip in the sierra?" Ramirez asked the nurse as he finished stitching the woman's leg. "Any scandals?"

"Well, I'll tell you one thing: they never paid Margarito Díaz the reward for finding the dead journalist," she said.

Her words struck like a dagger in my heart. We had paid the reward money—not once but twice, most recently to Samuel Salvador, the Huichol university professor who had assured Gatins that he had delivered the 10,000 pesos and my gift of turkey feathers to Díaz. How could we return to the sierra offering a second reward for the capture of Chivarra and Hernandez if the Huichols believed we had cheated Díaz out of his reward?

Outside the clinic, I told Ramirez that I was carrying enough pesos to pay for the airplane and to pay Díaz once and for all, if we could find him. The doctor announced to the group of Huichols who gathered around us outside the clinic that we intended to hike to the neighboring village of Popotito, which he had said would take us an hour or two.

"Why walk?" one of the men asked. Ramirez seemed confused. "There's a road there. You can get a ride and be there in fifteen minutes."

We stood in the back of a pickup after paying 300 pesos for the round trip, about $27 U.S., the high price a reflection of how scarce gasoline is in the sierra. Once in Popotito, we found Julian Carrillo, the clinic assistant, who welcomed us into his brick home perched atop a hill. One half of the house served as a small general store. His wife and the couple's two young girls sat outside, enjoying a mesmerizing view of the canyon in the mid-morning sun.

Carrillo was related to Díaz, who had sought him out at the clinic after discovering True's corpse. He too said that Díaz had never been paid and looked surprised when I explained our two previous efforts to pay the reward. Carrillo whistled down the slope to a woman walking along and asked her to fetch Díaz from his nearby house.

"He said for you to come down, he doesn't want to walk up there," she hollered a few minutes later, her smile visible even from the hilltop.

We met Díaz halfway on the road, where he greeted Ramirez and then turned to me and told me he remembered me. I recounted our efforts to pay him and said I now had come to get the job done in person. With Schiller taking photographs, we sat down in the shade of an adobe wall, out of view of the increasingly curious villagers, who knew Díaz had never received the reward and now suspected a large sum of money, at least by local standards, might be changing hands. I counted out the money in 200-peso bills. Díaz gratefully took each increment of a thousand pesos, recounted it, and smiled at me with a nod.

Afterward, I gave him a paternalistic talk about guarding his long overdue money, word of which would quickly spread through the sierra. I asked him what he intended to do with it, and he told me he wanted to laminate his home with corrugated metal. I suggested he invest in cattle and avoid loaning cash to others, especially anyone who seemed like a long lost friend suddenly resurfacing. Díaz just smiled.

I gave him my business card and said, "I don't want you to forget my name." I used my finger to slowly underline my first name, letter by letter.

"Soy Robert, o Roberto," I said, assuming he could not read.

Díaz took the card and glanced at it. "Editor, eh?" he asked.

I stood up, feeling foolish, and wished him well. We embraced, and then he disappeared around the corner, eager to hide his new wealth.

Carrillo's eyes widened when we showed him the poster with the large numerals announcing the peso reward. He asked for more copies to share with others.

A Huichol man in the village told us he had seen Chivarra and Hernandez at their ranch and fishing in the river as recently as late November and believed they were still there. Most Huichols, he said, thought the two men had been absolved of the charges and set free. No one seemed to know they were fugitives, but that quickly changed. We returned to San Miguel to distribute posters and I took the opportunity to introduce myself once again to the villagers and then explained our previous unsuccessful attempts to pay the reward. People in both villages knew Salvador, the professor, and hung on every word. I also told them that I had just paid Díaz and fulfilled the newspaper's obligation, and now was eager to pay an even larger sum if True's killers were captured.

We didn't want to draw undue attention to Díaz, but it was important that word spread through the sierra of our efforts to get the money to him, which might encourage other Huichols to set out to earn the larger reward. Once that would have been impossible. But as I watched Ramirez and several villagers punch one another's numbers into their cell phone memories, I was happy we had posted a variety of telephone numbers on the posters that would put the Huichols in touch with the authorities.

The nurse pleaded with us to join her family for a communal meal. We were pressed for time, with a lot of ground to cover before sunset, but we readily accepted the invitation. It struck me that all along his way, True had found no such welcome. In the company of Ramirez, we were no longer strangers. Now I found children following me and women proudly displaying their beadwork and other *artesanía*, which we eagerly purchased. Inside the one-room home, part of a larger compound, we took seats at a long table filled with Huichols of all ages. A stack of steaming blue corn tortillas awaited us, along with a bowl of beans and macaroni noodles cooked in a wild tomato sauce. A spicy salsa made from chili peppers I didn't recognize caused me to break into an intense sweat, delighting the young children who devoured small purple seed pods freshly harvested from a tree that I could not name. After eating, I visited the small, smoky kitchen to thank the three generations of women at work there, one of them nursing a six-month-old boy. We then invited the children down to the plane to collect the balls and watch our takeoff.

Girls and boys alike struggled to carry a ball under each arm before we boarded and then ascended into the air. López gained altitude and opened his window. It was time to test Schiller's tubes. For the next two hours we flew between soaring peaks and wide cliffs, swooping over small villages and settlements, unloading tubes as curious Huichols who heard our approach emerged and watched the tubes tumble end over end before they hit the ground. After finishing our work, we overflew the canyon bottom that was once True's grave, the river now sparkling in peace.

That afternoon, we flew west into the setting sun and landed in Tepic, satisfied that we had paid the reward to Díaz once and for all and that our reward posters had generated so much interest among the Huichols. In the course of my second brief visit to the Chapalagana, I had glimpsed the old and the new in the sierra. Soon the roads, the schools, the electricity and cell phones, and satellite television would transform the Huichol world forever. I couldn't say if it was good or bad. I only knew that twice now I had been privileged to experience life in this other world so important to True. My first visit ended in tragedy. My second visit ended with hope.

"I don't know if they will call anyone listed on the posters," Ramirez said, "but I wouldn't be surprised if I get a call in a few days or weeks. They know you paid Díaz and they know you will pay again. People here could do a lot with that money."

Epilogue
The Search Ends

To continue the theater of history is to be condemned and to condemn the country, dramatically or grotesquely, to endless repetition. There has been and there is a different possibility. Mexican society could finally reconcile itself with its origins. . . Then Mexicans could begin to compose a new history for themselves, free of that part of the past that is only weight and sickness. The history of Mexico could then begin to be a story of all Mexican lives. Democracy would print a final period.

—Enrique Krauze, *Mexico: The Biography of Power*

Any worthwhile quest challenges body and spirit, whether the journey is a hundred-mile trek through the Sierra Madre or years spent searching for justice through the Mexican judicial labyrinth. Lose the trail and despair, True wrote as he contemplated his ascent in the Chapalagana. Find it again, and move ahead. Where does the trail end?

Gaining a sense of finality takes time. What began six years earlier cannot be shelved like a finished book. Did we win? Did they lose? Winning and losing now seem like empty words.

Regret never quite retreats from conscious memory. Regret for not knowing True better while he lived. Regret at not understanding the emotions and life experiences that sent him on his fatal walk into the sierra. Regret that he was lost before we began our search.

Martha and Teo have much to look ahead to in life, but she will experience the future without her husband and her son will grow up without his father. These are empty spaces as big as any natural chasm or gorge, and no guilty verdict can fill them. Martha has memories of her time with Philip. Teo will have his father's stories, and now the story of his father.

All of True's friends and fellow workers over his fifty-year lifetime are part of his story, even if many of them, like my family, came to understand him better in death than life.

Miguel and Ruby Gatins walked down one path; when it led them to a truth they never expected, they summoned the moral courage to find the right path. Their lives move on, and they can focus their energy on their two wonderful children as they approach adulthood and their college years. In their parents, Francis and Remy have great models.

Patricia Morales hopes to expand the reach of her charitable institute. Despite the time we spent together in Mexico, our telephone conversations, and our e-mail exchanges, she remains an enigma. Morales embodies all that I love and loathe about Mexico, its ancient spirit and mysticism, and its shallow retreats from the truth and deep ambivalence toward the rule of law.

Si dios quiere, if God is willing, as the Mexicans say, there will be no more trips to Guadalajara to argue our case—perhaps one final trip to the sierra to pay a 50,000-peso reward. All the actors in this drama now know the ending, even if it is not the one they envisioned. Juan Chivarra de la Cruz and Miguel Hernandez de la Cruz murdered Philip True, even if motive and the details of the actual act of his taking his life resist complete revelation or comprehension.

There is the satisfaction of prevailing in a Mexican court of law, even more the satisfaction that comes from not dropping out of the race. Our most important achievement, however, was not the verdict alone. It was the light we cast on Mexico's system of justice, too often a system of injustice. Some in Mexico did not welcome our efforts, believing we cast the country in the worst light. Others urged us on, hoping the case would hasten reform. By fighting for our rights as victims, by fighting to convict and punish True's killers, we fought for every Mexican denied his or her own day in court, and certainly every Mexican journalist whose murder has gone unpunished. More Mexican journalists have been murdered since we lost True, five in 2004 alone. Not one of their killers has been brought to justice. Even as the violence continues, we can hope we made it easier for the next victim, the next family and colleagues of a slain reporter, to demand and win justice.

Everyone is entitled to an opinion about Philip True and his quest to hike the length of the Huichol sierra. The Philip True I came to know during the course of this investigation was a man of passion, a good husband, a dedicated reporter, someone who still believed one person can make the world a better place. He also was a human being, a victim of unforgettable abuse in his childhood. He made his fair share of mistakes and missteps, sometimes hurting those closest to him. The man who married Martha and set out to build a family with her is someone to admire for all he overcame on life's path. The *San Antonio Express-News* was fortunate to have True as one of its reporters for six years. He helped make it a better newspaper. Someday there will be no one left in the newsroom who knew True, but his spirit will endure.

Mexico, as President Fox told the U.S. Congress, wants to be trusted and respected as an equal partner. There is so much to admire about Mexico, its people, its culture, and its history, with so many qualities and characteristics that we cannot find in ourselves north of the border. As Mexico continues on its own path, Americans have much to learn about injustices Mexicans have suffered at our hands over the past two centuries and that they continue to suffer. There is, in short, much to be done on our side of the border before we can hope to earn the trust of the Mexicans.

But what separates us today, more than distrust and our history of intervention, is that Mexico is not a nation with the rule of law. It is a country where justice is the exception to the rule, where people are preyed on by the very forces that exist to protect them. Mexico, like True, needs to find a way to put together the pieces of its broken soul.

Those of us living north of the border, where cocaine and heroin consumption fuels so much trouble to the south, are linked to that quest. It is a journey worth making together.

Marriage made Chivarra and Hernandez members of the same ostracized clan, regarded as troublemakers by other Huichols long before True was killed. The two brothers-in-law deserve what befalls them. Their violence brought far more attention to the Huichol communities than True ever imagined when he wrote his story proposal. Far more people, including myself, gained an appreciation of the colliding forces that define and threaten the Huichol way of life, yet the killing only made the larger Huichol community feel more threatened by these outside forces. The Huichol story is an important story, both inspiring and sad. I only wish them peace and solitude.

The two killers cannot escape their crime. Their community now knows them as the killers of the American journalist. Chivarra and Hernandez will drag their heavy burden of guilt along in life just as they once struggled to drag True's corpse down into the depths of the Chapalagana. They will have no more luck hiding their deed than they did in hiding True's shallow grave. Their own shame is a prison that surrounds them even in the most remote canyon country.

We do not consider the case closed. That will come when the guilty are punished. Last summer, after the verdict and while we awaited word from the arrest party, I allowed my mind to wander through a world of magical realism as I floated in the cool, shallow currents of the Llano River and gazed into the vast blue sky of the Texas Hill Country. I imagined a mythic Huichol world, shrouded in a veil of peyote-induced hallucination, of shamans and ancient souls communing, the long-vanished deer of creation summoned, all set free to roam the unconquerable sierra of the heart. Only Juan Chivarra and Miguel Hernandez fare differently. A trail of feathers follows the killers everywhere they go, even into their dreams.

Acknowledgments

This book would not have been possible without the support of Martha True. I hope I have repaid her generosity of spirit by bringing the story of her husband's life and death and our shared search for justice to a wider audience. I also hope this book one day will help Philip Theodore True Jr., "Teo," to appreciate the father he never met. Bonnie True Biggs, Philip's sister and only surviving family member, welcomed me with an open heart and a treasure trove of letters, photographs, and family contacts and memories.

True's friends, former girlfriends and co-workers in southern California and Long Island trusted me with their own memories and, in some cases, the letters from True they still hold. They were instrumental in helping me understand True's development as a wilderness devotee and his eventual conversion to newspaper journalism. The editors at *La Tribuna Hispana*, the Spanish-language weekly on Long Island, provided me with True's earliest published news stories.

Hilde Maeckle, my mother-in-law, provided me with the initial research of the Bleibtreu family in Leipzig, Germany and translated the inscription on the pocket watch True inherited after his father's death. Fran Bumann, director, and T. Maureen Schoenky, German studies researcher, at the Southern California Gene Genealogical Society, did extensive work on the Bleibtreu name and German immigration to the United States in the nineteenth century. Heather Tunender, a database researcher at UC-Irvine, unearthed True's otherwise lost account of his arrest at a Berkeley antiwar demonstration that was published in a now-defunct campus newspaper.

Countless editors and reporters in Texas and Mexico lent insight on True's years as a newspaperman. Two of his fellow Mexico City correspondents, Dudley Althaus of the *Houston Chronicle* and Tracey Eaton of the *Dallas Morning News*, were especially committed to our search for justice in the case. The intrepid Alan Zarembo, then of *Newsweek* and now at the *Los Angeles Times*, located True's overlooked journal, a find that provided further circumstantial evidence against True's killers. Paul Kvinta, writing for *Outside* magazine, wrote a superb article after trekking through the Huichol sierra in an effort to reconstruct True's journey. Evan Smith, editor of *Texas Monthly* magazine, helped bring the True story to a wider audience.

Three important press organizations lent considerable support and guidance throughout the case: The Miami-based Inter American Press Association, the Committee to Protect Journalists in New York, and the American Society of Newspaper Editors in Roslyn, Virginia. Three former IAPA presidents, Jorge Fascetto, owner and publisher of *El Día* in Rio Plata, Argentina; Edward Seaton of the *Manhattan Mercury*; and, Tony Pederson, former executive editor of the *Houston Chronicle* and now the Belo Distinguished Professor of Journalism at Southern Methodist University in Dallas, traveled to Mexico to push for action in the case. Alberto Ibarguen, the former publisher of the *Miami Herald* and now the head of the Knight Foundation; Rich Oppel of the *Austin-American Statesman* and onetime ASNE president; and Ann Cooper and Joel Simon, of CPJ, all showed steadfast support and are great defenders of press freedom, especially in the Americas.

Many Mexicans in and outside the government and the press were helpful during the six-year life of the case. Without the support of President Zedillo and his advisors, I doubt we would have found True's remains or identified his killers. Fox's former foreign minister, Jorge Castañeda, and his deputy, Enrique Berruga, now Mexico's ambassador to the United Nations, received me at a time when our cause seemed lost. Both men are dedicated to building a more democratic Mexico. Dr. Mario Melgar, director of the San Antonio campus of the Universidad Nacional Autonomo de Mexico, edited all Spanish usage. Former mayor of Oaxaca and Consul General de Mexico in San Antonio, Carlos Sada, and the current consul general, Ambassador Martha Lara, assisted me in the same spirit. Sara Delano Rojas, the Mexico City therapist, educated me on the disturbing and complex issue of incest and sexual abuse. Two U.S. ambassadors to Mexico, Jeffrey Davidow under President Clinton, and Tony Garza under George W. Bush, offered support and friendship over the years.

In Guadalajara, Miguel and Ruby Gatins displayed great moral courage by coming forward with the truth and later by reviewing the manuscript. Once adversaries, we are now friends. Dr. Phil Weigand, the dean of U.S. anthropologists who have studied the Huichols, and Dr. Paul Liffman, who gave me his unpublished dissertation on the Huichols, greatly deepened my understanding of Huichol culture and history. They also read, corrected, and improved the manuscript.

My name is on the book, but it would not have been possible to write it without the support of so many friends and colleagues, past and present, at the *San Antonio Express-News*. They are too many to name, but some must be singled out: Susana Hayward, now reporting from Mexico City for Knight-Ridder Newspapers, was the first reporter to go south in search of True. Her later stories from Mexico City, Guadalajara, and Colotlán were essential building blocks for the book. Dane Schiller, who replaced her in Mexico City, accompanied me back into the Chapalagana in January 2005. Marie Martinez Couch, my administrative assistant in San Antonio, did more for me than I can say. Minea Nieto, office manager of the *Express-News*'s

Mexico bureau, also labored tirelessly. Both arranged travel, appointments, and kept the case files. Sean Mattson, our freelance correspondent in Guadalajara, always made himself available to help with the case. Craig Thomason, the venerable city editor, has edited my Sunday columns, more than a few about the True case. Carmina Danini, the newspaper's Mexico City correspondent before True, corrected my translations of columns I wrote for publication in Mexican newspapers, and fine-tuned my correspondence with Mexican presidents, attorneys general, and governors.

I could not have pursued the case with the same intensity had it not been for the leadership of Brett Thacker, the managing editor. My other partners at the *Express-News*, Larry Walker, publisher and CEO, and Tom Stephenson, general manager and COO, supported my direct involvement in the True case until its end. Big media companies make easy targets, but I am proud to be part of the Hearst team, where the senior leadership in New York displayed the same resolve and support from the day True disappeared. Many thanks to Frank Bennack, Vic Ganzi, George Irish and Steve Swartz for their support and commitment to quality journalism in San Antonio.

Speaking of distinguished newspapermen, I am indebted to Peter Osnos, one-time *Washington Post* senior editor and founder and CEO of PublicAffairs, who took a chance on a Texas newspaperman and his first book. Under the guidance of Lisa Kaufman, my editor and vice president at PublicAffairs, what began as a story slowly evolved into a book. Lisa is old school, a gifted and challenging hands-on editor with unyielding standards; other published authors tell me such editors are a disappearing breed. Robert Kimzey, PublicAffairs' managing editor, and Melissa Raymond, production editor, meticulously edited and re-edited the manuscript.

Thanks to my agent David McCormick of Collins/McCormick for taking my clumsy book proposal and guiding me through countless rewrites until we had something good enough to win the attention of a publisher. Thanks to Texas journalist, author, and friend Jan Jarboe Russell, who introduced us.

Then there are my manuscript readers, a network of friends and colleagues, good editors all: Thacker, David Sheppard, Dane Schiller and Lisa Sandberg at the *Express-News*; Jeff Cohen, editor of the *Houston Chronicle*; Elizabeth Perry, friend and fellow traveler in Central America; Edward Seaton in Kansas; and Krystina Sibley, who ought to come back to journalism.

Above all, there is my family. Monika, Nick, and Alex formed my most important support group, who endured my frequent absences, lost nights, weekends and vacations spent reporting and writing.

I reserve my final sentiments for Philip True. We are proud to have had him as our reporter. He and his work at the *San Antonio Express-News* will not be forgotten.

Bibliography

Abbey, Edward. *Beyond the Wall*. New York: Holt, 1971.

———*The Journey Home*. New York: Dutton, 1977.

———*Desert Solitaire*. Tucson: University of Arizona Press, 1988.

Aguayo, Sergio. *Myths and [Mis]Perceptions: Changing U.S. Elite Visions of Mexico*. Translated by Julián Brody. San Diego: Center for U.S.-Mexican Studies, 1998.

Barry, Tom. *Mexico: A Country Guide*. Albuquerque: Inter-Hemispheric Education Resource Center, 1992.

Castañeda, Jorge. *Somos Muchos*. Colina, Fla.: Editorial Planeta Mexican, 2004.

Chasan, Alice. *Attacks on the Press in 1998: A Worldwide Survey by the Committee to Protect Journalists*. New York: Committee to Protect Journalists, 1999.

Chávez, Jorge Humberto. *La ciudad y el viaje interminable*. México: Entrelíneas Editores, 2003.

Cohen, Tony. *On Mexican Time*. New York: Broadway, 2000.

Collings, Peter. *The Huichol of Mexico*. Mexico: Casa Isabel, 2000.

Collins, Patrick, Christine Gilbert, and Germaine Curry, eds. *Border-lands: Texas Poetry Review.* Austin: Morgan, 1997.

Coyle, Philip E., and Paul Liffman, eds. "Ritual and Historical Territoriality of the Náyari and Wixárika Peoples." *Journal of the Southwest,* special issue, 42, no. 1 (2000).

Davidow, Jeffrey. *El Oso y El Puercoespín.* Mexico: Editorial Grijalbo, 2003.

Downie, Leonard Jr., and Robert G. Kaiser. *The News About the News.* New York: Knopf, 2002.

Ehrenreich, Barbara. *Nickel and Dimed: On (Not) Getting By in America.* New York: Metropolitan, 2001.

Fehrenbach, T. R. *Fire and Blood: A History of Mexico.* New York: Da Capo, 1995.

Fletcher, Colin. *The Man Who Walked Through Time.* New York: Vintage, 1989.

Fletcher, Colin, and Chip Rawlins. *The Complete Walker IV.* New York: Knopf, 2002.

Fuentes, Carlos. *The Old Gringo.* Translated by Margaret Sayers Peden. New York: Farrar Straus Giroux, 1985.

———. *Terra Nostra.* Translated by Margaret Sayers Peden. Illinois: Dalkey Archive Press, 2003.

Greene, Graham. *The Lawless Roads.* New York: Penguin, 1982.

Griswold Del Castillo, Richard. *The Treaty of Guadalupe Hidalgo: A Legacy of Conflict.* Norman: University of Oklahoma Press, 1990.

Hamnett, Brian. *A Concise History of Mexico.* New York: Cambridge University Press, 1999.

Heath, Jonathan. *Mexico and the Sexenio Curse: Presidential Successions and the Economic Crises in Modern Mexico.* Washington D.C.: Center for Strategic and International Studies, 1999.

Kaiser, Charles. *1968 in America: Music, Politics, Chaos, Counterculture, and the Shaping of a Generation.* New York: Grove, 1997.

Kovach, Bill, and Tom Rosenstiel. *The Elements of Journalism.* New York: Crown, 2001.

Krauze, Enrique. *Mexico: Biography of Power: A History of Modern Mexico, 1810–1996.* Translated by Hank Heifetz. New York: HarperCollins, 1997.

———*La presidencia imperial: Ascenso y caída del sistema politico mexicano (1940–1996)*. México: Tusquets Editores, 1997.

Langewiesche, William. *Cutting for Sign*. New York: Pantheon, 1993.

Lawson, Chappell H. *Building the Fourth Estate: Democratization and the Rise of a Free Press in Mexico*. Berkeley: University of California Press, 2002.

Lewis, Oscar. *The Children of Sanchez: Autobiography of a Mexican Family*. New York: Vintage, 1963.

Liffman, Paul. "Territoriality and Historical Consciousness in Beatriz Rojas' *Los huicholes en la historia.*" *Journal of the Southwest,* spring 2000, 167–180.

——— "Huichol Territoriality: Land Conflict and Cultural Representation in Western Mexico," chap. 4. Ph.D. diss., University of Chicago, 2002.

Lopez, Barry. *Desert Notes*. New York: Avon, 1976.

Lumholtz, Carl. *Unknown Mexico: A Record of Five Years' Exploration Among the Tribes of the Western Sierra Madre*. New York: Scribner's, 1902.

McCarthy, Cormac. *Cities of the Plain*. New York: Knopf, 1998.

Meyer, Michael C., and William H. Beezley. *The Oxford History of Mexico*. New York: Oxford University Press, 2000.

Miller, Tom. *On the Border*. New York: Harper & Row, 1981.

Monasterio, Pablo Ortiz. *Corazón de venado*. México: Casa de las Imágenes, 1998.

Monsiváis, Carlos. *Mexican Postcards*. Translated by John Kraniauskas. New York: Verso, 1997.

Montejano Y Aguiñaga, Rafael. *Real de Catorce: El real de minas de la purisima concepcion de los catorce, S.L.P.* San Luis Potosi: Academia de Historia Potosina, 1974.

Neruda, Pablo. *The Yellow Heart*. Translated by William O'Daly. Port Townsend, Wash.: Copper Canyon, 1990.

Oppenheimer, Andres. *Bordering on Chaos: Mexico's Roller-Coaster Journey Toward Chaos*. New York: Little, Brown, 1996.

Paz, Octavio. *The Labyrinth of Solitude*. New York: Grove, 1985.

——— *Piedra del sol*. New York: New Directions, 1987.

Preston, Julia, and Samuel Dillon. *Opening Mexico: The Making of a Democracy.* New York: Farrar, Straus & Giroux, 2004.

Reid, Jan. *The Bullet Meant for Me.* New York: Broadway, 2002.

Riding, Alan. *Distant Neighbors.* New York: Vintage, 1986.

Rulfo, Juan. *Pedro Páramo.* Austin: University of Texas Press, 2002.

Simon, Joel. *Endangered Mexico: An Environment on the Edge.* San Francisco: Sierra Club Books, 1997.

Solomon, Joel. *Systemic Injustice: Torture, "Disappearance," and Extrajudicial Execution in Mexico.* New York: Human Rights Watch, 1999.

Stilwell, Hart. *Border City.* Garden City, N.Y.: Country Life Press, 1945.

Trotti, Ricardo. *Impunity No More: Unpunished Crimes Against Journalists.* Miami: Inter American Press Association, 1999.

———*Press Freedom in the Americas: Annual Report.* Miami: Inter American Press Association, 1999, 2002.

Tuck, Jim. *Pancho Villa and John Reed: Two Faces of Romantic Revolution.* Tucson: University of Arizona Press, 1984.

Weigand, Phil C. *Co-Operative Labor Groups in Subsistence Activities Among the Huichol Indians of the Gubernancia of San Sebastian Teponahuastlan, Municipio of Mezquitic, Jalisco, Mexico.* Carbondale: Southern Illinois University Press, 1972.

Notes

As editor of the *San Antonio Express-News,* as a member of the search party that located True's grave, and as a representive of my employer in pursuing justice in the Mexican courts, I had a unique opportunity to engage in original reporting throughout the six-year ordeal. My growing interest in True's early life and his adult years before he became a newspaper reporter led me to track down former friends, roommates, coworkers, and others. It was rewarding to return to my roots as a reporter. Wherever and whenever possible, I relied on my own reporting, even when it required independently interviewing key figures previously written about in news accounts. Still, this book also depends in no small part on the good work of other newspaper and magazine journalists, notably Susana Hayward, Mexico City bureau chief of the *San Antonio Express-News* from 1998 to 2002. The work of my colleagues Dane Schiller, the current Mexico City correspondent, and John MacCormack, based in San Antonio, also merits individual acknowledgment. Wherever I have used direct quotes from the work of others, I have listed the specific article in the chapter notes. Whenever appropriate, I also have credited the individual reporter in the actual text.

Chapter 1

Descriptions of True's morning work habits and his home environment are drawn from my interviews with Martha True, my visits to the house on Calle Sierra Amatepec, and my interview with Fred Bonavita, True's supervising editor. True's March 1998 story proposal is reprinted in its entirety. His November 1998 e-mail to editors complaining that his Mexico stories were being underplayed also is reprinted verbatim. Accounts of tensions between True and editors in the home office came from Brett Thacker, then assistant managing editor and now managing editor; David Sheppard, projects editor; Nora Lopez, state editor; and Dane Schiller, then our Laredo correspondent and now Mexico City correspondent. I learned of the existence of True's undelivered performance evaluation in my interview with Bonavita and later found it in our files. All other quotes in the book come from my own interviews with the individuals. U.S. anthropologist and Huichol expert Paul Liffman disputes the translation of "Chapalagana" as "Twisted Serpent," although he offers no alternative translation. Huichol Indians in our small search party who spoke Spanish as well as Huichol translated Chapalagana to mean "Serpiente Torcida."

Chapter 2

I wrote my description of the Avenida Reforma and all its street activity and distractions, as well as the ambience found in Las Lomas de Chapultepec, after three separate outings in which I retraced True's ten-mile training route, an extended version of his regular seven-mile jogging route. Mexico City has been familiar ground for me since the early 1980s, and anyone who has visited the park and its immediate environs with any regularity will have his or her own memories of the fire-eaters and other street spectacles. Martha True also spoke to me about her husband's October–November training routine. Finally, I visited the taxi *sitio* around the corner from the True's home on two different occasions, each time interviewing drivers who had been hired by True and were familiar with his planned journey, his training regimen, and his death on the trail. Philip and Martha's last trip together, visiting the Northeast and Canada in October 1998, was recounted in interviews I conducted with Martha, Sonia Cantú Wieloch in Connecticut, and Bob Horchler and his wife, Julie McDonald, in Baldwin, Long Island. Details of Martha's pregnancy and how she and Philip felt about his trek are drawn from interviews with Martha and Joel Simon, who lived in Mexico while researching a book on the environment, and Dudley Althaus, Mexico City correspondent for the *Houston Chronicle*. Both reporters told me about the weekly *cantina* and their conversations in mid- and late 1998 with True about Martha's pregnancy and his looming trip to the Huichol sierra. Martha also recounted for me the Thanksgiving Day meal prepared by Philip. The Brownsville and Matamoros passages are drawn from my interviews with Martha, Kim Garcia, Lavis Laney, Rebecca Thatcher, Martha True, and Juanita Serrano. Accounts of True's preparation for departure and previous trip to the edge of the Huichol sierra with Martha are drawn from my interviews with her. True's planned itinerary is taken from his route map.

CHAPTER 3

Reconstruction of events surrounding the memorial service for Theodore True, Philip's father, was drawn from my interviews with Bronwen Heuer in Boston and Bonnie True Biggs in Reno, Nevada. Hilde Maeckle translated the inscription on the heirloom German pocket watch. The Bleibtreu, Minear, and True family histories and the story of the family chicken farm come from Bonnie, as well as from notations on family photographs she loaned me and my original research. Fran Bumann and T. Maureen Schoenky, of the Southern California Genealogical Society and Family Research Library in Burbank, California, kindly assisted me in researching the Bleibtreu family tree and the family's move from Illinois down through Missouri and out west to California. All quotes in this chapter are drawn from my interviews with Peter and Grace Harris in Seattle, Bonnie True Biggs in Reno, Nevada, Annette Fuentes in New York, Sara Delano Rojas in Mexico City and San Antonio, and Joe Vasquez in Sacramento.

Biggs provided me with Philip's last letter to her, written in January 1998. Information about True's attendance at Los Angeles Valley Junior College and the University of California–Irvine came from Vasquez, Heuer, and academic transcripts released to me at Martha's request.

CHAPTER 4

The description of UC–Irvine in the late 1960s is drawn from interviews with Joe Vasquez, Peter and Grace Harris, Bronwen Heuer, and other True friends from that period. True's published letter in the *New University*, a now defunct campus newspaper, and his subsequent bylined story in the same publication about the arrest of UC–Irvine students at an antiwar rally, were located by Heather Tunender, intrepid UC–Irvine electronic services researcher. Details of True's relationship with Kathleen Sullivan are drawn from my interview with her and access she gave me to correspondence she received from True over the years. Details of True's relationship with Cathy Bell and his first move to Long Island are drawn from my interview with Cathy Bell Thomson in Huntington Beach, Orange County. True's use of psychedelics came from Peter Harris. Details of the move to Long Island by the Harrises and then by True and Heuer come from the Harrises, Bell, and Heuer. True's habitual pot use in his early Long Island years came from my interviews with Heuer and Fuentes and was confirmed by various other True friends from that period. The account of True's hitchhiking trip with his dog, Alice, from Long Island to Tennessee and back came from a journal of his made available to me by Heuer, who also gave me access to correspondence she had from True over the years. Accounts of True's life and travels during the years he was with Annette Fuentes came from various interviews with Fuentes; Mike Collins, a True friend who led him to become a paper hanger; noted writer and feminist Barbara Ehrenreich, who once rented a basement room to True; and Brian Donovan, former *Newsday* reporter who hired True to wallpaper his home. The account of True's relationship with Sandy Weber and their camping trip to Nova Scotia is drawn from my interview with her. Weber, Fuentes, and Vasquez, among others, recounted to me True's decision to undergo therapy, but none knew the identity of his Long Island therapist, whom I was unable to locate. Vasquez told me about his reunion with True. Fred Chase and two editors at *La Tribuna Hispana* on Long Island, Emilio Ruiz and Jose Oquendo, told me about True's early work as a freelance reporter and his first forays into Central America. Details of True's move to Brownsville, Texas, are drawn from interviews with Bob Horchler on Long Island, Fred Chase, and Rebecca Thatcher.

CHAPTER 5

The account of True's marriage is drawn from interviews with Martha and Juanita Serrano. The account of the newlyweds' visit with True's mother and sister in Reno is drawn from my interviews with Martha and Bonnie. The account of True's telephone conversation with Bonavita about his new job is drawn from my interviews with Martha and Bonavita. True's work in Laredo for the *Express-News* is reconstructed from original articles found in the *Express-News* archives. Chase told me about his own move to Laredo, and Bonavita, Chase, and *Express-News* photographer Jerry Lara recounted for me True's first work in Chiapas after the Zapatista uprising. My family's visit to Laredo and Nuevo Laredo to dine with the Trues is drawn from my own recollections, my wife, Monika, and Martha. The road trip to Seattle is drawn from my interviews with Martha and with the Harrises. The quote from Tim Padgett, *Newsweek* magazine, comes from a December 20, 1998, story, "Mourners recall True's love of Mexican back country," by John MacCormack, *Express-News* senior reporter.

CHAPTER 6

The account of Martha's actions when Philip failed to contact her or return from his trek after ten days is drawn from my interviews with Martha, Rojas, Serrano, Obaya, Chase, and Bonavita. The account of Bonavita and other editors informing me that True was missing is based on my contemporary notes, and my interviews with Bonavita and other editors.

CHAPTER 7

The account of my conversations with Larry Walker and Tom Stephenson at the *Express-News* in the days after we learned of True's disappearance is based on my contemporary notes and the recollections of my two colleagues. The account of the initial search efforts by Manuel Obaya and Fred Chase with pilot Chuy López is based on interviews I conducted with all three men. The account of Martha's activities during this same time period is drawn from my interviews with her and Juanita. My account of Susana Hayward joining the search team is based on their recollection, my interview with Bonavita, and contemporary conversations between Hayward and myself during the search effort.

CHAPTER 8

The account of the Philip Truempler incident is taken from my contemporary notes at the True house and my interviews with Martha and Juanita, David Nájera in Mexico City, and Bonavita in San Antonio. The comments from President Zedillo after his election came during an interview with *Express-News* representatives, including Walker and myself.

CHAPTER 9

All material and quotes in this chapter are drawn from my contemporary reporting on scene in December 1998.

CHAPTER 10

All material and quotes about the first autopsy are drawn from my own reporting. The passage revealing that President Zedillo and his team learned True was murdered from television news reports rather than state

officials is drawn from my interviews with Zedillo and Nájera. The statement made by Dr. Rivas Souza that True's death was a homicide in his
Televisa interview was reported by the *Express-News* and other media at
the time; I myself noted it while watching the interview in Guadalajara.
My conversation with Dr. Phil Weigand, an anthropologist and noted
Huichol authority, was the source of much of my writing about Huichol
history and customs, but many other sources, Mexican and U.S., inform
my writing on the subject and not all of the experts or other observers of
Huichol life agree on everything. My book is bound to fuel additional
debate over a number of issues, including ritual peyote use, Huichol attitudes toward outsiders entering their territory, and the clash between the
ancient and the modern that is changing Huichol society so rapidly. The
account of Lieutenant Colonel Roberto Aguilera, chief of police of the
Mexican army at the Defense Ministry, visiting Guadalajara to arrange
for a second autopsy comes from State Department cables released
under the Freedom of Information Act. Interestingly, to this date the FBI
has refused to release any information about its role in the True case, and
an FBI spokeswoman at headquarters in Washington, D.C., accused me
of threatening the agency when I wrote that the FBI's continued refusal
to comply with the law would result in a notation of same in my book.

CHAPTER 11

The excerpt from True's final bylined story is taken from the *Express-
News* archives, "Private campaign, government effort help in Mexican
preserve's recovery," published December 6, 1998. The excerpt from the
Rick Casey column is taken from *Express-News* archives, "Celebrating, in
death, curiosity and anger," published December 18, 1998. Readers interested in reading more of True's stories can go to www.mysanantonio.com
(registration required), go to special sections, and click on the photo of
True. My account of our first report that True's killers had been detained
is drawn in part on contemporary conversations with Bonavita and Hayward and from the *Express-News* archives, "2 reportedly admit killing
news writer; pair believed in custody of Mexican military," by senior

reporter Carmina Danini, published December 26, 1998. My press statement was published in various U.S. and Mexican media, including the
Danini story.

<h2 style="text-align:center">CHAPTER 12</h2>

My account of the arraignment of Juan Chivarra de la Cruz and Miguel
Hernandez de la Cruz and their initial confession in Guadalajara is
drawn from two Hayward stories in the *Express-News:* "Journalist's action
cited in murder. Officials say 2 men were angered because True was taking photos," published December 28, 1998; and "Pair arraigned in death
of correspondent," published December 29, 1998. The second version of
their confession is drawn from a third story by Hayward, "New motive
reported in True slaying," published December 31, 1998, and from various
Mexican newspapers, including *La Jornada* in Mexico City, in which I
cite its own headline dated December 31, 1998. I also draw on the actual
signed confessions as entered into evidence in the trial documents. Dr.
Gary W. Kunsman's remarks regarding postmortem alcohol production in
a corpse to Don Finley, an *Express-News* reporter and editor, appeared in
the December 31 story by Hayward. Observations about True falling
behind schedule on the trail are my own, based on the confessions. The
Gloria Ferniz quote is from my interview with her. My observations here
and elsewhere in the book about the shortcomings of Mexico's judicial
system and comments about badly needed reforms come from personal
experience, various Mexican authorities, including President Vicente
Fox, and author and former Foreign Minister Jorge Castañeda and his
excellent book *Somos Muchos,* published in Mexico in 2004. The defendants' claims of being tortured were first made in a December 29, 1998,
story in the Guadalajara newspaper *Publico.* I also quote an excerpt from
a statement released by the Jalisco State Human Rights Commission
detailing the defendants' claims of torture and abuse against themselves,
other family members, and a village leader. Here and elsewhere n the
book I try to present all viewpoints on this issue. My account of the controversy surrounding the second autopsy is drawn from a January 6,

1999, story by Dane Schiller datelined Mexico City, "Mexico officials to attempt consensus on True's death." The same article surfaces tensions between federal and state forensics experts on the actual cause of True's death. Schiller filed a second story the next day, January 7, "Jalisco coroner not called to meeting on True's death," reporting that Dr. Rivas Souza, the state coroner, was not invited to a meeting between federal and state officials to reconcile the forensics issues in dispute. Schiller filed a third story on January 8, "Alcohol poisoning cited in True death," that included his interview with Dr. Emma Lew, the FBI consultant. Schiller filed a fourth story, January 9, "Mexican officials say blows to head, back killed True," that was based on public statements by officials with the federal attorney general. I also relied on official statements about the autopsy posted on the ministry's website. Dr. Vincent DiMaio, the chief coroner in Bexar County, was interviewed by Schiller for his January 12 story, "Expert says True's cause of death may never be known." The excerpt from Arnoldo Kraus's column in the Mexico City newspaper *La Jornada*, "The True Case, the Mexico case," appeared December 29, 1998. All references regarding the trip to the suspects' ranch in the sierra by Tracey Eaton, the *Dallas Morning News* bureau chief in Mexico, are dawn from my interview with him and his excellent article, "True's murder far from resolved," which appeared in the *Morning News* and also was printed in the *Express-News* on March 1, 1999. My observations about the Chivarra family and relations between the neighboring counties of San Sebastián and San Miguel come from a variety of on-the-record sources, such as Dr. Phil Weigand, the noted Huichol anthropologist, and individuals in and near the Huichol county of San Sebastián who spoke to me on condition of anonymity.

CHAPTER 13

True's original journal, as far as I know, remains unaccounted for, although multiple copies of it were made; both Martha and I have copies. *Newsweek's* Alan Zarembo quoted liberally from it in his account, and other excerpts have appeared in the *Express-News*, other U.S. and

Mexican newspapers, and magazines. I include extensive passages not previously deciphered or published. Hoffman Reporting and Video Services in San Antonio, a firm specializing in court reporting and bilingual documentation, provided valuable handwriting analysis in helping me read previously unreadable passages in the journal. Only a few words in True's hand elude us to this day. All Zarembo quotes are drawn from my interview with him. All quotes from Paul Kvinta, a contributing writer to *Outside* magazine, also come from my interview with him. The account of his journey along True's route appeared in the magazine's June 1999 edition and represents the most exhaustive effort by any of the journalists who entered the Huichol sierra after True was killed. Quotes by Paul Liffman, Ph.D., are drawn from my interview with him. My comments about Real de Catorce benefited from Phil Weigand and Alicia García de Weigand, "Huichol Society before the Arrival of the Spanish," Paul Liffman, "Gourdvines, Fires, and Wixárika Territoriality," Olivia Selena Kindl, "The Huichol Gourd Bowl as a Microcosm," and Johannes Neurath, "Tukipa Ceremonial Centers in the Community of Tuapurie: Cargo Systems, Landscape and Cosmovision," *Journal of the Southwest*, spring 2000, published by the Southwest Center at the University of Arizona at Tucson, as cited in the bibliography under Coyle, Philip E.

Chapter 14

Hayward's first interview with the suspects appeared in her April 3 story, "True suspects alter story again," from which I recount the defendants' demeanor and comments to her and *Express-News* chief photographer Bob Owen. My account of the IAPA delegation's meetings with Attorney General Jorge Madrazo and President Ernesto Zedillo is drawn from my contemporary notes and from subsequent conversations and interviews with other participants, including Jorge Fascetto and Tony Pederson, and a later exchange of correspondence with President Zedillo before and after he left office, and in addition to an interview with David Nájera after he left office. I also drew on a June 2, 1999 story by Hayward, "Media group to address slayings," and her June 3 story, "Zedillo assures media group on slayings." My account of our meeting in Guadalajara with the governor and state attorney general also is drawn from my notes, conversations with my fellow delegates, and from a Hayward story that appeared June 4, "Media delegation is assured of justice in reporter's death." Gary R. Martin, Washington bureau chief for the *Express-News,* filed an April 23, 1999, story, "Alamo City lawmaker presses for answers in True's death," including the FBI spokesman who wrote a letter stating that the agency believed the suspects were guilty of killing True. Ambassador Jeffrey Davidow's remarks occurred in conversation with me during a visit he made to San Antonio. My account of Martha receiving a posthumous honor for Philip's work at the annual IAPA delegation held in Houston was drawn from my personal notes and a story by John MacCormack that appeared on October 21, 1999, "True's widow accepts award in his name." My account of Hayward's second trip to Colotlán to interview the two suspects is drawn from her December 5, 1999, story, "Journalist's 1998 murder case 'moving along.'" Tony Pederson's quote comes from a May 28, 2000, story in the *Express-News* by Hayward, "Delegation to seek status of True case; Newspaper leaders going to Mexico." Quotes attributed to Solís come from her May 31 story, "August completion eyed for True case." The excerpt attributed to Rich Oppel, executive editor of the *Austin American-Statesman,* is drawn from his June 4, 2000, column, "Case of slain journalist a test for Mexico." Quotes from President Zedillo taken during our June 1 meeting, and from delegation members afterward, are from my notes and the June 2 story by Hayward, "Mexico president pledges resolution of True case; Zedillo calls killing atypical."

CHAPTER 15

My account of President Fox's victory in the 2000 presidential elections is based on my own observation of the election, general U.S. and Mexico media coverage, including the *Express-News,* and Julia Preston and Sam Dillon's excellent inside account of Mexican politics in their book *Opening Mexico,* cited in the bibliography. The quote attributed to President Zedillo from his national television address is my translation of his

statement as posted on the presidential website. The quotes from
Colotlán prosecutor Jaime Ruiz Sandoval and the suspects' defense
lawyer, Juan Pedro Salas Castillo, are drawn from Hayward's September
7, 2000, story, "End of True case seen despite defense's legal delays."
Describing my open letter of petition to Fox, the excerpt I use is from
my own Sunday column of December 10, "Mr. Fox, please accept our
petition." With Martha along, both Hayward and I took notes of our subsequent meeting with President Fox in his office. Quotes are from my
notes, the transcribed conversation, and Hayward's February 14, 2001,
story, "Fox lends a hand in slaying case; True widow, officials in Jalisco to
meet."

CHAPTER 16

All details about the involvement of Miguel and Ruby Gatins and Patricia
Morales in the case—from the outset through the release of the two suspects and their respective family histories—come from extensive interviews with all three of them. Morales reconstructed her meetings with the
suspects in the jail during our interviews. I also relied on the five stories
filed by Hayward from the August 4, 2001, release of the suspects through
August 12, including her interview with Chivarra and Hernandez after they
were freed. I also reference an incisive profile of Miguel Gatins by John
MacCormack published August 12, 2001, "Man of strong convictions; Huichols' benefactor was brought up to question those in power." Hayward
and Gatins each dispute the other's account of their initial telephone conversation, when Gatins called her to disclose his role in the case. Hayward
and I also differ on whether she sent me a contemporary e-mail recounting
the conversation. In the end, all of us at the *Express-News* failed to understand the role of Gatins and Morales in the case, or anticipate the impact
they would have on the outcome. My account of Gatins's subsequent telephone call to Martha in Brownsville is based on interviews with both of
them. Comments by Reyes Contreras to Hayward were reported in her
June 15, 2001, story, "True case in judge's hands." Denis Rodriguez's Aug. 3,
2001, story in *Mural,* "Torturan a un huichol por la muerte de True,"

focused on a claim by a physician retained by the defense team that Hernandez was tortured before confessing his role. Martha True's reaction and my own reaction to the release of the two suspects were quoted in various media, including the *Express-News*. Gatins himself confirmed for me that both Hayward and MacCormack told him separately that he had succeeded in helping two guilty men win their freedom, comments they had told me about that came back to haunt Gatins. The comment by Homero Aridjis came from Hayward's August 12, 2001, story, "Who killed Philip True? Truth may be a casualty in the dismissal of a murder case in the writer's death." Cables from consular officials to Washington were obtained under an FOI request.

CHAPTER 17

This chapter is based on my own reporting, my published columns on the Montesinos case that appeared in *Reforma* and *El Norte* in Mexico, and my column in the *Express-News* about the de Haro killing, "Injustice can occur on either side of the border," published August 26, 2001.

CHAPTER 18

President Fox's state visit to Washington and his appearance before the Congress is taken, in part, from Gary R. Martin's September 7, 2001, story, "Fox takes his case to Congress; lawmakers cheer call by Mexico's president to ease suspicion." I canceled my plans to attend the September 24, 2001, appeals court hearing in Guadalajara after the terrorist attacks on September 11. My account of the hearing is drawn from Hayward's September 30, 2001, story, "Photos called proof E-N writer murdered; Pictures in True case appeal reportedly back up first autopsy." Later I also interviewed Ochoa, Solís, and Gatins. MacCormack and Hayward teamed up for their October 14, 2001, story, "Reviews indicate E-N writer was murdered; experts say first autopsy suggests a homicide." I thought it was a brilliant move by MacCormack to send forensics experts in this country the autopsy photos for their review and comment.

Reyes Contreras had ignored the photos as evidence during the trial. The story scored big in the court of public opinion. The press conference that Martha and I held in Guadalajara to pressure the appeals court for a ruling was covered by Hayward in her November 22, 2001, story, "E-N editor asks new ruling in writer True's death; case has been in courts for three years." Coverage of the appeals court verdict and aftermath is drawn from Hayward's May 31, 2002, story, "Tribunal issues guilty verdicts in True case." I also drew on my June 2, 2002, column, "Note of sadness is gone from the voice of reporter's widow." Coverage of President Fox's aborted trip to Texas and the Crawford ranch of President Bush is based on stories published in the *San Antonio Express-News* and one particular analysis written by Richard Boudreaux of the *Los Angles Times* on August 18, 2002, "Domestic politics strain U.S.-Mexico relations." My account of a federal court sending the case back yet again to the state appeals court was drawn from Dane Schiller's February 19, 2003, story, "E-N writer's convicted killers still free; case is sent back to lower court because of conflict of interest." My account of Governor Ramirez's speech at St. Mary's University in San Antonio is drawn from *Express-News* reporter Lucy Hood's February 20, 2003, story, "Mexico official defends handling of True case."

CHAPTER 19

This chapter draws on my e-mail exchanges with Patricia Morales and my first meeting with her in Guadalajara. Events at the canceled appeals court hearing were drawn from my own notes and from Dane Schiller's April 10, 2003, story, "Case of E-N writer takes another twist; Politically connected defense attorney gets magistrates removed."

CHAPTER 20

This chapter is based on an e-mail exchange between Morales and me after my return to San Antonio, e-mails sent by Gatins, my contemporary notes, and Gatins's October 2003 visit to San Antonio and the *Express-*

News. Martha's comments are drawn from our e-mail exchange planning the next visit to Guadalajara.

CHAPTER 21

Coverage of the Guadalajara press conference attended by Martha, myself, Gatins, and Morales is drawn from my own notes and prepared statements read by all four participants. Also, Schiller's November 25, 2003, story, "Suspects in True case lose backer's support; Man who bankrolled defense now believes pair are guilty of E-N writer's killing," and his November 26, 2003, story, "Investigator says pair strangled E-N writer; Woman working for defense team says Huichols told her of killing True." Also, my November 29, 2003, column, "Old adversaries are new allies in the search for justice for True." My account of the dinner late that night is based on my own notes and my later interviews with Gatins and Morales. My account of President Fox's historic speech on judicial reform is drawn from the official presidential website and two articles by Schiller before and after the speech: his March 28, 2004, story, and March 30, 2004, story, "Fox makes his push for judicial overhaul: he says, 'This is the moment to prove that together, we can end the corruption.'" My own account of the final verdict is drawn from my May 2, 2004, column, "Justice finally served in True case, but it's hard to celebrate." Ambassador Tony Garza's remarks following the final verdict were contained in an official embassy press release.

CHAPTER 22

This chapter is based on my interviews with Gatins and Morales, as well as conversations with Schiller and chief photographer Bob Owen. I also draw on various published stories about the search for the two killers: *Express-News* staff writer Jeorge Zarazua's May 4, 2004, story, "No arrest yet in True's murder; Judge says he won't issue warrants until he receives court's ruling"; a May 8, 2004, story by Sean Mattson, our freelance contributor in Guadalajara, "Hunt to start for E-N writer's killers; A lawyer says they'll probably surrender peacefully;" and Mattson's May 11 story, "Talks fail to deliver E-N journalist's killers." A May 30, 2004, story by Dane Schiller, "Searching for killers in lawless land; Cops in E-N writer's case on their own in Huichol country," is the best account of the failed search effort. Morales's images of Huichol spiritualism and her account of Chivarra's boyhood are contained in an exchange of e-mails between us around the time of the search. My further observations about Huichol society are based on various readings and my interviews with anthropologists Phil Weigand and Paul Liffman and with Dr. Sergio Ramirez, who lived with the Huichols for one year in 1998.

Chapter 23

This chapter recounts the January 2005 trip Dane Schiller and I took to Guadalajara to meet with Governor Ramirez and Attorney General Solís to express our frustration at the lack of efforts to capture the two killers and our subsequent journey into the Huichol sierra with Dr. Ramirez to distribute reward posters and fly over the Chapalagana, where True died and his remains were recovered. I rely again on my own notes and my January 16, 2005, column, "After 6 years, a return to Chapalagana Canyon seeking justice."

All thoughts here are mine.

Index

PublicAffairs is a publishing house founded in 1997. It is a tribute to the standards, values, and flair of three persons who have served as mentors to countless reporters, writers, editors, and book people of all kinds, including me.

I.F. STONE, proprietor of *I. F. Stone's Weekly*, combined a commitment to the First Amendment with entrepreneurial zeal and reporting skill and became one of the great independent journalists in American history. At the age of eighty, Izzy published *The Trial of Socrates*, which was a national bestseller. He wrote the book after he taught himself ancient Greek.

BENJAMIN C. BRADLEE was for nearly thirty years the charismatic editorial leader of *The Washington Post*. It was Ben who gave the *Post* the range and courage to pursue such historic issues as Watergate. He supported his reporters with a tenacity that made them fearless and it is no accident that so many became authors of influential, best-selling books.

ROBERT L. BERNSTEIN, the chief executive of Random House for more than a quarter century, guided one of the nation's premier publishing houses. Bob was personally responsible for many books of political dissent and argument that challenged tyranny around the globe. He is also the founder and longtime chair of Human Rights Watch, one of the most respected human rights organizations in the world.

For fifty years, the banner of Public Affairs Press was carried by its owner Morris B. Schnapper, who published Gandhi, Nasser, Toynbee, Truman, and about 1,500 other authors. In 1983, Schnapper was described by *The Washington Post* as "a redoubtable gadfly." His legacy will endure in the books to come.

Peter Osnos, *Founder and Editor-at-Large*